Pro Jakarta Tomcat 5

MATTHEW MOODIE

Apress®

Pro Jakarta Tomcat 5

ISBN (pbk): 1-59059-331-6

Printed and bound in the United States of America 9 8 7 6 5 4 3 2 1

Lead Editor: Steve Anglin

Technical Reviewer: Scott Davis

Project Manager: Tracy Brown Collins

Copy Edit Manager: Nicole LeClerc

Copy Editor: Kim Wimpsett

Production Manager: Kari Brooks-Copony

Production Editor: Katie Stence

Compositor: Susan Glinert

Proofreader: Liz Welch

Indexer: Kevin Broccoli

Artist: April Milne

Cover Designer: Kurt Krames

Manufacturing Manager: Tom Debolski

Distributed to the book trade in the United States by Springer-Verlag New York, Inc., 233 Spring Street, 6th Floor, New York, NY 10013, and outside the United States by Springer-Verlag GmbH & Co. KG, Tiergartenstr. 17, 69112 Heidelberg, Germany.

In the United States: phone 1-800-SPRINGER, fax 201-348-4505, e-mail orders@springer-ny.com, or visit http://www.springer-ny.com. Outside the United States: fax +49 6221 345229, e-mail orders@springer.de, or visit http://www.springer.de.

For information on translations, please contact Apress directly at 2560 Ninth Street, Suite 219, Berkeley, CA 94710. Phone 510-549-5930, fax 510-549-5939, e-mail info@apress.com, or visit http://www.apress.com.

The source code for this book is available to readers at http://www.apress.com in the Downloads section.

To Laura

Contents at a Glance

Contents

About the Author

MATTHEW MOODIE is a native of southwest Scotland and is a graduate of the University of Edinburgh, where he obtained a master's degree in linguistics and artificial intelligence.

Matthew enjoys a life of fun in Glasgow, Scotland. He's a keen novice gardener with a houseful of plants.

About the Technical Reviewer

SCOTT DAVIS is a senior software engineer and instructor in the Denver, Colorado, area. He has worked on a variety of Java platforms, including J2EE, J2SE, and J2ME (sometimes all on the same project). He's a frequent presenter at national conferences and local user groups. He was the president of the Denver Java Users Group (`http://www.denverjug.org`) in 2003 when it was voted one of the top-ten JUGs in North America. Keep up with him at `http://www.davisworld.org`.

Acknowledgments

Matthew would like to thank Laura for her love and friendship.

Love to his mum, Valla, Alexandra, Harcus, Angus, Howard and his grandparents. Thanks go to Andrew, Brian, Katy, Lindsey and Disco Robot Craig for the good times. Big shout out to the Lochmaben boys Billy and Dave. See you down the gaff. And not forgetting the Lockerbie whistle posse of Pete, Broon, Stuart and Mark (Carrutherstown doesn't count).

CHAPTER 1

■ ■ ■

Introducing Tomcat

This, as befits a first chapter in a book on Tomcat, is a short history of dynamic Web content and how Tomcat fits into that history. Once you've dealt with that, you'll learn about Tomcat's architecture and its modular approach to configuration.

Understanding the Web Today

The Web isn't solely made up of static pages that show the same document to every user; many pages contain content generated independently for each viewer. Although static files still have their place, many useful and necessary Web sites would be unable to function without dynamic content. For example, Amazon.com is one of the major success stories of the Web and is often the reason people go online for the first time. Without dynamic content, such as shopping baskets, personal recommendations, and personalized welcome messages, Amazon.com wouldn't be the success it has been, and many people wouldn't be online.

The Common Gateway Interface (CGI) was the original dynamic content mechanism that executed programs on a Web server and allowed Webmasters to customize their pages, which was extremely popular in the early days of the Web. The CGI model is as follows:

1. The browser sends a request to the server just as it would for a Hypertext Markup Language (HTML) page.
2. The server maps the requested resource to an external program.
3. The server runs the external program and passes it the original Hypertext Transfer Protocol (HTTP) request.
4. The external program executes and sends its results to the server.
5. The server passes the program's output to the browser as an HTTP response.

CGI has been implemented in many programming languages, but Perl was, and still is, the most popular language for developing CGI applications. However, CGI isn't very efficient; each time the server receives a request, it must start a new copy of the external program.

So, if only a small number of users request a CGI program simultaneously, it's not too big of a problem. However, it's a different story if hundreds or thousands of users request the resource simultaneously. Every copy of the program requires a share of the server's processing power, which is rapidly used up as requests pile up. The situation is made even worse with CGI programs that are written in interpreted languages such as Perl, which result in the launch of large runtime interpreters with each request.

Looking Beyond CGI

Many alternative solutions to CGI have been developed since the Web began. The more successful of these provide an environment that exists inside an existing server or even functions as a server on its own.

Many CGI replacements have been built on top of the Apache server (`http://www.apache.org`) because of Apache's popular modular application programming interface (API). Developers can use the API to extend Apache's functionality with persistent programs, and thus it's ideal for creating programs that create dynamic content. Apache loads modules into its memory when it starts and passes the appropriate HTTP requests to them as appropriate. It then passes the HTTP responses to the browser once the modules have processed the requests. Because the modules are already in the server's memory, the cost of loading an interpreter is removed and scripts can execute faster.

Although few developers actually create modules themselves (they're relatively difficult to develop), many third-party modules provide a basis for applications that are much more efficient than normal CGI. The following are a few examples:

- `mod_perl`: This maintains the Perl interpreter in memory, thus removing the overhead of loading a new copy of the Perl interpreter for each request. This is an incredibly popular module.
- `mod_php4`: This module speeds up PHP in the same way that `mod_perl` speeds up Perl.
- `mod_fastcgi`: This is similar to straight CGI, but it keeps programs in memory rather than terminating them when each request is finished.

Microsoft provides an interface to its Internet Information Services (IIS) Web server, called the Internet Server Application Programming Interface (ISAPI). This API doesn't have the following that Apache's API has because of its complexity, but it's nevertheless a high-performance API. However, IIS is widely used, mainly because it comes as part of many versions of Windows. In Chapter 9 you'll configure Tomcat to work with IIS so you can combine the best features of both.

Microsoft also developed the Active Server Pages (ASP) technology, which lets you embed scripts, typically VBScript, into standard HTML pages. This model has proved extremely successful and was the catalyst for Java Web technology, which I'll discuss next.

Introducing Java on the Web

Java was initially released in the mid-1990s as a way to liven up static Web pages. It was platform independent and allowed developers to execute their programs, called *applets*, in the user's browser. An incredible amount of hype surrounded applets: that they would make the Web more exciting and interactive, that they would change the way people bought computers, and that they would reduce all the various operating systems into mere platforms for Web browsers.

Applets never really caught on; in fact, other technologies, such as Macromedia Flash, became more popular ways of creating interactive Web sites. However, Java isn't just for writing applets: you can also use it to create stand-alone platform-independent applications.

The main contribution of Java to the Web is *servlets*, which are another alternative technology to CGI. Just as CGI and its other alternatives aren't stand-alone programs (because they require a Web server), servlets require a servlet container to load servlets into memory. The servlet container then receives HTTP requests from browsers and passes them to servlets that generate the response. The servlet container can also integrate with other Web servers to use their more efficient static file abilities while continuing to produce the dynamic content. You'll find an example of this in Chapter 9 when you integrate Tomcat with Apache and IIS.

Unfortunately, although servlets are an improvement over CGI, especially with respect to performance and server load, they too have a drawback. They're primarily suitable for processing logic. For the creation of content (that is, HTML), they're less usable. First, hard-coding textual output, including HTML tags, in code makes the application less maintainable. This is because if text in the HTML must be changed, the servlet must be recompiled.

Second, this approach requires the HTML designer to understand enough about Java to avoid breaking the servlet. More likely, however, the programmer of the application must take the HTML from the designer and then embed it into the application: an error-prone task if ever there was one.

To solve this problem, Sun Microsystems created the JavaServer Pages (JSP) technology.

Adding to Servlets: JavaServer Pages

Although writing servlets requires knowledge of Java, a Java newbie can quickly learn some useful JSP techniques. As such, JSP represents a viable and attractive alternative to Microsoft's ASP.

Practically speaking, JSP pages are compiled into servlets, which are then kept in memory or on the file system indefinitely, until either the memory is required or the server is restarted. This servlet is called for each request, thus making the process far more efficient than ASP, since ASP requires the server to parse and compile the document every time a user comes to the site. This means that a developer can write software whose output is easy to verify visually and that the result works like a piece of software. In fact, JSP took off mainly as a result of its suitability for creating dynamic visual content at a time when the Internet was growing in popularity.

One major practical difference between servlets and JSP pages is that servlets are provided in compiled form and JSP pages are often not (although precompilation is possible). What this means for a system administrator is that servlet files are held in the private resources section of the servlet container, and JSP files are mixed in with static HTML pages, images, and other resources in the public section of servlet container.

Introducing Servlet Containers

JSP pages and servlets require a servlet container to operate at all. Tomcat, the subject of this book, is the reference implementation (RI) servlet container, which means that Tomcat's first priority is to be fully compliant with the Servlet and JSP specifications published by Sun Microsystems. However, this isn't to say that Tomcat isn't worthy of use in production systems. Indeed, many commercial installations use Tomcat.

An RI has the added benefit of refining the specification, whatever the technology may be. As developers add code per the specifications, they can uncover problems in implementation requirements and conflicts within the specification.

As noted previously, the RI is completely compliant with the specification and is therefore particularly useful for people who are using advanced features of the specification. The RI is released with the specification, which means that Tomcat is always the first server to provide the new features of the specification when it's finished.

Looking at Tomcat

Tomcat has its origins in the earliest days of the servlet technology. Sun Microsystems created the first servlet container, the Java Web Server, to demonstrate the technology, but it wasn't terribly robust. At the same time, the Apache Software Foundation (ASF) created JServ, a servlet engine that integrated with the Apache Web server.

In 1999, Sun Microsystems donated the Java Web Server code to the ASF, and the two projects merged to create Tomcat. Version 3.*x* was the first Tomcat series and was directly descended from the original code that Sun Microsystems provided to the ASF. It's still available and is the RI of the Servlet 2.2 and JSP 1.1 specifications.

In 2001, the ASF released Tomcat 4.0, which was a complete redesign of the Tomcat architecture and which had a new code base. The Tomcat 4.*x* series is the RI of the Servlet 2.3 and JSP 1.2 specifications.

Tomcat 5.*x* is the current Tomcat version and is the RI of the Servlet 2.4 and JSP 2.0 specifications. As such, this is the version of Tomcat you'll use in this book. Note that two branches of Tomcat 5.*x* exist: Tomcat 5.0.*x* and Tomcat 5.5.*x*. Tomcat 5.5.*x* branched at Tomcat 5.0.27 and is a refactored version that's intended to work with the proposed Java 2 Platform Standard Edition 5.0 (though you can use it with Java 2 Standard Edition 1.4). You should get no discrepancy between the servers when they run Web applications. The main differences are in configuration. Where a configuration discrepancy exists, I'll give the relevant details.

Understanding Tomcat's Architecture

The latest version of Tomcat is 5.*x*, which supports the Servlet 2.4 and JSP 2.0 specifications. It consists of a nested hierarchy of components.

- *Top-level components* exist at the top of the configuration hierarchy in a rigid relationship with one another.
- *Connectors* connect the servlet container to requests, either from a browser or another Web server that's handling the static resources.
- *Container components* contain a collection of other components.
- *Nested components* can reside in containers but can't contain other components.

Figure 1-1 illustrates the structure of a Tomcat configuration.

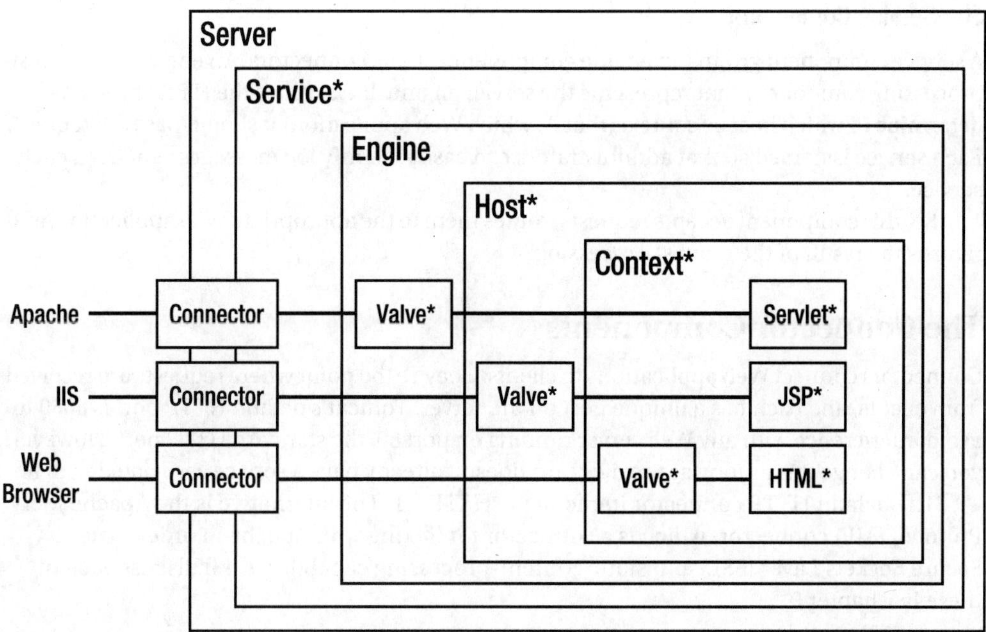

Figure 1-1. *An example Tomcat configuration. The components marked with a star can occur multiple times.*

When configuring Tomcat, you can remove some of these objects without affecting the server. Notably, the engine and host may be unnecessary if you're using a Web server such as Apache.

You won't be surprised to hear that Tomcat is configured with an Extensible Markup Language (XML) file that mirrors the component hierarchy. You'll learn about this file, called `server.xml`, in Chapter 4.

In the next couple of sections, you'll look into each component in turn.

Top-Level Components

The top-level components are the Tomcat server, as opposed to the other components, which are only parts of the server.

The Server Component

The server component is an instance of the Tomcat server. You can create only one instance of a server inside a given Java virtual machine (JVM).

You can set up separate servers configured to different ports on a single server to separate applications so that you can restart them independently. So, if a given JVM crashes, the other applications will be safe in another instance of the server. This is sometimes done in hosting environments where each customer has a separate instance of a JVM so that a badly written application won't cause others to crash.

The Service Component

A service component groups an engine component with its connectors. An engine is a request-processing component that represents the servlet engine. It examines the HTTP headers to determine to which host or context (that is, which Web application) it should pass the request. Each service is named so that administrators can easily identify log messages sent from each service.

So, this component accepts requests, routes them to the appropriate Web application, and returns the result of the request processing.

The Connector Components

Connectors connect Web applications to clients. They're the point where requests are received from clients, and each has a unique port on the server. Tomcat's default HTTP port is 8080 to avoid interference with any Web server running on port 80, the standard HTTP port. However, you can change this as long as the new port doesn't already have a service associated with it.

The default HTTP connector implements HTTP 1.1. The alternative is the Apache JServ Protocol (AJP) connector, which is a connector for linking with Apache in order to use its Secure Sockets Layer (SSL) and static content-processing capabilities. I'll discuss each of these in Chapter 9.

The Container Components

The container components receive the requests from the top-level components as appropriate. They then deal with the request process and return the response to the component that sent it to them.

The Engine Component

The engine component is the top-level container and can't be contained by another container component. Only one may be contained in each service component.

The top-level container doesn't have to be an engine, because it only has to implement the container interface. This interface ensures the object implementing it is aware of its position in the component hierarchy, provides a realm for user authentication and role-based authorization, and has access to a number of resources including its session manager and some important internal structures.

The container at this level is usually an engine, so you'll see it in that role. As mentioned earlier, the container components are request-processing components, and the engine is no exception. In this case it represents the Catalina servlet engine. It examines the HTTP headers to determine to which virtual host or context to pass the request. In this way you can see the progression of the request from the top-level components down the hierarchy of components.

If Tomcat is used as a stand-alone server, the defined engine is the default. However, if Tomcat is configured to provide servlet support with a Web server providing the static pages, the default engine is overridden, as the Web server has normally determined the correct destination for the request.

The host name of the server is set in the engine component if required. An engine may contain hosts representing a group of Web applications and contexts, each representing a single Web application.

The Host Component

A host component is analogous to the Apache virtual host functionality. This allows multiple servers to be configured on the same physical machine and be identified by separate Internet Protocol (IP) addresses or host names. In Tomcat's case, the virtual hosts are differentiated by a fully qualified host name. Thus, you can have `http://www.apress.com` and `http://www.moodie.com` on the same server. In this case, the servlet container routes requests to the different groups of Web applications.

When you configure a host, you set its name; the majority of clients will usually send both the IP address of the server and the host name they used to resolve the IP address. The engine component inspects the HTTP header to determine which host is being requested.

The Context Component

The final container component, and the one at the lowest level, is the context, also known as the Web application. When you configure a context, you inform the servlet container of the location of the application's root folder so that components that contain this component can route requests effectively. You can also enable dynamic reloading so that any classes that have changed are reloaded into memory. This means the latest changes are reflected in the application. However, this is resource intensive and isn't recommended for deployment scenarios.

A context component may also include error pages, which will allow you to configure error messages consistent with the application's look and feel.

Finally, you can also configure a context with initialization parameters for the application it represents and for access control (authentication and authorization restrictions). More information on these two aspects of Web application deployment is available in Chapter 5.

The Nested Components

The nested components are nested within container components and provide a number of administrative services. You can't nest all of them in every container component, but you can nest many of them this way. The exception to the container component rule is the global resources component, which you can nest only within a server component.

The Global Resources Component

As already mentioned, this component may be nested only within a server component. You use this component to configure global Java Naming and Directory Interface (JNDI) resources that all the other components in the server can use. Typically these could be data sources for database access or serverwide constants for use in application code.

The Loader Component

The loader component may be nested only within a context component. You use a loader to specify a Web application's class loader, which will load the application's classes and resources into memory. The class loader you specify must follow the Servlet specification, though it's unlikely you'll find it necessary to use this component, because the default class loader works perfectly well.

The Logger Component

This component is available only in Tomcat 5.0.*x* and not in Tomcat 5.5.*x*. You should use a logging implementation such as Log4J with Tomcat 5.5.*x*, more of which is covered in Chapter 4.

A logger component reports on the internal state of its parent component. You can include a logger in any of the container components. Logging behavior is inherited, so a logger set at the engine level is assigned to every child object unless overridden by the child. The configuration of loggers at this level can be a convenient way to decide the default logging behavior for the server.

This allows you to configure a convenient destination for all logging events for the components that aren't configured to generate their own logs.

The Manager Component

The manager component represents a session manager for working with user sessions in a Web application. As such, it can be included only in a context container. A default manager component is used if you don't specify an alternative, and, like the loader component mentioned previously, you'll find that the default is perfectly good.

The Realm Component

The realm for an engine manages user authentication and authorization. As part of the configuration of an application, you set the roles that are allowed to access each resource or group of resources, and the realm is used to enforce this policy.

Realms can authenticate against text files, database tables, Lightweight Directory Access Protocol (LDAP) servers, and the Windows network identity of the user. You'll see more of this in Chapter 11.

A realm applies across the entire container component in which it's included, so applications within a container share authentication resources. By default, a user must still authenticate separately to each Web application on the server. (This is called *single sign-on.*) You'll see how you can change this in Chapter 7.

The Resources Component

You can add the resources component to a context component. It represents the static resources in a Web application and allows them to be stored in alternative formats, such as compressed files. The default is more than sufficient for most needs.

The Valve Component

You can use valve components to intercept a request and process it before it reaches its destination. Valves are analogous to filters as defined in the Servlet specification and aren't in the JSP or Servlet specifications. You may place valve components in any container component.

Valves are commonly used to log requests, client IP addresses, and server usage. This technique is known as *request dumping*, and a request dumper valve records the HTTP header information and any cookies sent with the request. Response dumping logs the response headers and cookies (if set) to a file.

Valves are typically reusable components, so you can add and remove them from the request path according to your needs; Web applications can't detect their presence, so they shouldn't affect the application in any way. (However, performance may suffer if a valve is added.) If your users have applications that need to intercept requests and responses for processing, they should use filters as per the Servlet specification.

You can use other useful facilities, such as listeners, when configuring Tomcat. However, filters aren't defined as components. You'll deal with them in Chapter 7.

Summary

This chapter was a quick introduction to dynamic Web content and the Tomcat Web server. You learned about the emergence of CGI, its problems, and the various solutions that have been developed over the years. You saw how servlets are Java's answer to the CGI problem and that Tomcat is the reference implementation of the Servlet specification as outlined by Sun Microsystems.

The chapter then discussed Tomcat's architecture and how all its components fit together in a flexible and highly customizable way. Each component is nested inside another to allow for easy configuration and extensibility.

Now that you're familiar with Tomcat, you'll learn about how to install it on various platforms.

CHAPTER 2

■ ■ ■

Installing Tomcat

In the previous chapter you saw a brief history of the Internet and the Web that built up to the development of servlets and the release of Tomcat. Continuing in this abstract manner, you learned about Tomcat's modular architecture. However, none of this is useful if you don't have the Tomcat server, so in this chapter you'll do the following:

- You'll install Java if you haven't done so already.
- You'll install Tomcat on your platform of choice.
- You'll install the Ant build tool.

You'll also see how to compile Tomcat from the source code provided on the Tomcat Web site. This process is the same on Windows and Linux and requires the Ant build tool, so you'll see how to do it once all the other installation techniques have been covered.

Installing Java

Your choice of JVM can significantly affect the performance of your Tomcat server, and it's worth evaluating a few to see which gives you the best performance. This is a subject that many people don't concern themselves with or have never thought about, so you won't be alone if you think that this isn't an issue. Sun Microsystems' JVM is all you need, right?

Well, if performance is really an issue and you want to squeeze as much out of your server setup as possible, you should look into this area. You can find a lot of information on the Internet, and Sun provides its own guidance at `http://java.sun.com/docs/performance/`.

IBM (`http://www.ibm.com/developerworks/java/jdk/`) and the Blackdown project (`http://www.blackdown.org`), which is a Linux port of source donated by Sun Microsystems, provide the main alternatives to Sun Microsystems' Java development kit (JDK).

Installing Java on Windows

Download the Java installer from `http://java.sun.com/j2se/downloads/`. You can choose either JDK 1.4 or JDK 5.0, though the latter option isn't a final release and you must use Tomcat 5.5.*x*.

The Java installer on Windows is a standard installation package with easy-to-follow steps. Start the installation by double-clicking the downloaded installer, and you'll shortly have the JDK installed. Choose the folder where you want to install Java, which is referred to as `%JAVA_HOME%`. The `%JAVA_HOME%\bin` directory is where the installer places all the Java executables, including the JVM, the compiler, the debugger, and a packaging utility.

You'll probably have noted that the installation directory was specified as if it were an environment variable. This is because you now have to add the installation folder as an environment variable called `%JAVA_HOME%` so that Windows can find the Java executables. Java itself doesn't need this environment variable, but many third-party packages need to know where Java is, and Tomcat is no exception. Finally, add the `%JAVA_HOME%\bin` directory to the Windows path. This avoids clashes with other JVMs that may be on the system.

Setting Environment Variables

To set environment variables, select Start ➤ Settings ➤ Control Panel, and choose the System option. Now choose the Advanced tab, and click the Environment Variables button. You'll see a screen like the one in Figure 2-1.

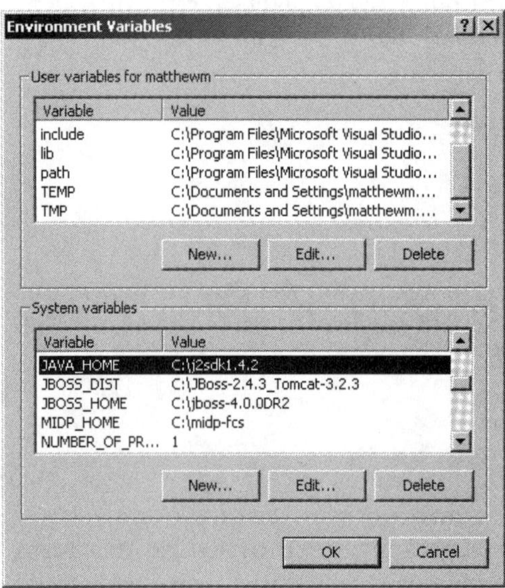

Figure 2-1. *The Windows Environment Variables dialog box*

The top window contains variables for the user you're logged in as, which will be available only when you're logged in as this user, and the bottom window contains system environment variables, which are available to all users. To add `%JAVA_HOME%` so that every user has access to it, click the New button below the bottom window; then enter **JAVA_HOME** as the variable name, and enter the directory where Java was installed as the value.

Next, modify the `%Path%` variable to include `%JAVA_HOME%\bin`, making sure it's the first entry in the path to avoid any naming clashes. Adding this directory to the path will make the Java executables available at the command prompt. To test the installation, open an instance of the command prompt and type the following:

```
> java -version
```

You should then see version information as follows:

```
java version "1.4.2_03"
Java(TM) 2 Runtime Environment, Standard Edition (build 1.4.2_03-b02)
Java HotSpot(TM) Client VM (build 1.4.2_03-b02, mixed mode)
```

In this example, JDK 1.4.2_03 is installed as the default Java. If you have the wrong version information, check that you've added the correct Java to the Windows path.

Setting Environment Variables in Windows 9x

In Windows 9*x*, you set the environment variables by editing the `c:\autoexec.bat` file. Open the file, and add the following path to your installation:

```
set JAVA_HOME=c:\j2sdk1.4.2
```

For Windows ME, you can use the System Configuration utility to set environment variables. To run it, choose Start ➤ Programs ➤ Accessories ➤ System Tools ➤ System Information. You'll see a Microsoft help and support page, from which you should select the Tools menu and then the System Configuration utility. From here, select the Environment tab, and set the `JAVA_HOME` variable to point to your Java installation directory. Test the installation as mentioned previously.

Installing Java on Linux

Download a suitable distribution from `http://java.sun.com/j2se/downloads/`. Two types of download exist: a self-extracting binary file and an RPM package for systems supporting RPMs. You can choose either JDK 1.4 or JDK 5.0; the latter option isn't a final release, and you must use Tomcat 5.5.*x*.

Installing Java Using the Self-Extracting Binary

Once you've obtained the self-extracting binary, you must set its execute permissions. Note that you don't need to be a root user to install Java using the self-extracting binary, though you do need to be a root user if you want to install it in a system directory such as `/usr/local`; this is because the binary won't overwrite any system files otherwise. To change the execute permissions, type the following command from the directory where the binary is located:

```
# chmod +x j2sdk-1_4_2-linux-i586.bin
```

Now change the directory to the one where you want to install Java and execute the binary. You must prefix the binary's filename with any path information that's necessary, like so:

```
# ./j2sdk-1_4_2-linux-i586.bin
```

This command will display a license agreement and, once you've agreed to the license, install Java in a `j2sdk-1_4_2` directory in the current directory.

You need to add the `$JAVA_HOME` environment variable to your system to specify the location of the JDK. So, if you installed it in `/usr/java/j2sdk-1_4_2_05-linux-i386`, you should give `$JAVA_HOME` this value. To add it permanently, you can add it to your `~/.bashrc` file or, if you want all users to have access to Java, to `/etc/profile`.

Alternatively, /etc/profile runs any shell scripts in /etc/profile.d, so you can add the following lines to a file named tomcat.sh:

```
JAVA_HOME=/usr/java/j2sdk-1_4_2_05-linux-i386/
export JAVA_HOME
PATH=$JAVA_HOME/bin:$PATH
export PATH
```

You may have to log out and log in again for your system to read /etc/profile or tomcat.sh. You should also add execute permissions for the $JAVA_HOME/bin folder for all the users who will be using Java as appropriate.

To test the installation, type the following:

```
# java -version
```

If the installation succeeded, you'll see version information.

Installing Java Using the RPM Installer

To install the JDK using the RPM, you must first download the file. Unlike with the self-extracting binary, you must be a root user to install the RPM.

Sun Microsystems supplies the RPM as an executable to allow you to agree to the licensing terms. If you agree to the licensing terms, the RPM installer decompresses an RPM into the current directory. Before you can run the RPM, you have to set execute permissions for the file, like so:

```
# chmod a+x j2sdk-1_4_2-linux-i586-rpm.bin
# ./j2sdk-1_4_2-linux-i586-rpm.bin
# rpm -iv jdk-1_4_2-linux-i586.rpm
```

The RPM will install Java as a replacement of the Linux system version. You should now follow the previous instructions to add execute permissions for the JDK executables and modify the path to include them. Again, you can test the installation as described previously.

Installing Tomcat

Now that you've installed Java, it's time for you to install the Tomcat server. The Windows installations are first, followed by instructions for Linux.

The first step for all systems is obtaining the appropriate distribution. This may be a binary or source distribution, depending on your needs. Whatever your requirements, Tomcat is available from http://jakarta.apache.org/site/binindex.cgi. Choose the most stable version of Tomcat 5.0.*x* or Tomcat 5.5.*x* provided. The choice will largely depend on what version of Java you're using. If you have JDK 5, then choose Tomcat 5.5.*x*; otherwise you can pick either, because Tomcat 5.5.*x* can be modified to work with earlier versions of Java (download the appropriate compatibility zipped file).

You can select a binary installer if you're a Windows user and want to use Tomcat as a service, or you can select a zipped version of the binaries for any system.

If you're interested in the latest version of Tomcat or want to download an older version, you'll find both of these options below the binary downloads.

Note Tomcat 5.5 doesn't come with documentation for Tomcat's internal APIs. If you require this documentation, click the title link for the Tomcat 5.5 distribution (the link above the list of download options starting with KEYS). This will take you to a directory listing of an Apache download mirror. Click bin, and then select `jakarta-tomcat-5.5.x-fulldocs.tar.gz`. This is a Web application to replace the default `tomcat-docs` Web application.

You'll also require Ant for various deploy and build tasks later in the book. Ant is a build tool like `make` and is another excellent Jakarta project.

Installing Tomcat on Windows Using the Installer

If you choose to install Tomcat with the installer, save it in a convenient location and double-click it to begin installation. As always, you must agree with the license agreement before you can continue with the installation.

Figure 2-2 shows the screen where you choose which components to install.

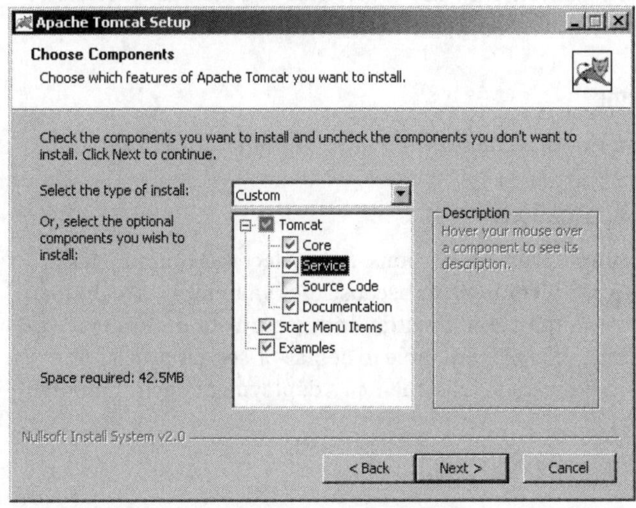

Figure 2-2. *Tomcat's installation options*

Installing Tomcat As a Service

If you select the Service option, as shown in Figure 2-2, you'll install Tomcat as a service, with all the functionality that entails. This is a useful option if you want Tomcat to run every time you start your machine or if you want it to run as a unique user so you can track its behavior. Remember that this isn't available on Windows 98 and its derivatives. However, you'll see a work-around for this a bit later in the "Running Tomcat in the Background" section.

Tomcat will run at startup and will run in the background even when no user is logged in. This is the option you'd use on a deployment server, but it's probably not the option you'd use on a development machine.

■ **Note** The installer will install Tomcat as a service whether you check this box or not. The difference is that the installer will install the service to start automatically by default if you check the box. Otherwise it's set to manual startup.

Installing Tomcat's Source Code

If you want to compile Tomcat from source, select this option. Note that you'll require Ant for this process, which I'll cover in the "Installing Tomcat from Source" section.

Installing Tomcat's Documentation

You should install the Tomcat documentation; it's a useful resource and includes the Servlet and JSP API javadocs. You'll find these invaluable if you do any Web development.

Installing Tomcat's Start Menu Items

If you want to add shortcuts to Windows' Start menu, then select this option.

Installing Tomcat's Example Web Applications

If you want to examine Tomcat's example Web applications, then select this option. This is unlikely if you'll be using Tomcat as a production server because they will simply take up space and are certainly a security risk. The examples aren't written with security or performance in mind, and, as well-known applications, they're vulnerable to denial-of-service attacks and attempts to gain root access. If your users want to have them in a deployment environment, by all means let them.

Finishing the Installation

Once you've chosen the components you want to install, click Next. The installer will then ask you for information on installation directories, the location of Java, an administrator's username and password, and the port details. Fill in these as appropriate for your installation.

Note All public Web servers run on port 80, which is the default HTTP port. When a browser attempts to connect to a Web site, it uses port 80 behind the scenes; that is, you don't have to specify it. Tomcat's HTTP service runs on port 8080 by default to avoid a clash with other Web servers that may already be running. You'll see how to change this in Chapter 4.

If you're using Tomcat 5.5.*x* and JDK 1.4, then extract the contents of `jakarta-tomcat-5.5.x-compat.zip` to the appropriate subdirectory of `%CATALINA_HOME%`. You can see where the files are to be placed in Figure 2-3.

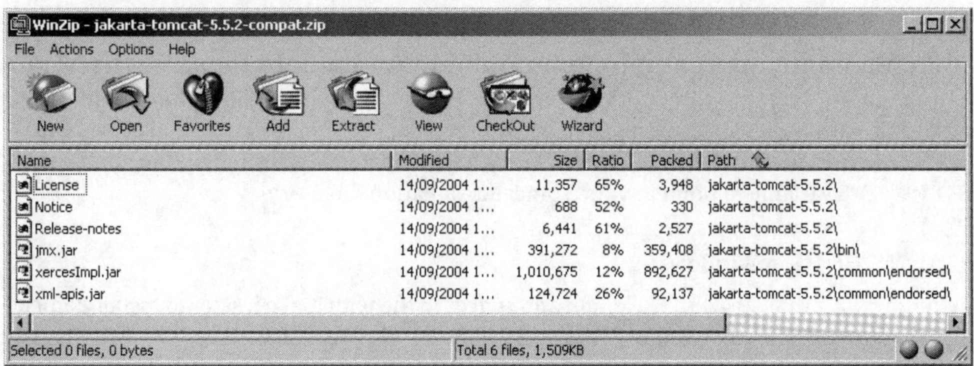

Figure 2-3. *Tomcat 5.5.x compatibility file for JDK 1.4*

Here `jakarta-tomcat-5.5.2` is `%CATALINA_HOME%`, so move the files to the corresponding directory of your `%CATALINA_HOME%` like this:

- `%CATALINA_HOME%\bin\jmx.jar`
- `%CATALINA_HOME%\common\endorsed\xercesImpl.jar`
- `%CATALINA_HOME%\common\endorsed\xml-apis.jar`

These APIs are now part of the new Java specification and as such are missing from Tomcat 5.5.*x*.

Setting Environment Variables

The scripts provided with Tomcat will usually be able to guess at your setup so that no further intervention is strictly necessary. However, it's prudent to add the following environment variables.

Adding the CATALINA_HOME Environment Variable

%CATALINA_HOME% is the directory where you chose to install Tomcat. Tomcat needs to know this information to find the resources that are referenced as relative paths to this folder. If you chose the default directory while installing, this will be C:\Program Files\Apache Software Foundation\Tomcat 5.x.

To add the environment variable in Windows XP, navigate to Start ➤ Settings ➤ Control Panel, and choose System. Now choose the Advanced tab, and click the Environment Variables button. Click the New button in the System Variables section, call the new variable CATALINA_HOME, and enter the path to your installation.

In Windows 98, set the environment variables in c:\autoexec.bat. Open the file, and add the following path to your installation:

```
set CATALINA_HOME=c:\tomcat5.x
```

For Windows ME, you can use the System Configuration utility to set environment variables. To run it, choose Start ➤ Programs ➤ Accessories ➤ System Tools ➤ System Information. You'll see a Microsoft help and support page, from which you should select the Tools menu and then the System Configuration utility. From here, select the Environment tab, and set the CATALINA_HOME variable to point to your Tomcat installation directory.

CATALINA_HOME in Windows 9x

In Windows 9*x*, problems with file length and spaces in the path make it safer to install Tomcat directly onto c:\ rather than under Program Files. You'll also need to increase the default environment space to Tomcat by opening a DOS prompt window, right-clicking it, choosing Properties, selecting the Memory tab, and setting the initial environment to 4096 bytes (4 kilobytes).

Testing the Installation

To test the installation, you must first start the server. You can start the server in two ways: manually or as a service.

Starting the Server Manually

You can start the server manually by selecting Start ➤ Programs ➤ Apache Tomcat 5.*x* and then selecting the Tomcat 5.*x* Program Directory option. Navigate to the bin directory, and double-click startup.bat. A new terminal window will start that shows the server is running. You can also run it from a command prompt, like so:

```
> %CATALINA_HOME%\bin\startup.bat
```

Note that if the window appears and promptly disappears again, you can try the tips in the "Troubleshooting and Tips" section.

If you want to shut down the server, use the `shutdown.bat` file in the `bin` directory.

Starting the Server As a Service

If you want to start the server as a service, you have three choices. First, you could have selected to start the server at the end of installation.

Second, choose Start ➤ Settings ➤ Control Panel, and select Administrative Tools. You then select the Services icon, which will contain an entry for Tomcat, as shown in Figure 2-4.

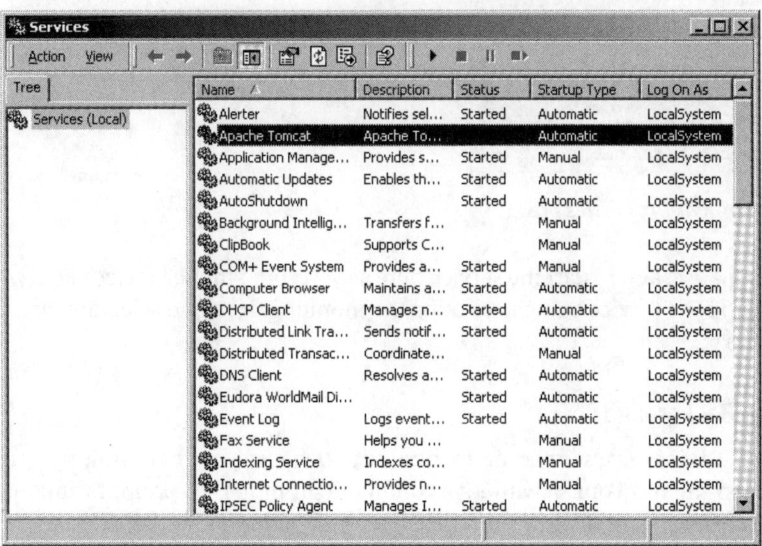

Figure 2-4. *The Services administrative tool with the Tomcat service highlighted*

To start the service, right-click the Tomcat entry, and then choose Start. You won't see a console window, as described previously, because the server is running as a service. Once you've started the service, you can then restart and stop it by right-clicking the service's entry in the Services window.

You can also start and stop the service using the Tomcat monitor. To start the monitor, select Start ➤ Programs ➤ Apache Tomcat 5.*x* ➤ Monitor Tomcat. You'll see a new icon in your system tray with a red stop sign on it. You can double-click the icon to display the Apache Tomcat Properties box, as shown in Figure 2-5.

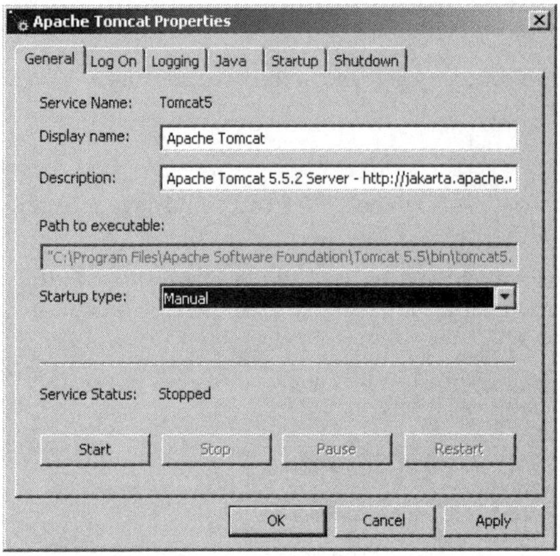

Figure 2-5. *The Apache Tomcat Properties box*

You can start, stop, pause, and restart the service here as you could in the Services utility. You can also start and stop the service by right-clicking the monitor's icon and selecting the action you want to perform.

Running Tomcat in the Background

If you don't want to run Tomcat as a service, or are unable to because you're running Windows 9*x*/ME, you can still run Tomcat without a command prompt/DOS prompt window open while Tomcat is running by modifying the `catalina.bat` file in `%CATALINA_HOME%\bin`. Replace the following text:

```
%_RUNJAVA%
```

with this:

```
%_RUNJAVAW%
```

This command calls the windowless version of the `java` executable. Tomcat will now start with no attached Tomcat window, but one will appear and disappear.

You should now check that the server is indeed running (the absence of a window makes it hard to check by the usual means) by going to the server's home page as described in the next section. If you find a problem, run the startup batch file from the `%CATALINA_HOME%\bin` directory and note the error messages.

Viewing the Default Installation

Tomcat, like most servers, comes with a default home page that you can use to check the installation. Enter the following address in a browser: `http://localhost:8080/`. You should see a page similar to the one in Figure 2-6.

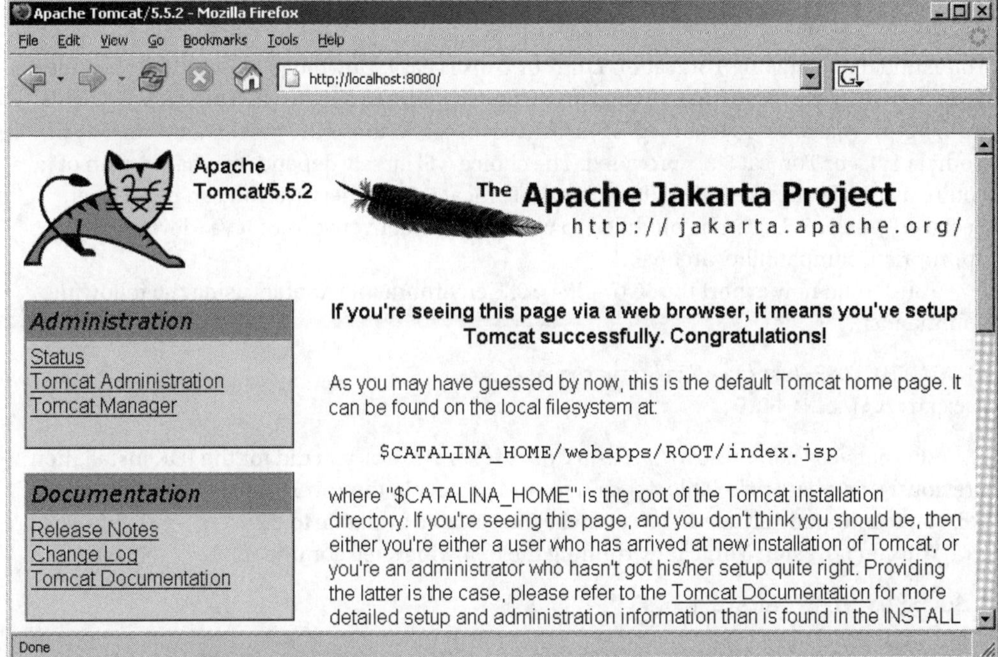

Figure 2-6. *The Tomcat default home page*

As mentioned, Tomcat connects to port 8080 by default. This is to avoid problems with other servers, such as Apache or IIS, that may be running on the machine.

If you have any problems, refer to the "Troubleshooting and Tips" section later in this chapter.

Installing Tomcat on Windows Using the Zipped File

Installing Tomcat using the zipped file is extremely straightforward. It's significantly bigger than the executable installer but has the same contents. All you have to do to install Tomcat from the zipped file is to uncompress the contents to a convenient directory.

The final step of installation is to add the `%CATALINA_HOME%` environment variable as described previously. To start the server, you need to navigate to `%CATALINA_HOME%\bin` (no shortcut this time, though you should create your own).

Now start the server as per the previous manual instructions; that is, double-click `startup.bat`. A new terminal window will start that shows the server is running.

You can also run it from a command prompt, like so:

```
> %CATALINA_HOME%\bin\startup.bat
```

If you're using Tomcat 5.5.*x* and JDK 1.4, then extract the contents of `jakarta-tomcat-5.5.x-compat.zip` to the same location as the Tomcat zipped file. You can see where to place the files in Figure 2-3. The Tomcat zipped file and the compatibility zipped file have the same structure so that installation is simple.

Installing Tomcat on Linux

You'll find that installing Tomcat on Linux or Unix is easy. Download either the zipped file or the gzipped tar file if you have GNU gzip. Whatever your requirements, Tomcat is available from `http://jakarta.apache.org/site/binindex.cgi`. Choose the most stable version of Tomcat 5.0.*x* or Tomcat 5.5.*x* provided. The choice will largely depend on what version of Java you're using. If you have JDK 5, then choose Tomcat 5.5.*x*; otherwise you can pick either, because Tomcat 5.5.*x* can be modified to work with earlier versions of Java (download the appropriate compatibility archive).

You should now export the `$CATALINA_HOME` environment variable, using the following commands:

```
# CATALINA_HOME=/usr/java/jakarta-tomcat-5.x
# export CATALINA_HOME
```

Alternatively, add these to `~/.bashrc` or `/etc/profile` as you did for the JDK installation previously, or create a shell file, `tomcat.sh`, and place it in the `/etc/profile.d`. `/etc/profile` will run it automatically at startup to make the variable available to all users.

You can now start Tomcat by running the following shell command:

```
# $CATALINA_HOME/bin/startup.sh
```

You can shut down Tomcat using `$CATALINA_HOME/bin/shutdown.sh`.

If you're using Tomcat 5.5.*x* and JDK 1.4, then extract the contents of `jakarta-tomcat-5.5.x-compat.tar.gz` to the same location as the Tomcat zipped file. You can see where to place the files in Figure 2-3. The Tomcat zipped file and the compatibility file have the same structure so that installation is simple.

■ **Note** All public Web servers run on port 80, which is the default HTTP port. When a browser attempts to connect to a Web site, it uses port 80 behind the scenes; that is, you don't have to specify it. Tomcat's HTTP service runs on port 8080 by default to avoid a clash with other Web servers that may already be running. Another reason is that Linux and Unix systems require a user to have root permission to assign port numbers below 1024 to a process. You'll see how to change this in Chapter 4.

Viewing the Default Installation

To check that Tomcat is running, point your browser to `http://localhost:8080`. You should see a screen like the one in Figure 2-6.

To check that the dynamic side of Tomcat's functionality is working, choose the JSP Examples link from the menu on the left and select some of the examples. Check that they run without error messages. Do the same with the Servlet Examples link to test this functionality.

If you have any problems, refer to the "Troubleshooting and Tips" section later in this chapter.

Running Tomcat with the Server Option

You can run Tomcat with Java's server option, which will increase efficiency and thus increase performance. To run Tomcat with the server option, you'll need to modify a number of files in the bin directory. For Windows, you need to edit setclasspath.bat. Change the last three lines as follows:

```
set _RUNJAVA="%JAVA_HOME%\bin\java" -server
set _RUNJAVAW="%JAVA_HOME%\bin\javaw" -server
set _RUNJDB="%JAVA_HOME%\bin\jdb" -server
```

Of course this assumes you're starting Tomcat manually.

The process is similar in Linux. This time you modify setclasspath.sh, like so:

```
_RUNJAVA="$JAVA_HOME"/bin/java -server
_RUNJDB="$JAVA_HOME"/bin/jdb -server
```

Installing Ant

Before you install Tomcat from source, or indeed before you start any serious Java-based project, you should install Ant. Ant is a Java-based build tool that has become ubiquitous. You use it to build and deploy applications. It benefits from platform independence and can use a single build file on multiple platforms. However, the build files must minimize dependency on a specific file path. (Windows paths, for example, will cause problems on Linux, and vice versa.)

You can download the latest binary distribution of Ant from http://ant.apache.org/bindownload.cgi. Ant is easy to install; simply unpack the distribution to a convenient location.

Because Ant is a program that you'll use on a number of projects, you should make it available from any directory. To do this, add it to your path and then add an ANT_HOME environment variable as you did with CATALINA_HOME. It's a good idea to set the entry in the path to ANT_HOME\bin to allow for any updates to Ant that you may make.

To test that you've installed Ant, type **ant -version** in a terminal window. If everything has gone to plan, you'll see Ant's usage message.

You won't use Ant for anything but compiling the source code and deploying Web applications in this book, so you won't see the details of it. However, you should be aware that it uses an XML file, called build.xml by default, to carry out its tasks.

Installing Tomcat from Source

If you want to obtain the latest version of Tomcat with the newest bug fixes and upgrades, then installing it from the source code is a good option. In Linux it's far more common for servers to be built for the system. However, this isn't strictly necessary for a Java-based server such as Tomcat.

Tomcat is easily built using the Ant build utility. You use Ant for automated project building, including compilation and deployment. It has all the system-independent benefits that Java enjoys because it's written in Java.

You can also use Ant to carry out a number of administrative actions on Tomcat, each of which is described in Chapter 6. The `deployer` application mentioned previously also uses Ant.

It used to be the case that you had to manually download a huge number of libraries from many different sources to compile Tomcat, but now Ant can do it for you. In fact, it will even download the Tomcat's source for you.

All you need to download and build Tomcat is the `http://jakarta.apache.org/tomcat/tomcat-5.0-doc/build.xml` file (or `http://jakarta.apache.org/tomcat/tomcat-5.5-doc/build.xml`) and a file called `build.properties` that you create for the purpose. Download the `build.xml` file to a convenient directory where you'll carry out the build. Create a `build.properties` file in the same directory with the appropriate lines from Listing 2-1. Those with # marks are commented out and can be ignored if they don't apply to your installation. You should ensure that `base.path` points to the place you want to download.

Listing 2-1. *Ant's `build.properties` File*

```
# ----- Default Base Path for Dependent Packages -----
# ----- Linux/Unix path -----
base.path=/usr/share/java
# ----- Windows path -----
#base.path=C://TomcatBuild

# ----- Proxy setup -----
# Uncomment if using a proxy server
#proxy.host=proxy.domain
#proxy.port=8080
#proxy.use=on
```

Once you're satisfied with your setup, you can build Tomcat using the following line in the base directory:

```
> ant
```

The build will take a few minutes, and the resultant build is the subdirectory `jakarta-tomcat-5/build`. To deploy the new server, move (and rename) it out of the source folder and into a folder of its own, and set the `CATALINA_HOME` variable using the instructions given previously.

If you want to update the source code and recompile it, use the following commands in the source directory:

```
> ant checkout
> ant build
```

The second command will compile only those files that have changed, so you can also use it to compile the server if you've made any changes of your own to the source.

Troubleshooting and Tips

Finally, before I close this chapter, I'll cover the typical problems that may occur when you install Tomcat. If you have further problems, you can find more material on the Tomcat Web site at `http://jakarta.apache.org/tomcat/` and at `http://java.sun.com` as well as on various forums. You should also read the release notes available with each download.

The following are a number of problems typically encountered when first installing Tomcat.

The Tomcat Window Disappears

This is particularly difficult to diagnose and applies especially to Windows. Since the problem usually has one of two causes, however, you can start by diagnosing it and then move on to the known solutions.

If Tomcat doesn't start, it can be run in the current shell or command prompt so you can see what the problem is. Type the following on Linux:

```
# $CATALINA_HOME/bin/catalina.sh run
```

Or type the following on Windows:

```
> %CATALINA_HOME%/bin/catalina run
```

This will produce the normal startup messages, and any errors will be displayed. These errors also appear in the log file in the `CATALINA_HOME/logs` directory. (You may have to set up logging for Tomcat 5.5.*x*; see Chapter 4.)

Check that you're using the correct version of Java for the Tomcat version you're trying to run. If you're using JDK 1.4 with Tomcat 5.5, make sure the following files exist:

- `CATALINA_HOME\bin\jmx.jar`
- `CATALINA_HOME\common\endorsed\xercesImpl.jar`
- `CATALINA_HOME\common\endorsed\xml-apis.jar`

If not, download the compatibility files from the Jakarta Web site.

The Port Number Is in Use

Tomcat uses port 8080 by default, as mentioned previously. You can check if another program is using this port by using `netstat`. Typing **netstat** (**netstat -ln** on Linux) into your shell/command prompt will list open ports on your system and should show the process that's interfering with Tomcat. You have two options: shut the process down or change Tomcat's port as described earlier.

A common problem is trying to start a new Tomcat instance when one is still running. This is especially true if it's running as a daemon thread. If you suspect this is the case, you can check it by using `telnet` to connect to the socket, as follows, and see if you're given a connection:

```
$ telnet localhost 8080
```

If you're awarded a connection, the screen goes blank rather than giving an error.

When you're connected, type **GET /** and press Return or Enter. (Echo is turned off by default on Windows, so it looks a little strange because typing doesn't appear to achieve anything.) On Windows, this results in the following output:

```
HTTP/1.0 302 Found
Content-Type: text/html
Location: http://127.0.0.1:8080/
/index.jsp
Content-Length: 167
Servlet-Engine: Tomcat Web Server/3.2.1 (JSP 1.1; Servlet 2.2; Java 1.3.0; Windows

2000 5.0 x86; java.vendor=Sun Microsystems Inc.)

<head><title>Document moved</title></head>
<body><h1>Document moved</h1>
This document has moved <a href="http://127.0.0.1:8080/
/index.jsp">here</a>.<p>
</body>

Connection to host lost.

>
```

In this case, you have an instance of Tomcat 3.2.1 running in the background that's stopping the new Tomcat instance from booting.

Even if you're refused a connection, this indicates that a process is sitting on that port. If the connection fails, then try one of the other possibilities.

Summary

I've gone through a great deal of information in the course of this chapter to select and install a JDK, Ant, and Tomcat in a variety of ways. In the majority of cases, the installation of the server is a straightforward process, because binary versions are available for the common platforms.

If you have any problems, `http://jakarta.apache.org` has a number of lists that can be helpful to the beginner. The user list is also archived, and you'll find that most questions have been asked, and answered, before.

CHAPTER 3

Examining Tomcat's Directories

In the previous chapter you saw how to install Tomcat on various platforms, using the binaries or the source as the fancy takes you. Now it's time to look at the directories that make up the Tomcat installation. You'll be introduced to the main configuration files and the structure of a Web application. However, I'll leave the details on configuration until Chapter 4.

In this chapter you'll do the following:

- You'll examine the default Tomcat installation.
- You'll learn about the generic Web application structure, both unpacked and packed.

Looking at CATALINA_HOME

The best place to start a discussion of Tomcat's directory structure is in the default installation directory, commonly called `CATALINA_HOME`. If you've installed Tomcat, then you'll have an environment variable pointing to this directory. Let's start by examining the `bin` directory and all the scripts it contains.

The bin Directory

The `bin` directory contains many scripts (in Windows they're called *batch files*, but the term *scripts* will do for the sake of brevity) for starting Tomcat in different modes and for stopping Tomcat, a number of utilities, and some Windows-specific executables.

The catalina and catalina.50 (Tomcat 5.0.*x* Only) Scripts

You can use the `catalina` script to start and stop the server. In addition, a number of the other scripts in the `bin` directory call it. `catalina.50` does the same job as `catalina` but has the following command-line parameter removed:

```
-Djava.endorsed.dirs="%JAVA_ENDORSED_DIRS%"
```

This means you use `catalina.50` to start Tomcat without enabling its endorsed mechanism. Therefore, Tomcat won't load any of the classes in `CATALINA_HOME/common/endorsed`. You may want to do this to force Web applications to use Java's default classes. However, none of the other scripts refers to this file; they still use `catalina`. Tomcat 5.5 doesn't contain the new script at all. From now on, `catalina` is the only script that will be referenced.

You can use it to start Tomcat in a variety of modes. For example, you can start it with or without debugging, with or without a security manager, and in embedded mode to use it as part of a bigger application.

The `catalina` script has a number of options associated with it, as described in Table 3-1.

Table 3-1. *The Options for the `catalina` Script*

Option	Description
`debug`	Runs Tomcat in a debugger.
`debug -security`	Runs Tomcat in a debugger with the security manager.
`jpda start`	Runs Tomcat in the Java Platform Debugger Architecture (JPDA) debugger. This API allows a developer to write custom debugging applications.
`run`	Runs Tomcat in the current window. This option is useful for debugging startup issues because you can see any error messages without the window vanishing.
`run -security`	Runs Tomcat in the current window with the security manager.
`start`	Runs Tomcat in a new window.
`start -security`	Runs Tomcat in a new window with the security manager.
`stop`	Stops Tomcat.
`version`	Shows the version of Tomcat.

The cpappend Script

Other scripts use the `cpappend` script to create the classpath dynamically before starting the server. You can override the setting provided here to allow each user to have personalized configuration files for the same server installation, whether for different instances of the server running at the same time or for a development environment for nonconcurrent users. This means each user can configure the server without affecting the work of other users.

The digest Script

You can use the `digest` script to create digested passwords. This is a particularly useful feature if you're using Tomcat's security features and want to implement container-managed security. By digesting a user's password, you make it harder for someone to obtain it, especially if you're using the file-based version of container-managed security. Plain-text passwords in text files are very vulnerable. Digesting a password doesn't mean that the password can't be discovered, but it does make it more difficult. Chapter 12 covers container-managed security.

The following is an example of digesting a password with the MD5 algorithm:

```
> digest -a md5 tomcat
```

The -a switch specifies the algorithm to use and is mandatory. The following is the result, with the clear-text password followed by a colon and then the digested password:

```
tomcat:1b359d8753858b55befa0441067aaed3
```

The digest script also supports the SHA algorithm, like so:

```
> digest -a sha tomcat
tomcat:536c0b339345616c1b33caf454454d8b8a190d6c
```

The service Script

The `service` script is a Windows-only script. You can use it to install and remove Tomcat as an NT service. Table 3-2 describes the options.

Table 3-2. *The Options for Running the `service` Script*

Option	Description
`install`	Installs Tomcat as a service called `Tomcat5` unless an alternative name is given
`remove`	Removes the Tomcat service called `Tomcat5` unless an alternative name is given

The following is an example of installing a service called `TomcatServ` and then removing it:

```
service install TomcatServ
service remove TomcatServ
```

The setclasspath Script

The `catalina` script calls the `setclasspath` script to check that all the necessary binaries, such as the Java compiler, are on the system, to set any Java options that have been specified, and to set its classpath.

The startup and shutdown Scripts

You can use the `startup` and `shutdown` scripts to start and stop the server, just as you could use the `catalina` script. However, in this case you don't have to specify any command-line options, so you can create shortcuts to start and stop Tomcat.

The startup-using-launcher and shutdown-using-launcher Scripts (Tomcat 5.0.*x* Only)

You can use the `startup-using-launcher` and `shutdown-using-launcher` scripts to start and stop the server using Ant's launcher mechanism. The `catalina.xml` file in the `bin` directory is used as the Ant project file. For this to work, you must place the `ANT_HOME/lib/ant-launcher.jar` file in your path. Note that this isn't the classpath, because the `ant-launcher.jar` file is considered an executable in this case.

Windows users should note that they may have to change the `shutdown-using-launcher.bat` file as follows for the shutdown command to work. Delete the following bold line:

```
rem %0 must have been found by DOS using the %PATH% so we assume that
rem setenv.bat will also be found in the %PATH%
call setenv.bat
goto doneSetenv
```

However, in most cases the script will complete its execution with an error message as follows:

```
'setenv.bat' is not recognized as an internal or external command,
operable program or batch file.
```

The tomcat5 Windows Executable

You can use the `tomcat5` executable to run the server if it's installed as an NT service. You can install Tomcat as a service either when you first install Tomcat, as described in the previous chapter, or using the `service.bat` file as described earlier in this chapter.

Note that the name of this executable must be the same as that of the service you want to start. So, if you install the service as `TomcatServ`, you must rename this file `TomcatServ.exe` if you want to use its services.

The tomcat5w Windows Executable

You can use the `tomcat5w` executable to run the Tomcat Properties box if Tomcat is installed as a service. Chapter 2 described this utility. You can use it to start and stop the service and set other options.

Note that the name of this executable must be the same as that of the service you want to start, with a `w` appended. So, if you install the service as `TomcatServ`, you must rename this file `TomcatServw.exe` if you want to use its services.

The tool-wrapper and tool-wrapper-using-launcher (Tomcat 5.0.*x* Only) Scripts

This script allows command-line tools to be called in the same environment as Tomcat so that they have a common set of references. For example, command-line analysis tools may need to run within the same environment as Tomcat to identify problems that are specific to Tomcat. If the classpath for the analysis tool isn't the same as for the server, then obviously classpath issues can't be identified, and so on.

The same instructions apply for the launcher version of this script as for the startup and shutdown scripts described previously. Windows users should remove the line that called `setenv.bat`.

The version Script

The `version` script calls the `version` option of the `catalina` script and produces the same results.

The common Directory

The common directory contains three subdirectories: classes, endorsed, and lib. Tomcat 5.5 also has the i18n directory. Classes in the subdirectories of common will be available to Tomcat and all the Web applications running on the server. Common contents of these directories, bar the defaults that come with Tomcat, will be database drivers for serverwide data sources.

You should place class files in the classes folder and utility Java archive (JAR) files (that is, packaged classes and supporting resources) in lib. Never place application-specific classes in either of these directories. The endorsed directory is a special case for working with JDK 1.4 and later.

JDK 1.4 (and later JDKs) comes packaged with a number of APIs, the most important of which, from your point of view, are XML parsers. It used to be the case that to change the systemwide XML parser you simply dropped the new parser's JAR files into common/lib. However, the class-loading mechanism always prefers the JDK's XML parser to any other XML parser in the classpath. The good news is that the JDK allows you to override this setting, and Tomcat does so by providing the endorsed directory and the following switch to the startup command in the bin/catalina script (though not the catalina.50 script for Tomcat 5.0.*x*, as explained previously):

```
-Djava.endorsed.dirs="%JAVA_ENDORSED_DIRS%"
```

You can set the JAVA_ENDORSED_DIRS variable in the bin/setclasspath script.

If you place JAR files here, they will be used by the class loader in preference to the JDK's classes and will be available to all Web applications running on the server.

The Tomcat 5.5 i18n directory contains optional internationalization messages that Tomcat uses to customize its output when dealing with browsers from a country other than your own. They can be removed if you don't require them.

The conf Directory

The conf directory contains the following Tomcat configuration files:

- catalina.policy sets up the necessary permissions for Catalina when it's run within the context of a security manager.
- catalina.properties sets the locations of the various class loader directories. The defaults are the common, server, and shared directories and their subdirectories. The settings in this file determine which classes are available to all Web applications and which classes are available to Tomcat. In other words, these settings configure the classpath of Tomcat and all Web applications.
- context.xml is a Tomcat 5.5–only file that sets the defaults for individual contexts.
- jk2.properties sets the properties for the Tomcat connector that connects to an external Web server. You'll see more of this in Chapter 9.
- server.xml is the main configuration file for Tomcat and is discussed in detail in Chapter 4. You use it to configure everything from the shutdown command to logging, filtering, connections to other Web servers, the port and host on which the server is running, and the location of each Web application's files.

- server-minimal.xml is a minimal version of server.xml.
- tomcat-users.xml is the default user database for container-managed authentication. You can change the name and location of the file in server.xml. You'll see more on this mechanism in Chapter 4.
- web.xml is the default deployment descriptor for all Web applications. Tomcat processes it before processing the web.xml files in the server's Web applications.

The Subdirectories of the conf Directory

If you have to configure a Web application context, you should place the XML configuration file for that context in the conf/[Service_name]/[Host_name] subdirectory.

Tomcat 5.5 also allows you to configure host-level context defaults by placing the context.xml file in conf/[Service_name]/[Host_name]. This is analogous to the context.xml file described in the previous section. You'll see how to do all this in Chapter 5.

The logs Directory

The logs directory is the default location for application log files. The default Tomcat 5.0.*x* installation generates time-stamped logs for the localhost host (the default home of the server). You can easily configure logs for each component of the server using logger components in conf/server.xml. Tomcat 5.5 uses a different mechanism that you'll learn about in Chapter 4.

You may have to schedule housekeeping tasks to ensure that the size of the logs directory doesn't grow out of hand.

The server Directory

The server directory contains three subdirectories: classes, lib, and webapps. Classes in the subdirectories of server will be available to Tomcat only.

You should place class files in the classes folder and utility JAR files (that is, packaged classes and supporting resources) in lib.

The webapps directory contains classes and resources for admin and manager, Tomcat's two admin Web applications. If you're using Tomcat 5.5, you'll have to download the admin application separately. However, the source distribution of Tomcat 5.5 includes the admin application, which means you will install it if you build Tomcat 5.5 from source.

The shared Directory

The shared directory contains two subdirectories: classes and lib. Classes in the subdirectories of shared will be available to all the Web applications running on the server but not to Tomcat.

You should place class files in the classes folder and utility JAR files (that is, packaged classes and supporting resources) in lib. Never place application-specific classes in either of these directories.

The temp Directory

Tomcat uses the temp directory for storing temporary files.

The webapps Directory

The `webapps` directory is the default location of Tomcat's Web applications. You can change this location, and it's recommended that you do so, as you can then separate the application files that change relatively frequently from the server files that don't tend to change much. As a bonus, the installation directory for Tomcat can be kept as read/write for the administrator only, thus maintaining greater security—read/write access for other users need be provided only for the now separate `webapps` folder.

You can deploy Web applications in `webapps` by placing them here, in both packaged and unpackaged formats, and they will be automatically deployed at the next server bootup. This is an alternative to the `conf/[Service_name]/[Host_name]` method and the various deployer (such as Ant and the Tomcat `manager` application) methods.

The work Directory

The `work` directory is where Tomcat places the JSP code after it has been converted into servlet code. Once a JSP page has been visited, Tomcat also stores the compiled servlet here.

Understanding Web Application Structure

A Web application is a collection of Web resources, such as JSP pages, HTML pages, servlets, and configuration files, organized into a hierarchy as specified in the Servlet specification. You have two ways in which to organize a Web application: packed and unpacked. The packed form is called a Web archive (WAR) file, and the unpacked form is a collection of directories stored on the file system.

The unpackaged format is convenient for Web application developers, as it allows them to replace individual files while the application is being developed and debugged.

However, in a deployment environment, it's often more convenient to provide a single file that can be automatically deployed. This reduces the deployment process to placing the file and setting up system resources. Tomcat can also automatically expand a Web application once the server has booted. The automatic expansion of WAR files is configured in the `server.xml` file as part of the `<Host>` element that configures hosts.

Web Application Context

Each Web application corresponds to a context component, as discussed in Chapter 1, and you assign a context path to each. The default context is called `ROOT` and corresponds to the name of the server with no other context information. For example, the `ROOT` Web application on your local machine will correspond to `http://localhost:8080`. If you've configured Domain Name System (DNS) settings for your server, it may also be accessible from a location such as `http://www.companyname.com/`.

Users access other Web applications by requesting a context relative to the server. For example, users can access Tomcat's `manager` Web application with the following URL: `http://localhost:8080/manager/`.

Applications that you place in the `webapps` folder are named after the directory they're in. So, you can access the Web application in the `tomcat-docs` directory with the following: `http://localhost:8080/tomcat-docs/`. Each application on the server is known by its name, and users can access resources according to the remainder of the uniform resource locator (URL) after the Web application's name.

This setup has a slight problem, however. If the ROOT Web application contains a subdirectory that has the same name as a Web application, and that Web application and that subfolder have filenames in common, then the applications won't work as expected. For example, the following are two Web applications that could cause confusion:

```
webapps/
        ROOT/
             tomcatBook/
                        index.html
        tomcatBook/
                   index.html
```

In this case http://localhost:8080/tomcatBook/ could map to both files and could cause confusion. Tomcat will display the index.html page from the tomcatBook Web application and will ignore the folder in the ROOT Web application. If your users are expecting the ROOT version, then they will be disappointed.

The WEB-INF Directory

The Servlet specification sets out how you partition Web applications into public and private areas. You store the private resources in a directory called WEB-INF in the root of the Web application. This is where you store all the Web application–specific configuration files, application classes, and application-specific utilities. Users may only access these resources indirectly (for example, through servlet mappings).

WEB-INF has a number of specialized subdirectories, where you store specific files, such as tag files and tag library descriptors (TLDs). These are defined in the appropriate specification, be it for servlets or JSP pages. You'll deal with them in detail in Chapter 5 when you configure a Web application, but here's a quick rundown:

```
webAppX/
        WEB-INF/
                classes/
                lib/
                tags/
```

The classes and lib directory follow the usual pattern in Tomcat; you place class files in classes and JAR files in lib. tags is a special directory for tag files, which are a new part of the JSP 2.0 specification.

The META-INF Directory

The `META-INF` directory is placed at the root of a Web application when it's deployed as a WAR file. This is where you place tag TLDs and tag files so that they can be found using a unique uniform resource indicator (URI). If no context XML files for this WAR file exist, then you can also place one in this directory. You'll find more details of this directory in Chapter 5.

Summary

This chapter outlined the contents of Tomcat's installation directory, its subdirectories, and the scripts they contain. This information is all you need to manage Tomcat's operation, from startup to shutdown.

The chapter also covered the structure of a Web application, without going into the details of configuration. It should have given you a familiarity with Tomcat's internals and prepared you for the coming chapters.

CHAPTER 4

Working with Tomcat's Configuration Files

In this chapter, you'll focus on basic Tomcat configuration by examining the files found in `CATALINA_HOME/conf`. The default installation of Tomcat uses these files to configure the server when it starts up; therefore, it's of the utmost importance that you understand what the default configuration will do and how you can modify it.

You'll see the main configuration file, `server.xml`, and Tomcat's other configuration files. As you saw in Chapter 1, Tomcat uses a component-based, hierarchical architecture. This model greatly simplifies the configuration of the complex server.

You'll see the top-level components and the hierarchy of containers below them, as well as the nested components, all of which should be familiar to you from Chapter 1. By the end of this chapter, you'll be comfortable with the default configuration of Tomcat, and you'll also be able to modify this configuration for your own needs.

The final part of the chapter will cover Windows service configuration and how you can modify this option for your own needs.

Examining Tomcat's Configuration Files

Tomcat's configuration directory is `CATALINA_HOME/conf`. It contains the following files:

- `catalina.policy`
- `catalina.properties`
- `context.xml` (Tomcat 5.5 only)
- `jk2.properties` (Tomcat 5.0.*x* only)
- `server.xml`
- `server-minimal.xml`
- `tomcat-users.xml`
- `web.xml`

Using catalina.policy for Access Control

Because you'll see more on Tomcat security in a later chapter, in this chapter you'll take only a quick look through catalina.policy to learn how it provides fine-grained access control to a Tomcat server administrator through the built-in security model of Java 2.

Any access to system resources that isn't explicitly allowed is prohibited; therefore, you must anticipate all the resources that Tomcat will need and explicitly grant permission for it to do so. By default, Tomcat starts without security. To start it with security, use the -security switch.

```
> $CATALINA_HOME/bin/startup security
```

Tomcat only reads, processes, and enforces the catalina.policy file when started in the security manager in this manner. The general policy entry is in the following form:

```
grant <security principal> { permission list... };
```

Here <security principal> is typically a body of trusted code.

Looking at the catalina.policy file, the first set of permissions grants access to all resources for code from the Java compiler directories; this is essentially the Java compiler and runtime system code. (See http://java.sun.com/j2se/1.4.2/docs/guide/security/permissions.html for details of permissions.)

```
// These permissions apply to javac
grant codeBase "file:${java.home}/lib/-" {
        permission java.security.AllPermission;
};

// These permissions apply to all shared system extensions
grant codeBase "file:${java.home}/jre/lib/ext/-" {
        permission java.security.AllPermission;
};

// These permissions apply to javac when ${java.home] points at $JAVA_HOME/jre
grant codeBase "file:${java.home}/../lib/-" {
        permission java.security.AllPermission;
};

// These permissions apply to all shared system extensions when
// ${java.home} points at $JAVA_HOME/jre
grant codeBase "file:${java.home}/lib/ext/-" {
        permission java.security.AllPermission;
};
```

As these directories have access to the entire system, it's vital that you protect them using your operating system file protection features (see Chapter 12 for details). Without this precaution, malicious code could run unchecked on your system.

The next section of catalina.policy grants the Catalina server and API libraries access to all resources.

```
// These permissions apply to the launcher code
grant codeBase "file:${catalina.home}/bin/commons-launcher.jar" {
        permission java.security.AllPermission;
};

// These permissions apply to the daemon code
grant codeBase "file:${catalina.home}/bin/commons-daemon.jar" {
        permission java.security.AllPermission;
};

// These permissions apply to the commons-logging API
grant codeBase "file:${catalina.home}/bin/commons-logging-api.jar" {
        permission java.security.AllPermission;
};

// These permissions apply to the server startup code
grant codeBase "file:${catalina.home}/bin/bootstrap.jar" {
        permission java.security.AllPermission;
};

// These permissions apply to the JMX server
grant codeBase "file:${catalina.home}/bin/jmx.jar" {
        permission java.security.AllPermission;
};

// These permissions apply to the servlet API classes
// and those that are shared across all class loaders
// located in the "common" directory
grant codeBase "file:${catalina.home}/common/-" {
        permission java.security.AllPermission;
};

// These permissions apply to the container's core code, plus any additional
// libraries installed in the "server" directory
grant codeBase "file:${catalina.home}/server/-" {
        permission java.security.AllPermission;
};
```

Again, you must secure the previous directories on the file system, thus avoiding the possibility of an attacker adding malicious code to them. Any class files you place in these directories will be granted access to all system resources.

The final set of permissions in `catalina.policy` contains the default Web application permissions. They're significantly more restrictive than those shown previously. In other words, they're never granted the `java.security.AllPermission` super permission.

The first section enables access to system properties that enable Java Naming and Directory Interface (JNDI) and JDBC access.

```
grant {
    // Required for JNDI lookup of named JDBC DataSource's and
    // javamail named MimePart DataSource used to send mail
    permission java.util.PropertyPermission "java.home", "read";
    permission java.util.PropertyPermission "java.naming.*", "read";
    permission java.util.PropertyPermission "javax.sql.*", "read";
```

The next section enables read-only access to some operating system description properties: the type of operating system Tomcat is running under and what this operating system uses to separate file extensions in a filename.

```
// OS-specific properties to allow read access
permission java.util.PropertyPermission "os.name", "read";
permission java.util.PropertyPermission "os.version", "read";
permission java.util.PropertyPermission "os.arch", "read";
permission java.util.PropertyPermission "file.separator", "read";
permission java.util.PropertyPermission "path.separator", "read";
permission java.util.PropertyPermission "line.separator", "read";
```

The third section enables read-only access to some JVM-specific properties that are often used in application programming:

```
// JVM properties to allow read access
permission java.util.PropertyPermission "java.version", "read";
permission java.util.PropertyPermission "java.vendor", "read";
permission java.util.PropertyPermission "java.vendor.url", "read";
permission java.util.PropertyPermission "java.class.version", "read";
permission java.util.PropertyPermission "java.specification.version", "read";
permission java.util.PropertyPermission "java.specification.vendor", "read";
permission java.util.PropertyPermission "java.specification.name", "read";

permission java.util.PropertyPermission "java.vm.specification.version", "read";
permission java.util.PropertyPermission "java.vm.specification.vendor", "read";
permission java.util.PropertyPermission "java.vm.specification.name", "read";
permission java.util.PropertyPermission "java.vm.version", "read";
permission java.util.PropertyPermission "java.vm.vendor", "read";
permission java.util.PropertyPermission "java.vm.name", "read";
```

The next two sections provide access for JavaBean `getAttribute` methods and the XML parser debug, frequently required during code development (see the JavaBean and JAXP specifications for more details on these properties).

```
// Required for OpenJMX
permission java.lang.RuntimePermission "getAttribute";

// Allow read of JAXP-compliant XML parser debug
permission java.util.PropertyPermission "jaxp.debug", "read";
```

The final section gives permission to the Jasper runtime classes for precompiled JSP pages. Internal Tomcat classes aren't available by default, but they can be made available in the catalina.properties file, which is described next.

```
    // Precompiled JSPs need access to this package.
    permission java.lang.RuntimePermission
      "accessClassInPackage.org.apache.jasper.runtime";
    permission java.lang.RuntimePermission
      "accessClassInPackage.org.apache.jasper.runtime.*";

};
```

These are the minimal permissions that are granted by default to Web applications. Your secured production configuration may require additional access to a JDBC server or network access to an external authentication system. You can find examples of these at the end of catalina.policy.

```
// The permissions granted to the context root directory apply to JSP pages.
// grant codeBase "file:${catalina.home}/webapps/examples/-" {
//      permission java.net.SocketPermission "dbhost.mycompany.com:5432", "connect";
//      permission java.net.SocketPermission "*.noaa.gov:80", "connect";
// };
//
// The permissions granted to the context WEB-INF/classes directory
// grant codeBase "file:${catalina.home}/webapps/examples/WEB-INF/classes/-" {
// };
//
// The permission granted to your JDBC driver
// grant codeBase "jar:file:${catalina.home}
    /webapps/examples/WEB-INF/lib/driver.jar!/-" {
//      permission java.net.SocketPermission "dbhost.mycompany.com:5432", "connect";
// };
// The permission granted to the scrape taglib
// grant codeBase "jar:file:${catalina.home}
    /webapps/examples/WEB-INF/lib/scrape.jar!/-" {
//      permission java.net.SocketPermission "*.noaa.gov:80", "connect";
// };
```

Using catalina.properties to Configure Tomcat's Class Loaders

You use the catalina.properties file to configure Tomcat's class loaders. These determine which classes are available to different parts of the server. In the previous chapter, you saw the three directories, common, server, and shared, that are set as the path for the class loaders by default. You can change these directories in catalina.properties.

Another setting you can alter here is the classes that are available to Web applications running on the server. When a class loader tries to load a forbidden class, a `java.security.AccessControlException` is thrown. This setting applies only if you start Tomcat in security mode.

The first section lists the forbidden packages. By default, Tomcat won't allow Web applications to load any of Tomcat's internal classes.

```
# List of comma-separated packages that start with or equal this string
# will cause a security exception to be thrown when
# passed to checkPackageAccess unless the
# corresponding RuntimePermission ("accessClassInPackage."+package) has
# been granted.
package.access=sun.,org.apache.catalina.,org.apache.coyote.,
org.apache.tomcat.,org.apache.jasper.,sun.beans.
```

If a Web application on your server wants to have access to an internal class, say `org.apache.tomcat.util.IntrospectionUtils`, and you're happy about letting it, then you would add the following to `catalina.policy`:

```
// Permission for org.apache.tomcat. package
permission java.lang.RuntimePermission
  "accessClassInPackage.org.apache.tomcat.util";
```

The next section disallows users from defining classes in certain restricted packages.

```
# List of comma-separated packages that start with or equal this string
# will cause a security exception to be thrown when
# passed to checkPackageDefinition unless the
# corresponding RuntimePermission ("defineClassInPackage."+package) has
# been granted.
#
# by default, no packages are restricted for definition, and none of
# the class loaders supplied with the JDK call checkPackageDefinition.
#
package.definition=sun.,java.,org.apache.catalina.,org.apache.coyote.,
  org.apache.tomcat.,org.apache.jasper.
```

This section is here for completeness only and doesn't affect Tomcat's operation.

The next section defines Tomcat's common class loader, which in this case corresponds to the `common` directory and its subdirectories.

```
# List of comma-separated paths defining the contents of the "common"
# class loader. Prefixes should be used to define what is the repository type.
# Path may be relative to the CATALINA_HOME path or absolute. If left as blank,
# the JVM system loader will be used as Catalina's "common" loader.
# Examples:
#     "foo": Add this folder as a class repository
#     "foo/*.jar": Add all the JARs of the specified folder as class
#                  repositories
```

```
#     "foo/bar.jar": Add bar.jar as a class repository
common.loader=${catalina.home}/common/classes,${catalina.home}
  /common/endorsed/*.jar,${catalina.home}/common/lib/*.jar
```

Tomcat 5.5 has a slightly different setting to account for its different directory structure.

```
# Tomcat 5.5
common.loader=${catalina.home}/common/classes,
  ${catalina.home}/common/i18n/*.jar,
  ${catalina.home}/common/endorsed/*.jar,
  ${catalina.home}/common/lib/*.jar
```

Any classes placed in these directories will be available to Tomcat's internal classes as well as all Web applications.

The next section defines Tomcat's server class loader, which in this case corresponds to the server directory and its subdirectories.

```
# List of comma-separated paths defining the contents of the "server"
# class loader. Prefixes should be used to define what is the repository type.
# Path may be relative to the CATALINA_HOME path or absolute. If left as blank,
# the "common" loader will be used as Catalina's "server" loader.
# Examples:
#     "foo": Add this folder as a class repository
#     "foo/*.jar": Add all the JARs of the specified folder as class
#                  repositories
#     "foo/bar.jar": Add bar.jar as a class repository
server.loader=${catalina.home}/server/classes,${catalina.home}/server/lib/*.jar
```

Any classes placed in these directories will be available to Tomcat's internal classes only.

The final section of this file defines Tomcat's shared class loader, which in this case corresponds to the shared directory and its subdirectories. If this definition is left out, the common class loader will be used.

```
# List of comma-separated paths defining the contents of the "shared"
# class loader. Prefixes should be used to define what is the repository type.
# Path may be relative to the CATALINA_BASE path or absolute. If left as blank,
# the "common" loader will be used as Catalina's "shared" loader.
# Examples:
#     "foo": Add this folder as a class repository
#     "foo/*.jar": Add all the JARs of the specified folder as class
#                  repositories
#     "foo/bar.jar": Add bar.jar as a class repository
shared.loader=${catalina.base}/shared/classes,${catalina.base}/shared/lib/*.jar
```

Any classes placed in these directories will be available to Web applications but not Tomcat's internal classes.

Using jk2.properties to Connect to Apache

This file configures the Jk2 connector that allows Tomcat to work with the Apache Web server. In this setup, Tomcat handles the dynamic content, and Apache serves the static content. You'll see more of this file in Chapter 9.

Using server.xml to Configure Tomcat

Tomcat's component-based architecture considerably simplifies configuration. Any properties that are set on the outer components are inherited by the inner components. For example, a listener that's configured in an engine will be used by a nested host component.

However, if you need a lower-level component to have its own setup, you can override the outer configuration by adding components to the inner component. For example, you could set a realm on a context component to override the realm configured at the engine level. This means that the Web applications running within this context will use the newly defined realm instead of the outer one.

This component-based model lends itself to XML configuration because of XML's hierarchical nature. Each component is represented by an element in an XML file, which makes it easy to insert and remove components from a server as appropriate. The name of the file that does this job in Tomcat is `server.xml`, which Tomcat reads at startup.

■ **Note** No DTD or schema exists for `server.xml` because the attributes of certain elements depend on the class implementing the component that the element represents.

Tomcat comes bundled with a default `server.xml` file ready to run on your machine. It defines a "Catalina" service, a "Catalina" engine, and a "localhost" host. It also contains two loggers (Tomcat 5.0.*x* only), one for the engine and one at the host level, which overrides the engine's logger, and a memory realm for user authentication. A number of other options have been commented out by default but are well commented.

Tomcat also comes with a file called `server-minimal.xml`, which is a stripped-down version of the configuration file on which you can base your own settings.

Configuring a Server

Let's take a closer look at how to configure a server by going through the `server.xml` file that comes with Tomcat. As you'll recall from Chapter 1, a server component is a top-level component, and any Tomcat instances can have only one server component. This means that the `<Server>` element in `server.xml` is the root element.

```
<Server port="8005" shutdown="SHUTDOWN" debug="0">
```

The <Server> element represents the JVM and listens to port 8005 for a shutdown command, which will contain the text SHUTDOWN. This provides a graceful way for an administrator (or management console software) to shut down this Tomcat server instance. The server instance won't print debugging messages to the log because debug is set to 0. Note that at the time of writing Tomcat 5.5 still has the debug attribute set, even though it does nothing. (This caveat applies to all the components in Table 4-1.)

Table 4-1 lists the possible attributes of the <Server> element.

Table 4-1. *The Attributes of the <Server> Element*

Attribute	Description	Required?
className	The Java class for the server to use. This class must implement the org.apache.catalina.Server interface. The standard implementation is used by default.	No
debug	Tomcat 5.0.*x* only. The level of debug information logged by the server. The levels are 1 (errors), 2 (warnings), 3 (information), and 4 (debug). These correspond to the levels of debugging in the logger component. The default is zero, meaning no debugging (though the associated logger will still log fatal messages).	No
port	The TCP/IP port to listen to for the command specified by the shutdown attribute before shutting down gracefully. This command must come from the same physical server machine on which Tomcat is running. This provides a certain level of security when used in combination with the shutdown attribute.	Yes
shutdown	The command string that must be sent to the port number specified by the port attribute.	Yes

Table 4-2 lists the subelements of the <Server> element.

Table 4-2. *The Subelements of the <Server> Element*

Subelement	Description	Number
<GlobalNamingResources>	The global JNDI resources for this server	1
<Service>	A grouping of connectors associated with an engine	1 or more

Configuring Global Naming Resources

JNDI is an API used for looking up information via a naming and directory service. It's a platform-independent API, much like JDBC, and it's designed to work with any compatible naming and directory service—regardless of its native interface API. Some common information you can store and retrieve through JNDI includes the following:

- Usernames and passwords
- An access control policy, such as the Tomcat user and role mechanism
- Organizational directories
- Servers (databases, and so on)
- Printers
- Java objects, such as EJBs

JNDI allows you to avoid the problem of programming for the native interfaces of specific platforms and as such simplifies the process immeasurably. JNDI acts as a layer on top of the native interfaces and translates between the Java classes and the naming servers on the server platform, thus presenting Tomcat with a uniform view of the naming and directory service no matter what the underlying system is.

Additionally, many Java applications use JNDI to locate resources without the need for an underlying naming service. This means a Java application can access resources without knowing their underlying setup or location. For example, a database reference is looked up using its JNDI name only, so it doesn't matter what the underlying database is or what the driver is. This allows programmers to decouple their applications from hard-coded system resources. Figure 4-1 shows JNDI as a directory service and as a Java lookup mechanism.

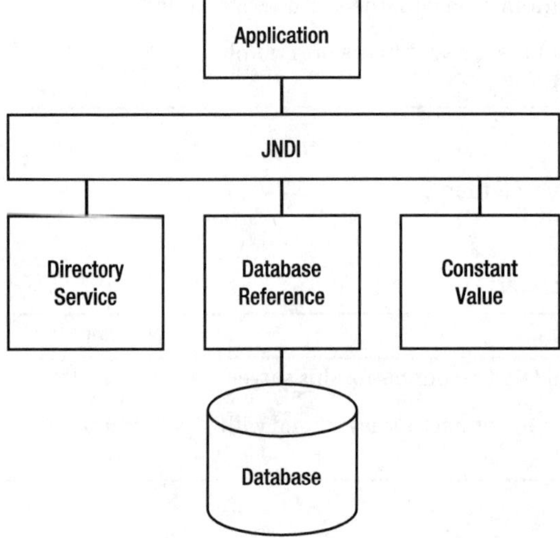

Figure 4-1. *JNDI*

Once the application has the database reference, it can connect to the database directly using JDBC. A constant stored as a JNDI resource can be used across all the Web applications running on a server, as well as by any other Java applications that require it.

Tomcat, and the Web applications that run on it, uses the JNDI resource lookup mechanism extensively.

You configure the server's global JNDI resources with the `<GlobalNamingResources>` element.

```
<GlobalNamingResources>
```

Table 4-3 shows the subelements of `<GlobalNamingResources>`.

Table 4-3. *The Subelements of the `<GlobalNamingResources>` Element*

Subelement	Description	Number
`<Environment>`	A global variable	0 or more
`<Resource>`	A global JNDI resource	0 or more

Configuring Environment Entries

The first type of resource is a serverwide variable. This variable must be of one of the primitive wrapper types that are specified for environment entries in the Servlet specification. You use an `<Environment>` entry to specify this kind of resource.

```
<Environment name="simpleValue" type="java.lang.Integer" value="30"/>
```

This environment entry is called `simpleValue`, is of type `java.lang.Integer`, and has the value 30. It's looked up using the `java:comp/env/simpleValue` string.

Table 4-4 specifies the attributes that `<Environment>` can take.

Table 4-4. *The Attributes of the `<Environment>` Element*

Attribute	Description	Required?
`description`	A description of this environment entry.	No
`name`	The name of the environment entry, relative to the `java:comp/env` context.	Yes
`override`	Set this to `false` if you don't want a Web application deployment descriptor to override this value. The default is `true`.	No
`type`	The fully qualified Java class type of this entry. Must be one of the legal values specified in the Servlet specification for Web application deployment descriptor environment entries: `java.lang.Boolean`, `java.lang.Byte`, `java.lang.Character`, `java.lang.Double`, `java.lang.Float`, `java.lang.Integer`, `java.lang.Long`, `java.lang.Short`, and `java.lang.String`.	Yes
`value`	The value of this entry.	Yes

Configuring a Global Resource

Global resources can include JDBC data sources, Enterprise JavaBean (EJB) references, and user authentication databases. You define them with a <Resource> element, and you must also define a set of resource parameters to configure the object factory for this resource type. You'll see how this is done next.

```
<Resource name="UserDatabase" auth="Container"
          type="org.apache.catalina.UserDatabase"
          description="User database that can be updated and saved">
</Resource>
```

This is a user database for authenticating users against and is set as the default for the Catalina engine further down in `server.xml`.

Table 4-5 describes the attributes that a <Resource> element can take.

Table 4-5. *The Attributes of the <Resource> Element*

Attribute	Description	Required?
`auth`	Specifies whether the Web application signs onto the corresponding resource manager programmatically or whether the container will sign onto the resource manager on behalf of the application. The value of this attribute must be `Application` or `Container`. This attribute is required if the Web application uses a <resource-ref> element in the Web application deployment descriptor but is optional if the application uses a <resource-env-ref> instead.	No
`description`	A description of this resource.	No
`name`	The name of the resource to be created.	Yes
`scope`	Specifies whether connections obtained through this resource manager can be shared. The value of this attribute must be `Shareable` or `Unshareable`. The default is `Shareable`.	No
`type`	The fully qualified Java class name of this resource.	Yes

Configuring Resource Parameters in Tomcat 5.0.*x*

To configure the parameters that go along with a global JNDI resource, you use the <ResourceParams> element.

```
  <ResourceParams name="UserDatabase">
    <parameter>
      <name>factory</name>
      <value>org.apache.catalina.users.MemoryUserDatabaseFactory</value>
    </parameter>
    <parameter>
      <name>pathname</name>
      <value>conf/tomcat-users.xml</value>
    </parameter>
  </ResourceParams>

</GlobalNamingResources>
```

These resource parameters are associated with the UserDatabase resource. They specify the factory class for providing instances of the resource class and specify where the user authentication file can be found, relative to CATALINA_HOME. You'll see more of tomcat-users.xml shortly.

Table 4-6 describes the attribute of the <ResourceParams> element.

Table 4-6. *The Attribute of the <ResourceParams> Element*

Attribute	Description	Required?
name	The name of the resource that these parameters belong to.	Yes

As shown in the previous example from server.xml, <ResourceParams> uses subelements to set the parameters for the resource. Table 4-7 describes these subelements.

Table 4-7. *The Subelements of the <ResourceParams> Element*

Subelement	Description	Number
parameter	Represents a parameter of this resource. It has no attributes and the two subelements listed next.	1 or more
name	The name of the parameter.	1
value	The value of the parameter.	1

Configuring Resource Parameters in Tomcat 5.5

Tomcat 5.5 no longer uses the <ResourceParams> element. Instead, you provide the information with the <Resource> element's attributes.

```
<Resource name="UserDatabase" auth="Container"
          type="org.apache.catalina.UserDatabase"
          description="User database that can be updated and saved"
          factory="org.apache.catalina.users.MemoryUserDatabaseFactory"
          pathname="conf/tomcat-users.xml" />
```

Note how the values here correspond to those previously and thus perform the same function.

Configuring a JDBC Data Source

Web applications running on your server may use common databases and as such will benefit from a JDBC data source. In fact, even if an application is the only one that uses a database, it will benefit from making it into a data source. This makes it easy for you as the administrator to change the underlying database without disturbing Web applications.

Another advantage of data sources is that Tomcat can use connection pooling with them, which means database connections can be recycled once they've finished executing. This in turn leads to improved performance. Tomcat uses the Jakarta Commons Database

Connection Pool mechanism, which you can find in CATALINA_HOME/common/lib/commons-collections-2.1.1.jar, commons-dbcp-1.2.1.jar, and commons-pool-1.2.jar.

The first step to data source configuration is to place the required JDBC driver in CATALINA_HOME/common/lib. This will allow Tomcat to find and access this driver.

As you saw earlier, you can configure the JNDI resource factory using the <Resource> and <ResourceParams> elements. Listing 4-1 shows you a MySQL data source defined for the whole server. This instance of the database will be shared between all the Web applications running on the server. Note that you can also place this definition in context XML files, Tomcat 5.5's default context.xml files, and Tomcat 5.0.*x*'s <DefaultContext> element.

Listing 4-1. *Configuring a JDBC Data Source*

```
<Server port="8005" shutdown="SHUTDOWN" debug="0">
  <GlobalNamingResources>

    <Resource name="jdbc/CatalogDB" auth="SERVLET"
              type="javax.sql.DataSource"/>

    <ResourceParams name="jdbc/CatalogDB">
      <parameter>
        <name>driverClassName</name>
        <value>com.mysql.jdbc.Driver</value>
      </parameter>
      <parameter>
        <name>url</name>
        <value>jdbc:mysql://localhost:3306/catalog</value>
      </parameter>
    </ResourceParams>
  </GlobalNamingResources>
```

This defines a data source called jdbc/CatalogDB and sets its drivers and connection URL. This illustrates how you could change the underlying database without affecting Web applications. In this case, the parameters shown in Table 4-8 are allowed.

Table 4-8. *The Parameters for Use with a JDBC Data Source*

Parameter	Description	Required?
driverClassName	Java class name of the JDBC driver. This driver should be placed in CATALINA_HOME/common/lib.	Yes
logAbandoned	Determines whether Tomcat should log a stack trace of the code that abandoned a connection (see removeAbandoned). The default is false.	No
maxActive	The maximum number of active connections in this pool.	No
maxIdle	The maximum number of idle connections in this pool.	No

Table 4-8. *The Parameters for Use with a JDBC Data Source (Continued)*

Parameter	Description	Required?
`maxWait`	The time in milliseconds that the driver should wait for a connection before throwing an exception.	No
`user`	The user ID used to log onto the database.	No
`password`	The password used to log onto the database.	No
`removeAbandoned`	Sets whether abandoned database connections are removed and recycled. An abandoned connection occurs if a Web application forgets to close it; if this situation continues, there will be no connections left in the pool. Removing and recycling connections avoids this situation. The default is `false`.	No
`removeAbandonedTimeout`	The number of seconds that a connection has been idle before it's classed as abandoned. The default is `300`.	No
`url`	The URL of the database server to be used.	Yes
`validationQuery`	A SQL query used to validate a connection. The factory will perform this query and ensure that rows are returned before considering the connection valid.	No

In addition to the previous configuration, the developer must declare the use of the resource in the application's `web.xml` using a `<resource-ref>` element, as shown in Listing 4-2.

Listing 4-2. *Configuring a Reference to a JDBC Data Source in* `web.xml`

```
<?xml version="1.0" encoding="ISO-8859-1"?>
<web-app xmlns="http://java.sun.com/xml/ns/j2ee"
         xmlns:xsi="http://www.w3.org/2001/XMLSchema-instance"
         xsi:schemaLocation="http://java.sun.com/xml/ns/j2ee
         http://java.sun.com/xml/ns/j2ee/web-app_2_4.xsd" version="2.4">

  <!-- Describe a DataSource -->
  <resource-ref>
    <description>
      Resource reference to a factory for java.sql.Connection
      instances that may be used for talking to a particular
      database that is configured in the tomcatBook.xml file.
    </description>
    <res-ref-name>
      jdbc/CatalogDB
    </res-ref-name>
    <res-type>
      javax.sql.DataSource
    </res-type>
```

```
    <res-auth>
      SERVLET
    </res-auth>
  </resource-ref>

  <!-- Define a Security Constraint on this Application -->
  <security-constraint>
    <web-resource-collection>
      <web-resource-name>Tomcat Book Application</web-resource-name>
      <url-pattern>/*</url-pattern>
    </web-resource-collection>
    <auth-constraint>
       <role-name>tomcat</role-name>
    </auth-constraint>

    <user-data-constraint>
      <description>
       Constrain the user data transport for the whole application
      </description>
      <transport-guarantee>CONFIDENTIAL</transport-guarantee>
    </user-data-constraint>

  </security-constraint>

  <!-- Define the Login Configuration for this Application -->
  <login-config>
    <auth-method>FORM</auth-method>
    <realm-name>Tomcat Book Application</realm-name>
    <form-login-config>
      <form-login-page>/ch12/login.jsp</form-login-page>
      <form-error-page>/ch12/error.jsp</form-error-page>
    </form-login-config>
  </login-config>

  <!-- Security roles referenced by this web application -->
  <security-role>
    <description>
      The role that is required to log in to the Tomcat Book Application
    </description>
    <role-name>tomcat</role-name>
  </security-role>

</web-app>
```

Configuring Mail Sessions

JavaMail is a standard programming API that can be used to create and send e-mails. Tomcat supports JavaMail by allowing you to configure a JavaMail session as a JNDI resource. Web applications can then use JNDI to look up and use this session.

You can configure JavaMail sessions that Web applications can use much in the same way as you can configure JDBC data sources. The theory and practice in both configurations are similar. In the case of JavaMail sessions, the Web application obtains a reference to the mail session without needing to know about the underlying implementation. Again, this allows you to change the underlying mail server without compromising any Web applications.

As already mentioned, the process of setting up a JavaMail session is analogous to setting up a JDBC data source. First, you must place the JavaMail API in `CATALINA_HOME/common/lib` so that Tomcat and Web applications can use its classes. It's available from `http://java.sun.com/products/javamail/downloads/` as `mail.jar`.

Second, configure the mail session in `server.xml` as shown in Listing 4-3.

Listing 4-3. *Configuring a Mail Session*

```
<Resource name="mail/Session" auth="Container"
          type="javax.mail.Session"/>

<ResourceParams name="mail/Session">
  <parameter>
    <name>mail.smtp.host</name>
    <value>localhost</value>
  </parameter>
</ResourceParams>
```

By convention, you configure mail sessions to resolve to the `mail` subcontext. The snippet in Listing 4-3 configures the `mail/Session` context, which refers to an SMTP server running on `localhost`. You can modify the SMTP port (if it isn't at the standard port 25) by setting the `mail.smtp.port` parameter.

Finally, set the JNDI resource in `web.xml`. Listing 4-4 shows the `mail/Session` reference.

Listing 4-4. *Configuring a Reference to a JavaMail Session in `web.xml`*

```
<resource-ref>
  <res-ref-name>mail/Session</res-ref-name>
  <res-type>javax.mail.Session</res-type>
  <res-auth>Container</res-auth>
</resource-ref>
```

Configuring a Service

A service component groups together all the connectors that may be used with an engine.

```
<Service name="Catalina">
```

This service is called Catalina. This name will be visible in logs and error messages, clearly identifying the component. Service management software can also use it to identify the service instance.

Table 4-9 describes the attributes of the `<Service>` element.

Table 4-9. *The Attributes of the <Service> Element*

Attribute	Description	Required?
`className`	The Java class name for the service class to use. The default is `org.apache.catalina.core.StandardService`.	No
`debug`	Tomcat 5.0.*x* only. The level of debugging for this service. The levels are 1 (errors), 2 (warnings), 3 (information), and 4 (debug). These correspond to the levels of debugging in the logger component. This attribute applies to the standard implementation (see `className` next). It may not exist if another implementation is used. The default is zero, meaning no debugging (though the associated logger will still log fatal messages).	No
`name`	The service name, used in logging and management. If more than one `<Service>` element appears inside the `<Server>` element, you must make sure their `name` attributes are different.	Yes

Table 4-10 describes the subelements that a `<Service>` element can have.

Table 4-10. *The Subelements of the <Service> Element*

Subelement	Description	Number
`Connector`	Connects Tomcat to request, either from users or from another Web server.	1 or more
`Engine`	This is Tomcat's request-processing machinery.	1

Configuring a Connector

The following are the two connection points where a request enters Tomcat:

- From a front-end Web server, which could be Apache, IIS, or any other Web server
- From a Web browser

One way to handle these connection requirements is to create a customized version of Tomcat for each situation. This is inefficient and hard to maintain. This is where connectors come in: a connector adapts an engine to the outside world by passing requests into the engine and passing responses out to the user. The connector handles the protocol, connection conventions, and so on, so that the engine doesn't have to handle them.

You can associate more than one connector with a single engine. For example, you may want to provide an HTTP service and an HTTPS service to your users from the same server. In this case, you configure an HTTP connector and an SSL connector in the same engine. You'll see more on this in Chapter 9. For the meantime, let's look through `server.xml` and see the default settings.

A number of different options are available to you when you configure a connector. `server.xml` shows four of the most common.

- An HTTP connector
- An SSL connector
- An AJP 1.3 connector for connecting to another Web server
- A proxy connector

The default connector for the Catalina engine is an HTTP/1.1 connector.

```
<!-- Define a non-SSL Coyote HTTP/1.1 Connector on port 8080 -->
<Connector port="8080"
           maxThreads="150" minSpareThreads="25" maxSpareThreads="75"
           enableLookups="false" redirectPort="8443" acceptCount="100"
           debug="0" connectionTimeout="20000"
           disableUploadTimeout="true" />
```

This sets a connector to listen on port 8080 for HTTP requests. Table 4-11 describes the attributes that are common to all connectors, and Table 4-12 describes the HTTP connector's attributes after the descriptions of the other `<Connector>` elements in `server.xml`.

```
<!-- Define a SSL Coyote HTTP/1.1 Connector on port 8443 -->
<!--
<Connector port="8443"
           maxThreads="150" minSpareThreads="25" maxSpareThreads="75"
           enableLookups="false" disableUploadTimeout="true"
           acceptCount="100" debug="0" scheme="https" secure="true"
           clientAuth="false" sslProtocol="TLS" />
-->
```

This sets a secure SSL connector to listen on port 8443 for HTTPS requests. It shares all the attributes of an ordinary HTTP connector but has some unique SSL attributes all its own. Table 4-13 describes these.

```
<!-- Define a Coyote/JK2 AJP 1.3 Connector on port 8009 -->
<Connector port="8009"
           enableLookups="false" redirectPort="8443" debug="0"
           protocol="AJP/1.3" />
```

This sets up an AJP 1.3 connector listening on port 8009. This type of connector allows Tomcat to connect to an Apache Web server to provide JSP pages and servlets while Apache provides HTML pages and important user-management functionality. Table 4-14 describes the AJP connector's attributes.

```
<!-- Define a Proxied HTTP/1.1 Connector on port 8082 -->
<!-- See proxy documentation for more information about using this. -->
<!--
<Connector port="8082"
           maxThreads="150" minSpareThreads="25" maxSpareThreads="75"
           enableLookups="false"
           acceptCount="100" debug="0" connectionTimeout="20000"
           proxyPort="80" disableUploadTimeout="true" />
-->
```

The final connector setup in server.xml configures a connector to work with a proxy server. This allows the proxy to provide a firewall.

All these connectors are configured to automatically send errors and logging information to the logger associated with their engine.

As promised, Table 4-11 describes the common attributes that are shared by all the connectors described previously.

Table 4-11. *The Common Attributes of the* <Connector> *Element*

Attribute	Description	Required?
address	For servers with more than one IP address, this attribute specifies which address will be used for listening on the specified port. By default, this port will be used on all IP addresses associated with the server.	No
allowTrace	A Boolean value that enables or disables the TRACE HTTP method (which prompts the server to return a copy of the request back to the client for inspection). The default is false.	No
enableLookups	Sets whether the DNS hostname of the client can be looked up. false skips the DNS lookup and returns the IP address as a string (thereby improving performance). The default is true.	No
maxPostSize	The maximum size in bytes of a POST request. You can disable this by setting this attribute to a value less than or equal to zero. The default is 2097152 (2 megabytes).	No
redirectPort	If this connector supports non-SSL requests and a request is received that requires SSL transport, Tomcat will automatically redirect the request to the port number specified here.	No
scheme	The name of the protocol you want to use for this connector. For example, you'd set this attribute to https for an SSL connector. The default is http.	No
secure	If you want to have calls to request.isSecure() return true (which is the case for an SSL connector), set this to true. The default is false.	No

Table 4-11. *The Common Attributes of the* `<Connector>` *Element (Continued)*

Attribute	Description	Required?
`URIEncoding`	The character encoding to use to decode the URI bytes. The default is `ISO-8859-1`.	No
`useBodyEncodingForURI`	This specifies if the encoding specified in `contentType` should be used for URI query parameters, instead of using the `URIEncoding`. This setting is for compatibility with Tomcat 4.1.*x*, where the encoding specified in the `contentType` was also used for the parameters from the URL. The default is `false`.	No

The default HTTP connector has the attributes described in Table 4-12.

Table 4-12. *The Attributes of the HTTP* `<Connector>` *Element*

Attribute	Description	Required?
`acceptCount`	The maximum queue length for incoming connection requests when all possible request-processing threads are in use. Any requests received when the queue is full will be refused. The default is `10`.	No
`bufferSize`	The size (in bytes) of the buffer to be provided for input streams created by this connector. The default is `2048`.	No
`compressableMimeTypes`	The value is a comma-separated list of MIME types for which HTTP compression may be used. The default is `text/html,text/xml,text/plain`.	No
`compression`	The connector may use HTTP/1.1 GZIP compression in an attempt to save server bandwidth. The acceptable values for the parameter are `off` (disables compression), `on` (allows compression, which causes text data to be compressed), `force` (forces compression in all cases), or an integer (which is equivalent to `on` but specifies the minimum amount of data before the output is compressed). If the content length isn't known and compression is set to `on` or more aggressive, the output will also be compressed. The default is `off`.	No
`connectionLinger`	The number of milliseconds during which the sockets used by this connector will linger when they are closed. The default is `-1` (socket linger is disabled).	No
`connectionTimeout`	The number of milliseconds this connector will wait, after accepting a connection, for the request URI line to be presented. The default is `60000` (that is, 60 seconds).	No
`debug`	Tomcat 5.0.*x* only. The debugging level for log messages generated by this component. The levels are 1 (errors), 2 (warnings), 3 (information), and 4 (debug). These correspond to the levels of debugging in the logger component. The default is zero, meaning no debugging (though the associated logger will still log fatal messages).	No

Table 4-12. *The Attributes of the HTTP <Connector> Element (Continued)*

Attribute	Description	Required?
disableUploadTimeout	Used to set a connection timeout while a servlet is being executed. This gives the servlet longer to complete its execution or allows a longer timeout during data upload. The default is false.	No
maxHttpHeaderSize	The maximum size of the request and response HTTP header, specified in bytes. The default is 4096.	No
maxKeepAliveRequests	The maximum number of HTTP requests that can be maintained until Tomcat closes the connection. A setting of 1 will disable HTTP/1.0 and HTTP/1.1 keep-alive and pipelining. A setting of -1 will allow an unlimited amount of pipelined or keep-alive HTTP requests. The default is 100.	No
maxSpareThreads	The maximum number of unused request-processing threads that will be allowed to exist until the thread pool stops the unnecessary threads. The default is 50.	No
maxThreads	The maximum number of request-processing threads to be created, which therefore determines the maximum number of simultaneous requests that can be handled. The default is 200.	No
minSpareThreads	The number of request-processing threads created when this connector starts. The connector will also make sure it has the specified number of idle processing threads available. This attribute should be set to a value smaller than maxThreads. The default is 4.	No
noCompressionUserAgents	A comma-separated list of regular expressions matching HTTP user-agents for which compression should not be used. The default is an empty string.	No
port	The port on which this connector will create a server socket and await incoming connections. Only one application may listen to a particular port number on a particular IP address.	Yes
protocol	Must be HTTP/1.1 to use the HTTP handler, which is the default.	No
proxyName	If this connector is being used in a proxy configuration, configure this attribute to specify the server name to be returned for calls to request.getServerName().	No
proxyPort	If this connector is being used in a proxy configuration, configure this attribute to specify the server port to be returned for calls to request.getServerPort().	No
restrictedUserAgents	A comma-separated list of regular expressions matching HTTP user-agents for which HTTP/1.1 or HTTP/1.0 keep-alive should not be used, even if they advertise support for these features. The default is an empty string.	No
server	Tomcat 5.5 only. The Server header for the HTTP response.	No

Table 4-12. *The Attributes of the HTTP <Connector> Element (Continued)*

Attribute	Description	Required?
strategy	Tomcat 5.5 only. The thread-pooling strategy to be used. The default strategy doesn't use a master thread. However, you can use a more conventional strategy with a master listener thread by setting this attribute's value to ms. The master strategy will work significantly better if you also use the threadPriority attribute, which will apply only to the thread that listens on the server socket. The default is lf.	No
socketBuffer	The size (in bytes) of the buffer to be provided for socket output buffering. A setting of -1 disables the use of a buffer. The default is 9000.	No
tcpNoDelay	If set to true, the TCP_NO_DELAY option will be set on the server socket, which improves performance under most circumstances. The default is true.	No
threadPriority	The priority of the request-processing threads within the JVM. The default is java.lang.Thread#NORM_PRIORITY. See the documentation for the java.lang.Thread class for more details on what this priority means.	No

An SSL connector has a number of unique attributes, as described in Table 4-13.

Table 4-13. *The Attributes of an SSL-Enabled <Connector> Element*

Attribute	Description	Required?
algorithm	The certificate algorithm to be used. The default is SunX509.	No
clientAuth	Set to true if you require a valid certificate chain from the client before accepting a connection. false won't require a certificate chain unless the client requests a resource protected by a security constraint that uses CLIENT-CERT authentication. The default is false.	No
keystoreFile	The path to the keystore file where you have stored the server certificate to be loaded. The default is .keystore in the home directory of the user that's running Tomcat.	No
keystorePass	The password used to access the server certificate from the specified keystore file. The default is changeit.	No
keystoreType	The type of keystore file to be used for the server certificate. The default is JKS.	No
sslProtocol	The version of the SSL protocol to use. The default is TLS.	No
ciphers	A comma-separated list of the encryption ciphers that may be used. Any available cipher may be used by default.	No

The final set of attributes belongs to the AJP connector and is described in Table 4-14. Remember that this connector also has the common attributes described in Table 4-11.

Table 4-14. *The Attributes of an AJP1.3 <Connector> Element*

Attribute	Description	Required?
`debug`	Tomcat 5.0.*x* only. The debugging detail level of log messages generated by this component. The levels are 1 (errors), 2 (warnings), 3 (information), and 4 (debug). These correspond to the levels of debugging in the logger component. The default is zero, meaning no debugging (though the associated logger will still log fatal messages).	No
`protocol`	Must be `AJP/1.3` to use the AJP handler.	Yes

Configuring an Engine

You can have as many connectors as you need in a service to handle the different connection requirements for a server, but you can have only one engine. An engine executes Web applications when processing incoming requests and generating outgoing responses.

```
<!-- Define the top level container in our container hierarchy -->
<Engine name="Catalina" defaultHost="localhost" debug="0">
```

An engine represents a running instance of the servlet processor; in other words, it's the servlet engine. The default engine in `server.xml` is called Catalina. The `defaultHost` is the host component to which this engine will direct a request if it's not for a known host on this server. The `debug` attribute here specifies that there will be no debug messages for this engine written by the logger to the log.

Table 4-15 describes the attributes of the `<Engine>` element.

Table 4-15. *The Attributes of the <Engine> Element*

Attribute	Description	Required?
`backgroundProcessorDelay`	Represents the delay in seconds between the invocation of the `backgroundProcess()` method on this engine and its child containers, including all hosts and contexts. Child containers will be invoked if their delay value is negative (which would mean they're using their own processing thread). Setting this to a positive value will cause a thread to be spawned. After waiting the specified amount of time, the thread will invoke the `backgroundProcess()` method on this engine and all its child containers. The default is `10`.	No
`className`	Class name of the implementation to use. The default is `org.apache.catalina.core.StandardEngine`.	No

Table 4-15. *The Attributes of the <Engine> Element (Continued)*

Attribute	Description	Required?
debug	Tomcat 5.0.*x* only. The level of debugging for this engine. The levels are 1 (errors), 2 (warnings), 3 (information), and 4 (debug). These correspond to the levels of debugging in the logger component. This is an attribute of the standard implementation and may change if you're using another implementation. The default is zero, meaning no debugging (though the associated logger will still log fatal messages).	No
defaultHost	The default hostname. This host will process requests directed to host names on this server but that aren't configured in `server.xml`. This name must match the name of one of the host elements nested in this engine.	Yes
jvmRoute	The identifier that must be used in load balancing to enable session affinity. This value must be unique across all Tomcat 5 servers that participate in the cluster. It will be appended to the generated session identifier, therefore allowing the front-end proxy to forward a particular session to the same Tomcat 5 instance.	No
name	Name of this engine, used in log and error messages.	Yes

The `<Engine>` element has the subelements described in Table 4-16.

Table 4-16. *The Subelements of the <Engine> Element*

Subelement	Description	Number
DefaultContext	Tomcat 5.0.*x* only. Creates a default context for Web applications that are automatically deployed when Tomcat starts. Its settings are a subset of a context's, so it will be covered in the next chapter. Tomcat 5.5 uses an external default context file.	0 or 1
Logger	Tomcat 5.0.*x* only. The logging component instance used by this engine for logging messages. Unless overridden by inner containers, this is the default logger instance for any nested components inside the engine.	0 or 1
Realm	The user-authentication realm used by Tomcat's declarative security support.	0 or 1
Host	Each `<Host>` element is a virtual host handled by this engine. Tomcat can handle multiple virtual hosts per engine instance.	1 or more
Listener	Lifecycle listeners monitor the starting and stopping of the engine. You'll see one use for listeners in Chapter 9.	0 or more
Valve	Valves add processing logic into the request- and response-handling pipeline at the engine level. Standard valves are used to perform access logging, request filtering, implementing single sign-on, and so on.	0 or more

Configuring a Logger (Tomcat 5.0.x Only)

The first subelement inside the <Engine> is the default logger.

```
<!-- Global logger unless overridden at lower levels -->
<Logger className="org.apache.catalina.logger.FileLogger"
        prefix="catalina_log." suffix=".txt"
        timestamp="true"/>
```

A logger is a nested component that collects log information (debug or error messages) from Tomcat and Web application code and writes it to log files. Log files are placed in the `CATALINA_HOME/logs` directory by default. You can change this location with the `directory` attribute.

The default configuration uses the standard `FileLogger` class and configures the log name to be of the form `catalina_log.DATE.txt`.

More than one kind of logger exists, but all <Logger> elements have common attributes, as described in Table 4-17.

Table 4-17. *The Common Attributes of* <Logger>

Attribute	Description	Required?
`className`	The Java class to use for this instance of the logger.	Yes
`verbosity`	The level of logging are as follows: 0: Fatal messages only 1: Error messages 2: Warning messages 3: Information messages 4: Debug information The numbers are cumulative. (That is, 4 logs all messages, 3 logs everything but debug information, and so on.) The default is `1`.	No

As you can see from Table 4-17, the <Logger> element must specify a `className` attribute. You use this attribute to choose the standard logger implementation for this component. The `className` attribute can contain one of the classes shown in Table 4-18.

Table 4-18. *The Possible Values of the* `className` *Attribute*

Class Name	Description
`org.apache.catalina.logger.FileLogger`	Logs to a file
`org.apache.catalina.logger.SystemErrLogger`	Logs to the standard error stream.
`org.apache.catalina.logger.SystemOutLogger`	Logs to the standard output stream

The only one of these loggers that has any attributes is `org.apache.catalina.logger.FileLogger`. Table 4-19 describes these attributes.

Table 4-19. *The Attributes of `org.apache.catalina.logger.FileLogger`*

Attribute	Description	Required?
`directory`	The location of the log files. You may use relative or absolute paths. Relative paths are interpreted in relation to `CATALINA_HOME`. The default is `CATALINA_HOME/logs`.	No
`prefix`	The prefix for the log filenames. The default is `catalina`.	No
`suffix`	A suffix for the log filenames. The default is `.log`.	No
`timestamp`	Set to `true` to add a date and time stamp to each filename. Best practice dictates that you add a time stamp to your log files. The default is `false`.	No

Although this is a perfectly adequate logging mechanism, you can also configure Tomcat 5.0.*x* to use Log4J as described next. This is a much more powerful and flexible mechanism, so you may be tempted.

Tomcat 5.5 Logging

Tomcat 5.5 doesn't include the logger component and relies instead on the Jakarta Commons logging mechanism. This mechanism is a thin bridge between logging libraries and allows you to use any logging toolkit you want. The two most common are the Java 1.4 (and onward) built-in logging feature and the Apache Log4J toolkit. It's the latter that's most often used with Tomcat, so it's the one described in this section.

The first step is to download the Log4J classes from `http://logging.apache.org/log4j/`. Tomcat 5.5 uses the Commons logging mechanism during bootup, so if you want to use Log4J to harness the commons logging messages, you must also include it at bootup. To do this, add the `log4j.jar` binary to the boot classpath in the `catalina.bat`/`catalina.sh` script.

```
rem catalina.bat
set CLASSPATH=%CLASSPATH%;
%CATALINA_HOME%\bin\bootstrap.jar;
%CATALINA_HOME%\bin\log4j.jar

# catalina.sh
CLASSPATH="$CLASSPATH":
"$CATALINA_HOME"/bin/bootstrap.jar:
"$CATALINA_HOME"/bin/commons-logging-api.jar:
"$CATALINA_HOME"/bin/log4j.jar
```

Change the path to your Log4J binary.

The version of the Commons logging that Tomcat uses when booting up is a stripped-down version for simple logging to the console (`CATALINA_HOME/bin/commons-logging-api.jar`). Log4J, on the other hand, uses the full functionality of the logging mechanism. This means you must download the full distribution from http://jakarta.apache.org/commons/logging/. Copy the commons-logging.jar file to CATALINA_HOME/common/lib, where Tomcat, user applications, and Log4J can see it.

You can't replace the stripped-down version of the logging API in the bin directory directly. The steps described previously will carry out this task during bootup.

■ **Note** If you're using Tomcat 5.0.x, you don't need to do any of this. However, you need to copy log4j.jar to CATALINA_HOME/common/lib. Also remember to remove any <Logger> elements in server.xml.

The final step of configuration is to add a Log4J configuration file as shown in Listing 4-5. Call this file log4j.properties, and place it in CATALINA_HOME/common/classes. This places it in the same scope as the rest of the logging mechanism.

Listing 4-5. *CATALINA_HOME/common/classes/log4j.properties*

```
# Set the root logger for Tomcat
log4j.rootLogger=INFO, Tomcat

# Log to a file
log4j.appender.Tomcat=org.apache.log4j.FileAppender
log4j.appender.Tomcat.File=C:/jakarta-tomcat-5.5.3/logs/tomcat.log

# Use the simple layout
log4j.appender.Tomcat.layout=org.apache.log4j.SimpleLayout
```

This is a simple configuration that sets the level of logging and the log file for Tomcat to use. The logging levels are, in ascending order of severity, as follows: ALL, DEBUG, INFO, WARN, ERROR, FATAL, and OFF. Be careful and set logging to only the level you require because there can be severe performance penalties if you choose too low a level; at the same time, you may miss crucial information if you set the level too high.

Start Tomcat, and open the log file you configured previously. You should see the usual Tomcat startup messages, as shown in Listing 4-6.

Listing 4-6. *The Log Messages from* tomcat.log

```
INFO - Initializing Coyote HTTP/1.1 on http-8080
INFO - Initialization processed in 3004 ms
INFO - Starting service Catalina
INFO - Starting Servlet Engine: Apache Tomcat/5.5.3
INFO - XML validation disabled
INFO - org.apache.webapp.balancer.BalancerFilter: init():
  ruleChain: [org.apache.webapp.balancer.RuleChain:
  [org.apache.webapp.balancer.rules.URLStringMatchRule:
  Target string: News / Redirect URL: http://www.cnn.com],
  [org.apache.webapp.balancer.rules.RequestParameterRule:
```

```
  Target param name: paramName / Target param value: paramValue /
  Redirect URL: http://www.yahoo.com],
  [org.apache.webapp.balancer.rules.AcceptEverythingRule:
  Redirect URL: http://jakarta.apache.org]]
INFO - ContextListener: contextInitialized()
INFO - SessionListener: contextInitialized()
INFO - ContextListener: contextInitialized()
INFO - SessionListener: contextInitialized()
INFO - Starting Coyote HTTP/1.1 on http-8080
INFO - JK2: ajp13 listening on /0.0.0.0:8009
INFO - Jk running ID=0 time=0/101
  config=C:\jakarta-tomcat-5.5.3\conf\jk2.properties
INFO - Server startup in 5789 ms
```

If you had set the debug level higher than INFO, then there will be no messages in the log file.

You aren't limited to using the simple text file. For example, the previous listing has no dates or times. To change this, you can use a pattern layout, which uses pattern characters just as C does. Table 4-20 describes those characters relevant to Tomcat logging. See http://logging.apache.org/log4j/docs/api/org/apache/log4j/PatternLayout.html for more details on Log4J's logging patterns.

Table 4-20. *Pattern Layout Placeholders*

Pattern Character	Description
c	The category of the logging event. In Tomcat terms, this displays the component that made the log entry. You can configure the precision of the category name by placing an integer in brackets after the character. In this case, only the corresponding number of rightmost components of the category name will be printed. For example, for the category log4j.logger.org.apache.catalina.core.ContainerBase, the pattern %c{1} will print ContainerBase. This is a useful pattern character when you want to find out from where a certain log message has come.
d	The date of this log entry, which may be followed by a date format enclosed between braces—for example, %d{HH:mm:ss} or %d{dd MMM yyyy HH:mm:ss}. If no format is given, then ISO8601 format is used. For better results you should use the Log4J date formatters. These are ABSOLUTE, DATE, and ISO8601, for specifying AbsoluteTimeDateFormat, DateTimeDateFormat, and ISO8601DateFormat, respectively—for example, %d{ISO8601} or %d{ABSOLUTE}. ABSOLUTE is HH:mm:ss,SSS. DATE is dd MMM YYYY HH:mm:ss,SSS. ISO8601 is YYYY-MM-dd HH:mm:ss,SSS.
F	The filename where the logging request was issued. This can be slow, so you should avoid using this option unless execution speed isn't an issue.

Table 4-20. *Pattern Layout Placeholders (Continued)*

Pattern Character	Description
l	The location of the caller that generated the logging event. The location information depends on the JVM implementation but usually consists of the fully qualified name of the calling method, followed by the filename and line number between parentheses. Here's an example: `org.apache.jk.server.JkMain.start(JkMain.java:355)`. The location information can be useful, but obtaining it is extremely slow.
L	The line number where the logging request was issued. Obtaining caller location information is extremely slow.
m	The application-supplied message associated with the logging event.
M	The method name where the logging request was issued. Obtaining caller location information is extremely slow.
n	The platform-dependent line separator character or characters. This conversion character offers practically the same performance as using nonportable line separator strings such as `\n` or `\r\n`. Thus, it's the preferred way of specifying a line separator.
p	Used to output the priority of the logging event.
r	Used to output the number of milliseconds elapsed since the start of the application until the creation of the logging event.
t	Used to output the name of the thread that generated the logging event.
%	The sequence `%%` outputs a single percent sign.

Listing 4-7 shows how to put these characters into action.

Listing 4-7. *CATALINA_HOME/common/classes/log4j.properties*

```
# Set the root logger for Tomcat
log4j.rootLogger=INFO, Tomcat

# Log to a pattern file
log4j.appender.Tomcat=org.apache.log4j.FileAppender
log4j.appender.Tomcat.File=C:/jakarta-tomcat-5.5.3/logs/tomcat.pattern.log

# Use a pattern layout
log4j.appender.Tomcat.layout=org.apache.log4j.PatternLayout
log4j.appender.Tomcat.layout.ConversionPattern=%d{ISO8601} : %p : %m %n
```

In this case, you're logging the date in ISO8601 format, followed by the priority of the message (`%p`) and message itself (`%m`). The line is ended with a newline character (`%n`). Start Tomcat, and examine `tomcat.pattern.log`. It should look something like Listing 4-8.

Listing 4-8. *tomcat.pattern.log*

```
2004-10-03 20:50:19,527 : INFO : Initializing Coyote HTTP/1.1 on http-8080
2004-10-03 20:50:19,617 : INFO : Initialization processed in 2293 ms
2004-10-03 20:50:20,128 : INFO : Starting service Catalina
2004-10-03 20:50:20,138 : INFO : Starting Servlet Engine: Apache Tomcat/5.5.3
2004-10-03 20:50:20,168 : INFO : XML validation disabled
2004-10-03 20:50:22,562 : INFO : org.apache.webapp.balancer.BalancerFilter:
  init(): ruleChain: [org.apache.webapp.balancer.RuleChain:
  [org.apache.webapp.balancer.rules.URLStringMatchRule: Target string: News /
  Redirect URL: http://www.cnn.com],
  [org.apache.webapp.balancer.rules.RequestParameterRule:
  Target param name: paramName / Target param value: paramValue /
  Redirect URL: http://www.yahoo.com],
  [org.apache.webapp.balancer.rules.AcceptEverythingRule:
  Redirect URL: http://jakarta.apache.org]]
2004-10-03 20:50:22,942 : INFO : ContextListener: contextInitialized()
2004-10-03 20:50:22,942 : INFO : SessionListener: contextInitialized()
2004-10-03 20:50:23,773 : INFO : ContextListener: contextInitialized()
2004-10-03 20:50:23,773 : INFO : SessionListener: contextInitialized()
2004-10-03 20:50:24,504 : INFO : Starting Coyote HTTP/1.1 on http-8080
2004-10-03 20:50:25,115 : INFO : JK2: ajp13 listening on /0.0.0.0:8009
2004-10-03 20:50:25,135 : INFO : Jk running ID=0 time=0/90
  config=C:\jakarta-tomcat-5.5.3\conf\jk2.properties
2004-10-03 20:50:25,215 : INFO : Server startup in 5598 ms
```

Here you can see the pattern has been applied to each of the log entries.

If you want, you can also output to HTML. Listing 4-9 shows this configuration.

Listing 4-9. *CATALINA_HOME/common/classes/log4j.properties*

```
# Set the root logger for Tomcat
log4j.rootLogger=INFO, Tomcat

# Log to an HTML file
log4j.appender.Tomcat=org.apache.log4j.FileAppender
log4j.appender.Tomcat.File=C:/jakarta-tomcat-5.5.3/logs/tomcat.log.html

# Set the layout to HTML and specify a title
log4j.appender.Tomcat.layout=org.apache.log4j.HTMLLayout
log4j.appender.Tomcat.layout.Title=Apress Tomcat Log
```

Figure 4-2 shows the results.

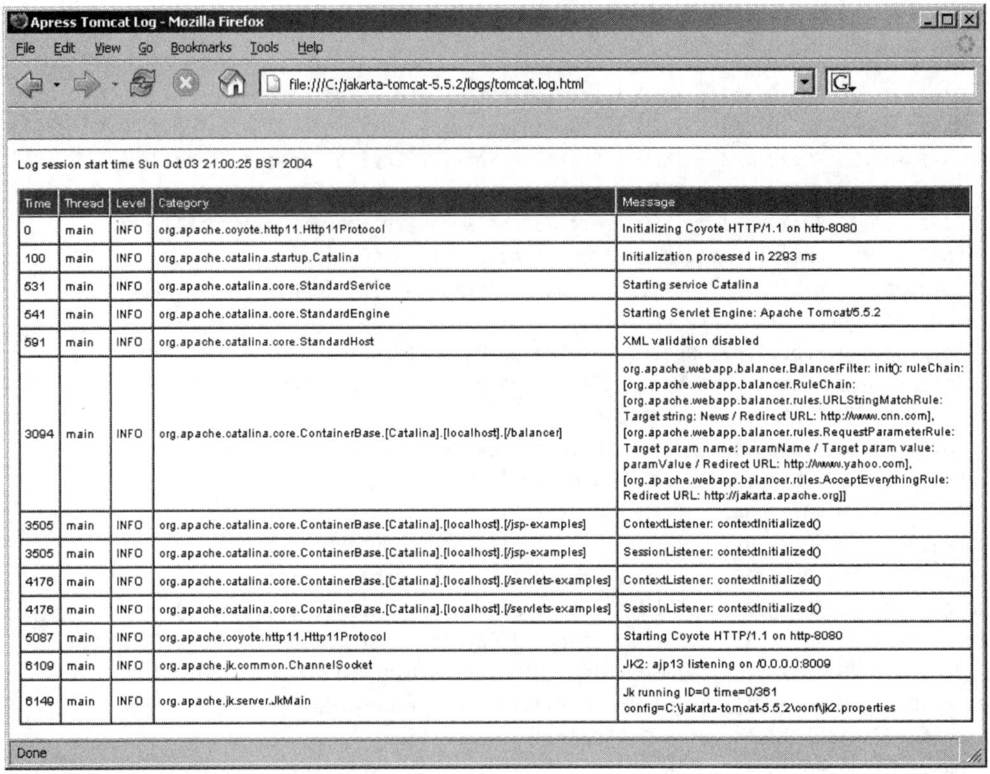

Apress Tomcat Log - Mozilla Firefox

File Edit View Go Bookmarks Tools Help

file:///C:/jakarta-tomcat-5.5.2/logs/tomcat.log.html

Log session start time Sun Oct 03 21:00:25 BST 2004

Time	Thread	Level	Category	Message
0	main	INFO	org.apache.coyote.http11.Http11Protocol	Initializing Coyote HTTP/1.1 on http-8080
100	main	INFO	org.apache.catalina.startup.Catalina	Initialization processed in 2293 ms
531	main	INFO	org.apache.catalina.core.StandardService	Starting service Catalina
541	main	INFO	org.apache.catalina.core.StandardEngine	Starting Servlet Engine: Apache Tomcat/5.5.2
591	main	INFO	org.apache.catalina.core.StandardHost	XML validation disabled
3094	main	INFO	org.apache.catalina.core.ContainerBase.[Catalina].[localhost].[/balancer]	org.apache.webapp.balancer.BalancerFilter: init(): ruleChain: [org.apache.webapp.balancer.RuleChain: [org.apache.webapp.balancer.rules.URLStringMatchRule: Target string: News / Redirect URL: http://www.cnn.com], [org.apache.webapp.balancer.rules.RequestParameterRule: Target param name: paramName / Target param value: paramValue / Redirect URL: http://www.yahoo.com], [org.apache.webapp.balancer.rules.AcceptEverythingRule: Redirect URL: http://jakarta.apache.org]]
3505	main	INFO	org.apache.catalina.core.ContainerBase.[Catalina].[localhost].[/jsp-examples]	ContextListener: contextInitialized()
3505	main	INFO	org.apache.catalina.core.ContainerBase.[Catalina].[localhost].[/jsp-examples]	SessionListener: contextInitialized()
4176	main	INFO	org.apache.catalina.core.ContainerBase.[Catalina].[localhost].[/servlets-examples]	ContextListener: contextInitialized()
4176	main	INFO	org.apache.catalina.core.ContainerBase.[Catalina].[localhost].[/servlets-examples]	SessionListener: contextInitialized()
5087	main	INFO	org.apache.coyote.http11.Http11Protocol	Starting Coyote HTTP/1.1 on http-8080
6109	main	INFO	org.apache.jk.common.ChannelSocket	JK2: ajp13 listening on /0.0.0.0:8009
6149	main	INFO	org.apache.jk.server.JkMain	Jk running ID=0 time=0/361 config=C:\jakarta-tomcat-5.5.2\conf\jk2.properties

Done

Figure 4-2. *The HTML layout log*

If you want to log to the console window, you have two choices: don't use Log4J and rely on the default logging or use the console logger from Log4J. The advantage of using Log4J is that you can use custom layouts and change the level of the logging threshold. Listing 4-10 shows how to log to the console.

Listing 4-10. *CATALINA_HOME/common/classes/log4j.properties*

```
# Set the root logger for Tomcat
log4j.rootLogger=INFO, Tomcat

# Log to the console
log4j.appender.Tomcat=org.apache.log4j.ConsoleAppender
log4j.appender.Tomcat.Target=System.out

# Set a custom layout level
log4j.appender.Tomcat.layout=org.apache.log4j.PatternLayout
log4j.appender.Tomcat.layout.ConversionPattern=%d{ISO8601} : %p : %m %n
```

The pattern here is the same as that for the pattern layout file, so the output to the console will be identical.

Now that you know how to log to different media, you can send different levels of messages to different destinations. In the example shown in Listing 4-11, all messages of level `INFO` and higher are logged to a file, and those of `ERROR` and higher are logged to the console for immediate attention.

Listing 4-11. *CATALINA_HOME/common/classes/log4j.properties*

```
# Send all INFO messages and above to a file and
# all ERROR messages and above to the console
log4j.rootLogger=INFO, TomcatINFO, TomcatERROR

# Use a pattern file for the INFO messages
log4j.appender.TomcatINFO=org.apache.log4j.FileAppender
log4j.appender.TomcatINFO.File=C:/jakarta-tomcat-5.5.3/logs/tomcat.pattern.log
log4j.appender.TomcatINFO.layout=org.apache.log4j.PatternLayout
log4j.appender.TomcatINFO.layout.ConversionPattern=%d{ISO8601} : %p : %m %n

# Use the console for ERROR messages
log4j.appender.TomcatERROR=org.apache.log4j.ConsoleAppender
log4j.appender.TomcatERROR.Target=System.out
log4j.appender.TomcatERROR.layout=org.apache.log4j.PatternLayout
log4j.appender.TomcatERROR.layout.ConversionPattern=%p: %m: %d{ABSOLUTE} %n
log4j.appender.TomcatERROR.Threshold=ERROR
```

You can use a huge number of variations with Log4J, such as using the Windows system log and Unix syslog, though such exhaustive treatment is beyond the scope of this chapter.

So far you've seen how to log Tomcat's log messages, no matter where they originated, to one or more destinations. However, you may want to log messages from different locations to different files. For example, in previous versions of Tomcat, you could place loggers at each component level to log to different log files. This meant you could see what was occurring in each component. To replicate this, you must assign a component's Log4J logger (different from a logger component of old) to an appender. The configuration is then the same as previously.

To assign a logger to an appender, use the following convention:

```
log4j.logger.LOGGER_NAME=[LOGGING_LEVEL],APPENDER_NAME
```

The `LOGGER_NAME` is usually the fully qualified class name of the component you want to log, with the exception of engines, hosts, and contexts. The following is an example of the `tomcatBook` context's logger, assuming it's in the Catalina engine and the localhost host:

```
org.apache.catalina.core.ContainerBase.[Catalina].[localhost].[/tomcatBook]
```

Putting all this together, the following will assign the `tomcatBook` context's log messages to the `tomcatBook` appender with a default debug level of `INFO`:

```
log4j.logger.org.apache.catalina.core.ContainerBase.
[Catalina].[localhost].[/tomcatBook]=INFO,tomcatBook
```

Listing 4-12 shows a `log4j.properties` file that sets a master log file that will log everything and a context-specific log file that logs only messages to that context.

Listing 4-12. *A log4j.properties That Logs Context-Specific Messages*

```
# Set the root logger for Tomcat
log4j.rootLogger=INFO, Tomcat

# Log to a file
log4j.appender.Tomcat=org.apache.log4j.FileAppender
log4j.appender.Tomcat.File=C:/jakarta-tomcat-5.5.3/logs/tomcat.log

# Use the simple layout
log4j.appender.Tomcat.layout=org.apache.log4j.SimpleLayout

log4j.logger.org.apache.catalina.core.ContainerBase.
[Catalina].[localhost].[/tomcatBook]=INFO,tomcatBook

# Log to a file
log4j.appender.tomcatBook=org.apache.log4j.FileAppender
log4j.appender.tomcatBook.File=C:/jakarta-tomcat-5.5.3/logs/tomcatBook.log

# Use the pattern layout
log4j.appender.tomcatBook.layout=org.apache.log4j.PatternLayout
log4j.appender.tomcatBook.layout.ConversionPattern=%c{3}: %m %n
```

The `tomcatBook` appender will display the last three sections of the component that created the log message, followed by the message. Here's an example log message in `CATALINA_HOME/logs/tomcatBook.log`:

```
[Catalina].[localhost].[/tomcatBook]: REQUEST URI=/tomcatBook/
```

You can configure other components in the same way. Appendix A contains details of Tomcat's Log4J loggers for your reference.

The one slight drawback of this approach is that you repeat the logging activity if you set the same levels of logging for the two log files. In the previous example, all messages on the server of level `INFO` and higher, including those for the `tomcatBook` context, are logged to the `tomcat.log` file. The logging messages from the `tomcatBook` context are also logged to the `tomcatBook.log` file, which means your server will be working hard to log double the amount of log messages for that context.

One solution is to reserve a serverwide log file for serious log messages, perhaps of level `ERROR` and higher, and have a log file for each context with `INFO` messages. Of course, you may not even need this level of logging for all your contexts once they're deployed.

Configuring a Realm

The next entry in `server.xml` is a realm, which is used for user authentication.

```
<!-- Because this Realm is here, an instance will be shared globally -->

<!-- This Realm uses the UserDatabase configured in the global JNDI
     resources under the key "UserDatabase".  Any edits
     that are performed against this UserDatabase are immediately
     available for use by the Realm.  -->
<Realm className="org.apache.catalina.realm.UserDatabaseRealm"
       debug="0" resourceName="UserDatabase"/>
```

Note that this realm uses the global resource you looked at earlier in the "Configuring a Global Resource" section. This realm is therefore attaching the global resource to the engine in which it resides.

Tomcat uses realms to perform authentication and implement container-managed security. They map usernames to passwords (for authentication) and usernames to user roles (for container-managed security). This means that Tomcat can then determine that users are who they say they are, using authentication, and determine which areas of the server are available to them, using container-managed security.

The user database is only one implementation of a realm. Others are data source realm, JDBC realm, JNDI realm, and JAAS realm. Tomcat 5 supports the memory realm for backward compatibility with Tomcat 4, but it's inefficient and insecure, so you shouldn't use it.

The various realms are described briefly next but will be dealt with in more detail in Chapter 11.

Configuring a User Database Realm

The user database realm is an upgraded version of the memory realm and is backward compatible with the memory realm. It comes with the same caveats as the memory realm.

Configuring a Data Source Realm

Data source realms use JDBC data sources stored with JNDI names to authenticate users. This allows you to change the underlying storage mechanism without having to change the settings on your realms.

Configuring a JDBC Realm

JDBC realms access relational databases to obtain authentication information. You can use any source of data that can be accessed with JDBC. This includes ODBC sources, such as Excel or comma-separated files, accessed with the JDBC-ODBC bridge. `server.xml` has a number of example JDBC realms commented out. The following uses a MySQL database instead of a text file:

```
<!--
<Realm  className="org.apache.catalina.realm.JDBCRealm" debug="99"
        driverName="org.gjt.mm.mysql.Driver"
        connectionURL="jdbc:mysql://localhost/authority"
        connectionName="test" connectionPassword="test"
        userTable="users" userNameCol="user_name"
        userCredCol="user_pass"
        userRoleTable="user_roles" roleNameCol="role_name" />
-->
```

Configuring a JNDI Realm

You can configure a JNDI LDAP service provider to provide user information from an existing directory service. This would allow you to use employee information that's already available.

Configuring a JAAS Realm

You can use the JAAS realm to authenticate users using the Java Authentication and Authorization Service (JAAS). This allows you to use any authentication mechanism you choose, but you have to write your own authentication module to implement whichever one you choose.

Configuring a Host

A host component represents a single virtual host running on this server.

```
<Host name="localhost" debug="0" appBase="webapps"
      unpackWARs="true" autoDeploy="true"
      xmlValidation="false" xmlNamespaceAware="false">
```

This virtual host is localhost. The applications running in this host are located in the CATALINA_HOME/webapps directory.

The unpackWARs attribute tells Tomcat to unpack any packaged WAR files found in the appBase directory if it's set to true. A value of false means that Tomcat will execute the Web applications without unpacking them, which saves space but increases response time.

A <Host> element is a container and has the attributes described in Table 4-21. These are the attributes of all hosts, and custom implementations of hosts are possible.

Table 4-21. *The Common Attributes of the <Host> Element*

Attribute	Description	Required
appBase	The base directory for this virtual host. This is a directory that may contain Web applications to be deployed on this virtual host. You may specify an absolute pathname or a pathname relative to the CATALINA_HOME directory.	Yes
autoDeploy	This flag value indicates whether new Web applications added to the appBase directory while Tomcat is running should be deployed automatically. The default is true.	No
background-ProcessorDelay	The delay in seconds between the invocation of the backgroundProcess() method on this host and its child containers, including all contexts. Child containers will be invoked if their delay value is negative (which would mean they're using their own processing thread). A positive value will cause a thread to be spawned. After waiting the specified amount of time, the thread will invoke the backgroundProcess() method on this host and all its child containers. A host will use background processing to perform live Web application deployment–related tasks. The default is -1, which means the host will rely on the background-processing thread of its parent engine.	Yes
className	Class name of the implementation to use. The default is org.apache.catalina.core.StandardHost.	No

Table 4-21. *The Common Attributes of the* <Host> *Element (Continued)*

Attribute	Description	Required
deployOnStartup	Set to true to automatically deploy Web applications on startup. The default is true.	No
name	The name of this virtual host, as configured with DNS. One of the hosts nested within an engine must have a name that matches the defaultHost attribute of that engine.	Yes

In addition, the standard host has the attributes defined in Table 4-22.

Table 4-22. *The Attributes of the Standard* <Host> *Element*

Attribute	Description	Required
debug	Tomcat 5.0.*x* only. The level of debugging logged by the associated logger. The levels are 1 (errors), 2 (warnings), 3 (information), and 4 (debug). These correspond to the levels of debugging in the logger component. The default is zero, meaning no debugging (though the associated logger will still log fatal messages).	No
deployXML	false disables the ability to deploy applications using an XML configuration file. This also prohibits the manager application from deploying Web application directories or WAR files that aren't located in CATALINA_HOME/conf/[Engine_name]/[Host_name]. XML-configured applications are deployed with Tomcat's security permissions, so you should set this to false if untrustworthy users can manage Web applications. The default is true.	No
errorReportValveClass	Class name of the error-reporting valve that will be used by this host. You can use this property to customize the look of the error pages that will be generated by Tomcat. The class must implement the org.apache.catalina.Valve interface. The default is org.apache.catalina.valves.ErrorReportValve.	No
unpackWARs	Set to true if you want to unpack WAR files in the appBase directory into a corresponding directory structure. false tells Tomcat to run such Web applications directly from their WAR file. The default is true.	No
workDir	A scratch directory to be used by applications running in this host. Each application will have its own directory with temporary read/write use. Configuring a working directory for a context will override this value. This directory is visible to servlets in the Web application as a servlet context attribute (of type java.io.File) named javax.servlet.context.tempdir as described in the Servlet specification. The default is a suitable directory underneath CATALINA_HOME/work.	No

Table 4-23 describes the subelements that can be placed inside a `<Host>` element.

Table 4-23. *The Subelements of the `<Host>` Element*

Subelement	Description	Number
`Context`	A context defines a Web application deployed within this host. When using Tomcat 5, you shouldn't place any context entries in `server.xml` because `server.xml` isn't reloaded after changes are made. Use XML configuration files or deployment tools, such as the `manager` application, instead.	0 or more
`DefaultContext`	Tomcat 5.0.*x* only. The default context is a set of property values for a Web application that's deployed within this host but doesn't have its own context specified. Typically, this default context is used for Web applications that are part of the standard behavior of the Tomcat server, and Web applications that are automatically deployed. Tomcat 5.5 uses external default context files.	0 or 1
`Logger`	Tomcat 5.0.*x* only. A default logger that's configured for this host. Overrides any previously specified logger.	0 or 1
`Realm`	A realm that can be accessed across all the Web applications running within this host—unless a lower-level component specifies its own realm.	0 or 1
`Valve`	You can add a valve to monitor access, filter requests, and implement single sign-on.	0 or more
`Listener`	You can add a listener to monitoring lifecycle events, such as this host starting or stopping, and to implement user Web applications.	0 or more
`Alias`	Defines an alias for this host if two or more network names need to apply to it.	0 or more

You'll cover context configuration in Chapter 5 when you'll learn how to configure Web applications.

Configuring a Valve

A valve is a Tomcat-specific interception mechanism for catching requests and responses. Any requests destined for the localhost host will be passed through the valve defined here, if it were to be uncommented.

```
<!--
<Valve className="org.apache.catalina.valves.AccessLogValve"
         directory="logs"  prefix="localhost_access_log."
         suffix=".txt"
         pattern="common" resolveHosts="false"/>
-->
```

The `org.apache.catalina.valves.AccessLogValve` valve creates access log files in the same format as Apache's log file. The previous configuration will create log files, in the common format, in `CATALINA_HOME/logs`. They will be named in the form `localhost_access_log.DATE.txt`.

You can also install valves at the engine level. Any valve that's installed at the engine level will have access to every request handled by the engine, regardless of which connector the request comes through. Therefore, you must test the valve thoroughly and make sure it doesn't require a lot of processor time to complete its operation. The standard valves that come with Tomcat have been designed and tested for efficiency.

■ **Note** Valves are specific to Tomcat and not part of the Servlet specification. Application programmers can use filters as a similar interception mechanism. They are part of the Servlet specification and reside within a Web application.

You'll see how to configure and use the standard valves in Chapter 7.

Configuring a Listener

If a user has an object that needs to know about server lifecycle events, then they need to implement a listener. The basic listener configuration is as follows:

```
<Listener className="com.acme.listeners.Listener" />
```

The `className` attribute is required. You can add other attributes according to the properties of the class. They're matched with the standard JavaBean naming mechanism.

Configuring an Alias

If you need to map more than one network name to a single virtual host, then you need to configure an alias. For example, say you want to map `www.company.com` and `www.company.org` to the same host; you'd do the following:

```
<Host name="www.company.com" ...>
  <Alias>www.company.org</Alias>
</Host>
```

Understanding Authentication and the tomcat-users.xml File

Tomcat's user database realm uses the `tomcat-users.xml` file by default and reads the entire file into memory. Once the realm has loaded the file into memory, no modification to the `tomcat-users.xml` file will be reflected until the next server restart. Here's `tomcat-users.xml`:

```
<?xml version='1.0' encoding='utf-8'?>
<tomcat-users>
  <role rolename="tomcat"/>
  <role rolename="role1"/>
  <user username="tomcat" password="tomcat" roles="tomcat"/>
  <user username="both" password="tomcat" roles="tomcat,role1"/>
  <user username="role1" password="tomcat" roles="role1"/>
</tomcat-users>
```

Each role that a user can play is defined with a `<role>` element, and each user has a `<user>` entry. Note how a user can have more than one role by adding a comma-separated list to the `roles` attribute.

Configuring Web Application Defaults with web.xml

Every Servlet 2.4 Web application must contain a `web.xml` deployment descriptor. This file must be placed in the `WEB-INF` directory of the Web application.

However, Tomcat comes with a default `web.xml` in `CATALINA_HOME/conf`. This file is similar to a Web application's `web.xml` file but is used to specify the default properties for all Web applications that are running within this server instance.

To gain an understanding of what you can do with this file, let's look at it. The file starts with the standard XML header and a reference to a DTD. Unlike `server.xml`, `web.xml` can be formally validated against a corresponding DTD.

```
<?xml version="1.0" encoding="ISO-8859-1"?>
<Web-app xmlns="http://java.sun.com/xml/ns/j2ee"
    xmlns:xsi="http://www.w3.org/2001/XMLSchema-instance"
    xsi:schemaLocation="http://java.sun.com/xml/ns/j2ee
http://java.sun.com/xml/ns/j2ee/Web-app_2_4.xsd"
    version="2.4">
```

The most noteworthy thing about this is that the default Web application version is 2.4.

Default Servlet Definitions

The default servlet that invokes any resources not mapped to any other servlet, either in this `web.xml` file or in an application's `web.xml` file, is defined in the first `<servlet>` definition. This includes all static resources. You'll see the mappings later.

```
<web-app>
  <servlet>
    <servlet-name>default</servlet-name>
    <servlet-class>
      org.apache.catalina.servlets.DefaultServlet
    </servlet-class>
    <init-param>
      <param-name>debug</param-name>
      <param-value>0</param-value>
    </init-param>
    <init-param>
      <param-name>listings</param-name>
      <param-value>true</param-value>
    </init-param>
    <load-on-startup>1</load-on-startup>
  </servlet>
```

Next comes the invoker servlet, which loads and executes anonymous servlets directly using the servlet's filename. This mechanism is inherently unsafe, because any class that exists in Tomcat's classpath can be invoked in this way, so the invoker servlet has been commented out of recent versions of Tomcat.

```
<!--
<servlet>
  <servlet-name>invoker</servlet-name>
  <servlet-class>
    org.apache.catalina.servlets.InvokerServlet
  </servlet-class>
  <init-param>
    <param-name>debug</param-name>
    <param-value>0</param-value>
  </init-param>
  <load-on-startup>2</load-on-startup>
</servlet>
-->
```

Just as servlets have their default servlet, JSP pages have a servlet that compiles them into servlets and executes them.

```
<servlet>
  <servlet-name>jsp</servlet-name>
  <servlet-class>org.apache.jasper.servlet.JspServlet</servlet-class>
  <init-param>
    <param-name>fork</param-name>
    <param-value>false</param-value>
  </init-param>
  <init-param>
    <param-name>xpoweredBy</param-name>
    <param-value>false</param-value>
  </init-param>
  <load-on-startup>3</load-on-startup>
</servlet>
```

The next set of servlets is commented out by default. You should uncomment them if you plan to add Apache-style Server Side Include (SSI) features to the stand-alone Tomcat server or process CGI. You'll see more of this in later chapters.

Matching URLs: Servlet Mappings

Servlet mappings specify which servlets are to process incoming requests, as defined by the request URL.

```
<!-- The mapping for the default servlet -->
<servlet-mapping>
  <servlet-name>default</servlet-name>
  <url-pattern>/</url-pattern>
</servlet-mapping>
```

The previous <servlet-mapping> element maps the pattern / to the default servlet defined earlier in web.xml. So, www.apress.com/tomcat/ will map to the default servlet, which will process the request.

The second <servlet-mapping> maps all requests that end in /servlet/* to the invoker servlet defined earlier in web.xml.

```
<!-- The mapping for the invoker servlet -->
<!--
<servlet-mapping>
  <servlet-name>invoker</servlet-name>
  <url-pattern>/servlet/*</url-pattern>
</servlet-mapping>
-->
```

The next <servlet-mapping> specifies that all URLs containing *.jsp and *.jspx should be passed to the servlet named jsp for processing:

```
<!-- The mapping for the JSP servlet -->
<servlet-mapping>
  <servlet-name>jsp</servlet-name>
  <url-pattern>*.jsp</url-pattern>
</servlet-mapping>

<servlet-mapping>
  <servlet-name>jsp</servlet-name>
  <url-pattern>*.jspx</url-pattern>
</servlet-mapping>
```

Configuring Session Timeout

The <session-config> element configures how long Tomcat will maintain a session on the server side on behalf of a client. For example, if the user leaves a service registration transaction in the middle and doesn't return to the cart for 30 minutes, all their information will be lost.

You must be careful to balance the <session-timeout> value with the potential of overloading the server with too many stale sessions.

```
<session-config>
  <session-timeout>30</session-timeout>
</session-config>
```

Configuring Mime Mappings

The <mime-mapping> elements that make up a large chunk of web.xml help Tomcat serve static files with specific extensions to the client. It will generate an HTTP Content-Type header when transmitting the file to the client. Most browsers will use a helper application to process the file being transmitted if it recognizes the Content-Type specified. For example, a browser may start Adobe Acrobat when it detects the application/pdf content type.

```
  <mime-mapping>
    <extension>abs</extension>
    <mime-type>audio/x-mpeg</mime-type>
  </mime-mapping>
... and so on ...
```

Configuring Welcome Files

To be compatible with the default behavior of most modern Web servers, including Apache, the default servlet will display a welcome file if the incoming URI is terminated in /—for example, `http://www.apress.com/`.

The default servlet will examine the root directory of the named virtual host and look for `index.html`, `index.htm`, or `index.jsp` in turn to be displayed. Each Web application may override this list in its own deployment descriptor file.

```
  <welcome-file-list>
    <welcome-file>index.html</welcome-file>
    <welcome-file>index.htm</welcome-file>
    <welcome-file>index.jsp</welcome-file>
  </welcome-file-list>
</web-app>
```

Changing NT Service Options

When you install Tomcat as a service, it's set to start automatically, which means that if you were to restart the computer, Tomcat would start automatically. From now on, every time Windows is started, Tomcat will automatically start up at boot time and will be available then.

You can further customize the service by choosing the Properties option from the context menu. This allows you to change the startup type to manual or entirely disable the service, plus it allows you to choose to automatically restart the service should it crash. This last option is especially useful as it also allows you to run a script should the server fail. You also have the option to reboot the computer. (However, you should consider seriously what you put in this script because it can offer a security hole if the script does something that may be used as a denial-of-service attack.)

It also allows you to carry out different actions depending on how many times it has failed (by choosing the Recovery tab), so you can initially request a reboot of the service and then request a reboot of the machine. Then, any subsequent failures will cause a script to run that perhaps alerts you of the failure.

The only possible reason for restarting the machine is if the applications that are running on Tomcat depend on an ordered bootup and no loss of connections between the applications and their various resources. This means that, on the whole, writing a script that flashes a warning or similar is more desirable than rebooting the system.

If you want to set the recovery options, right-click the Tomcat service entry in the list and choose Properties. In the window that opens, choose Recovery, and you'll see the options shown in Figure 4-3.

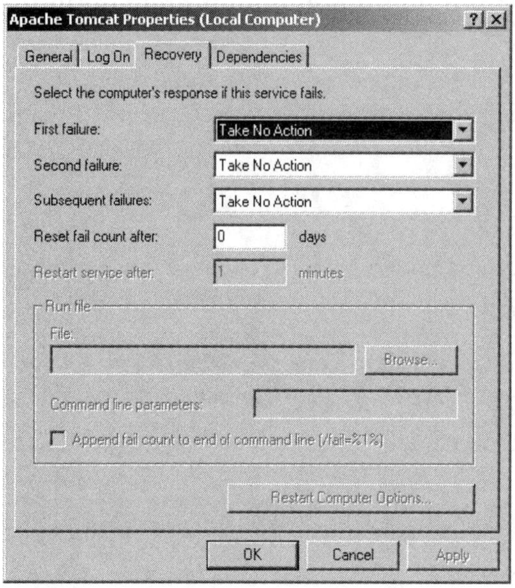

Figure 4-3. *The Tomcat service's recovery options*

The default is for no action to be taken. You're going to change this behavior and restart the server a maximum of twice and then run a script on the third and subsequent failures. Select the First Failure drop-down box, and choose Restart the Service. Do the same for the second box. Set the time after the crash that the service should be restarted to one minute. This should give any external resources enough time to notice the failure and respond if necessary.

If this is a stable server that rarely fails, set the reset level high, say, to 20 days, which should mean that consistent failures are noticed and addressed. It may be that it fails only occasionally—you want to know nevertheless. Setting the reset level high maximizes the chance that the third option will run, thus alerting you to the problem. Remember that the script can easily be responsible for restarting the server so that users feel a minimal downtime, yet you're still notified. In fact, this option may be preferable to having the system automatically restart the server without explicit notification of problems.

If the server fails often, it may be necessary to turn the reset level down so that failures can be noticed.

Now choose Run a File from the Subsequent Failures option menu. This will enable the Run File menu where you can choose the file to run (normally a batch file). The fail count is passed to the file as a command-line parameter for the script to report.

For the moment, assuming that you haven't specified any other command-line prompts, you can discover the failure count using a file such as the following:

```
@echo off
if NOT %1==/fail goto end
echo Number of failures to date is %2 >> T4.fail
:end
cd "c:\jakarta-tomcat\bin\"
start startup
```

The previous file is the simplest possible reporting script that merely appends the failure count to a file named `T4.fail` each time a failure occurs before restarting the server (but not as a service, rather as a manual start in a new command prompt window). In the first line you turn off `echo`, the second line checks that the first command-line argument (%1) is equal to `/fail` and if so prints the following line:

```
Number of failures to date is %x%
```

where `x` is the number of failures. Notice that `>> T4.fail` makes sure that `echo` is added to the `T4.fail` file and that the output is appended to, rather than replaces, the existing contents of the file. A single > would replace the file contents.

The result of multiple failures with this file, as set previously to run on the third failure, would be something along the lines of this:

```
Number of failures to date is %3%
Number of failures to date is %4%
Number of failures to date is %5%
Number of failures to date is %6%
```

Alternatively, you can run a Java class that extracts the information and perhaps e-mails the failure to you. To do this, simply forward the fail count to your program, calling it as follows:

```
@echo off
if NOT %1==/fail goto end
java ReportTomcatFailure %2
:end
cd "c:\jakarta-tomcat\bin\"
start startup
```

The number of failures is now available as `ReportTomcatFailure`'s first command-line argument (accessible as `args[0]`).

In addition to the security risk involved in having the computer automatically reboot itself, it's not entirely necessary. Since Tomcat runs within a JVM, unless you're doing something unusual, a failure of the Tomcat instance is isolated from the rest of the system and a soft reboot should suffice for most problems. This puts hardware reboots in the very serious category, and, as such, they're something you probably want to control manually.

Summary

In this chapter, you've seen all the configuration files in Tomcat's `CATALINA_HOME/conf` directory. `server.xml` is the main configuration file for Tomcat, and `server-minimal.xml` is a blank template from which you can create your own custom `server.xml` configuration.

The `tomcat-users.xml` file is used by the default user authentication mechanism in Tomcat. In a production system, you should use a more robust implementation of a realm, such as a JDBC realm or a JNDI realm.

The default `web.xml` file in `CATALINA_HOME/conf` specifies properties that are used in every Web application running on the server. Many of the default servlets configured here provide Web serverlike features (serving static content, SSI, CGI, and so on) for running Web applications.

Tomcat starts in an unsecured mode, but the catalina.policy file is vitally important in a secured Tomcat installation. It specifies who can access what, and anything else that isn't specified can't be accessed. Tomcat takes advantage of the sophisticated, built-in security infrastructure of Java 2.

The other two files in CATALINA_HOME/conf are catalina.properties and jk2.properties. catalina.properties configures Tomcat's class loaders as well as what classes can be executed by application code. By default, Tomcat internals are barred. jk2.properties defines a connector to the Apache Web server.

In the next chapter, you'll see how to administer a Web application.

CHAPTER 5

Administering Web Applications

It may seem as if it's not the administrator's job to look after a developer's application once it's deployed. But, as Web applications are run on the server you have responsibility for, it's important to know how they're structured so that you can administer them effectively. In an ideal world, the developer will have set up the Web application so that it runs smoothly as soon as it goes live. However, this isn't always the case.

A lot of code running on the server will have hard-coded paths to resources, which means that most applications won't be happy when you move files. The developer may even have to recompile and redeploy the application. Therefore, knowing about administering Web applications is a useful skill to have.

In this chapter I'll cover how to configure a context. (Remember, I didn't cover this in Chapter 4 because a context is configured in a separate file to `server.xml`.) To do all of this, however, you'll need to know where the various files are placed within a Web application, which has a well-defined structure.

Configuring Contexts

In the past, you may have configured contexts in `server.xml`, but this is no longer recommended. The main reason is that Tomcat reads `server.xml` only when it starts and doesn't reload it at any point of the server's life. This means that any changes, including new context definitions, won't be registered.

The new procedure requires you to use the same context definition as before but this time in its own XML file in the `CATALINA_HOME/conf/[Engine_name]/[Host_name]` directory. For the default setup, this is `CATALINA_HOME/conf/Catalina/localhost`.

The XML file may be called whatever you want and has the `<Context>` element as its root element. The name of this file is important in Tomcat 5.5 because it's used to name the Web application that the context XML file describes.

Configuring Default Contexts

Before you see how to configure a context, I'll discuss how Tomcat deploys contexts and how this affects the default settings. Tomcat uses a set sequence when it automatically deploys Web applications at startup (configured with the host's `deployOnStartup` attribute). To start with, it reads any context XML files in the `CATALINA_HOME/conf/[Engine_name]/[Host_name]` directory for each host. The `docBase` attribute of the `<Context>` element (see Table 5-1 in the next section) points to a WAR or directory where the application files are located. Tomcat then deploys this Web application using the settings in the context XML file.

The next step in the sequence is to expand any WAR files in the application base directory that don't have a corresponding directory (assuming the host's `unpackWARs` attribute is true). This means you have to remove any expanded Web applications if you add a new WAR file.

The final step in Web application deployment is the one that's most relevant to this section. Any expanded directories and WARs in the application base directory that don't have a corresponding context XML file are given a default implicit `<Context>` element. You configure this default element differently depending on the version of Tomcat you're using.

Tomcat 5.0.*x* has a `<DefaultContext>` element in `server.xml` that you use to define default context settings. This element uses a subset of the `<Context>` element's attributes. These are marked with an asterisk in Table 5-1.

Tomcat 5.5 uses an external default context XML file, which has the `<Context>` element as its root element. The default file for the entire server is `CATALINA_HOME/conf/context.xml`, and the default file for a host is `CATALINA_HOME/conf/[Engine_name]/[Host_name]/context.xml.default`. You may also place a `context.xml` file in a Web application's `META-INF` directory, though this is read only if there's no application context file as described previously. This file will apply only to that Web application.

The settings in `context.xml` override any in `context.xml.default` and `META-INF/context.xml`, even if you explicitly set the `override` attribute described in Table 5-1. However, `override` works for application context XML files. Figure 5-1 shows this process.

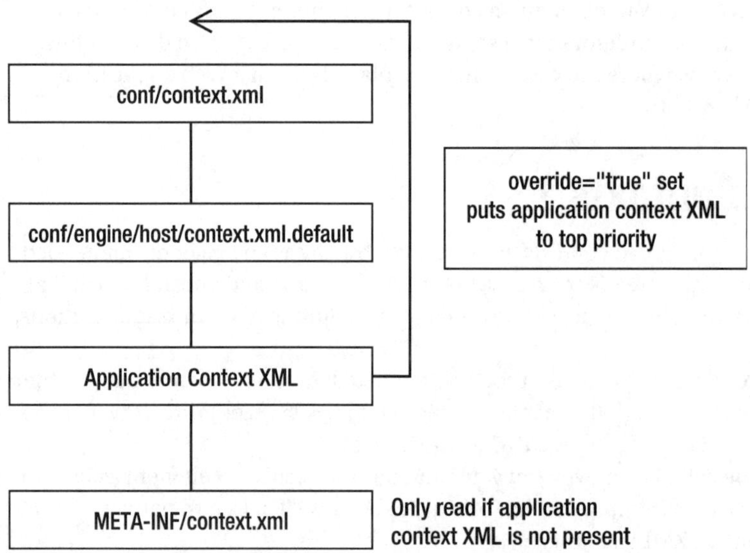

Figure 5-1. *The context file hierarchy in Tomcat 5.5*

These rules also apply to applications that are deployed after startup. That is, they apply to directories and WAR files that you drop into the Web application base directory, assuming autodeployment is enabled with the host's `autoDeploy` attribute. If autodeployment is disabled, then you can use tools such as the manager application and Ant to deploy applications, and the same process occurs.

Web applications are also restarted and redeployed if their web.xml file is changed, their WAR is updated, or their context XML file is updated, though you can also configure the web.xml reload using the <WatchedResource> element as described in the "Configuring a Watched Resource" section.

The Context Element

Tomcat's standard <Context> element has the attributes described in Table 5-1. Those marked with an asterisk are available to the Tomcat 5.0.*x* <DefaultContext> element.

Table 5-1. *The Attributes of the Standard <Context> Element*

Attribute	Description	Required?
allowLinking (*)	If true, symlinks pointing to resources outside the Web application base path are allowed for this Web application. This flag shouldn't be set to true on Windows, as it will disable case-sensitivity checks, allowing JSP source code disclosure, among other security problems. The default is false.	No
backgroundProcessorDelay	The delay in seconds between the invocation of the backgroundProcess() method on this context and its child containers, including all wrappers. Child containers will be invoked if their delay value is negative (which would mean they're using their own processing thread). Setting this to a positive value will cause a thread to be spawned. After waiting the specified amount of time, the thread will invoke the backgroundProcess() method on this host and all its child containers. A context will use background processing to perform session expiration and class monitoring for reloading. The default is -1, which means the context will rely on the background processing thread of its parent host.	No
cacheMaxSize (*)	Maximum size of the static resource cache in kilobytes. The default is 10240.	No
cacheTTL (*)	Time in milliseconds between cache entries revalidation. The default is 5000.	No
cachingAllowed (*)	If true, the cache for static resources will be used. The default is true.	No
caseSensitive (*)	If true, all case-sensitivity checks will be disabled. This flag shouldn't be set to true on Windows, as it will disable case-sensitivity checks, allowing JSP source code disclosure, among other security problems. The default value is true.	No

Table 5-1. *The Attributes of the Standard* `<Context>` *Element (Continued)*

Attribute	Description	Required?
`className`	Class name of the implementation to use. The default is `org.apache.catalina.core.StandardContext`.	No
`cookies (*)`	Set to `true` if you want cookies to be used to identify sessions (if supported by the client). Set to `false` if you want to disable the use of cookies for session identification and rely only on URL rewriting. The default is `true`.	No
`crossContext (*)`	Set to `true` if you want calls within this application to `ServletContext.getContext()` to successfully return a request dispatcher for other Web applications running on this virtual host. Set to `false` in security-conscious environments. The default is `false`.	No
`debug`	Tomcat 5.0.*x* only. The level of debugging for this context. The levels are 1 (errors), 2 (warnings), 3 (information), and 4 (debug). These correspond to the levels of debugging in the logger component. This is an attribute of the standard implementation and may change if you're using another implementation. The default is zero, meaning no debugging (though the associated logger will still log fatal messages).	No
`docBase`	The document base (or context root) directory for this Web application or the pathname to its WAR file. You can specify an absolute pathname for this directory or WAR file, or you can specify a pathname that's relative to the `appBase` directory of the owning host.	Yes
`managerChecksFrequency (*)`	Tomcat 5.0.*x* only. Frequency of the session expiration and related manager operations. Manager operations will be carried out once for the specified amount of `backgroundProcess()` calls (that is, the lower the amount, the more frequent the checks). The minimum value is `1`. The default is `6`.	No
`override`	In Tomcat 5.0.*x*, set to `true` to have explicit settings in this context override any corresponding settings in the `<DefaultContext>` element associated with the owning host. In Tomcat 5.5 this setting overrides the settings in all three default context files. The default is `false`.	No
`privileged`	Set to `true` to allow this context to use container servlets, like the manager servlet. The default is `false`.	No
`path`	The context path of this Web application, which is matched against the beginning of each request URI. All the context paths within a particular host must be unique. If you specify an empty string (`""`), you're defining the default Web application for this host, which will process all requests not assigned to other contexts. In Tomcat 5.5, the path of a Web application is inferred from the name of the context XML file or the file specified in `docBase`. Therefore, you shouldn't need to set a value for this attribute.	Yes (Tomcat 5.0.*x*) No (Tomcat 5.5)

Table 5-1. *The Attributes of the Standard <Context> Element (Continued)*

Attribute	Description	Required?
processTlds	Specify whether the context should process TLDs on startup. false is intended for special cases where you know in advance that TLDs aren't part of the Web application. The default is true.	No
reloadable (*)	Set to true if you want Tomcat to monitor classes in /WEB-INF/classes and /WEB-INF/lib for changes and automatically reload the Web application if a change is detected. This feature is useful during development, but it requires significant runtime overhead and isn't recommended for use on deployed production applications. Use the manager application to reload applications if this is required. The default is false.	No
swallowOutput (*)	If true, the output to System.out and System.err will be redirected to the Web application logger. The default is false.	No
tldNamespaceAware	If true, XML validation of TLDs will be namespace aware. If you turn this flag on, you should also turn tldValidation on, though setting it to true will incur a performance penalty. The default is false.	No
tldValidation	If true, TLDs will be XML validated on context startup. Setting it to true will incur a performance penalty. The default is false.	No
useNaming (*)	Set to true to have Tomcat enable a JNDI InitialContext for this Web application. The default is true.	No
workDir	The pathname to a scratch directory to be provided by this context for temporary read-write use by servlets. This directory is visible to servlets through a servlet context attribute (of type java.io.File) named javax.servlet.context.tempdir as described in the Servlet specification. The default is a suitable directory underneath CATALINA_HOME/work.	No
wrapperClass (*)	The Java class name of the org.apache.catalina.Wrapper implementation class that will be used for servlets managed by this context. The default is org.apache.catalina.core.StandardWrapper.	No

Tomcat 5.5 introduces a number of new attributes to the context element (see Table 5-2).

Table 5-2. *The New Attributes of Tomcat 5.5's Standard <Context> Element*

Attribute	Description	Required?
antiJARLocking	If true, Tomcat's class loader will take extra measures to avoid JAR file locking when JARs are accessed through URLs. This will slow application startup times but can prove useful on platforms or configurations where file locking can occur. The default is false.	No
antiResourceLocking	If true, Tomcat will prevent file locking. This will significantly slow application startup time but allows full hot deploy and undeploy on platforms or configurations where file locking can occur. The default is false.	No
unpackWAR	If true, Tomcat will unpack this Web application, if it's compressed, before running it. If the host's unpackWARs attribute is false, this setting has no effect. The default is true.	No

A context is a container and can have the nested components described in Table 5-3.

Table 5-3. *The Subelements of the <Context> Element*

Subelement	Description	Number
Environment	A global variable. See Chapter 4 for details.	Zero or more
Listener	You can add a listener to monitor lifecycle events, such as this host starting or stopping, and to implement user Web applications. See Chapter 4 for details.	Zero or more
Loader	Configures the Web application class loader. It's unlikely that you'd want to specify your own class loader. See the Tomcat documentation if this is a necessity.	Zero or one
Logger	Tomcat 5.0.*x* only. A logger to be used with this Web application. This element overrides any logger defined in the enclosing <Host> or <Engine> elements. See Chapter 4 for details.	Zero or one
Manager	A custom session manager to handle session persistence for this Web application. This is a technique used by programmers to overcome HTTP's stateless nature. It's unlikely you'd want to specify your own session manager. See the Tomcat documentation if this is a necessity.	Zero or one
Parameter	A value that will be available to the Web application as a named variable.	Zero or more
Realm	An authentication realm to be used within this Web application. This will override any previous realm definitions in the enclosing <Host> or <Engine> definitions. See Chapter 4 for details.	Zero or one
Resource	A JNDI resource. See Chapter 4 for details.	Zero or more
ResourceLink	A link to a global JNDI resource.	Zero or more

Table 5-3. *The Subelements of the* `<Context>` *Element (Continued)*

Subelement	Description	Number
`ResourceParams`	Parameters that go along with the named JBDI resource. See Chapter 4 for details.	Zero or more
`Resources`	A resource manager for accessing static resources (for serving static Web pages, graphics, and so on) within the Web application. It's unlikely you'd want to specify your own resource manager. See the Tomcat documentation if this is a necessity.	Zero or one
`Valve`	You can add a valve to monitor access, filter requests, and implement single sign-on. See Chapter 4 for details.	Zero or more

Configuring a Parameter

You can add servlet context initialization parameters in your context definition. These will be available to servlets throughout the application.

Table 5-4 describes the attributes of the `<Parameter>` element.

Table 5-4. *The Attributes of the* `<Parameter>` *Element*

Attribute	Description	Required?
`description`	Human-readable description of this context initialization parameter.	No
`name`	The name of the context initialization parameter to be created.	Yes
`override`	Sets whether a `<context-param>` element in the application's `web.xml` file can override the value specified here. The default is `true`.	No
`value`	The value that will be available to the application.	Yes

Configuring a Resource Link

A resource link references a global JNDI variable and makes it available under the new name.

Table 5-5 describes the attributes of a `<ResourceLink>` element.

Table 5-5. *The Attributes of the* `<ResourceLink>` *Element*

Attribute	Description	Required?
`global`	The name of the global JNDI resource	Yes
`name`	The name of the variable to be created, relative to the `java:comp/env` context	Yes
`type`	The class name expected by the Web application when it performs a lookup for this resource link	Yes

Configuring a Watched Resource (Tomcat 5.5 Only)

Tomcat, if set to autodeploy, will monitor the specified static resource of the Web application for updates and will reload the Web application if it's updated. The content of this element must be a string, and it has no attributes or subelements. You may have more than one watched resource per Web application as shown in the default server `context.xml` file.

```
<WatchedResource>WEB-INF/web.xml</WatchedResource>
<WatchedResource>META-INF/context.xml</WatchedResource>
```

This tells Tomcat to reload the Web application when the specified files are changed. Thus Tomcat reloads a Web application when its individual settings are changed.

Examining a Web Application

HTML and JSP pages belong to the public resources that a client may request directly. Servlets, JavaBeans, and other resources within a Web application's `WEB-INF` directory are private resources. You may allow the client to access these resources indirectly by mapping a URL to a servlet or including the page in a JSP page. However, private resources can't be served to the client without some type of intervention.

The following is a typical makeup of a Web application required by the Servlet 2.4 specification:

```
webapps/
        pics/
             index.html
             gallery/
                     index.html
                     images/
                            pic01.jpg
                            pic02.jpg
             images/
                    code.gif
                    execute.gif
                    read.gif
                    return.gif
             WEB-INF/(*)
                     web.xml(*)
                     classses/(*)
                              com/
                                  Controller.class
                              actions/
                                      ViewGalleryAction.class
```

```
            jsp/
                catalog.jsp
            lib/(*)
                jstl.jar
                standard.jar
            tags/(*)
                simpleTag.tag
            tlds/
                simple.tld
    META-INF/(*)
```

Not all these files and directories are required. Those marked with (*) are part of the Servlet specification and can't be renamed or moved, though some of them may be omitted. The `WEB-INF` folder, its subdirectories, and the `META-INF` folder are private areas that can be accessed only indirectly through application code or special configuration. A Web application deployed on Tomcat 5.5 as a WAR file may have a `META-INF` folder with a default `context.xml` file that provides context configuration information. Expanded Web applications may also use this mechanism, though providing a separate context XML file is the preferred method in this case.

This Web application is deployed in a folder named after the Web application (in this case it's called `pics`), and this folder is required. You'd access this Web application using the following URL: `http://servername:8080/pics/`. The `pics/` section is called the *context path*, and Tomcat uses this to resolve any paths contained within the Web application.

When a user requests a resource on the server (that is, an HTML document, a servlet, a JSP page, and so on), they type the path to it on the file system, relative to the context path. For example, if the user wants to request the `C:\jakarta-tomcat\webapps\tomcatBook\ch05\login.html` file, they'd type `http://servername:8080/tomcatBook/ch05/login.html`. In other words, the server directory structure overlays the file system structure from the contents of the `webapps` directory down.

■ **Note** This generality applies to the default setup but doesn't strictly apply to JSP pages. While the path to the resource is the same in the server and on the file system, the JSP page is processed into a servlet and compiled before it's returned as a response. Therefore, there isn't a one-to-one mapping between the requested resource and the resource that returns content. This distinction isn't relevant to your users, as they won't notice the difference, but it's a fact worth knowing.

This default behavior is a problem if a Web application is running servlets, because they reside in the private `WEB-INF` area and can't be accessed directly by users. In times past, the solution was to use the invoker servlet, but this isn't recommended. The answer is servlet mappings.

Mapping URLs to Resources

If a Web application uses servlets, users need some way to access them. The answer lies in web.xml, the Web application deployment descriptor. You can set a series of URL mappings to make servlets available to users.

So, for the previous example Web application, you need to define a servlet and give it a name.

```
<servlet>
  <servlet-name>
    Controller
  </servlet-name>
  <servlet-class>
    com.Controller
  </servlet-class>
</servlet>
```

The name of the servlet must be unique within the Web application and can't clash with those in the default web.xml file described in Chapter 4. The <servlet-class> element must contain the fully qualified class name. The previous servlet has a fully qualified class name with the package name (com) followed by the class name (Controller). The package name may be longer (for example, com.apress.servlets).

You have to perform one more step to make this named servlet available to your users. You must map it to a URL.

```
<servlet-mapping>
  <servlet-name>Controller</servlet-name>
  <url-pattern>/Controller</url-pattern>
</servlet-mapping>
```

This says that the http://servername:8080/pics/Controller URL should be passed to a servlet named Controller.

The mapping can use wildcards (*) to specify that you want to match any file, and you can use this with directories as well. This means you can cover whole directories with a mapping. For example, *.do is a common mapping used by the Apache Struts framework. This means that all requests ending in .do are routed to the specified servlet.

You can also map requests to JSP (or HTML) pages in the same manner. For example, say you want to show an index page for any requests that don't correspond to a resource. This means users never see a directory listing of the server and won't see a 404 error. Here's the resource definition in web.xml:

```
<servlet>
  <servlet-name>
    index
  </servlet-name>
  <jsp-file>
    /index.html
  </jsp-file>
</servlet>
```

This specifies that the index.html file in the root of the Web application is called index for the purpose of this configuration file. Just as you did for the servlet, you must now map URLs to this resource.

```
<servlet-mapping>
  <servlet-name>
    index
  </servlet-name>
  <url-pattern>
    /*
  </url-pattern>
</servlet-mapping>
```

So, you've mapped the resource called index to the wildcard URL /*. This pattern matches every resource, so all requests, no matter if they point to a file that exists or not, will return the index.html page. However, the servlet engine will get to this entry only if there are no more-specific entries. This allows you to have fine-grained control over your resources.

If you have both of the previous settings in your web.xml file, then http://servername:8080/pics/Controller will display the results of the Controller servlet, and http://servername:8080/pics/Controller2, http://servername:8080/pics/blah, or any other URL that points to the pics context will display the index page. This is because the Controller mapping is more specific than the index mapping.

Examining the WEB-INF Folder

The WEB-INF folder contains at least four subfolders and the web.xml file.

Examining the classes Folder

The classes directory is in the Web application's classpath, as are all of its subdirectories. This is why it contains servlets and the utility classes for the application, and it may also contain a number of resource files needed by these classes. It's also a subdirectory of WEB-INF, making it a private resource. Users may not access any of the resources here. You saw an example of this earlier in the "Examining a Web Application" section.

Java classes in the classes directory follow the same package structure as any other classes. That is, they're stored in a directory hierarchy within classes just as they would be in a regular setup. So, com.apress.PackageServlet is stored in the classes/com/apress directory.

Ideally, you don't need to be concerned with the contents of the classes directory.

Examining the lib Folder

The lib folder is also in the Web application's classpath. This is where you place JAR files that are required by the Web application.

Examining the tags Folder

As of JSP 2.0, developers can write tag extensions in JSP syntax without the need to know Java. Traditionally a tag extension was a Java class that defined the functionality of a custom markup tag. For example, a developer may write a tag that displayed the date, like so:

```
<date:today/>
```

These tag extensions are grouped together in tag libraries, which are a convenient way to group code that has similar functionality, much like a Java package does.

It's in the `tags` folder, and its subdirectories, that the developers place these JSP-syntax tag extensions so that the container can find them. Again, you shouldn't have many dealings with this folder.

Examining the tlds Folder

The `tlds` folder contains the configuration files for traditional Java-coded tag libraries. Each configuration file maps tag names to their implementation class so that the container can recognize which class to invoke when it comes across the tag. These configuration files are TLDs and have a `.tld` extension. The configuration of a tag library is the territory of developers and designers so you won't have many dealings with them.

Examining the web.xml File

You shouldn't have many dealings with a Web application's `web.xml` file, as it's the realm of the application's developer. However, certain aspects on the server are definitely your concern, so the following sections will go into the relevant sections in `web.xml`. They will be illustrated where possible by examples from Tomcat's default `web.xml` file.

<distributable>

The `<distributable>` element, if present, declares that this Web application can be deployed in a distributed servlet container or servlet container executing across multiple JVMs either running on the same host or different hosts. This Boolean value is `false` by default.

<context-param>

The `<context-param>` element declares a context initialization parameter, much as the previous `<Parameter>` element does. It contains the following:

- A `<param-name>` element containing the parameter's name
- A `<param-value>` element containing the parameter's value
- An optional `<description>` element

<filter>

The <filter> element declares a filter. A filter is a Java class that preprocesses the request data received from clients. This preprocessing may include decryption, formatting, or other processes. This element contains the following:

- An optional <icon> element
- A <filter-name> element containing the filter's name
- An optional <display-name> element
- An optional <description> element
- A <filter-class> element containing the filter's class name
- Zero or more <init-param> elements containing initialization parameters for the filter

Each <init-param> element contains the following:

- A <param-name> element containing the parameter name
- A <param-value> element containing the parameter value
- An optional <description> element

Chapter 7 describes a filter for working with requests. Its <filter> entry would be as shown in Listing 5-1.

Listing 5-1. *An Entry for a Filter*

```
<filter>
  <filter-name>requestFilter</filter-name>
  <filter-class>com.apress.admin.filters.RequestFilter</filter-class>
  <init-param>
    <param-name>allow</param-name>
    <param-value></param-value>
  </init-param>
  <init-param>
    <param-name>deny</param-name>
    <param-value>127.0.0.1</param-value>
  </init-param>
  <init-param>
    <param-name>blockPage</param-name>
    <param-value>/blocked.html</param-value>
  </init-param>
</filter>
```

<filter-mapping>

The `<filter-mapping>` element maps a filter to a servlet or a set of URLs. It contains the following:

- A `<filter-name>` element containing the name of a filter declared by a `<filter>` element.
- Either a `<url-pattern>` element containing a URL pattern to match or a `<servlet-name>` element containing the name of a servlet declared by a `<servlet>` element.
- Zero to four `<dispatcher>` elements; it can have one of the following values: `FORWARD`, `REQUEST`, `INCLUDE`, and `ERROR`. `FORWARD` applies the filter to `RequestDispatcher.forward()` calls, `REQUEST` applies the filter to ordinary client calls to the path or servlet, `INCLUDE` applies the filter to `RequestDispatcher.include()` calls, and `ERROR` applies the filter to the error page mechanism.

If the `<dispatcher>` element is omitted, the default value is `REQUEST`.

The previous filter would have the filter mapping as shown in Listing 5-2.

Listing 5-2. *An Example Filter Mapping*

```
<filter-mapping>
  <filter-name>requestFilter</filter-name>
  <url-pattern>/*</url-pattern>
</filter-mapping>
```

This maps all requests in the Web application to the filter.

<servlet>

Because you've already seen the `<servlet>` element in action, I won't discuss it in detail here. It contains the following:

- An optional `<icon>` element
- A `<servlet-name>` element containing the servlet's name
- An optional `<display-name>` element
- An optional `<description>` element
- Either a `<servlet-class>` element containing the listener's class name or a `<jsp-file>` element containing the location within the Web application of a JSP file
- `<init-param>` elements
- An optional `<load-on-startup>` element indicating that the servlet should be loaded when the Web application starts up and containing an optional positive integer value that indicates the order in which servlets should be started. If a `<jsp-file>` was specified, then the JSP should be precompiled and loaded.
- `<security-role-ref>` elements

- An optional <run-as> element that specifies the identity under which the servlet should run

Each <init-param> element contains the following:

- A <param-name> element containing the parameter name
- A <param-value> element containing the parameter value
- An optional <description> element

A <security-role-ref> element maps a role name called from within the servlet and maps the name of a security role defined for the Web application. It contains the following:

- An optional <description> element
- A <role-name> element containing the role name used within the servlet
- An optional <role-link> element containing the name of a role defined in a <security-role> element

Tomcat's default web.xml file contains many <servlet> entries. The first is for the default servlet, as shown in Listing 5-3.

Listing 5-3. *The Default Servlet <servlet> Setting*

```
<servlet>
  <servlet-name>default</servlet-name>
  <servlet-class>
    org.apache.catalina.servlets.DefaultServlet
  </servlet-class>
  <init-param>
    <param-name>debug</param-name>
    <param-value>0</param-value>
  </init-param>
  <init-param>
    <param-name>listings</param-name>
    <param-value>true</param-value>
  </init-param>
  <load-on-startup>1</load-on-startup>
</servlet>
```

<servlet-mapping>

The <servlet-mapping> element maps a servlet to a URL pattern. It contains the following:

- A <servlet-name> element containing the name of a servlet declared by a <servlet> element
- A <url-pattern> element containing a URL pattern to match

The previous default servlet has a corresponding <servlet-mapping> entry, as shown in Listing 5-4.

Listing 5-4. *The Default Servlet <servlet-mapping> Setting*

```
<servlet-mapping>
  <servlet-name>default</servlet-name>
  <url-pattern>/</url-pattern>
</servlet-mapping>
```

<session-config>

An administrator should be aware of the session settings of a Web application because it can have performance and security implications. A huge number of long-lasting sessions may cause problems for performance, but a session that never expires means that a user is always recognized. The latter means that any user who has access to the original user's machine can access the Web application as that user.

The <session-config> element contains the following:

- An optional <session-timeout> element containing the default session timeout for this Web application, which must be a whole number of minutes. The default behavior of the container without this attribute is never to time out.

Listing 5-5 shows the default session setting from Tomcat's default web.xml file.

Listing 5-5. *The Default Session Setting for Tomcat*

```
<session-config>
  <session-timeout>30</session-timeout>
</session-config>
```

<mime-mapping>

Browsers use MIME types to recognize the file type returned by the server so that the browser can handle the response correctly. That is, the browser chooses whether to display it (HTML, plain text, images), send it to a plug-in (such as Flash), or prompt the user to save it locally.

As you saw in Chapter 4, CATALINA_HOME/conf/web.xml comes with many MIME mappings set. However, you can configure additional MIME mappings in each Web application with the <mime-mapping> element.

The <mime-mapping> element contains the following:

- An <extension> element containing a filename extension
- A <mime-type> element containing a defined MIME type

Tomcat has many MIME mappings set, one of which is shown in Listing 5-6. This tells Tomcat to treat *.bmp files as the image/bmp type.

Listing 5-6. *A Default Tomcat MIME Mapping*

```
<mime-mapping>
  <extension>bmp</extension>
  <mime-type>image/bmp</mime-type>
</mime-mapping>
```

<welcome-file-list>

The <welcome-file-list> element defines an ordered list of welcome files to display if no filename is specified. It contains the following:

- One or more <welcome-file> elements containing a filename to use as a welcome file

Tomcat has a default setting for welcome files, as shown in Listing 5-7.

Listing 5-7. *Tomcat's Default Welcome Files*

```
<welcome-file-list>
  <welcome-file>index.html</welcome-file>
  <welcome-file>index.htm</welcome-file>
  <welcome-file>index.jsp</welcome-file>
</welcome-file-list>
```

These files are checked in the order they appear.

<error-page>

Web application developers can configure error pages to provide a user-friendly mechanism for informing the users about any problems and allowing them to continue using the application. The errors are mapped to the HTTP specification error mappings: a code for a resource that can't be found, a malfunctioning server, authentication issues, resource issues, and so on.

In addition, since there are no one-to-one correspondences between HTTP errors and Java exceptions, the exception class type may be specified; this allows error pages that are generic and follows good programming practice. Someone without an understanding of the application's internals can configure them.

The <error-page> element contains the following:

- Either an <error-code> element containing an HTTP error code or an <exception-type> element containing the class name of a Java exception type
- A <location> element containing the location of the error page resource within the Web application

Listing 5-8 shows an example of an error page setting. In this case any 404 errors generated by Tomcat will return the myError.jsp page to the client.

Listing 5-8. *An Error Page Configuration*

```
<error-page>
  <error-code>404</error-code>
  <location>/myError.jsp</location>
</error-page>
```

<resource-env-ref>

The <resource-env-ref> element declares that the Web application references an administered object such as a user database. This is defined in the <GlobalNamingResources> element of the server component. It contains the following:

- An optional <description> element
- A <resource-env-ref-name> element containing the name of the resource environment
- A <resource-env-ref-type> element containing the type of the resource environment reference

The manager application configures a reference to a global resource, as shown in Listing 5-9.

Listing 5-9. *The Manager Web Application's <resource-env-ref> Setting*

```
<resource-env-ref>
  <description>
    Link to the UserDatabase instance from which we request lists of
    defined role names.  Typically, this will be connected to the global
    user database with a ResourceLink element in server.xml or the context
    configuration file for the manager Web application.
  </description>
  <resource-env-ref-name>users</resource-env-ref-name>
  <resource-env-ref-type>
    org.apache.catalina.UserDatabase
  </resource-env-ref-type>
</resource-env-ref>
```

<resource-ref>

The <resource-ref> element declares that the Web application references an external resource such as a data source reference. This is typically configured in a context entry using the <Resource> element. It contains the following:

- An optional <description> element.
- A <res-ref-name> element containing the name of the resource factory reference.
- A <res-type> element specifying the type of the data source.

- A `<res-auth>` element indicating whether the application code signs onto the resource programmatically or whether the container should sign on based on information supplied by the application deployer. Contents must be either `Application` or `Container`.

- An optional `<res-sharing-scope>` element specifying whether connections can be shared. Contents must be either `Shareable` (the default) or `Unshareable`.

Listing 5-10 shows an example.

Listing 5-10. *A Reference to a JDBC Data Source*

```
<resource-ref>
  <description>
    Resource reference to a factory for java.sql.Connection
    instances that may be used for talking to a particular
    database that is configured in the tomcatBook.xml file.
  </description>
  <res-ref-name>
    jdbc/CatalogDB
  </res-ref-name>
  <res-type>
    javax.sql.DataSource
  </res-type>
  <res-auth>
    SERVLET
  </res-auth>
</resource-ref>
```

<security-constraint>

Web resources may be associated with some security constraints for user authentication and access control. The constraints limit access to the resource according to user roles, such as manager, administrator, user, and guest, and by transport guarantee, which can include SSL secure data transmission, guaranteeing delivery and noninterference.

The `<security-constraint>` element contains the following:

- An optional `<display-name>` element

- One or more `<web-resource-collection>` elements

- An optional `<auth-constraint>` element

- An optional `<user-data-constraint>` element

A `<web-resource-collection>` element identifies a set of resources within the application; it can be qualified by specifying particular HTTP method(s) such as GET or POST. (By default, the security constraint applies to all HTTP methods.) It contains the following:

- A `<web-resource-name>` element containing the name of the Web resource collection
- An optional `<description>` element
- One or more `<url-pattern>` elements, each containing a URL pattern to match
- Zero or more `<http-method>` elements, each containing the name of an HTTP method

An `<auth-constraint>` element indicates that certain user roles should be permitted to access these Web resources. It contains the following:

- An optional `<description>` element
- Zero or more `<role-name>` elements, each containing a role referenced in a `<security-role-ref>` element or the special name * that indicates all roles in this application

A `<user-data-constraint>` element indicates how data transmitted between the client and the application should be protected. It contains the following:

- An optional `<description>` element
- A `<transport-guarantee>` (can have one of the three values in Table 5-6)

Table 5-6. *<transport-guarantee> Values*

Value	Description
NONE	No transport guarantee is required.
INTEGRAL	The data must not be changed in transit.
CONFIDENTIAL	Others may not view the data en route.

The `manager` Web application contains a security constraint on all its resources, as shown in Listing 5-11.

Listing 5-11. *The Manager Web Application's Security Constraint*

```
<security-constraint>
  <web-resource-collection>
    <web-resource-name>HTMLManager and Manager command</web-resource-name>
    <url-pattern>/jmxproxy/*</url-pattern>
    <url-pattern>/html/*</url-pattern>
    <url-pattern>/list</url-pattern>
    <url-pattern>/sessions</url-pattern>
    <url-pattern>/start</url-pattern>
    <url-pattern>/stop</url-pattern>
    <url-pattern>/install</url-pattern>
    <url-pattern>/remove</url-pattern>
    <url-pattern>/deploy</url-pattern>
```

```
    <url-pattern>/undeploy</url-pattern>
    <url-pattern>/reload</url-pattern>
    <url-pattern>/save</url-pattern>
    <url-pattern>/serverinfo</url-pattern>
    <url-pattern>/status/*</url-pattern>
    <url-pattern>/roles</url-pattern>
    <url-pattern>/resources</url-pattern>
  </web-resource-collection>
  <auth-constraint>
     <!-- NOTE:  This role isn't present in the default users' file -->
     <role-name>manager</role-name>
  </auth-constraint>
</security-constraint>
```

<login-config>

The <login-config> element configures the authentication mechanism for this application. It contains the following:

- An optional <auth-method> element specifying the authentication mechanism; it must contain the text BASIC, DIGEST, FORM, or CLIENT-CERT. They're plain text, digested text, HTML form, and certificate based, respectively.
- An optional <realm-name> element specifying the realm name for HTTP basic authorization.
- An optional <form-login-config> element to configure form-based authentication. It contains a <form-login-page> element specifying the login page and a <form-error-page> element specifying the error page used if login is unsuccessful.

The manager application defines a <login-config> to go along with the security constraint described previously (see Listing 5-12).

Listing 5-12. *The Manager Web Application's Login Configuration*

```
<login-config>
  <auth-method>BASIC</auth-method>
  <realm-name>Tomcat Manager Application</realm-name>
</login-config>
```

<security-role>

The <security-role> element declares a security role used in the Web application's security-constraints. It contains the following:

- An optional <description> element
- A <role-name> element containing the name of the role

The manager application defines a security role to go along with the security constraint described previously (see Listing 5-13).

Listing 5-13. *The Manager Web Application's Security Role*

```
<security-role>
  <description>
    The role that is required to log in to the Manager Application
  </description>
  <role-name>manager</role-name>
</security-role>
```

Summary

In this chapter, you saw the issues relevant to Web application configuration. Many of the configuration issues will depend on access to well-documented and well-designed application specifications or, if these aren't available, working hand-in-hand with a developer. As the application grows older, there will tend to be an increasing reliance on the experience of the administrator in the production environment to guide the administration of the application. Collaboration between the developers and system administration will necessarily increase.

It's likely that the administration of a Web application will mostly concern security configuration. This will also increasingly include the use of filters to given URL patterns, session configuration, error page configuration, the addition of tag libraries, and the administration of application initialization parameters to adapt to the server.

CHAPTER 6

Using Tomcat's Administration Tools

As Tomcat has evolved over the years, its administration tools have become more and more sophisticated. Tomcat 5's administration tools have been designed for use in a number of ways, each of which suits a different style of administration. In this chapter, you'll see the `manager` Web application, which you can use to deploy and manage Web applications, and the `admin` application, which you can use to configure Web applications.

Both these applications have Web interfaces you can use to administer the Tomcat server, but you can also use the `manager` application via HTTP request parameters or with Apache Ant. I'll discuss all these options.

Using the Manager Application

The `manager` application is provided as part of the Tomcat 5 distribution and is stored in the `CATALINA_HOME/server/webapps` directory by default. It's a special Web application that allows you to manage other Web applications while the Tomcat server is running. You can, for example, deploy, undeploy, start, and stop Web applications on the server using this tool.

The `manager` application is necessary for a number of reasons. First, without the `manager` application, you need write access to Tomcat's installation directory to deploy a Web application, because this is where you copy an expanded Web application, WAR file, or context XML file. This requires you to have access to the server's file system, which isn't always possible or desirable in a high-security environment.

Second, you can remove a Web application only by deleting the files on the server's file system. This has the same drawbacks as previously mentioned. However, Tomcat will still have the context name configured in memory, which may cause problems in future deployments if you try to add another application with the same name. Another problem with this approach is that the Web application is removed permanently from the server and not just made unavailable, which may be a better option.

Third, if the host's `autoDeploy` setting is `false`, then you can't deploy any applications on a running server, even if you have access to the file system.

Fourth, if the host's `deployOnStartup` setting is `false`, then no new Web applications will be deployed when the server starts up after being shut down. Both of these settings combined will make it more difficult for unauthorized users to deploy Web applications on the server, so they may be part of a secured server's setup.

As it stands, Tomcat seems to be fairly inflexible. You must have access to the file system, and the server must be configured to allow automatic deployment. This is where the manager application comes in. You can use it to solve all the problems mentioned and have a choice as to how to go about it.

The following is a list of the tasks you can carry out with the manager application:

- You can deploy a new Web application.
- You can list the currently deployed Web applications, with session information.
- You can reload a Web application.
- You can list the operating system and JVM properties.
- You can list the available global JNDI resources.
- You can list the available security roles.
- You can display session statistics.
- You can start a stopped application.
- You can stop an existing application.
- You can undeploy a Web application.

Setting Up the Manager Application

The manager application is a powerful addition to Tomcat's functionality. For this reason you can access it only if you're an authenticated user. The system of authentication is the same for the manager application as it is for other Web applications running on a Tomcat server, as described in Chapter 11.

The default realm for the manager application, as defined in CATALINA_HOME/conf/Catalina/localhost/manager.xml, is the user database defined in server.xml. Recall from Chapter 4 that this is conf/tomcat-users.xml.

By default, access to the manager application is disabled in Tomcat, by virtue of omitting any valid users or roles from tomcat-users.xml. To set up the manager application, add a user with the manager role to this file. You can, for example's sake, add the manager role and then alter an existing user, such as tomcat, as follows:

```
<role rolename="manager"/>
<user username="tomcat" password="tomcat" roles="tomcat, manager"/>
```

■ **Note** If you used the Windows installer, you would have already defined an admin password for Tomcat and tomcat-users.xml will be configured for you.

If Tomcat is running, restart it to read the updated `tomcat-users.xml`. Next, check the URL `http://localhost:8080/manager/html`. You'll be asked for a username and password, so enter the details of the user that you configured. If your details are correct, you'll see the screen as in Figure 6-1.

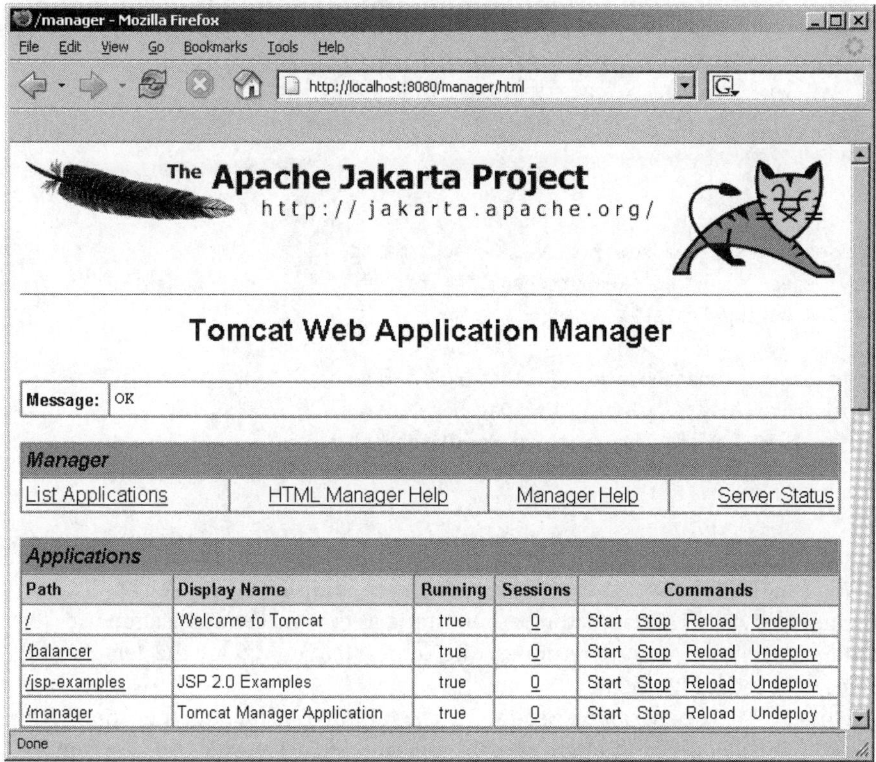

Figure 6-1. *The Tomcat* `manager` *application's HTML interface*

Configuring the Manager Application

As with other Web applications, you can change the settings for the security manager to suit your own preferences. The security manager comes with a context XML file and a deployment descriptor, both of which you can modify as you would any other configuration file. The default `manager.xml` file is in the `CATALINA_HOME/conf/Catalina/localhost` directory. Listing 6-1 shows the file for Tomcat 5.0.*x* and Tomcat 5.5.

Listing 6-1. *The Default* `manager.xml` *File*

```
<!-- Tomcat 5.0.x -->
<Context path="/manager" docBase="${catalina.home}/server/webapps/manager"
        debug="0" privileged="true">

  <!-- Link to the user database we will get roles from -->
  <ResourceLink name="users" global="UserDatabase"
                type="org.apache.catalina.UserDatabase"/>

</Context>

<!-- Tomcat 5.5 -->
<Context docBase="${catalina.home}/server/webapps/manager"
        privileged="true" antiResourceLocking="false"
        antiJARLocking="false">

  <!-- Link to the user database we will get roles from -->
  <ResourceLink name="users" global="UserDatabase"
                type="org.apache.catalina.UserDatabase"/>

</Context>
```

This file sets the name of the Web application to `manager`, tells Tomcat that it can find this Web application in `CATALINA_HOME/server/webapps/manager`, and allows this Web application access to container servlets. This last setting is important, as the `manager` application uses the manager container servlet to perform its duties. The Tomcat 5.5 settings are the defaults and allow resources to be locked by clients.

The `<ResourceLink>` element sets up a source of user information for authentication in this Web application. This can quite easily be changed to match any realm you've set up in `server.xml`. As it stands, this file allows you to use the `manager` application, assuming you've set up an authorized user as previously described.

If you want to allow more than one role to access the `manager` Web application, or you want to change the authentication mechanism to fit in with your server's setup, then you'll have to modify the `manager` application's `web.xml` file. Most of this file is given over to servlet definitions and servlet mappings, which you should leave as they are, but the end of the file contains security-related configuration.

Listing 6-2 shows the security-related configuration.

Listing 6-2. *Security-Related Configuration from the Manager Application's* `web.xml` *File*

```
  <!-- Define reference to the user database for looking up roles -->
  <resource-env-ref>
    <description>
      Link to the UserDatabase instance from which we request lists of
      defined role names. Typically, this will be connected to the global
      user database with a ResourceLink element in server.xml or the context
      configuration file for the manager Web application.
    </description>
```

```
    <resource-env-ref-name>users</resource-env-ref-name>
    <resource-env-ref-type>
      org.apache.catalina.UserDatabase
    </resource-env-ref-type>
  </resource-env-ref>

  <!-- Define a Security Constraint on this Application -->
  <security-constraint>
    <web-resource-collection>
      <web-resource-name>HTMLManager and Manager command</web-resource-name>
      <url-pattern>/jmxproxy/*</url-pattern>
      <url-pattern>/html/*</url-pattern>
      <url-pattern>/list</url-pattern>
      <url-pattern>/sessions</url-pattern>
      <url-pattern>/start</url-pattern>
      <url-pattern>/stop</url-pattern>
      <url-pattern>/install</url-pattern>
      <url-pattern>/remove</url-pattern>
      <url-pattern>/deploy</url-pattern>
      <url-pattern>/undeploy</url-pattern>
      <url-pattern>/reload</url-pattern>
      <url-pattern>/save</url-pattern>
      <url-pattern>/serverinfo</url-pattern>
      <url-pattern>/status/*</url-pattern>
      <url-pattern>/roles</url-pattern>
      <url-pattern>/resources</url-pattern>
    </web-resource-collection>
    <auth-constraint>
       <!-- NOTE:  This role isn't present in the default users' file -->
       <role-name>manager</role-name>
    </auth-constraint>
  </security-constraint>

  <!-- Define the Login Configuration for this Application -->
  <login-config>
    <auth-method>BASIC</auth-method>
    <realm-name>Tomcat Manager Application</realm-name>
  </login-config>

  <!-- Security roles referenced by this web application -->
  <security-role>
    <description>
      The role that is required to log in to the Manager Application
    </description>
    <role-name>manager</role-name>
  </security-role>

</web-app>
```

The `<resource-env-ref>` element defines the user database that Tomcat uses to authenticate users. Recall that the name `user` is defined in `manager.xml`, which in turn is a reference to the global user database. You'll find details of changing the user database to another type of authentication scheme in Chapter 11.

The `<security-constraint>` element defines the resources on the server that are covered by the security mechanism and sets which roles are allowed access to them. In this case, all the servlets defined earlier in `web.xml` are covered, and only users with the manager role are allowed to access them. This element works in combination with the `<security-role>` element, which defines the roles used in this Web application's authentication scheme.

If you change the `<auth-method>` element to anything other than BASIC, tools such as Ant won't be able to use the `manager` application because they can't use any other kind of authentication. Therefore, you must balance the security needs of your server with the way you administer using the `manager` application. Using DIGEST or FORM authentication makes the `manager` application more secure but prevents you from using Ant.

■ **Note** You'll see more mappings in `web.xml` than manager commands listed in this chapter. This is for backward compatibility with scripts that were written for older versions of Tomcat. The deprecated commands (`install` and `remove`) aren't available from the HTML interface, and `install` now calls `undeploy` in the manager servlet.

If you want to allow users with other roles to access the `manager` application, add `<role-name>` elements in the `<auth-constraint>` element. Once you've done this, add a `<security-role>` element, with appropriate subelements, for each role you want to add. For example, if you want to allow users with the admin role to use the `manager` application, alter `web.xml` as shown in Listing 6-3.

Listing 6-3. *Allowing a User with the Admin Role to Use the Manager Application*

```
  <auth-constraint>
     <!-- NOTE:  This role isn't present in the default users' file -->
     <role-name>manager</role-name>
     <role-name>admin</role-name>
  </auth-constraint>
</security-constraint>

...
<!-- Added as part of Tomcat Chapter 6 -->
<security-role>
  <description>
    The role that is required to log in to the Manager Application
  </description>
  <role-name>admin</role-name>
</security-role>
```

Using the Manager Application

The simplest way of using the manager application is through its Web interface. Once you've logged in at http://localhost:8080/manager/html, you'll see the Web interface as shown in Figure 6-1. All the functions of the manager application are available through this interface. Many of the HTML interface commands listed in this section will prompt you for confirmation. This is a sure sign that your actions may affect users accessing your server. If you want to continue, you should click OK.

It's also possible for you to use request parameters to administer the Web application with scripts. The manager application can provide its responses in plain text so that they can be parsed easily. Some of these plain text messages appear in the status message section of the Web interface, though the Web interface takes a number of the other responses and displays them in user-friendly HTML tables. An example of this is the list of deployed Web applications that you'll see in the "Listing Web Applications" section.

The manager application commands that are issued via the Web browser have the following format:

```
http://{hostname}:{port}/manager/{command}?{parameters}
```

The various parts of the URL are as follows:

- hostname: The host on which the Tomcat instance is running.
- port: The port on which the Tomcat instance is running.
- command: The manager command you want to run. The allowed values for command are deploy, list, reload, resources, roles, sessions, start, stop, and undeploy. You'll look at these in more detail later in the chapter. The manager application understands two other commands: install and remove. These are retained for backward compatibility, though install is now identical to undeploy and is mapped to the undeploy code in the manager servlet. remove is deprecated; you can still use it if you want, though you'll never feel the need. Therefore, I won't describe it in this chapter.
- parameters: The parameters passed to the commands listed previously. These are command specific and are explained in detail, along with the specific command, in a moment. Many of these parameters contain the context path to the Web application (the path parameter) and the URL to the Web application file (the war parameter). The context path for the ROOT application is an empty string. For all other Web applications, the context path must be preceded by /.

A number of problems could occur while working with the manager application. The "Troubleshooting" section lists the possible causes of failure.

Listing Web Applications

You can list the applications that are deployed on this server by clicking the List Applications link. This is the default when you first visit the Web interface (see Figure 6-2). You can click a Web application's name to run it. The HTML Manager Help and Manager Help links take you to help pages that are part of the manager Web application.

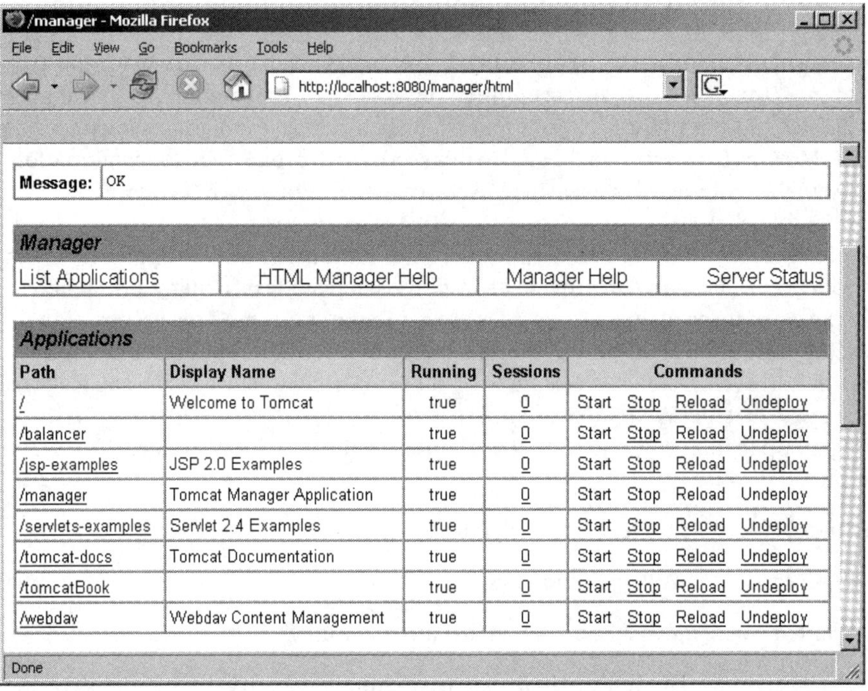

Figure 6-2. *Listing Web applications with the Web interface*

The message bar at the top of the page gives you a status message related to the commands you run. In this case, the listing was successful, so you get the "OK" status message.

To list the running applications using request parameters, use the following command:

```
http://localhost:8080/manager/list
```

For Tomcat 5.0.*x* this will list the running Web applications as shown in Figure 6-3.

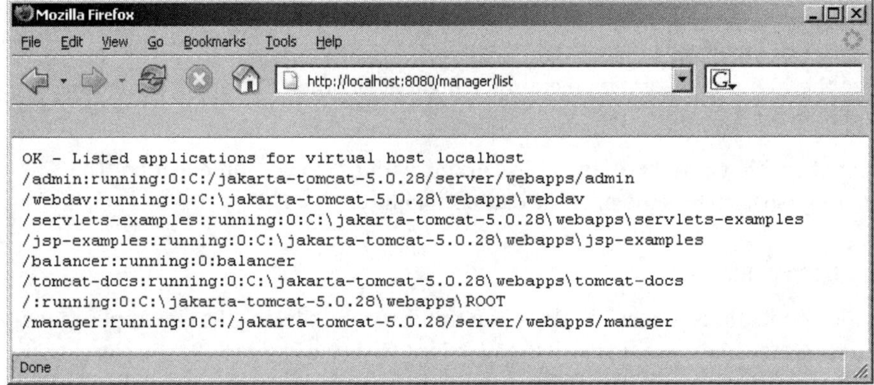

Figure 6-3. *Listing Web applications with the Tomcat 5.0.x* `manager` *application*

The listing has the following structure:

```
webapp name:status:number of active sessions:path to web application
```

For Tomcat 5.5 you'll see the running Web applications as shown in Figure 6-4.

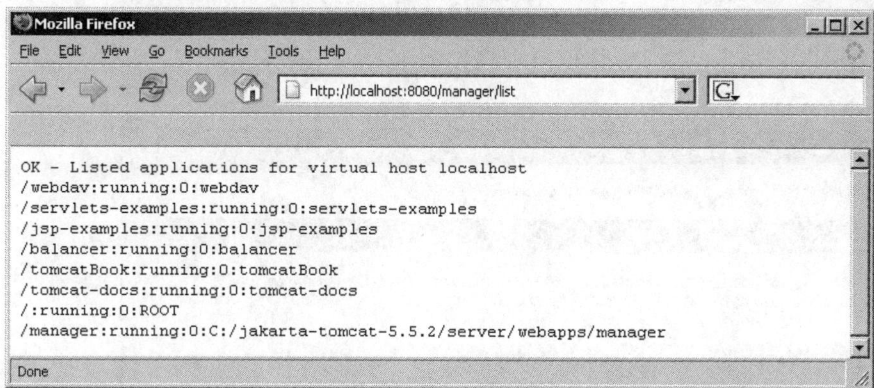

Figure 6-4. *Listing Web applications with the Tomcat 5.5* `manager` *application*

Here the path to the Web application is relative to the application base directory or an absolute path if the Web application isn't within the application base directory.

Checking the Status of the Server

Click on the Server Status link to check the server's status. You'll see a screen like that in Figure 6-5.

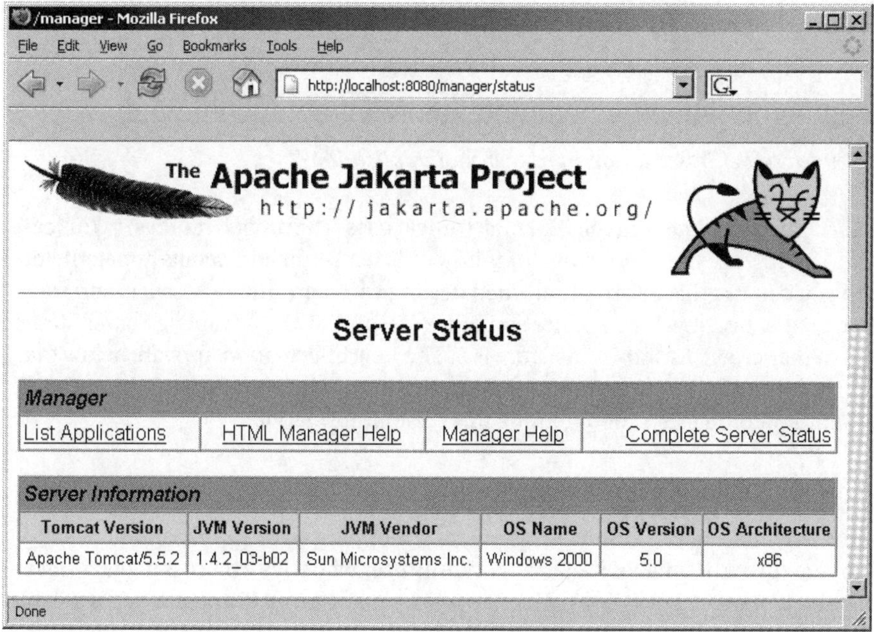

Figure 6-5. *Viewing the server's status with the* `manager` *application*

The sections shown in Figure 6-5 are straightforward and show the server version and other related information. You can find the real server information below these sections (see Figure 6-6).

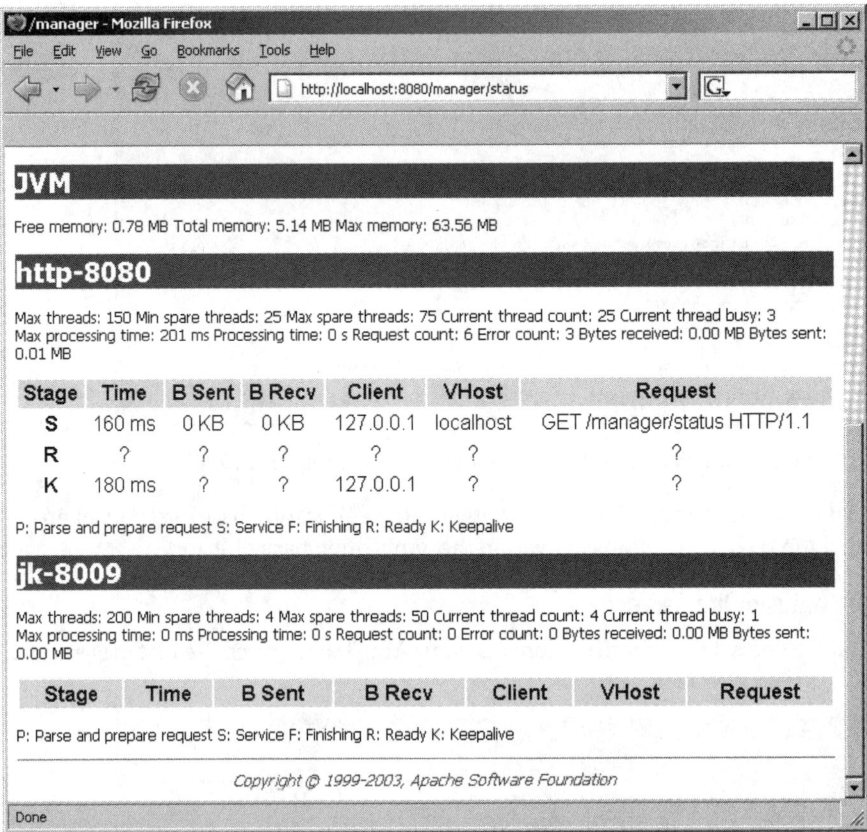

Figure 6-6. *Extended server information in the* `manager` *application*

The JVM section gives details of the JVM that Tomcat uses. The other headings, in this case `http-8080` and `jk-8009`, are the connectors for this host. Their setup and details appear below each one, and you can use this information when dealing with performance issues, and so on.

For a Web application–by–Web application breakdown, click the Complete Server Status link at the top of the screen, as shown in Figure 6-5. The new information appears below that as shown in Figure 6-6.

No alternative method exists for obtaining this server information.

Starting, Stopping, and Restarting Web Applications

The links under Commands are fairly self-explanatory. Stopping a Web application doesn't remove it from the server but makes it unavailable. Any user who tries to access it will be given a 503 unavailable error code. The Web application is still deployed, and its name is unavailable for new Web applications. Figure 6-7 shows the results of stopping a Web application.

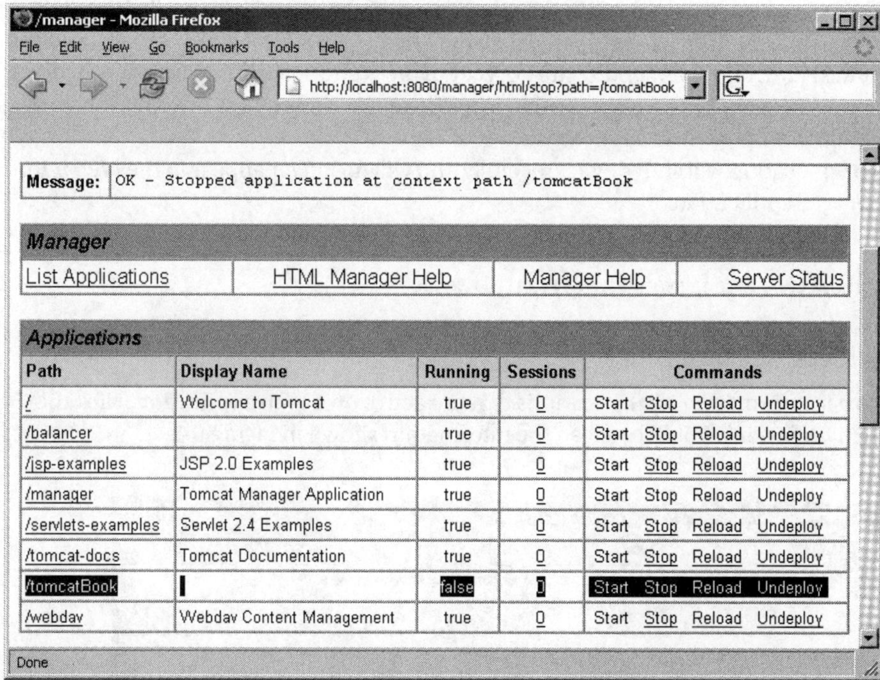

Figure 6-7. *Stopping a Web application with the* manager *application*

The running status of the tomcatBook Web application is now "false," and the Start link is activated. Again, note the status message that tells you the action completed successfully. Another important aspect of Figure 6-7 is the URL that the Web interface uses to stop the Web application. This is how you stop the Web application using HTTP request parameters to activate the manager application without the help of the Web interface.

The following is the stop command. Remember to start the Web application's path with /.

```
http://localhost:8080/manager/stop?path=/webapp
```

If the command is successful, you'll get the following message:

```
OK - Stopped application at context path /webapp
```

This success message is similar to those you'll receive for all the other commands.

Starting the Web application is just a matter of clicking the Start link, and if any configuration or code changes, you can restart it by clicking the Restart link.

You can also use the following:

```
http://localhost:8080/manager/start?path=/webapp
http://localhost:8080/manager/reload?path=/webapp
```

Undeploying Web Applications

If you want to permanently remove a Web application, click the Undeploy link. It's important to realize that this command will delete any files associated with the Web application, as long as they're in Tomcat's directory structure. In other words, the `manager` application will delete the expanded Web application if it's in `webapps`, delete the original WAR file if it's in `webapps`, and delete the context XML file in the subdirectory of `conf`. If the Web application is based elsewhere, the files aren't deleted, but the Web application is no longer available as a Web application and its name is available for new Web applications.

The Web application will shut down gracefully and will no longer appear in the Web interface of the `manager` application.

The HTTP request parameter version of this command is as follows:

```
http://localhost:8080/manager/undeploy?path=/webapp
```

Checking Session Information

If you want basic information on the sessions that are active on a Web application, click the number of active sessions. You'll be given the information shown in Figure 6-8.

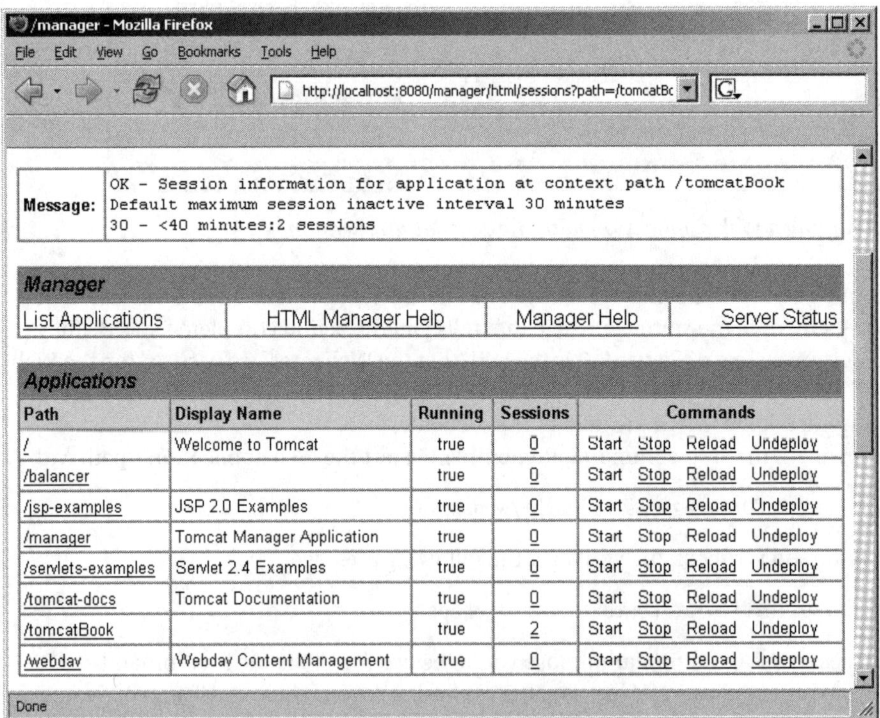

Figure 6-8. *Session information using the `manager` application*

In this case, the default session timeout is 30 minutes, and the `tomcatBook` Web application has two sessions listed. A session is listed if it's inactive for less than the timeout value plus ten minutes.

The following is the basic command:

```
http://localhost:8080/manager/sessions?path=/webapp
```

This will produce the same message as in Figure 6-8, though without any of the HTML wrapping.

Deploying Web Applications

The section below the Web application list allows you to deploy a new Web application. You can deploy a Web application using a context XML file, a WAR file, or a Web application directory, each of which must be on the server's machine. You can also deploy a WAR from a remote machine.

Figure 6-9 shows the options.

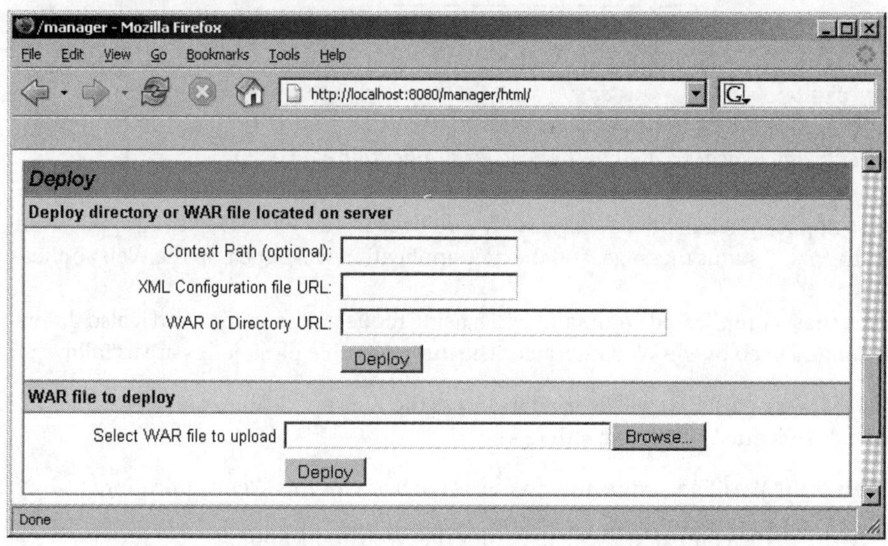

Figure 6-9. *The Web application deployment section of the `manager` application*

Deploying Web Applications from the Local Machine

The context path is optional; if you omit it, the `manager` application will assign the name of the directory, WAR file, or XML file to the Web application. You have the following two ways to specify the location of the Web application:

- As a file in the host's application base directory, which is `webapps` by default
- In the form `file:/absolute/path/to/application`

The second method applies to directories, WAR files, and context XML files. Figure 6-10 shows how to deploy a Web application from a WAR file in the `C:\dev\webapps` directory. Note the direction of the path separators and the use of the appropriate form field.

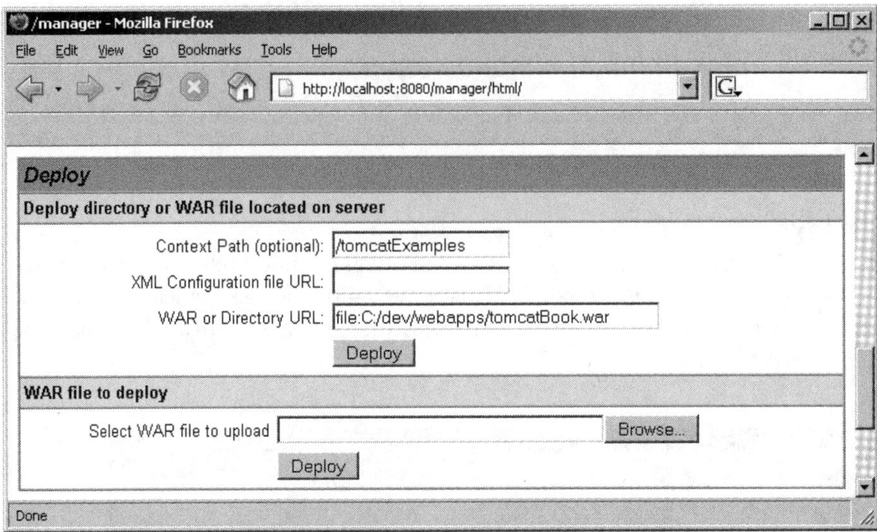

Figure 6-10. *Deploying a local WAR with the* `manager` *application*

If the Web application is installed successfully, you'll receive an "OK—Deployed application at context path /path" status message, and the new application will appear in the Web application list.

This is the most complicated command when using request parameters, and it also differs from the command used by the Web interface. The three possible parameters are as follows:

- `path`: This is the path that will be used to access the Web application once it has been deployed. This must be started with /.
- `war`: This is the WAR file or directory to use as the basis for this Web application.
- `config`: This is the context XML file to use for this Web application.

If you're using a context XML file this way, you must also use the `war` parameter and omit the `path` parameter. You can use the other two parameters by themselves.

The value of `war` can be in one of the following formats:

- `file:/absolute/path/to/a/directory`: This specifies the absolute path to a directory where a Web application is present in an unpackaged form. This entire path is then added as the context path of the Web application in Tomcat's configuration.
- `file:/absolute/path/to/a/webapp.war`: This specifies the absolute path to a WAR file.
- `directory`: This is a Web application directory in the host's Web application base directory (`webapps` by default).
- `webapp.war`: This is the name of a Web application WAR file in the host's Web application base directory (`webapps` by default).

The value of config can be as follows:

- file:/absolute/path/to/a/context.xml: This is the absolute path to a context XML file that contains the definition of this Web application's context container.

The simplest way to use this command is to deploy a Web application from the application base directory, either using an expanded directory or a WAR file. The first line of the following deploys the Cat.war file to the /Catalog path, and the second line deploys the Cat directory to the /Catalog path:

```
http://localhost:8080/manager/deploy?path=/Catalog&war=Cat.war
http://localhost:8080/manager/deploy?path=/Catalog&war=Cat
```

If you omit the path parameter, the application is given the name of the directory or WAR file as its path. For example, the following would deploy the bank.war file to the /bank path:

```
http://localhost:8080/manager/deploy?war=bank.war
```

You can use request parameters to deploy a Web application from anywhere on the server's local machine, just as you could with the Web interface. The commands are similar to those shown previously:

```
http://localhost:8080/manager/deploy?path=/Catalog&war=file:C:/dev/Cat.war
http://localhost:8080/manager/deploy?path=/Catalog&war=file:C:/dev/Cat
```

Note the absolute path to the WAR and directory. This creates a new context XML file in conf/[Engine_name]/[Host_name] for this Web application. This file is named after the context and contains a reference to the file you specified as the war parameter. Again, the path parameter is optional.

Using a context XML file is a slightly more complicated process. With Tomcat 5.0.*x* you must use both war and config but not the path parameter. (Using path won't result in an error, but equally it won't do anything else either.) This is because Tomcat 5.0.*x* makes the path attribute of <Context> mandatory, so it reads the context path from there. Tomcat 5.5 does use the path parameter with this command because you're encouraged not to use the path attribute of <Context>. (It's not mandatory in Tomcat 5.5.)

config should point to the XML file, and war should point to the application's files, whether they're in a directory or in a WAR. So, for Tomcat 5.0.*x*, you'd use http://localhost:8080/manager/deploy?config=file:C:/catalog.xml&war=file:C:/Catalog and http://localhost:8080/manager/deploy?config=file:C:/catalog.xml&war=file:C:/Catalog.war.

This copies the context XML to conf/[Engine_name]/[Host_name] and renames it after the context it configures. In other words, it's named after the value of its <Context> element's path attribute. For example, Listing 6-4 shows a context XML file called newwebapp.xml. However, it will be called form.xml once it's copied to the server because its path attribute is form. Remember that all this applies only to Tomcat 5.0.*x*.

Listing 6-4. *The newwebapp.xml File*

```
<?xml version='1.0' encoding='utf-8'?>
<Context path="/form" crossContext="false"
         debug="0"
         reloadable="true" >

</Context>
```

Without the path attribute in a context definition in Tomcat 5.5, you must use the path parameter to deploy a Web application, like so:

```
http://localhost:8080/manager/deploy?
  config=file:C:/catalog.xml&war=file:C:/Catalog&path=/catalogue
http://localhost:8080/manager/deploy?
  config=file:C:/catalog.xml&war=file:C:/Catalog.war&path=/catalogue
```

In both cases, the file will be renamed to the value of the path parameter. (In this example, this would be catalogue.xml.)

Deploying Web Applications from a Remote WAR File

The second section of the deploy section allows you to upload a WAR file to the server. This is particularly useful if you want to administer Tomcat remotely. The manager application will name the resultant Web application after the WAR file and receives the WAR file via the HTTP PUT method.

This method copies the WAR file to the server's application base directory and expands it. This action has a request parameter version, but it can be used only with tools, such as Ant, that can send PUT data to a server. You'll see this in the "Managing Applications with Ant" section.

Listing Resources

You can't list the JNDI resources on the server using the Web interface. To do so, use request parameters as follows:

```
http://localhost:8080/manager/resources
```

This will list all the JNDI resources on the server, with the name of the resource followed by a comma, then the fully qualified Java language type. If you want only to see resources of a certain type, then use the type parameter, like so:

```
http://localhost:8080/manager/resources?type=java.lang.Integer
```

This will display JNDI resources of type java.lang.Integer only. You can use this command to list user databases, JNDI data sources, and serverwide constants.

Listing Security Roles

Listing security roles is another request parameter–only command and lists all the roles defined on the server.

```
http://localhost:8080/manager/roles
```

This lists the security role name and an optional description. There's one security role listed per line, and the fields are separated by colons. Note that the roles are those defined in the user database for the `manager` application and may not be all the roles available to all Web applications.

Troubleshooting

A number of things could go wrong while working with the `manager` application. The possible causes of failure are as follows:

Application already exists at path `{context_path}`: The context path for each Web application must be unique, and this error indicates that another application with the same context path exists on the server. It's possible that this is the same application and you've tried to deploy it twice. To fix this, either undeploy the previous application or choose a different context path.

Encountered exception: The Tomcat log files will have error messages relating to the specific error. Typical causes of errors are missing classes/JAR files while loading the application, invalid commands in the application's `web.xml` file, and incorrect settings in a context XML file. For example, with Tomcat 5.0.*x* you may be trying to deploy from a `<Context>` element with no `path` attribute, and thus Tomcat can't assign a context path.

Invalid context path specified: The context path must start with `/`, except when the `ROOT` Web application is being deployed, in which case the context path must be a zero-length string.

No context path specified: You must specify a context path for the command you're attempting to run.

Document base does not exist or is not a readable directory: The value specified for the WAR file path/URL in the `war` parameter is incorrect. This parameter must point to an expanded Web application or an actual WAR file.

No context exists for path `{context_path}`: The context path is invalid, meaning there's no Web application deployed under this context path.

Reload not supported on WAR deployed at path `{context_path}`: The Web application had been installed from a WAR file, instead of from an unpacked directory.

No global JNDI resources: No JNDI global resources are configured for this Tomcat instance.

Can't resolve user database reference: There was an error looking up the appropriate user database.

No user database is available: The `<ResourceLink>` element hasn't been configured properly in the `manager.xml` configuration file. See the earlier "Configuring the Manager Application" section for more information.

Managing Applications with Ant

You can also use Ant to run the previous administration commands. This is convenient for development purposes, because an Ant build file could be used to compile, deploy, and even start a Web application. The steps for doing this once Ant is installed are as follows:

1. Copy the `CATALINA_HOME/server/lib/catalina-ant.jar` file into Ant's library directory (`ANT_HOME/lib`). This JAR file contains the Tomcat management task definitions for Ant.
2. Add `ANT_HOME/bin` to your path.
3. Add a user with the manager role to Tomcat's user database if such a user doesn't exist.
4. Now add `<taskdef>` elements to your custom `build.xml` script that call the Tomcat manager commands.

Listing 6-5 shows a sample `build.xml`. You could use it to build and deploy a Web application. As it stands, it simply allows you to use all the previous commands with Ant. A developer would typically give you the Ant script for building the application.

Listing 6-5. *A Sample `build.xml` File for Using the Manager Application*

```
<project name="ManagerApplication" default="list" basedir=".">

  <!-- Configure the context path for this application -->
  <property name="path"     value="/Catalog"/>
  <property name="build"     value="C:/dev"/>
  <property name="file"     value="Catalog.war"/>
```

The `<project>` tag has attributes for the name of the project and the default target. The default target in this case is called `list`. Running Ant with no options will invoke the tasks associated with this default target. The `basedir` attribute is the base directory for all path calculations in the Ant build script. This is set to `.` (the current directory), and therefore all the paths are taken to be relative to the directory from which you run Ant. You then define properties for the build (in this case the path of the Web application and the location of your Web application files).

The properties in Listing 6-6 specify the access URL and username/password for the `manager` application. At the end of this section you'll see how you can also pass the password from the command line.

Listing 6-6. *Defining the Properties for the Manager Application*

```
<!-- Configure properties to access the Manager application -->
<property name="url"      value="http://localhost:8080/manager"/>
<property name="username" value="tomcat"/>
<property name="password" value="tomcat"/>
```

Listing 6-7 specifies the task definitions for the `manager` application. Ant allows for custom tasks that extend its functionality. Tomcat implements the custom tasks shown in Listing 6-7 for executing the `manager` application commands. For example, `org.apache.catalina.ant.DeployTask` executes the `deploy` command against the `manager` application.

Listing 6-7. *Ant Task Definitions for Using the Manager Application*

```
<!-- Configure the custom Ant tasks for the Manager application -->
<taskdef name="deploy"
        classname="org.apache.catalina.ant.DeployTask"/>
<taskdef name="list"
        classname="org.apache.catalina.ant.ListTask"/>
<taskdef name="reload"
        classname="org.apache.catalina.ant.ReloadTask"/>
<taskdef name="resources"
        classname="org.apache.catalina.ant.ResourcesTask"/>
<taskdef name="roles"
        classname="org.apache.catalina.ant.RolesTask"/>
<taskdef name="start"
        classname="org.apache.catalina.ant.StartTask"/>
<taskdef name="stop"
        classname="org.apache.catalina.ant.StopTask"/>
<taskdef name="undeploy"
        classname="org.apache.catalina.ant.UndeployTask"/>
```

Next, Listing 6-8 shows the manager tasks for listing all Web applications and deploying/undeploying Web applications.

Listing 6-8. *The Manager Command Tasks*

```
  <target name="deploy" description="Deploy web application">
    <deploy url="${url}" username="${username}" password="${password}"
          path="${path}" war="file:${build}/${file}"/>
  </target>

  <target name="list" description="List all web applications">
    <list url="${url}" username="${username}" password="${password}"/>
  </target>

  <target name="reload" description="Reload web application">
    <reload url="${url}" username="${username}" password="${password}"
          path="${path}"/>
  </target>

  <target name="resources" description="List all JNDI resources">
    <resources url="${url}" username="${username}" password="${password}"/>
  </target>
```

```
  <target name="roles" description="List all roles">
    <roles url="${url}" username="${username}" password="${password}"/>
  </target>

  <target name="start" description="Start web application">
    <start url="${url}" username="${username}" password="${password}"
           path="${path}"/>
  </target>

  <target name="stop" description="Stop web application">
    <stop url="${url}" username="${username}" password="${password}"
          path="${path}"/>
  </target>

  <target name="undeploy" description="Undeploy web application">
    <undeploy url="${url}" username="${username}" password="${password}"
              path="${path}"/>
  </target>

</project>
```

The password property in the previous Ant script contains the password for the user with manager privileges. This is useful for development environments where you don't want to specify the password each time you build and deploy.

You can override this value from the command line, or even omit it from the build file altogether and pass it only from the command line. This avoids the security risk of putting the password in a text file. The following will stop the tomcatBook Web application using a username and password at the command line:

```
ant -Dpassword=tomcat -Dusername=tomcat -Dpath=/tomcatBook stop
```

Using the Tomcat Administration Tool

Tomcat also has a Web-based administration tool that you can use to administer the server and individual Web applications. In other words, it allows you to edit server.xml and Web application context settings remotely, as well as other server configuration files. If you're using Tomcat 5.5, you must download the admin tool separately from the main server. This is an indirect indication of the status of the admin tool, meaning that, as it stands, the admin tool isn't as essential or as useful as it may seem on the surface. The following description, the discussion of realms in Chapter 11, and the security discussion in Chapter 12 will cover the drawbacks of the admin tool.

■ **Note** The source distribution of Tomcat 5.5 includes the `admin` application, which means you'll install it if you build Tomcat 5.5 from source.

Before you run the `admin` application, you must add an admin role and assign it to a user in `tomcat-users.xml`, or whichever authentication mechanism you're using. As with the `manager` application's Web interface, the admin tool is a Web application running on the server. You can access it via the following URL:

```
http://localhost:8080/admin
```

Once you log in via the form, you'll see the admin Web interface similar to that shown in Figure 6-11. Tomcat 5.0.*x* users will see a debug-level setting as well.

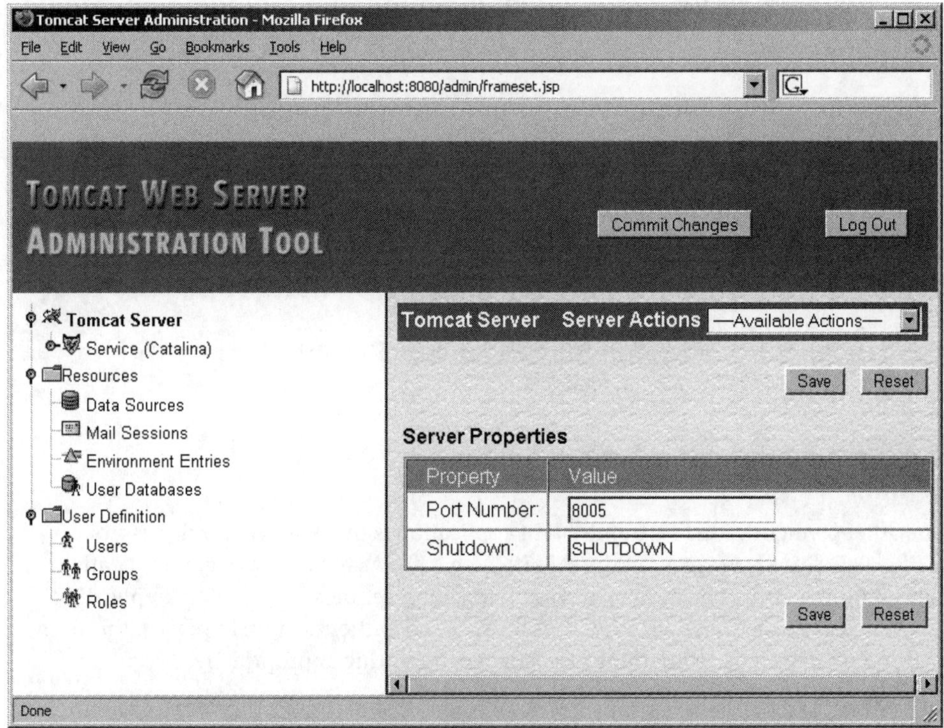

Figure 6-11. *The admin application Web interface*

You can configure the `admin` application in the `CATALINA_HOME/conf/[Engine_name]/[Host_name]/admin.xml` file. Listing 6-9 shows the contents.

Listing 6-9. *The* admin *Application's Context XML File*

```
<!-- Tomcat 5.0.x -->
<Context path="/admin" docBase="${catalina.home}/server/webapps/admin"
        debug="0" privileged="true">

  <!-- Uncomment this Valve to limit access to the Admin app to localhost
   for obvious security reasons. Allow may be a comma-separated list of
   hosts (or even regular expressions).
  <Valve className="org.apache.catalina.valves.RemoteAddrValve"
    allow="127.0.0.1"/>
  -->

  <Logger className="org.apache.catalina.logger.FileLogger"
           prefix="localhost_admin_log." suffix=".txt"
          timestamp="true"/>

</Context>

<!-- Tomcat 5.5 -->
<Context docBase="${catalina.home}/server/webapps/admin" privileged="true"
         antiResourceLocking="false" antiJARLocking="false">

  <!-- Uncomment this Valve to limit access to the Admin app to localhost
   for obvious security reasons. Allow may be a comma-separated list of
   hosts (or even regular expressions).
  <Valve className="org.apache.catalina.valves.RemoteAddrValve"
    allow="127.0.0.1"/>
  -->

</Context>
```

The other configuration file for the admin application is the deployment descriptor (CATALINA_HOME/server/webapps/admin/WEB-INF/web.xml). As with the manager application, you can alter the security constraints and authentication settings for the admin application here. In this case, the admin application uses form-based authentication to protect the admin pages. If you'd rather it use something else, change the setting appropriately.

Using the Administration Tool

Each node in the left pane represents a setting you can edit. The Service node corresponds to the <Service> element in server.xml, and its subnodes are the <Service> element's subelements. If you expand this node, you'll see each subelement, which you can then alter via commands in the right pane. There are few settings you can't alter, but changing the document base of a Web application is one of them. If you want to change the application's base directory, you'll have to undeploy it and redeploy it with new settings.

The next set of nodes after the Service node, under Resources, contains global settings for server.xml. Again, few settings can't be changed.

The final set of nodes corresponds to the settings in `tomcat-users.xml`. You can add users, roles, and groups here.

Each setting screen has a Save button and a Reset button. Clicking Save will commit any changes to the `admin` application's memory but won't write them to `server.xml`. Therefore, you can make all your changes before writing to disk. This is important because when the `admin` application writes the changes to `server.xml`, it restarts Tomcat to enable the changes to take effect. The restart will be graceful, but some users may experience problems with the restart, least of all you because you'll be logged out of the `admin` application.

To make the changes permanent, click the Commit Changes button at the top of the `admin` application screen. This makes the write to `server.xml`. However, the `admin` application creates a new `server.xml` file based on the settings it's holding in memory. It doesn't delete the old `server.xml`, but rather it renames it as follows:

```
server.xml.yyyy-MM-dd.hh-mm-ss
```

The new `server.xml` file won't have any comments in it and as such may be significantly smaller and less comprehensible to someone not familiar with your setup. It may be a good idea to copy the comments from the old file into the new one.

The exception to the previous discussion is editing users in the default user database. Clicking the Save button on a user's screen will commit the changes to `tomcat-users.xml` straightaway.

As you can see, the admin tool has some drawbacks, the least of which are still to be discussed in the security chapter. Careful consideration should go into whether you need the admin tool. Remote access is its biggest advantage.

Summary

This chapter covered the two tools supplied with Tomcat that allow you to manage the server remotely: the `manager` application and the `admin` application. The `manager` application provides you with a user-friendly Web interface that you can use to manage Web applications. Through this interface you can deploy new applications, undeploy old applications, start them, stop them, and list them. The `manager` application also comes with a stripped-down interface that you can use with scripts and Ant.

You can use the admin tool to work with Tomcat's configuration files, such as `server.xml` and `tomcat-users.xml`. Again, it's a Web interface, and you can access it and use it remotely.

CHAPTER 7

■ ■ ■

Configuring Tomcat

In the preceding chapters you saw how to install Tomcat and how to carry out basic administration tasks. These are the day-to-day tasks that an administrator would carry out, but Tomcat has other features you may have to work with from time to time. This chapter will show you these features and how to use them.

You'll see the following:

- Access log administration
- Request filtering
- Single sign-on
- JNDI resources
- Session managers

The first three of these topics are common administration tasks. The others are built into Tomcat to allow developers to use their features. These are all part of the Servlet and JSP specifications as defined by Sun Microsystems, and, as the reference implementation, Tomcat must include them.

Using Valves to Intercept User Requests

A Web server wouldn't be a Web server if it didn't allow you to intercept user requests, examine them, and log them. As mentioned in Chapter 4, Tomcat provides you with components called *valves* that you can place in the request-processing stream to do just that. Recall that valves can be configured at different levels within the Tomcat hierarchy and can be applied in chains so that requests go through more than one filter before reaching their destination. Figure 7-1 shows a set of valves in a Tomcat installation.

As Figure 7-1 shows, a valve configured at the engine level will intercept all requests to contexts on this engine, no matter what host or context they're bound for. The valve at the host level intercepts all requests to this virtual host, and the valves in the contexts intercept only requests that are specifically for them. This means valves can be chained together to work in conjunction with each other.

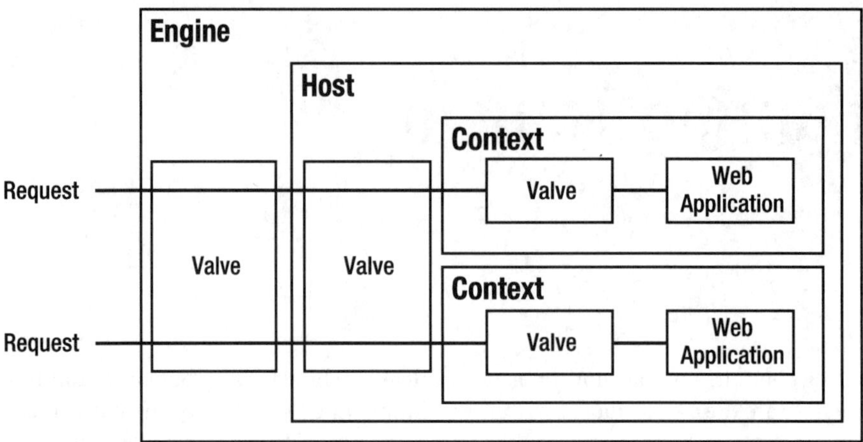

Figure 7-1. *Valves intercept requests for certain resources, and you can use them in conjunction with each other.*

Valves offer value-added functionality that includes the following:

- Access logging
- Single sign-on for all Web applications running on the server
- Requests filtering/blocking by IP address and hostname
- Detailed request dumps for debugging

Standard Valves

Valves are nested components in the Tomcat configuration hierarchy that can be placed inside `<Engine>`, `<Host>`, or `<Context>` containers. (Refer to Chapter 4 for details on containers.) Tomcat comes with the Java interface `org.apache.catalina.Valve`, which Java programmers can use to create their own valves. However, the functions that have already been mentioned are provided with Tomcat as standard. Table 7-1 describes these standard valves.

Table 7-1. *Standard Valves As Supplied by Tomcat*

Valve Name	Description
Access log valve	Logs requests.
Single sign-on valve	Lets you pass user login information to other Web applications on the server. This means the users need to log in only once, no matter how many Web applications they visit.
Request filter valves	Enables selective filtering of incoming requests based on IP addresses or hostnames.
Request dumper valve	Prints the headers and cookies of incoming requests and outgoing responses to a log.

Using Access Log Valves

Logging access to resources is a common activity for Web server administrators. As such, Tomcat comes with a valve for logging access to resources, be that at the engine level, the host level, or the context level. The location of a log valve is fairly important from a performance point of view, because each log entry requires Tomcat to write data to disk. If you have a logging valve at the engine level of a busy server, as well as logging valves for every context, the log will be written to many times and will grow very large. However, you may need to do this to monitor each individual context as well as the whole server. This just illustrates the need for careful planning when using valves.

An access log valve isn't a logger because a logger prints information and errors to a log file so that you can diagnose errors in Web applications. For example, if a component encounters problems and a user reports the error message to you, you'd look in the logger's log because this is where the error will be reported. However, if you wanted to see how often a client at a certain IP address requests a certain resource, you'd examine the access log valve's log file.

The logger's format also depends on the application in question. If it has been written properly, all errors will be written to the error log file in a standard way so that they can be investigated and rectified. If not, you may see nasty Java stacktraces with details of the error buried among it.

The typical format for an access log valve is the common log file format, which you can find at `http://www.w3.org/Daemon/User/Config/Logging.html#common-logfile-format`. You may already have an analysis tool that can analyze log files in this format. If not, don't worry—they're quite common. AWStats (`http://awstats.sourceforge.net`) is a great open-source option, though you'll need Perl to use it. Another option is Webalizer (`http://www.mrunix.net/webalizer/`).

Table 7-2 shows the attributes for the standard access log valve that's supplied with Tomcat. In this case, the `className` attribute must be `org.apache.catalina.valves.AccessLogValve`.

Table 7-2. *The Attributes for the Standard Access Log Valve*

Attribute	Description	Required?
`className`	The Java class of the valve. This must be `org.apache.catalina.valves.AccessLogValve`.	Yes
`condition`	Turns conditional logging on. If set, the access log valve logs requests only if `ServletRequest.getAttribute()` is `null`. For example, if this value is set to `userId`, then a particular request will be logged only if `ServletRequest.getAttribute("userId") == null`.	No
`directory`	The directory where the log files will be placed. Usually relative to the `CATALINA_HOME`, but you can also specify an absolute path instead. The default is `logs`.	No
`fileDateFormat`	Allows a customized date format in the access log filename. The date format also decides how often the file is rotated. If you want to rotate every hour, then set this value to `yyyy-MM-dd.HH`.	No

Table 7-2. *The Attributes for the Standard Access Log Valve (Continued)*

Attribute	Description	Required?
pattern	Specifies the format used in the log. You can customize the format, or you can use common or combined as the format (the common format plus the referrer and user-agent are logged). To customize the format, you can use any of the following patterns interspersed with a literal string: %a: Inserts remote IP address. %A: Inserts local IP address (of URL resource). %b: Inserts bytes sent count, excluding HTTP headers, shows - if zero. %B: Inserts bytes sent count, excluding HTTP headers. %D: Time taken to process the request, in milliseconds. %h: Inserts remote hostname (or IP address if the resolveHosts attribute is set to false). %H: Inserts the request protocol (HTTP). %l: Inserts remote logical user name (always '-'). %m: Inserts request method such as GET and POST. %p: Inserts the local TCP port where this request is received. %q: Inserts the query string of this request. %r: Inserts the first line of the request. %s: Inserts the HTTP status code of the response. %S: Inserts the user session ID. %t: Inserts the date and time in common log file format. %T: Time taken to process the request, in seconds. %u: Inserts the remote user that has been authenticated (otherwise it's -). %U: Inserts the URL path of the request. %v: Inserts the name of the local virtual host from the request. %{xxx}i: Use this for incoming headers, where xxx is the header. %{xxx}c: Use this for a specific cookie, where xxx is the name of the cookie. %{xxx}r: Use this for ServletRequest attributes, where xxx is the attribute. %{xxx}s: Use this for HttpSession attributes, where xxx is the attribute. The default is common, which is %h %l %u %t "%r" %s %b.	No
prefix	The prefix added to the name of the log file.	No
resolveHosts	Determines if the log will contain hostnames via a reverse DNS lookup. This can take significant time if enabled. The default is false.	No
rotatable	Determines if log rotation should occur. If false, then this file is never rotated and the fileDateFormat attribute is ignored. Use this attribute with caution because the log file could grow very large indeed. The default is true.	No
suffix	The extension added to the name of the log file.	No

Examining an Example Access Log Valve

This section contains an example access log valve to demonstrate the attributes listed in Table 7-2. By default, the access log valves in server.xml are commented out to disable them. This does, however, make it easy to activate them. Open server.xml, and navigate to the localhost <Host> entry. The access log valve is configured after the large comment section (see Listing 7-1).

Listing 7-1. *The Access Log Valve in server.xml*

```
<Valve className="org.apache.catalina.valves.AccessLogValve"
       directory="logs"
       prefix="localhost_access_log."
       suffix=".txt"
       pattern="common"
       resolveHosts="false"/>
```

You may not have this entry if you've previously used the admin Web interface. As noted in Chapter 6, the admin application rewrites a new server.xml once you've made any configuration changes. This means that comments are lost, even if they contain useful default components. The good news is that the old server.xml should have been saved under another name in the conf directory, so you can copy and paste the valve entry from there into the new server.xml.

Uncomment this entry, start/restart Tomcat, and point your browser to http://localhost:8080. You should see the default Tomcat welcome page. Now examine the CATALINA_HOME/logs directory, and open the localhost_access_log.DATE.txt file. You'll see the access log entry for the Web page itself, though you'll also see the entries for the associated image files, all in the common log file format, as shown in Listing 7-2.

Listing 7-2. *The localhost_access_log.DATE.txt Log File*

```
127.0.0.1 - - [01/Aug/2004:20:47:54 +0000]
"GET / HTTP/1.1" 200 9312
127.0.0.1 - - [01/Aug/2004:20:47:54 +0000]
"GET /tomcat.gif HTTP/1.1" 200 1934
127.0.0.1 - - [01/Aug/2004:20:47:54 +0000]
"GET /jakarta-banner.gif HTTP/1.1" 200 8584
127.0.0.1 - - [01/Aug/2004:20:47:54 +0000]
"GET /tomcat-power.gif HTTP/1.1" 200 2324
```

You may want to experiment further with other attributes of the standard access log valve by modifying the previous <Valve> entry. You should experiment with other access log valve configurations, such as valves at the context level, which you configure in the appropriate context XML file, and valves at the engine level. This way you can use tools to analyze access at various levels of the server.

Using Request Filter Valves

As a server administrator you'll often find it useful to restrict access to certain resources. You've already seen password protection for administration resources, but Tomcat also allows you to use request filter valves to block access so that a user doesn't even get as far as the password prompt. You can use this facility to block access to admin resources except for users who are on the local machine or an admin-only machine. Other options can include blocking denial-of-service (DoS) attacks or denying access to sales data for nonsales personnel, and so on.

Two types of request filter valves exist: the remote address valve and the remote host valve. The first of these filters requests by the client's IP address, and the second filters by the client's host. Table 7-3 shows the attributes of the remote address valve.

Table 7-3. *The Attributes of the Remote Address Request Filter Valve*

Attribute	Description	Required?
`allow`	A comma-separated list of regular expressions used to match the client's IP address. If there's a match, then the request is allowed through to its destination. If not, it's blocked. If this attribute isn't specified, then all requests are allowed except if they match a pattern in the `deny` attribute.	No
`className`	The Java class of the valve. This must be `org.apache.catalina.valves.RemoteAddrValve`.	Yes
`deny`	A comma-separated list of regular expressions used to match the client's IP address. If there's a match, then the request is blocked. If not, it's allowed.	No

It's now possible to see how you can allow access only to those users on a local or admin machine. In this example, you'd add the IP address of the local (or admin) machine to the `allow` list. Listing 7-3 shows the scenario where both conditions are allowed (assuming the admin machine has 192.168.0.73 as its IP address).

Listing 7-3. *An Example Remote Address Request Filter Valve*

```
<Valve className="org.apache.catalina.valves.RemoteAddrValve"
       allow="127.0.0.1,192.168.0.73"/>
```

Visit a page on the local Tomcat server. You should see the page as usual. Now remove the 127.0.0.1 portion, and restart Tomcat. Visit the same page, and you should be blocked, as shown in Figure 7-2.

■ **Note** If a blank page isn't a satisfactory way to indicate a blocked page, you should use servlet filters. These are part of a Web application and can be used to show custom error pages. If you're interested in using a filter for this task, one is provided on the Apress Web site that replicates the behavior described in this section.

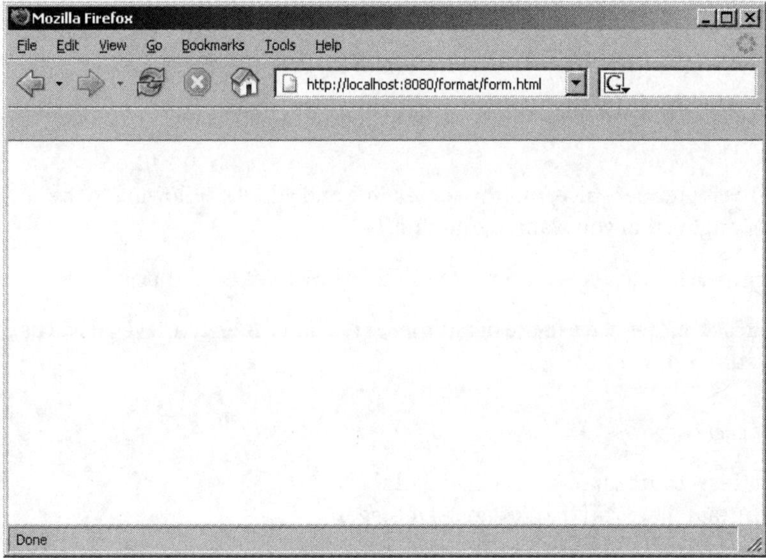

Figure 7-2. *A blocked URL using the remote address request filter valve*

You can also achieve this effect by denying access to the localhost:

```
<Valve className="org.apache.catalina.valves.RemoteAddrValve"
     deny="127.0.0.1"/>
```

Filtering by client host is just as easy. The only differences between the two are the class that implements the valve and the values of the regular expressions. In the case of the remote host request filter valve, the class is `org.apache.catalina.valves.RemoteHostValve`, and the regular expressions are hostnames instead of IP addresses.

```
<Valve className="org.apache.catalina.valves.RemoteHostValve"
     allow="*.com"/>
```

■ **Note** The remote host request filter requires a reverse DNS lookup, so the server must have access to DNS.

Request Dumper Valve

The request dumper valve allows you to debug Web applications by dumping the headers and cookies of requests and responses to a log. The request dumper valve uses whichever logging mechanism you've configured for the component that contains the valve, be that a `<Logger>` in Tomcat 5.0.*x* or Log4J in Tomcat 5.5 (see Chapter 4 for more information on logging).

You can use it for the following:

- Checking how the scope of a valve affects the requests that are processed
- Debugging other valves and any other request-processing components that are configured on the server

To configure a request dumper valve, modify `server.xml` and add the following to the context, virtual host, or engine that you want to examine:

```
<Valve className="org.apache.catalina.valves.RequestDumperValve"/>
```

If you add the request dumper valve to the default `server.xml` at the engine level, it will use the logger shown in Listing 7-4.

Listing 7-4. *An Engine-Level Logger*

```
<!-- Global logger unless overridden at lower levels -->
<Logger className="org.apache.catalina.logger.FileLogger"
       prefix="catalina_log." suffix=".txt"
       timestamp="true"/>
```

For Tomcat 5.0.*x*, if you configure it at the host level (for the `localhost` host) or the context level for the default Tomcat distribution, it will use the logger shown in Listing 7-5, unless you configure a new logger for the context.

Listing 7-5. *A Host-Level Logger*

```
<Logger className="org.apache.catalina.logger.FileLogger"
       directory="logs"  prefix="localhost_log." suffix=".txt"
       timestamp="true"/>
```

For Tomcat 5.5 you'd use the following logger for logging at the host level. Each line of the log has `INFO` priority.

```
log4j.logger.org.apache.catalina.core.ContainerBase.[Catalina].[localhost]
```

If you wanted logging at the context level, assuming that your context is called `tomcatBook`, you'd use the following:

```
log4j.logger.org.apache.catalina.core.ContainerBase.
[Catalina].[localhost].[/tomcatBook]
```

This means the request dumper valve inherits the logger from a higher-level component, which isn't always desirable if you're troubleshooting a specific Web application's request/response-processing pipeline.

Once you've set up the valve, visit a Web application that will be covered by the valve. Once your request has been processed, open the appropriate log file. You should see something similar to Listing 7-6. The version of Tomcat and the settings of your logger will affect this, though the messages will be the same.

Listing 7-6. *The Output of the Request Dumper Valve*

```
REQUEST URI=/tomcatBook/
authType=null
characterEncoding=null
contentLength=-1
contentType=null
contextPath=/tomcatBook
cookie=JSESSIONID=7F31F129712D208903FC6F50FD5143EA
header=host=localhost:8080
header=user-agent=Mozilla/5.0
(Windows; U; Windows NT 5.0; rv:1.7.3) Gecko/20040913 Firefox/0.10.1
header=accept=text/xml,application/xml,application/xhtml+xml,
text/html;q=0.9,text/plain;q=0.8,image/png,*/*;q=0.5
header=accept-language=en-us,en;q=0.5
header=accept-encoding=gzip,deflate
header=accept-charset=ISO-8859-1,utf-8;q=0.7,*;q=0.7
header=keep-alive=300
header=connection=keep-alive
header=cookie=JSESSIONID=7F31F129712D208903FC6F50FD5143EA
locale=en_US
method=GET
pathInfo=null
protocol=HTTP/1.1
queryString=null
remoteAddr=127.0.0.1
remoteHost=127.0.0.1
remoteUser=null
requestedSessionId=7F31F129712D208903FC6F50FD5143EA
scheme=http
serverName=localhost
serverPort=8080
servletPath=/index.jsp
isSecure=false
---------------------------------------------------------------
---------------------------------------------------------------
authType=null
contentLength=-1
contentType=text/html;charset=ISO-8859-1
message=null
remoteUser=null
status=200
===============================================================
```

As you can see, this contains a fair amount of information, all of which can be used to analyze a client's interaction with your server. A word of warning, though: this valve decodes any parameters sent with the request using the platform's default encoding. This may affect Web applications on the server because calls to `request.setCharacterEncoding()` will have no effect.

Using Single Sign-on Valves

Another standard valve that's frequently used is the single sign-on valve. Conventionally, whenever users of a Web application reaches a protected page, they will be required to log in, a process that's repeated if they browse to another Web application on the same server. Using single sign-on, it's possible to eliminate this repetition, provided that all the Web applications on a host use the same Tomcat realm.

The single sign-on valve caches the user's credentials on the server and will authenticate users as they move between Web applications on a host. The credentials are cached in the client's session, which means that a single sign-on will be effective throughout a session. The user's browser will send a cookie with a value that uniquely identifies this user as a user who has signed in. The valve then associates the new request with the existing user credentials and allows the user to visit protected resources. This is one of the main reasons for having a common realm for the host.

Table 7-4 describes the attributes of the single sign-on valve.

Table 7-4. *The Attributes of the Single Sign-on Valve*

Attribute	Description	Required?
`className`	The Java class of the valve. This must be `org.apache.catalina.authenticator.SingleSignOn`.	Yes
`debug`	Tomcat 5.0.*x* only. Level of debugging. The default is zero (no debugging).	No
`requireReauthentication`	Determines whether the valve should use the authentication realm to authenticate the user every time authentication is required. If `false`, the valve uses the cookie sent by the client and automatically authenticates the user without rechecking the realm. The default is `false`.	No

Configuring a Single Sign-on Valve

Before seeing what single sign-on does, you should first experience the problem that sometimes makes it necessary to configure single sign-on. You'll need two separate Web applications that are both protected. Luckily Tomcat comes with two such Web applications: the `manager` application and the `admin` application. If you're using Tomcat 5.5 you'll have to download the `admin` application or protect another application for this example to work.

You should already have a user who has the manager role required for access to the manager `application` and a user who has the admin role required for access to the `admin` application. You may even have a user who has both. If not, then you must create one in `tomcat-users.xml` now, as shown in Listing 7-7.

Listing 7-7. *A User with Manager and Admin Roles Defined in* `tomcat-users.xml`

```
<role rolename="manager"/>
<role rolename="admin"/>
<user username="tomcat" password="tomcat" roles="tomcat,manager,admin"/>
```

Here the tomcat user has three roles: tomcat, manager, and admin. Now start/restart Tomcat, and navigate to `http://localhost:8080/manager/html/`. You'll be asked for your user details as usual. Now sign in as the user with both roles. Once you've done so, you should see the Web interface of the `manager` application.

The next step is to navigate to `http://localhost:8080/admin/`. You'll be presented with the form for logging into the `admin` application, which means your login for the `manager` application hasn't carried over into the `admin` application despite the details being valid for both. This is where single sign-on comes in.

Open `server.xml`, and navigate to the valve as shown in Listing 7-8. It's the first valve in the `localhost` host, after the large commented-out section.

Listing 7-8. *The Single Sign-on Valve in* `server.xml`

```
<!-- Normally, users must authenticate themselves to each Web app
     individually. Uncomment the following entry if you would like
     a user to be authenticated the first time they encounter a
     resource protected by a security constraint, and then have that
     user identity maintained across *all* Web applications contained
     in this virtual host. -->
<!--
<Valve className="org.apache.catalina.authenticator.SingleSignOn"
          debug="0"/>
-->
```

Uncomment the valve, and restart Tomcat. Make sure you've closed your browser windows to start a new session, and navigate to `http://localhost:8080/manager/html/` as before. Log in as the user with both roles as before. Once you've logged in successfully, navigate to `http://localhost:8080/admin/`. This time you won't be asked to log in again because the valve will have recognized you from the cookie sent by your browser and will have authenticated you.

Configuring User Sessions

Sessions can play an important part in a server's performance and its ability to service client requests. When you shut Tomcat down, all session information is usually lost, and sessions that are idle take up valuable working memory until session timeout—which is typically a long period, since some users may leave their computers. Therefore, it'd be useful to save session information across restarts so that users don't experience a loss of service. Equally, it may be useful to remove idle sessions from memory and store them elsewhere to improve performance.

To solve these problems, Tomcat comes with session managers, which are works in progress, with features and configuration that are subject to change.

You can do the following with the session managers:

- You can swap inactive sessions onto disk, thereby releasing the memory consumed by them and making memory available for active sessions.
- You can save current sessions to disk when you shut Tomcat down; upon restart, the saved sessions are restored.
- You can save sessions lasting beyond a specified threshold period to disk, enabling the system to survive an unexpected crash.

The last two features enable you to give a reliable service to users despite minor server failures or restarts.

Tomcat also allows you to configure clustering so that you can replicate a user's session across more than one server, thus minimizing the risk of losing their information when one server crashes or becomes unavailable.

Configuring a Session Manager

The session manager is a context-level component, and you configure it in `server.xml` using the `<Manager>` element. Tomcat provides two types of session manager: the standard session manager and the persistent session manager. The standard session manager is the default session manager that Tomcat uses if you don't specify one of your own, and it doesn't allow for persistent session management, except that it can retain sessions across a restart. You can still configure a custom standard session manager for a Web application. The persistent session manager allows you to perform all the tasks described previously.

Both types of session manager share two attributes, as shown in Table 7-5.

Table 7-5. *The Common Session Manager Attributes*

Attribute	Description	Required?
`className`	The class that implements the session manager. The default is the standard session manager.	No
`distributable`	Sets whether the session manager should enforce the restrictions described in the Servlet specification for distributable applications. This means that all session attributes must implement `java.io.Serializable`. This setting can also be inherited from an application's `web.xml` file. The default is `false`.	No

If you want to configure the standard implementation, you must set the className attribute to org.apache.catalina.session.StandardManager. Table 7-6 describes its additional attributes.

Table 7-6. *The Standard Session Manager Attributes*

Attribute	Description	Required?
algorithm	Name of the message digest algorithm used to calculate session identifiers produced by this manager. This value must be supported by the java.security.MessageDigest class. The default is MD5.	No
checkInterval	The number of seconds between checks for expired sessions for this manager. The default is 60.	No
debug	Tomcat 5.0.*x* only. The level of debugging detail logged by this manager to the associated logger. Higher numbers generate more detailed output. The default is zero.	No
entropy	A String value that's used when seeding the random number generator used to create session identifiers for this manager. If not specified, a semi-useful value is calculated, but a long String value should be specified in security-conscious environments.	No
maxActiveSessions	The maximum number of active sessions that will be created by this manager. Use -1 (the default) for no limit.	No
pathname	Absolute or relative (to the work directory for this context, CATALINA_HOME/work/[Engine_name]/[Host_name]/[Webapp_name]) pathname of the file in which session state will be preserved across application restarts, if possible. You may disable restart persistence by setting this attribute to an empty string. The default is SESSIONS.ser.	No
randomClass	Java class name of the java.util.Random implementation class to use. The default is java.security.SecureRandom.	No

To configure a persistent session manager, you need to set the className attribute to org.apache.catalina.session.PersistentManager. Table 7-7 describes its additional attributes.

The differences between the standard session manager and the persistent session manager are illustrated by their attributes. The persistent session manager has options for saving sessions to permanent storage at any point in their life cycle, as well as when you shut down the server, using the maxIdleBackup attribute. It also has options to move sessions out of memory after a certain period, using the maxIdleSwap and minIdleSwap methods. You also have control over whether to save the sessions over a restart using the saveOnRestart attribute.

Table 7-7. *The Persistent Session Manager Attributes*

Attribute	Description	Required?
`algorithm`	Name of the message digest algorithm used to calculate session identifiers produced by this manager. This value must be supported by the `java.security.MessageDigest` class. The default is `MD5`.	No
`checkInterval`	The number of seconds between checks for expired sessions for this manager. The default is `60`.	No
`debug`	Tomcat 5.0.*x* only. The level of debugging detail logged by this manager to the associated logger. Higher numbers generate more detailed output. The default is zero.	No
`entropy`	A `String` value that's used when seeding the random number generator used to create session identifiers for this manager. If not specified, a semi-useful value is calculated, but a long `String` value should be specified in security-conscious environments.	No
`maxActiveSessions`	The maximum number of active sessions that will be created by this manager. Use `-1` (the default) for no limit.	No
`maxIdleBackup`	The time in seconds since the last access to a session before it's eligible for being persisted to the session store. `-1` (the default) disables this feature.	No
`maxIdleSwap`	The time in seconds since the last access to a session before it should be persisted to the session store and taken out of the server's memory. If this feature is enabled, the time interval specified should be equal to or longer than the value specified for `maxIdleBackup`. `-1` (the default) disables this feature.	No
`minIdleSwap`	The time in seconds since the last access to a session before it will be eligible to be persisted to the session store and taken out of the server's memory. If specified, this value should be less than that specified by `maxIdleSwap`. `-1` (the default) disables this feature and allows the swap at any time.	No
`processExpiresFrequency`	Tomcat 5.5 only. Frequency of the session expiration and related manager operations. Manager operations will be done once for the specified amount of background process calls. (That is, the lower the amount, the more often the checks will occur.) The minimum value is `1`. The default is `6`.	No
`randomClass`	Java class name of the `java.util.Random` implementation class to use. The default is `java.security.SecureRandom`.	No
`saveOnRestart`	Specifies whether all sessions should be persisted and reloaded when Tomcat is shut down and restarted or when this application is reloaded. The default is `true`.	No

One crucial difference between the sets of attributes is the absence of a location for storing the session in Table 7-7. In the case of the persistent session manager, you configure the session store using the `<Store>` subelement. Tomcat allows you to configure two types of store: a file store and a JDBC store.

The file store is the same mechanism used by the standard session manager, except you can use the extra functionality of the persistent session manager. To configure a file store, set the className attribute to org.apache.catalina.session.FileStore and use the attributes from Table 7-8.

Table 7-8. *The Persistent File Store Attributes*

Attribute	Description	Required?
checkInterval	The interval in seconds between checks for expired sessions among those sessions that are currently swapped out. The default is 60.	No
className	Java class name of the implementation to use.	Yes
debug	Tomcat 5.0.*x* only. The level of debugging detail logged by this store to the associated logger. Higher numbers generate more detailed output. The default is zero.	No
directory	Absolute or relative (to the temporary work directory for this Web application, CATALINA_HOME/work/[Engine_name]/[Host_name]/[Webapp_name]) pathname of the directory into which individual session files are written. The default is the temporary work directory assigned by the container.	No

The JDBC store uses JDBC to store the sessions in a permanent data store, usually a database. To configure a JDBC store, set the className attribute to org.apache.catalina.session.JDBCStore and use the attributes from Table 7-9.

Table 7-9. *The Persistent JDBC Store Attributes*

Attribute	Description	Required?
checkInterval	The interval in seconds between checks for expired sessions among those sessions that are currently swapped out. The default is 60.	No
className	Java class name of the implementation to use.	Yes
connectionURL	The connection URL that will be handed to the configured JDBC driver to establish a connection to the session database.	Yes
debug	Tomcat 5.0.*x* only. The level of debugging detail logged by this store to the associated logger. Higher numbers generate more detailed output. The default is zero.	No
driverName	Java class name of the JDBC driver to be used.	Yes
sessionAppCol	Name of the database column in the specified session table that contains the engine, host, and context name in the format /Engine/Host/Context.	Yes

Table 7-9. *The Persistent JDBC Store Attributes (Continued)*

Attribute	Description	Required?
sessionDataCol	Name of the database column in the specified session table that contains the serialized form of all the session attributes for a swapped-out session. The column type must accept a binary object (typically called a BLOB).	Yes
sessionIdCol	Name of the database column in the specified session table that contains the session identifier of the swapped-out session. The column type must accept character string data of at least as many characters as are contained in session identifiers created by Tomcat (typically 32).	Yes
sessionLastAccessedCol	Name of the database column in the specified session table that contains the lastAccessedTime property of this session. The column type must accept a Java long (64 bits).	Yes
sessionMaxInactiveCol	Name of the database column in the specified session table that contains the maxInactiveInterval property of this session. The column type must accept a Java integer (32 bits).	Yes
sessionTable	Name of the database table to be used for storing swapped out sessions. This table must contain (at least) the database columns that are configured by the other attributes of this element.	Yes
sessionValidCol	Name of the database column in the specified session table that contains a flag indicating whether this swapped-out session is still valid. The column type must accept a single character.	Yes

To use the JDBC store, you must create a suitable database in which to store sessions. Listing 7-9 shows an example SQL script for a MySQL database.

Listing 7-9. *A SQL Script for MySQL That Creates a JDBC Store-Compatible Database*

```
CREATE TABLE tomcat_sessions (
  session_id     VARCHAR(100) NOT NULL PRIMARY KEY,
  valid_session  CHAR(1) NOT NULL,
  max_inactive   INT(32) NOT NULL,
  last_access    INT(64) NOT NULL,
  app_name       VARCHAR(255),
  session_data   MEDIUMBLOB,
  KEY kapp_name(app_name)
);
```

Listing 7-10 shows how to configure a JDBC store in server.xml using this table.

Listing 7-10. *A Persistent Session Manager Using a JDBC Store in* `server.xml`

```
<Manager className="org.apache.catalina.session.PersistentManager"
         maxIdleBackup="300"
         minIdleSwap="0"
         maxIdleSwap="360">

  <Store className="org.apache.catalina.session.JDBCStore"
         connectionURL="jdbc:mysql://localhost:3306/tomcatSession"
         driverName="com.mysql.jdbc.Driver"
         sessionAppCol="app_name"
         sessionDataCol="session_data"
         sessionIdCol="session_id"
         sessionLastAccessedCol="last_access"
         sessionMaxInactiveCol="max_inactive"
         sessionTable="tomcat_sessions"
         sessionValidCol="valid_session"/>

</Manager>
```

Notice how the attributes of the `<Store>` element correspond to the columns created in Listing 7-9. The settings in the `<Manager>` element tell Tomcat that sessions left for five minutes (300 seconds) are eligible to be backed up to the store, that sessions can be taken out of memory and placed in the store at any time, and that sessions left for six minutes (360 seconds) should be taken out of memory and placed in the store.

If you use this setup and check the database periodically, you'll see that it's empty until either the session backup limit is reached or the server is shut down. Once either of these events occurs Tomcat will save the session to the database.

Configuring a Cluster

Tomcat also allows you to implement a clustered environment. You can then replicate user sessions across multiple servers to ensure that they don't lose any data. For clustering to work you'll have to use some form of load balancing and activate multicasting. Chapter 9 discusses this.

Each Tomcat instance is a node of the cluster and must report in on multicast ping. If a node fails to report for a certain amount of time, the other nodes don't attempt to replicate any session changes to it. Replicating user sessions across nodes is determined by a set of rules, which is described next. The clustering implementation uses a session manager that overrides any other session manager in the Tomcat instance.

A cluster is defined at the host level using the `<Cluster>` element, and Tomcat's default `server.xml` comes with an example and very serviceable cluster setup. Table 7-10 shows the attributes of the `<Cluster>` element using the standard implementation `org.apache.catalina.cluster.tcp.SimpleTcpCluster`.

Table 7-10. *The Attributes of the* `<Cluster>` *Element*

Attribute	Description	Required?
`className`	The class that implements this cluster. Use `org.apache.catalina.cluster.tcp.SimpleTcpCluster`.	Yes
`debug`	Tomcat 5.0.*x* only. Set the debug level for this component. The default is zero (no debugging).	No
`expireSessionsOnShutdown`	Set to `true` to remove sessions when this cluster node is shut down. The default is `true`.	No
`managerClassName`	The name of the manager class that looks after the sessions (see earlier for details on session managers). Use `org.apache.catalina.cluster.session.DeltaManager`, which is the default.	No
`clusterName`	Set the name of the cluster to join; if no cluster with this name is present, create one.	No
`notifyListenersOnReplication`	Tomcat 5.5 only. Set to `true` to notify attribute/context listeners upon replication of a session change. These listeners are configured on an application-by-application basis. The default is `true`.	No
`printToScreen`	Set to `true` to write session information to `std.out`. The default is `false`.	No
`protocol`	Sets the configurable protocol stack. However, this setting has no function at the time of writing.	No
`useDirtyFlag`	Set to `false` to replicate a session only after a call to `setAttribute()` or `removeAttribute()`. In other words, replicate only after session information has changed. Set to `true` to replicate the session after each request. The default is `false`.	No

Listing 7-11 shows the setting from Tomcat 5.5's `server.xml`.

Listing 7-11. *The Default Cluster Setting in Tomcat 5.5's* `server.xml`

```
<Cluster className="org.apache.catalina.cluster.tcp.SimpleTcpCluster"
        managerClassName="org.apache.catalina.cluster.session.DeltaManager"
        expireSessionsOnShutdown="false"
        useDirtyFlag="true"
        notifyListenersOnReplication="true">
```

These cluster settings should be the same for all nodes of the cluster.

Configuring a Node's Membership

Now you need to configure this node's membership credentials using a `<Membership>` element with the standard `org.apache.catalina.cluster.mcast.McastService` implementation. This is a subelement of `<Cluster>`, and Table 7-11 shows its attributes.

Table 7-11. *The Attributes of the `<Membership>` Element*

Attribute	Description	Required?
`className`	The class that implements this membership setting. Use `org.apache.catalina.cluster.mcast.McastService`.	Yes
`mcastAddr`	The multicast address that this cluster uses to maintain its cohesion. Each node will ping this address to inform the rest of the cluster that it's still active. This setting has to be the same for all the nodes.	Yes
`mcastBindAddr`	This setting binds the multicast socket to a specific address. The default is null.	No
`mcastDropTime`	The number of milliseconds from the last multicast heartbeat before a node is considered to be unavailable.	Yes
`mcastFrequency`	The number of milliseconds between each multicast heartbeat.	Yes
`mcastPort`	The multicast port that this cluster uses to maintain its cohesion. This setting has to be the same for all the nodes.	Yes
`mcastSoTimeout`	The multicast read timeout. The read of the pings by other nodes will last as long as this value. The default is `-1` (no timeout).	No
`mcastTTL`	The multicast time to live if you want to limit your broadcast. The heartbeat ping will last only as long as this value. The default is `-1` (no timeout).	No

Listing 7-12 shows the setting from Tomcat 5.5's `server.xml`.

Listing 7-12. *The Default Membership Setting in Tomcat 5.5's `server.xml`*

```
<Membership
  className="org.apache.catalina.cluster.mcast.McastService"
  mcastAddr="228.0.0.4"
  mcastPort="45564"
  mcastFrequency="500"
  mcastDropTime="3000"/>
```

All these settings should be the same for each node on the cluster.

Configuring a Node's Receiver

A node in a cluster receives replication information so that it can synchronize its sessions with the other nodes in the cluster. You achieve this by using a `<Receiver>` element with the standard `org.apache.catalina.cluster.tcp.ReplicationListener` implementation in `server.xml`. These settings are unique to a node, and Table 7-12 describes the relevant attributes.

Listing 7-13 shows the setting from Tomcat 5.5's `server.xml`.

Table 7-12. *The Attributes of the `<Receiver>` Element*

Attribute	Description	Required?
`className`	The class that implements this receiver. Use `org.apache.catalina.cluster.tcp.ReplicationListener`.	Yes
`isSenderSynchronized`	If set to `true`, then this node will send an acknowledgment to the replication sender. The default is `false`.	No
`tcpListenAddress`	The TCP address that this node will listen on for session replication. Setting this to `auto` means that the address is determined with a call to `InetAddress.getLocalHost().getHostAddress()`. In other words, the local address of the machine.	Yes
`tcpListenPort`	The TCP port that this node will listen on for session replication. The default is `0`, which lets the system pick up an ephemeral port.	No
`tcpSelectorTimeout`	The timeout in milliseconds for the `Selector.select()` method in case the operating system has a bug in `java.nio`. Set to `0` for no timeout, which is the default.	No
`tcpThreadCount`	The number of threads to handle incoming replication requests. The optimal setting would be the same amount of threads as nodes in this cluster. The default is `0`.	No

Listing 7-13. *The Default Receiver Setting in Tomcat 5.5's `server.xml`*

```
<Receiver
  className="org.apache.catalina.cluster.tcp.ReplicationListener"
  tcpListenAddress="auto"
  tcpListenPort="4001"
  tcpSelectorTimeout="100"
  tcpThreadCount="6"/>
```

Configuring a Node's Sender

Just as a node must receive replication information, it must send replication information when one of its sessions changes. You achieve this by using a `<Sender>` element with the standard `org.apache.catalina.cluster.tcp.ReplicationTransmitter` implementation in `server.xml`. Table 7-13 describes these settings.

Table 7-13. *The Attributes of the <Sender> Element*

Attribute	Description	Required?
`className`	The class that implements this sender. Use `org.apache.catalina.cluster.tcp.ReplicationTransmitter`.	Yes
`replicationMode`	Can be `pooled`, `synchronous`, or `asynchronous`. The default is pooled.	No

The settings for `replicationMode` are as follows:

`synchronous` ensures that the thread that executes the request is also the thread that replicates the data to the other nodes. It won't return until all the nodes in the cluster have received the information. It does this by waiting for an acknowledgment.

`pooled` uses several sockets in a synchronous way; that is, the data is replicated, then the receiving node sends an acknowledgment. This is the same as `synchronous` except that it uses a pool of sockets, meaning it's multithreaded. This is the fastest and safest configuration. Ensure that you have enough threads as advised previously.

`asynchronous` states that there's a specific sender thread for each node, so the request thread will queue the replication request and then return to the client. A session is added to the queue, and if the same session already exists in the queue from a previous request, that session will be replaced in the queue instead of replicating two requests. This almost never happens, unless there's a large network delay.

Listing 7-14 shows the setting from Tomcat 5.5's `server.xml`.

Listing 7-14. *The Default Sender Setting in Tomcat 5.5's `server.xml`*

```
<Sender
  className="org.apache.catalina.cluster.tcp.ReplicationTransmitter"
  replicationMode="pooled"
  ackTimeout="15000"/>
```

Configuring a Node's Replication Valve

It's not always necessary to replicate session state after every request. You've already seen the `useDirtyFlag` attribute of the `<Cluster>` element. This allows you to replicate session information only after a change in the session state.

You have other ways to save on the overhead and network traffic involved in session replication. One is to not replicate a session after a request for a static resource such as an HTML page or an image. This may not apply in all cases, but you can do it if you want to use a `<Valve>` element with the `org.apache.catalina.cluster.tcp.ReplicationValve` implementation. Table 7-14 describes its attributes.

Table 7-14. *The Attributes of the Replication <Valve> Element*

Attribute	Description	Required?
className	The class that implements this valve. Use org.apache.catalina.cluster.tcp.ReplicationValve.	Yes
filter	A set of regular expressions matching file extensions. The valve will intercept requests that match these regular exceptions and bypass the replication mechanism.	Yes

Listing 7-15 shows the setting from Tomcat 5.5's server.xml.

Listing 7-15. *The Default Replication Valve Setting in Tomcat 5.5's server.xml.*

```
<Valve className="org.apache.catalina.cluster.tcp.ReplicationValve"
       filter=".*\.gif;.*\.js;.*\.jpg;.*\.htm;.*\.html;.*\.txt;"/>
```

Here you can see that the filter won't allow replication after requests for images, JavaScript, HTML, and text files.

If you use this valve, the session replication algorithm is as follows. A session is replicated only if all the following conditions are met:

- useDirtyFlag is true *or* setAttribute has been called *or* removeAttribute has been called.
- *And* a session exists (has been created).
- *And* the request isn't trapped by the filter attribute of the replication valve.

Configuring a Node's Deployer

A node can also deploy and undeploy local Web applications across the cluster using WAR files. This allows you to quickly and easily drop a Web application into the cluster for immediate use and replication. You achieve this by using a <Deployer> element with the standard implementation org.apache.catalina.cluster.deploy.FarmWarDeployer in server.xml. Table 7-15 describes these settings.

Table 7-15. *The Attributes of the <Deployer> Element*

Attribute	Description	Required?
className	The class that implements this deployer. Use org.apache.catalina.cluster.deploy.FarmWarDeployer.	Yes
deployDir	The directory where this node will deploy the WAR once it has been dropped into the watchDir. The default is CATALINA_HOME/bin.	No
tempDir	The temporary work directory for this node. The default is null.	No
watchEnabled	Set to true to watch the watchDir for WAR files and changes to WAR files. The default is false.	No
watchDir	The directory where you place new WARs for deployment across the cluster.	Only if watchEnabled is true

When a WAR is dropped into `watchedDir`, Tomcat copies it to `deployDir` and creates a context XML file in `CATALINA_HOME/conf/[Engine]/[Host]`, which is named after the WAR file. The resultant `<Context>` element's `docBase` attribute will point to the WAR file in `deployDir`. Listing 7-16 shows an example.

Listing 7-16. *An Example Context XML File After a Node Has Deployed a WAR*

```
<?xml version='1.0' encoding='utf-8'?>
<Context docBase="/C:/JavaStuff/Tomcat/Tomcat29/deployDir/format.war"
         path="/format">
</Context>
```

Listing 7-17 shows the setting from Tomcat 5.5's `server.xml`.

Listing 7-17. *The Default Deployer Setting in Tomcat 5.5's* `server.xml`

```
<Deployer className="org.apache.catalina.cluster.deploy.FarmWarDeployer"
          tempDir="/tmp/war-temp/"
          deployDir="/tmp/war-deploy/"
          watchDir="/tmp/war-listen/"
          watchEnabled="false"/>
```

This doesn't watch for any WAR files and therefore won't deploy any applications to the cluster.

Summary

In this chapter you saw Tomcat's proprietary system of valves that you can use to intercept requests. The various types of valve can block access to a resource, log details of the intercepted request, and log details of Web application access. You can also use valves to implement single sign-on, where a user can log into every Web application running on a server.

You also saw Tomcat's session managers, which can ensure that user sessions are persisted across server restarts and crashes and can give Tomcat the ability to move inert sessions out of memory, thus boosting performance. You can configure the location of these sessions, with the choice being between files or JDBC data sources.

You also saw how you extend this mechanism with Tomcat's clustering mechanism. This allows you to provide a more robust service to your users.

CHAPTER 8

Understanding Tomcat's Class Loaders

Tomcat is intrinsically linked with the Java programming language; it's written in Java, and Java applications run on it. As such, it's governed by the rules and attributes of the Java specification, two of which are platform independence and suitability for distributed network architectures.

To fulfill both these goals, Java employs many innovative techniques, one of which is how it loads code libraries. If Java is to be platform independent, it can't rely on a specific type, or types, of file system. In addition, Java is designed to load code libraries from sources spread across a network, so it can't just load them from a single file system.

The Java architects introduced class loaders to deal with these issues. A *class loader* abstracts the process of loading classes, making the process completely independent of any type of underlying data store, be it a network or a hard drive. Notice the similarity to the JNDI and JDBC APIs discussed in Chapter 7. These APIs also abstract the details of the underlying system and allow Java to be independent of any type of underlying naming service or database.

Tomcat and its Web applications use class loaders just as any other Java application does. However, as a servlet/JSP container Tomcat must provide class loaders to its Web applications. You've already read a quick discussion of this in Chapter 3 where you saw the locations for Tomcat's class loaders. This chapter will expand on that discussion to give you a fuller picture of Tomcat and of class loaders, starting at the bottom with J2SE class loaders.

Examining the Standard J2SE Class Loaders

Since J2SE 1.2, the JVM has used three distinct class loaders.

- Bootstrap class loader
- Extension class loader
- System class loader

These class loaders sit in a hierarchy with the bootstrap class loader at the top and the system class loader at the bottom. They have parent-child relationships, so the parent of the system class loader is the extension class loader. The bootstrap class loader is written in native code and is included in the JVM, and the other two class loaders, as is the case with Tomcat's class loaders, are written in Java.

The Bootstrap Class Loader

The JVM uses the bootstrap class loader to load those Java classes that are necessary for it to function. This means the bootstrap class loader loads all the core Java classes (such as `java.lang.*` and `java.io.*`).

As noted previously, the bootstrap class loader is written in native code, so it solves the circular problem of loading Java-based class loaders when the initial class loader itself must be loaded. The classes it loads are located in different locations depending on the JVM vendor. They're always in JAR files, and Sun stores them in `JAVA_HOME/jre/lib/`.

The Extension Class Loader

J2SE 1.2 introduced the standard extension mechanism. Normally, when developers want the JVM to load class files that aren't in the bootstrap classpath, they use the `CLASSPATH` environment variable. Sun introduced the standard extension mechanism as an alternative method; you can drop JAR files into a standard extension directory, and the JVM will automatically find them.

The extension class loader is responsible for loading all the classes in one or more extension directories. Just as the bootstrap class loader's path can vary on different JVMs, so can the standard extension path. On Sun's JVM, the standard extension directory is `JAVA_HOME/jre/lib/ext/`.

One advantage with the standard extension mechanism is that developers don't have to struggle with a huge `CLASSPATH` environment variable as they add more and more libraries to their systems.

The System Class Loader

The system class loader places its classes in those directories and JAR files specified in the `CLASSPATH` environment variable. The system class loader is also used to load an application's main class and is the default class loader for loading any other classes not covered by the previous two class loaders.

The Delegation Model

So, J2SE has three different class loaders, but how does the JVM know which class loader to use? The answer is in the delegation model. In every version of Java since J2SE 1.2, whenever a class loader receives a request to load a class, it first asks its parent to fulfill the request. (In other words, it delegates the request to its parent class loader.) If the parent loads the class successfully, then the resulting class object is returned. The original class loader attempts to load the class itself only if its parent (and its parent's parent, and so on) fails to load the class.

Thus, when a developer references a class in a Java program, the JVM will automatically route a request to the system class loader to load the class. The system class loader will then request that the extension class loader load the specified class, which in turn will request that the bootstrap class loader load the class. The process stops with the bootstrap class loader, which will then check the core Java libraries for the requested class.

If the class doesn't exist in the core libraries, then the extension class loader will check the standard extensions for the class. If it's still not found, then the system class loader will check the locations specified by the `CLASSPATH` variable for the class. If the class still could not be located, then a `ClassNotFoundException` will be thrown.

The Endorsed Standards Override Mechanism

Following the previous discussion, when a developer uses a class in a Java application, the request to load it is passed up the class loader hierarchy. This means that if the bootstrap class loader can load a class, it will load it even if the class is present in the scope of another class loader. For example, J2SE 1.4 and 5 includes a Java API for XML Processing (JAXP) XML parser as standard, which as a consequence is loaded by the bootstrap class loader. In this case, developers can't place their preferred XML parser in an application's `CLASSPATH` because the system class loader always defers to the bootstrap class loader.

The Endorsed Standards Override Mechanism solves this problem. If a developer places JAR files that replace the standard XML parser in some specific location, the bootstrap class loader will load their class files instead. In J2SE 1.4 and 5, this location is `JAVA_HOME/lib/endorsed/`. Users can change the path for this mechanism by setting the `java.endorsed.dirs` property.

Before you start thinking about replacing any of the core libraries, Java allows you only to override certain packages. You can find the complete list of packages in the J2SE 1.4 documentation (`http://java.sun.com/j2se/1.4.2/docs/guide/standards/`) and the J2SE 5 documentation (`http://java.sun.com/j2se/1.5.0/docs/guide/standards/`). In summary, you can override only the CORBA classes and the XML parser classes with this mechanism.

Understanding Class Loader Attributes

Now that you've seen the standard Java class loaders and the delegation model that governs how these class loaders interact, let's talk more about how class loaders work.

Loading Classes on Demand

The three class loaders don't preload all the classes in their scope. Instead, they load the classes on demand. This is called *lazy loading* because the class loader doesn't load the data until it's requested. Although laziness in human beings is generally regarded as negative, it's actually quite a good thing for class loaders. The reasons are as follows:

- **Faster performance**: If each class loader had to load every class, it would take much longer to initialize the JVM.
- **Efficiency**: Loading in the classes would consume more memory than necessary if loaded early.
- **Flexibility**: JAR files and classes can be added to the search paths of all the class loaders even after the class loaders have been initialized.

Note that when a class is loaded, all its parent classes must also be loaded. Thus, if `ClassB` extends `ClassA`, and `ClassB` is loaded, then `ClassA` is also loaded.

Class Caching

The standard J2SE class loaders look up classes on demand, but once a class is loaded into a class loader, it will stay loaded (cached) for as long as the JVM is running.

Separate Namespaces

Each class loader has its own unique namespace. In other words, if the bootstrap class loader loads a class named `sun.misc.ClassA`, and the system class loader loads a class named `sun.misc.ClassB`, the two classes will be considered to be in distinct packages and each class won't have access to the other class's package-private members.

Creating a Custom Class Loader

A developer can even create custom class loaders, though it may seem like a pointless exercise. However, creating custom class loaders is fairly easy and doing so can in fact give an application an incredible amount of flexibility. While this is beyond the scope of this book, it's worth noting that Tomcat extensively uses custom class loaders.

Understanding Security and Class Loaders

Class loading is at the center of the Java security model. After all, if a rogue third party were to get an application to load a custom version of `java.lang.String` that had the nasty side effect of deleting the hard drive whenever it was instantiated, it would be problematic for users and for Sun. Understanding the security features of the class loader architecture will help you understand how Tomcat's class loader system works.

The Java class loader architecture tackles the security problem with the following strategies:

- Class loader delegation
- Core class restriction
- Separate class loader namespaces
- Security manager

Class Loader Delegation

The delegation model is often described as a security feature. After all, it seems like it should be: anyone trying to load false versions of the core Java classes will fail because the bootstrap class loader has priority and will always find the genuine copies of the core Java classes.

However, the delegation model is flawed as a security mechanism because class loaders aren't required to implement it. In other words, if you want to create a class loader that doesn't follow the delegation model, you're free to do so.

So, if a custom class loader doesn't have to delegate requests to the system class loader, what's to stop a custom class loader from loading its own copy of `java.lang.String`?

Core Class Restriction

Fortunately, it's not possible for any class loader written in Java to instantiate a core Java class. The `ClassLoader` abstract class, from which all class loaders must descend, blocks the creation of any class whose fully qualified name begins with `java`. Thus, no false `java.*` classes are allowed. As the bootstrap class loader isn't written in Java and doesn't descend from `ClassLoader`, it's not subject to this restriction.

By implication, this restriction indicates that all class loaders must at least delegate to the bootstrap class loader; otherwise, when the class is loaded, the class loader has no way to load `java.lang.Object`, from which all objects must descend.

Thus, the delegation model by itself doesn't provide security. It's the core class restriction mechanism that prevents rogue class loaders from tampering with the core Java libraries (at least at run time).

Separate Class Loader Namespaces

As you saw earlier, each class loader has its own namespace, so you can load two different classes with the same fully qualified name. Having separate namespaces is an important security feature because it prevents custom class loaders from stepping over each other or the system class loader. No matter how hard a renegade class loader may try, it can't replace a class loaded by a different class loader; furthermore, it can't access the package-private members in classes of a package with the same name that was loaded from a different location.

Security Manager

If developers really want to make sure no one can damage their programs with custom class loaders, they can simply disallow the use of custom class loaders altogether with the `SecurityManager` class. This is Java's general mechanism for applying security restrictions in applications.

With a security manager, and its associated policy files, you can disallow (or allow) a large number of tasks. For example, you can prevent a program from opening any socket to some network host or prevent it from opening any file on the local file system. More appropriately, you can also prevent an application from loading a class loader. In fact, you have the following options for preventing class loader–related operations:

- You can prevent the loading of any class loader.
- You can prevent a reference to any class loader being obtained (including the system class loader).
- You can prevent the context class loader of any thread being changed.

You have to perform only two steps.

1. Configure a policy file with the permissions you want for a given application.
2. Turn on the application's security manager.

There's a lot more to the security manager than this, but the complexity of the topic means that Chapter 12 is devoted to the subject.

Understanding Tomcat and Class Loaders

Tomcat builds on the standard Java class loaders by adding its own to the class loader hierarchy, as shown in Figure 8-1. They're the common class loader, the server class loader, the shared class loader, and the Web application class loader. These are the class loaders you saw in Chapter 3.

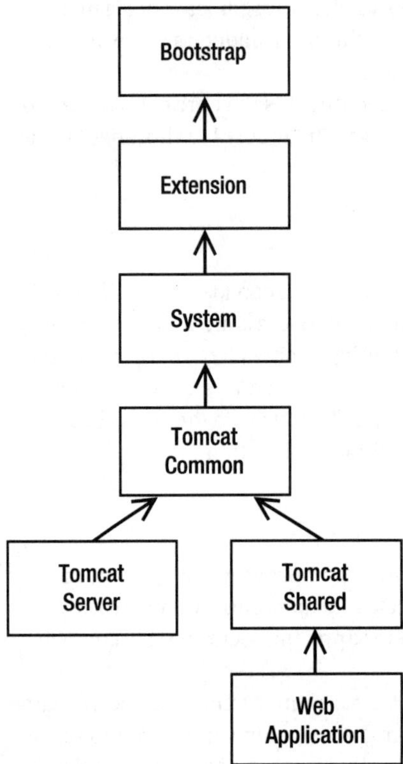

Figure 8-1. *Tomcat's class loaders in the class loader hierarchy*

As you can see, it's not the same model of direct delegation. The server class loader delegates to the common class loader, as do the shared and Web application class loaders. This means the shared and Web application class loaders don't have access to server internal classes, but the server class loader does.

Tomcat and the System Class Loader

Tomcat uses the default system class loader but clears the `CLASSPATH` environment variable in its startup file. In its place, Tomcat sets the `CLASSPATH` to the following:

- `CATALINA_HOME/bin/bootstrap.jar`
- `CATALINA_HOME/bin/commons-logging-api.jar`
- `JAVA_HOME/lib/tools.jar`

At the time of writing, `commons-logging-api.jar` is added only to the Linux startup files. However, it's added to the bootstrap classpath on all systems because of its presence in the `CATALINA_HOME/bin` directory (see the next section for details).

You'll recall that the system class loader searches the CLASSPATH, but since Tomcat sets the CLASSPATH to the previously listed files, the system CLASSPATH variable is ignored for the duration of Tomcat's life cycle. This is an unending source of problems with Web applications. As long as you remember that Tomcat has its own classpath that's separate from the system classpath, and that you can add classes to Tomcat's classpath by using the directories listed in the "Tomcat's Common Class Loader" section, you won't have any problems.

The bootstrap.jar file contains those classes necessary for Tomcat to start, and the tools.jar file contains the javac compiler, which is used to compile JSP pages into class files at run time. commons-logging-api.jar is used in Tomcat's bootstrap logging.

Tomcat and the Extension Class Loader

On startup, Tomcat sets the Endorsed Standards Override Mechanism to point to the following directories, rather than the default ones mentioned earlier: CATALINA_HOME/bin and CATALINA_HOME/common/endorsed. The net result is that Tomcat's XML parser is preferred to the one shipped with Java when using JDK 1.4. Tomcat 5.5 without the compatibility patch uses JDK 5's XML parser, as described in Chapter 2.

Tomcat's Common Class Loader

Next in the hierarchy is Tomcat's common class loader that loads those classes available to Tomcat and all Web applications. It loads these class files from the following locations:

- CATALINA_HOME/common/lib/: For JAR files
- CATALINA_HOME/common/classes/: For class files
- CATALINA_HOME/common/i18n/: For class files relating to internationalized messages (Tomcat 5.5 only)

Tomcat includes a number of JAR files in CATALINA_HOME/common/lib/, as shown in Table 8-1.

Table 8-1. *The Contents of CATALINA_HOME/common/lib/*

JAR File	Description
ant.jar	The popular Apache Ant build and deploy tool. Tomcat 5.0.*x* only.
ant-launcher.jar	Tomcat can be started using an Ant task, and this library is part of the process. Tomcat 5.0.*x* only.
commons-collections.jar	The Jakarta Commons library of general-purpose code; the collections component adds features to the standard J2SE collections framework. Tomcat 5.0.*x* only.
commons-dbcp.jar	As mentioned in Chapter 7, the Commons database connection pooling (DBCP) mechanism provides database and object pooling services. Tomcat 5.0.*x* only.
commons-el.jar	The JSP 2.0 specification includes the JSP Expression Language (EL) for the first time. This library enables the EL.
commons-pool.jar	Another object pooling service. Tomcat 5.0.*x* only.

Table 8-1. *The Contents of CATALINA_HOME/common/lib/ (Continued)*

JAR File	Description
jasper-compiler.jar	The Jasper compiler, which turns JSP files into servlets.
jasper-compiler-jdt.jar	Tomcat 5.5 uses the Eclipse compiler. This file allows Tomcat to run with just a JRE as opposed to a JDK. Tomcat 5.5 only.
jasper-runtime.jar	More Jasper files—these execute JSP pages that have compiled into servlets.
jsp-api.jar	The JSP API classes. Versions of Tomcat 5 separate these from the Servlet API classes. Older Tomcat versions don't.
naming-common.jar	JNDI implementation—used to provide the default JNDI naming context as mentioned in Chapter 4.
naming-factory.jar	More JNDI support files—these are object factories exposed via the default JNDI context.
naming-factory-dbcp.jar	JNDI object factories based on the Jakarta Commons DBCP connection pooling technology. Tomcat 5.5 only.
naming-java.jar	More JNDI support files. Tomcat 5.0.*x* only.
naming-resources.jar	JNDI directory context implementation—provides interface for retrieving static resources.
servlet-api.jar	The Servlet API classes. Note that the JSP-specific classes are in `jsp-api.jar`.

Although developers can reference all these APIs, you shouldn't allow them to place their own classes or JARs in `CATALINA_HOME/common/lib`. If developers need classes and JAR files to be visible to all Web applications, you should place them where the shared class loader can see them. Note that this doesn't apply to well-known third-party libraries such as database drivers because Tomcat often needs to have access to these classes, especially if you're providing JDBC data sources.

Putting custom classes in the common class loader path is to be discouraged for at least two reasons:

- The custom classes could conceivably cause compatibility problems with Tomcat. For example, if you placed your own XML parser in this directory and it wasn't tested with Tomcat, it could introduce hard-to-fix bugs. The same would be true if you introduced an older version of the Servlet API into these paths.
- It's easy to forget which classes/JAR files belong to developers and which belong to Tomcat. Maintenance is therefore tricky, especially for others who wouldn't expect user classes to be in those locations.

Tomcat's Server Class Loader

Tomcat uses the server class loader to load the server-specific classes that aren't available to Web applications, as specified in the Servlet specification. They're stored in `CATALINA_HOME/server/lib` and `CATALINA_HOME/server/classes` (see Table 8-2).

Table 8-2. *The Contents of* `CATALINA_HOME/common/lib/`

JAR File	Description
`catalina.jar`	Catalina servlet container classes.
`catalina-ant.jar`	Support files that enable easy deployment via Ant.
`catalina-cluster.jar`	Support for Tomcat clustering.
`catalina-i18n-XX.jar`	Internationalization classes for Tomcat in Spanish, French, and Japanese. Tomcat 5.0.*x* only. These have been moved into `CATALINA_HOME/common/i18n` in Tomcat 5.5.
`catalina-optional.jar`	Classes for Tomcat features that aren't part of an official specification. For example, these include the valves and session managers discussed in Chapter 7.
`commons-beanutils.jar`	Easy-to-use wrappers for the Java reflection and introspection APIs. Thus, Tomcat can work with JavaBeans. Tomcat 5.0.*x* only. Tomcat 5.5 doesn't have any use for these classes, though the `admin` application uses them.
`commons-digester.jar`	A digester for XML-to-Java mapping commonly used for parsing XML configuration files. Tomcat 5.0.*x* only. Tomcat 5.5 doesn't have any use for these classes, though the `admin` application uses them.
`commons-fileupload.jar`	A file-upload facility. Tomcat 5.0.*x* only. Tomcat 5.5 doesn't have any use for these classes, though the `admin` application uses them.
`commons-modeler.jar`	A mechanism to create MBeans compatible with the Java Management Extensions (JMX) specification.
`jakarta-regexp-1.3.jar`	Jakarta's well-known Java regular expression implementation. Used by the request filter valves for one. Tomcat 5.0.*x* only. Tomcat 5.5 doesn't have any use for these classes.
`jkconfig.jar`	Configuration classes for the JK connector. Tomcat 5.0.*x* only. Replaced with `tomcat-ajp.jar` in Tomcat 5.5.
`jkshm.jar`	Configuration classes for the JK connector. Tomcat 5.0.*x* only. Replaced with `tomcat-ajp.jar` in Tomcat 5.5.
`servlets-XXX.jar`	Some of Tomcat's basic services, such as using SSI, using CGI, and serving static content, are provided by servlets. These JAR files contain such servlets.
`tomcat-ajp.jar`	JK connector classes. Tomcat 5.5 only.
`tomcat-coyote.jar`	Coyote connector classes.
`tomcat-http.jar`	HTTP/1.1 connector classes. Tomcat 5.5 only.
`tomcat-http11.jar`	HTTP/1.1 connector classes. Tomcat 5.0.*x* only. Replaced by `tomcat-http.jar` in Tomcat 5.5.
`tomcat-jk.jar`	JK connector classes. Tomcat 5.0.*x* only. Replaced with `tomcat-ajp.jar` in Tomcat 5.5.
`tomcat-jk2.jar`	JK2 connector classes. Tomcat 5.0.*x* only. Replaced with `tomcat-ajp.jar` in Tomcat 5.5.
`tomcat-jni.jar`	Classes for working with the Java Native Interface. Tomcat 5.0.*x* only.
`tomcat-util.jar`	Shared classes for the various and sundry Tomcat connectors.

Tomcat's Shared Class Loader

Unlike the common class loader, developers can place their own classes and JAR files into the shared class loader directories. These classes are available to all Web applications. The shared class loader looks in `CATALINA_HOME/shared/lib` and `CATALINA_HOME/shared/classes`.

Tomcat's Web Application Class Loader

Each Web application also has its own class loader, which looks in `CATALINA_HOME/webapps/[webapp]/WEB-INF/lib` and `/WEB-INF/classes` for JARs and class files. Two things make the Web application class loader unique. First, each Web application has its own instance of this class loader, which means that Web applications can't see other people's class files.

Second, the Web application class loader doesn't use the delegation pattern that class loaders are encouraged to use. Instead, it tries to load classes first, before delegating the request to the other class loaders. This behavior makes it easy for Web applications to override classes in the shared and common class loaders on a per–Web application basis.

Note that this doesn't mean the Web application class loader can override Java base classes. It can't.

The other exception is that the Web application class loader will always delegate the following class patterns:

- `javax.*`
- `org.xml.sax.*`
- `org.w3c.dom.*`
- `org.apache.xerces.*`
- `org.apache.xalan.*`

If a parent class loader doesn't load these patterns, then the Web application class loader will attempt to load them.

Revisiting Class Loader Order

To review how these various Tomcat class loaders work together, you'll now see what happens when an individual application requests a class. The following is a list of class loaders that will look for a class in the order attempted to find it:

1. The bootstrap class loader looks in the core Java classes.
2. The system class loader looks in the following places:
   - `CATALINA_HOME/bin/bootstrap.jar`
   - `CATALINA_HOME/bin/commons-logging-api.jar`
   - `JAVA_HOME/lib/tools.jar`
3. The Web application class loader looks in `CATALINA_HOME/webapp/[webapp]/WEB-INF/classes` and `CATALINA_HOME/webapp/[webapp]/WEB-INF/lib`.

4. The common class loader looks in `CATALINA_HOME/common/classes`, `CATALINA_HOME/common/endorsed`, and `CATALINA_HOME/common/lib` (and `CATALINA_HOME/common/i18n` for Tomcat 5.5).

5. The shared class loader looks in `CATALINA_HOME/shared/classes` and `CATALINA_HOME/shared/lib`.

Dynamic Class Reloading

As discussed earlier, once a class loader has loaded a class, it caches the class. This means that future requests for the class always receive the cached copy; thus, if the class on the file system is changed while the JVM is running, the new class will be ignored.

However, because Tomcat uses its own class loader to load each Web application, it can accomplish dynamic class reloading simply by halting the Web application and then reloading it using a new class loader. The Web application's original class loader is then orphaned and thus garbage collected at the JVM's convenience. This eliminates the need to restart the JVM when new versions of classes are deployed.

You have two mechanisms for instructing Tomcat to reload a Web application.

- You can configure Tomcat to scan `WEB-INF/classes` and `WEB-INF/lib` for changes.
- You can explicitly reload the Web application with the Tomcat manager application.

Tomcat doesn't direct its class loaders to dump their caches and reload from disk, but, rather, when it detects a change or receives an explicit reload instruction, it reloads and restarts the entire Web application.

Avoiding Class Loader Pitfalls

A couple of common problems occur when dealing with Tomcat's class loaders. The solutions to these problems come from the information covered previously.

Packages Split Among Different Class Loaders

Each class loader has its own unique namespace, which has a practical application in Tomcat. If you have multiple classes in the same package, the same class loader must load them all for them to have access to other class loaders' private, protected, or package-private members.

Singletons

A *singleton* is a class designed that can be instantiated only one time in any given JVM. Say a developer wants to share a singleton among multiple Web applications and wants to maintain the contract that only one instance be created in a single JVM.

Placing this class in the Web application class loader path means that each Web application will create a new instance of this class, which isn't what the developer intends. This is because each Web application has its own class loader and class loaders maintain distinct namespaces.

The solution is to place this class in the shared class loader path, where the singleton will be shared among all Web applications, as they all share the same class loader.

Summary

In this chapter you learned how class loaders abstract the process of loading class files before the first instantiation and make them available for use. Java's class loaders support loading classes from the local file system to the network and also give developers the facility to create their own custom class loaders. The three basic class loaders are the bootstrap, extension, and system class loaders.

Class loaders use the delegation model where every class loader passes the request to its parent until the bootstrap class loader is reached, and then each class loader looks for the class; if it can't find it, it goes back down the chain. Implementing the delegation model is optional, but class loaders can't function if they don't delegate to the bootstrap class loader at some point. Also, some advantages exist of having a unique namespace for each class loader.

The Java security model prevents the misuse of custom class loaders by allowing only the bootstrap class loader to load classes that start with `java.*`. Also, by using the security manager, an application can forbid the use of custom class loaders.

Lastly you saw that Tomcat has four class loaders: common, server, shared, and Web application. To share classes with all Web applications, users should use the shared class loader.

CHAPTER 9

Using Tomcat's Connectors

When you use Tomcat out of the box to run Web applications, it's able to serve HTML pages without any additional configuration. This is because it comes with an HTTP connector that can handle requests from a user's Web browser. Because of this connector, Tomcat can function as a stand-alone Web server and serve static HTML pages in addition to handling servlets and JSP pages.

Tomcat connectors provide the external interface to Tomcat clients. Two kinds of connectors exist—those that implement an HTTP stack of their own (called *HTTP connectors*) and those that link Tomcat to an external Web server such as Apache or IIS (called *Web server connectors*).

In this chapter, you'll see how to configure both types of Tomcat connectors. As mentioned earlier, you don't have to do any additional configuration to get the HTTP connector working. So why do you need this chapter? This chapter is useful if you need to modify the HTTP connector configuration (for example, to create a secure HTTPS connection) and if you want to use Tomcat with an external Web server. The reasons for doing so will become clear shortly.

Note that this chapter contains a reference to the HTTPS-related configuration, but the details of SSL setup are in Chapter 12.

Using the HTTP Connector

The HTTP connector is a Java class that implements HTTP. The connector in Tomcat 5.0.*x* is HTTP/1.1 (`org.apache.coyote.tomcat5.CoyoteConnector`), which implements the HTTP/1.1 protocol and listens on the connector port for incoming HTTP requests. The Tomcat 5.5 version is `org.apache.catalina.connector.Connector`, which is used for all the connectors described next.

Configuring the HTTP/1.1 Connector

Listing 9-1 shows the default Coyote HTTP/1.1 connector configuration (from `CATALINA_HOME/conf/server.xml`).

Listing 9-1. *The Default HTTP/1.1 Connector*

```
<!-- Define a non-SSL Coyote HTTP/1.1 Connector on port 8080 -->
<Connector port="8080"
           maxThreads="150"
           minSpareThreads="25"
           maxSpareThreads="75"
           enableLookups="false"
           redirectPort="8443"
           acceptCount="100"
           debug="0"
           connectionTimeout="20000"
           disableUploadTimeout="true" />
```

As with many components in Tomcat's configuration, some of these attributes are common to all connectors and some are unique to the HTTP connector. Chapter 4 shows how to deal with all these attributes. However, in this case the attributes specify that this service should listen to port 8080 for HTTP requests, set thread-handling information, disallow DNS lookups, and assign a port to which SSL requests should be sent (8443), among other things.

Configuring SSL on Tomcat

The connector for the service that supports HTTPS connections must have its `secure` attribute set to `true` and its `scheme` attribute set to `https`.

Listing 9-2 shows the SSL connector from `server.xml`. Note that it's commented out by default. Uncomment it, and make changes if required. If you change the SSL port (8443) to something else, you need to change the `redirectPort` attribute for all the non SSL connectors to that port number, too. The non-SSL connectors redirect users to this port if they try to access pages with a security constraint that specifies that SSL is required.

Listing 9-2. *The Default SSL Connector*

```
<!-- Define a SSL Coyote HTTP/1.1 Connector on port 8443 -->
<!--
<Connector port="8443"
           maxThreads="150"
           minSpareThreads="25"
           maxSpareThreads="75"
           enableLookups="false"
```

```
           disableUploadTimeout="true"
           acceptCount="100"
           debug="0"
           scheme="https"
           secure="true"
           clientAuth="false"
           sslProtocol="TLS" />
-->
```

For details of these attributes, see Chapter 4. The two important attributes here are scheme and secure. As noted previously, they're used to indicate that this is an SSL-enabled connector.

Working with Keystores

To use an SSL connector with Tomcat, you'll need to create a keystore. This contains the server's digital certificates, which are used by clients to validate the server. Once clients have accepted a certificate, they can use the public key it contains to encrypt any data it wants to send. The server for its part holds a private key, which is the only way to decrypt the data. Chapter 12 covers this subject, as well as all aspects of Tomcat security, in more detail. I'll leave the details until then, but this chapter will get your SSL connector up and running.

Note If you're using JDK 1.3 or older, you'll need to install Java Secure Socket Extension (JSSE). Download the API from `http://java.sun.com/products/jsse/`, and install the JAR files from `JSSE_HOME/lib` to `JAVA_HOME/jre/lib/ext` or set a `JSSE_HOME` environment variable to point to the location of JSSE.

To create the keystore, use the following command (assuming the `JAVA_HOME/bin` directory is in your path). `keytool` is a utility that comes as part of the J2SE distribution.

```
> keytool -genkey -alias tomcat -keyalg RSA
```

This creates a public-private key pair (-genkey), for user tomcat, with the RSA algorithm. The MD5 algorithm is also available, but RSA is recommended for Web use because of its compatibility with other Internet-aware applications. This method creates what's called a *self-signed* certificate. If you were serious about your security, you'd use a certificate issued by a certificate authority, a process that's discussed in Chapter 12. For now, you can test the mechanism with a self-signed certificate.

You'll be asked for a password; make sure you specify something other than the default. Once you've done this, you'll be asked for some details. The first and last name question is really asking for the name of your host. If you don't put the name of your host, then clients will be warned and the certificate may not be accepted, as shown in Figure 9-1.

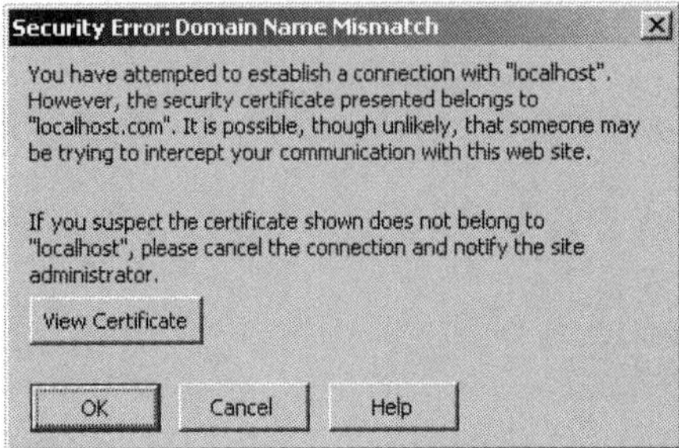

Figure 9-1. *A browser warning that the certificate may not be trustworthy*

Finally, add the password for the keystore to the SSL connector's entry in `server.xml`, as shown in Listing 9-3.

Listing 9-3. *Adding a Keystore Password to `server.xml`*

```
<Connector port="8443"
           maxThreads="150" minSpareThreads="25" maxSpareThreads="75"
           enableLookups="false" disableUploadTimeout="true"
           acceptCount="100" debug="0" scheme="https" secure="true"
           clientAuth="false" sslProtocol="TLS"
           keystorePass="tomcat"/>
```

Now start Tomcat, and visit `https://localhost:8443`. You'll be asked to accept the certificate because it's likely that your browser doesn't recognize your organization as a certificate authority. If you accept the certificate, you can continue to Tomcat's home page and view it using an SSL connection.

Running Tomcat Behind a Proxy Server

A common deployment scenario has Tomcat running behind a proxy server. In this kind of environment, the host name and port that the server should return to the client in the HTTP response should be those the client used in the original request and not the actual host name and port that on which Tomcat is running. This is controlled via the `proxyName` and `proxyPort` attributes of the connector.

Apache is a good candidate as a proxy server because of its robustness and all-around good grace. If you use Apache, you can use its proxy module (`mod_proxy`) to pass the servlet requests to the Tomcat server. Uncomment the following in Apache's `conf/httpd.conf` file:

```
LoadModule proxy_module libexec/mod_proxy.so
LoadModule proxy_http_module modules/mod_proxy_http.so
```

Next, add the following lines after the module definitions:

```
ProxyPass / http://localhost:8080/
ProxyPassReverse / http://localhost:8080/
```

The Apache server will now pass all requests to the Tomcat server.

On the Tomcat side, the configuration in `server.xml` for the HTTP connector is as shown in Listing 9-4.

Listing 9-4. *Defining a Proxy Name and Proxy Port in server.xml*

```
<!-- Define a non-SSL Coyote HTTP/1.1 Connector on port 8080 -->
<Connector port="8080"
        maxThreads="150" minSpareThreads="25" maxSpareThreads="75"
        enableLookups="false" redirectPort="8443" acceptCount="100"
        debug="0" connectionTimeout="20000"
        disableUploadTimeout="true"
        proxyName="localhost" proxyPort="80"/>
```

If you don't specify the `proxyName` and `proxyPort`, the response will indicate that it came from `http://localhost:8080` instead of `http://localhost`.

Using the AJP Connector

If you want another Web server, such as Apache or IIS, to handle the static content while Tomcat handles the dynamic content, you need the AJP connector. It works in conjunction with Apache's `mod_jk` or an IIS ISAPI module to deploy Web applications with the combination of Tomcat and another Web server. The following sections cover Apache 1.3.*x*, Apache 2.0.50, and IIS. A basic knowledge of Apache is assumed; the following URL may be of use as a quick reference: `http://httpd.apache.org/docs/install.html`.

Introducing mod_jk and mod_jk2

To integrate Tomcat with a Web server, you need a redirector module that will forward client requests for JSP pages and servlets from the Web server to Tomcat. You do this by matching the URL pattern of the request to a mapping in a configuration file. The JSP pages/servlets then handle the forwarded request, generate an appropriate dynamic response, and send it to the client via the module. To address this requirement, the Jakarta project provides modules called `mod_jk` and `mod_jk2`. The `mod_jk2` module is a refactored version of `mod_jk` and has been designed with Apache 2.0, Microsoft IIS, and other multithreaded Web servers in mind, though it still works with older Web servers such as Apache 1.3. Both modules use the same protocol to link Tomcat with the external Web server: the differences for the administrator are configuration and performance.

If you've previously configured Apache to use `mod_jserv`, remove any `ApJServMount` directives from your `httpd.conf` file. If you're including `tomcat-apache.conf` or `tomcat.conf`, you'll want to remove them as well, as they're specific to `mod_jserv`. These steps are necessary because the `mod_jserv` configuration directives aren't compatible with `mod_jk` and `mod_jk2`.

■ **Note** `mod_jserv` was a port of Apache JServ, the Apache server's servlet engine module. Unfortunately, this meant that a lot of unnecessary functionality was included with `mod_jserv`. After all, the idea was to talk to Tomcat, not do its job for it. This was not the only problem with the `mod_jserv` module. The fact that it could be used only on Apache running on Unix was a particularly limiting attribute.

The Apache JServ Protocol

The Apache JServ Protocol (AJP) is a packet-oriented, TCP/IP-based protocol. It provides a communication channel between the Apache Web server process and running instances of Tomcat. Various versions of this protocol are available, including versions 1.2, 1.3, and 1.4. AJP 1.3 is the most commonly used and well-tested version used by Tomcat, so it's the only version of the protocol I'll discuss.

AJP ensures good performance by reusing already open TCP-level connections with the Tomcat container and as such saves the overhead of opening new socket connections for each request. This is a concept similar to that of a connection pool and makes things simple by avoiding the cost of more opened connections. In the request-response cycle, when a connection is assigned to a particular request, it will not be reused until that request-response cycle is completed.

■ **Note** When integrating with IIS, you also use AJP as your protocol. Don't be deceived by the Apache in its name. This simply refers to the provider of the protocol and the module, not to the Web server.

Worker Implementations

A *worker* is a Tomcat instance that serves JSP/servlet requests coming from another Web server. In most cases, there's only a single Tomcat process, but sometimes you'll need to run multiple workers to implement load balancing or site partitioning (mainly required for sites with heavy traffic). You'll see how to achieve this with both versions of Apache and IIS in the following sections.

Each worker is identified by a host name/IP and port number combination. Here *host* means the machine on which the given Tomcat instance is running, and *port* refers to the port on which that instance is listening for any requests.

Multiple Tomcat Workers

You may use a multiple worker setup in a number of situations:

- You may want different contexts to be served by different Tomcat workers. This setup will provide a development environment where all the developers share the same Web server but own a Tomcat worker of their own.
- You may want different virtual hosts served by different Tomcat processes to provide a clear separation between sites belonging to different entities.

- You may want to provide load balancing, where you run multiple Tomcat workers each on a machine of its own (or maybe on the same machine) and distribute the requests between them.

Integrating Tomcat with Apache 1.3 Using mod_jk

mod_jk isn't available as a binary for Apache 1.3 if you're using Linux, though you can build it from source, as shown next. It's available as a binary for Apache 2.0. A Windows DLL (rename it to mod_jk.dll) and shared objects exist for other platforms. You can find all these via the Jakarta binaries download page. After downloading the DLL or shared object, move it to the modules subdirectory of Apache.

To build the module on Linux (and other Unix-like systems), extract the download to a convenient location and navigate to the jk/native subdirectory. Here you should run the following commands (modifying the path to your Apache 1.3 apxs):

```
> ./configure --with-apxs=/usr/sbin/apxs
> make
> cp ./apache-1.3/mod_jk.so /usr/lib/apache/modules
```

The first command configures the build so that the resultant module is compatible with Apache 1.3 (or whichever version of Apache you specify because this command is equally applicable to Apache 2.0). The make command builds the module, and the final command copies the built module to Apache's modules directory.

Configuring the AJP Connector in server.xml

The AJP connector configuration in server.xml is already present. This makes configuration easy, as you don't need to do anything at all.

Setting the workers.properties File

Each running Tomcat instance is represented as a single worker. You can set up Tomcat workers for the Web server plug-in by using a simple properties file called workers.properties, which is used only with mod_jk and not mod_jk2. This file consists of entries that will convey information about Tomcat workers to the Web server plug-in.

Format of workers.properties File

The format used by workers.properties for defining a list of available workers is as follows:

```
worker.list = <comma-separated list of worker names>
```

For example, here you define two workers named worker1 and worker2:

```
worker.list = worker1, worker2
```

You can also define a property for a given worker, as follows:

```
worker.<worker name>.<property> = <property value>
```

For example, you can assign the value `localhost` to the `host` attribute of `worker1`, like so:

```
worker.worker1.host = localhost
```

Types of Workers in mod_jk

Any defined Tomcat worker needs to be assigned a type. You can assign the following types to various Tomcat workers:

- `ajp13`: This type of worker uses the AJP 1.3 protocol to forward requests to out-of-process Tomcat workers.
- `lb`: This type of worker is used for load balancing. In a load-balancing scenario, this type of worker doesn't handle any processing; it just handles the communication between a Web server and other defined Tomcat workers of type `ajp13`. This kind of worker supports round-robin load balancing with a certain level of fault tolerance. You'll see this in more detail in the "Understanding Tomcat Load Balancing" section.

For example, the following line sets the type of `worker1` to `ajp13`, meaning it will use the AJP 1.3 protocol:

```
worker.worker1.type=ajp13
```

Worker Properties

After you've set a worker's type, you can set a number of other properties. You can set the port on which the worker listens as shown next. However, if your worker is of type `ajp13`, it will listen for AJP requests, by default, on port 8009.

```
worker.worker1.port=8009
```

Next you configure the host where the Tomcat worker is listening for requests. For example, if `worker1` is running on `localhost`, then set the entry as follows:

```
worker.worker1.host=localhost
```

When working with a load balancer worker, you need to set the load-balancing factor for this worker. For example, if `worker1` is running with a load balancer, then, depending on the hardware condition of the machine, you can set the corresponding load factor as follows:

```
worker.worker1.lbfactor=5
```

Some Web servers (for example, Apache 2.0 and IIS) are multithreaded, and Tomcat can take advantage of this by keeping a number of connections open as a cache, though you shouldn't use `mod_jk` with these servers because of `mod_jk2`'s superior multithreaded abilities. An appropriately high value based on the average number of concurrent users for Tomcat can prove beneficial from a performance point of view (the default is 1).

```
worker.worker1.cachesize=20
```

Configuring a Tomcat Worker

Create `workers.properties` in `CATALINA_HOME/conf`, as shown in Listing 9-5.

Listing 9-5. *`workers.properties` for mod_jk*

```
# For Windows:
# Setting Tomcat & Java Home
workers.tomcat_home="c:\jakarta-tomcat"
workers.java_home="c:\j2sdk1.4.2"
ps=\
worker.list=worker1
# Settings for worker1 worker
worker.worker1.port=8009
worker.worker1.host=localhost
worker.worker1.type=ajp13

# -----------------------

# For Linux/Unix systems:
# Setting Tomcat & Java Home
workers.tomcat_home=/usr/java/jakarta-tomcat
workers.java_home=/usr/java/j2sdk1.4.2
ps=/
worker.list=worker1
# Settings for worker1 worker
worker.worker1.port=8009
worker.worker1.host=localhost
worker.worker1.type=ajp13
```

The `ps=\` line sets the path separator for the operating system on which Tomcat is running.

Configuration Settings for Apache

Tomcat and Apache can communicate once the information about the available Tomcat workers is included in the `httpd.conf` Apache Web server configuration file. You have two ways in which to do this, both of which are discussed next.

Autogenerating Configuration Settings

You can configure Tomcat to automatically generate a configuration file called `mod_jk.conf`. You can then include this in the main Apache configuration file.

The mod_jk.conf file is created every time Tomcat starts, so make sure you really can afford this overhead. Also, this will reset all your deployment settings, as Tomcat overwrites the file every time.

To generate the settings, you need to add special listeners at the server and host levels. Just add the code in Listing 9-6 after the <Server port="8005"> declaration.

Listing 9-6. *A Listener That Will Autogenerate mod_jk Settings*

```
<Listener className="org.apache.jk.config.ApacheConfig"
    modJk="C:/Program Files/Apache Group/Apache/modules/mod_jk.dll"
    workersConfig="C:/jakarta-tomcat/conf/workers.properties"
    jkLog="C:/jakarta-tomcat/logs/mod_jk.log"
    jkDebug="info"
/>
```

Here you provide the necessary information to the listener. It creates appropriate entries, such as the LoadModule entries for mod_jk, in the autogenerated mod_jk.conf file using this information. Here you provide the location of the workers.properties file, the location of the mod_jk module, the location of the log file, and the level of logging information you require.

Table 9-1 describes the attributes supported by the ApacheConfig listener.

Table 9-1. *The Attributes of the ApacheConfig Listener*

Attribute	Description	Required?
configHome	The default parent directory for all the paths provided as attribute values. It's overridden when absolute paths are provided for any attribute value. The default is CATALINA_HOME.	No
jkConfig	The location of the Apache mod_jk.conf file. The default is CATALINA_HOME/conf/auto/mod_jk.conf.	No
workersConfig	The path to the workers.properties file used by mod_jk. The default is CATALINA_HOME/conf/jk/workers.properties.	No
modJk	The path to the Apache mod_jk module. If not set, this defaults to modules/mod_jk.dll on Windows and modules/mod_jk.so on Linux/Unix systems.	No
jkLog	The path to the log file that mod_jk uses.	No
jkDebug	The level of logging to be done by mod_jk. May be debug, info, error, or emerg. If not set, this defaults to emerg.	No
jkWorker	The desired worker. This must be set to one of the workers defined in the workers.properties file and defaults to ajp13.	No
forwardAll	If this is set to true (the default), mod_jk will forward all requests to Tomcat. This ensures that all the behavior configured in web.xml functions correctly. If false, Apache will serve static resources. Note that when set to false, some of Tomcat's configuration may not be duplicated in Apache, so check the generated mod_jk.conf file to see what configuration is actually being set in Apache.	No

Table 9-1. *The Attributes of the* `ApacheConfig` *Listener (Continued)*

Attribute	Description	Required?
`noRoot`	If this attribute is set to `true`, the `ROOT` context isn't mapped to Tomcat. If `false` and `forwardAll` is `true`, all requests to the `ROOT` context are mapped to Tomcat. If `false` and `forwardAll` is `false`, only JSP page and servlet requests to the `ROOT` context are mapped to Tomcat. When `false`, to correctly serve Tomcat's `ROOT` context, you must also modify the `DocumentRoot` setting in Apache's `httpd.conf` file to point to Tomcat's `ROOT` context directory. Otherwise, Apache will serve some content, such as `index.html`, before `mod_jk` can get the request and pass it on to Tomcat. The default is `true`.	No
`append`	Append the generated configuration file to the current configuration file. The default is `false`. Therefore, it's a good idea to back up the values in another file and reference it from Apache.	No

The next step is to create an Apache `<VirtualHost>` entry in the resultant `mod_jk.conf` file. This ensures that all requests to the Tomcat host are mapped to the Apache host correctly. Add a listener below each `<Host>` entry that you're integrating, as shown in Listing 9-7.

Listing 9-7. *A Listener That Will Define Virtual Hosts in* `mod_jk.conf`

```
<Listener className="org.apache.jk.config.ApacheConfig"
          append="true"
          jkWorker="worker1" />
```

You can also choose individual Tomcat contexts by adding the listener after the `<Context>` in the context XML file. Now start Tomcat, and open the `CATALINA_HOME/conf/auto/mod_jk.conf` file. If you had used the previous values, your file should look like the one in Listing 9-8.

Listing 9-8. *The Autogenerated* `mod_jk.conf` *File*

```
<IfModule !mod_jk.c>
  LoadModule jk_module "C:/Program Files/Apache Group/Apache/modules/mod_jk.dll"
</IfModule>

JkWorkersFile "C:/jakarta-tomcat/conf/workers.properties"
JkLogFile "C:/jakarta-tomcat/logs/mod_jk.log"

JkLogLevel info

<VirtualHost localhost>
    ServerName localhost
```

```
    JkMount /admin worker1
    JkMount /admin/* worker1

    JkMount /servlets-examples worker1
    JkMount /servlets-examples/* worker1

    JkMount /webdav worker1
    JkMount /webdav/* worker1

    JkMount /jsp-examples worker1
    JkMount /jsp-examples/* worker1

    JkMount /balancer worker1
    JkMount /balancer/* worker1

    JkMount /tomcatBook worker1
    JkMount /tomcatBook/* worker1

    JkMount /tomcat-docs worker1
    JkMount /tomcat-docs/* worker1

    JkMount /manager worker1
    JkMount /manager/* worker1
</VirtualHost>
```

The JkMount directive mounts a Tomcat directory onto the Apache root Web context. The other three JK directives are pretty self-explanatory.

```
JkWorkersFile "C:/jakarta-tomcat/conf/workers.properties"
JkLogFile "C:/jakarta-tomcat/logs/mod_jk.log"
JkLogLevel info
```

The log file is where any AJP-specific information is placed. Access logs for resources on Tomcat and Apache function as normal.

Each time Tomcat is started, it will write the configuration file to CATALINA_HOME/conf/auto/mod_jk.conf. As a result, your settings will be overwritten. Therefore, you should either disable the autogeneration option by commenting out the directive in server.xml or copy the file to another location.

The final step is to include this file in Apache's httpd.conf file as follows. Place this entry at the end of the file.

```
Include "C:/jakarta-tomcat/conf/auto/mod_jk.conf"
```

Adding Configuration Settings Manually

If you don't want to use ApacheConfig, you need to append the previous settings to the end of your httpd.conf or save them as mod_jk.conf in CATALINA_HOME/conf/auto.

Testing the Final Setup

Next, you'll see how Apache accepts every request. All the requests for any dynamic processing, like JSP pages or servlets, will be handed over to Tomcat. Similarly, any response from them will be sent to the client through Apache.

The first step for testing will be to check the JSP examples Web application by pointing a browser at http://localhost/jsp-examples/. If everything is set up correctly, you should see the list of examples.

This shows that the integrated combination of Tomcat and Apache is working fine for serving static content. Now check whether mod_jk is doing its job equally well for serving dynamic content by clicking one of the examples.

After testing the deployment from a local machine, test the installation from any other machine across the network. This will make sure the settings you made are working as expected.

Integrating Tomcat with Apache 2.0 Using mod_jk2

Using mod_jk2 is similar to the previous instructions, though Tomcat is no longer the place to generate mappings.

Configuring the AJP Connector in server.xml

The AJP connector configuration in server.xml is already present. This makes configuration easy, as you don't need to do anything at all.

Setting the workers2.properties File

Each running Tomcat instance is represented as a single worker. You can set up Tomcat workers for the Web server plug-in by using a simple properties file called workers2.properties. This file consists of entries that will convey information about Tomcat workers to the Web server plug-in. The workers2.properties is kept in Apache's conf directory by default.

Format of workers2.properties File

The format used by workers2.properties for defining a list of available workers is as follows:

```
[TYPE:NAME]
PROPERTY=VALUE
```

You also have the option of using the old format from mod_jk.

To define a connection to a running Tomcat instance, you should define a channel.socket component:

```
[channel.socket:localhost:8009]
```

This example will communicate with a Tomcat instance running on the localhost host that listens on port 8009. Once you've defined a connection, you must add a worker and assign it to an existing channel:

```
[ajp13:localhost:8009]
channel=channel.socket:localhost:8009
```

In this case, ajp13 is the type of worker and localhost:8009 is the name of the worker. The name has been chosen as a reminder of its host and port, though changing these in the name won't change the actual connection to the Tomcat instance.

Types of Workers in mod_jk2

Any defined Tomcat worker needs to be assigned a type. You can assign the following types to various Tomcat workers:

- ajp13: This type of worker uses the AJP 1.3 protocol to forward requests to out-of-process Tomcat workers.
- lb: This type of worker is used for load balancing. In a load-balancing scenario, this type of worker doesn't handle any processing; it just handles the communication between a Web server and other defined Tomcat workers of type ajp13. This kind of worker supports round-robin load balancing with a certain level of fault tolerance. You'll see this in more detail in the "Understanding Tomcat Load Balancing" section.
- status: This is an internal mod_jk2 worker, which displays monitoring information as HTML. As such, it doesn't connect to any Tomcat instance.

Worker Properties

After you've set a worker's type, you can set a number of other properties. The host and port on which the worker listens is defined on the channel to which it belongs.

When working with a load balancer worker, you need to set the load-balancing factor for this worker. For example, if localhost:8009 is running with a load balancer, then, depending on the hardware condition of the machine, you can set the corresponding load factor.

```
[ajp13:localhost:8009]
channel=channel.socket:localhost:8009
lb_factor=2
```

Some Web servers (for example, Apache 2.0 and IIS) are multithreaded, and Tomcat can take advantage of this by keeping a number of connections open as a cache. An appropriately high value based on the average number of concurrent users for Tomcat can prove beneficial from a performance point of view (the default is 0).

```
[ajp13:localhost:8009]
channel=channel.socket:localhost:8009
lb_factor=2
max_connections=10
```

Configuring a Tomcat Worker

Create workers2.properties in Apache 2.0's conf directory, as shown in Listing 9-9.

Listing 9-9. *workers2.properties*

```
[channel.socket:localhost:8009]

[ajp13:localhost:8009]
channel=channel.socket:localhost:8009

[status:statusWorker]
styleMode=1

[uri:/jkstatus]
group=status:statusWorker

[uri:/jsp-examples/*]
worker=ajp13:localhost:8009
```

This defines an ajp13 worker called localhost:8009 and a status worker called statusWorker. The [uri:] sections assign a URI to a worker. So, /jkstatus is assigned to statusWorker, and everything under /jsp-examples is assigned to localhost:8009. This configuration uses the default logger, which on an Apache server is the error.log log file.

Configuration Settings for Apache

Tomcat and Apache can communicate once the information about the available Tomcat workers is included in the httpd.conf Apache Web server configuration file. You have two ways to do this, both of which I discuss next.

Autogenerating Configuration Settings

You have two ways to autoconfigure settings, though they use the same Java class. This class is called org.apache.jk.config.WebXml2Jk, and it converts web.xml settings into mod_jk2 settings.

The first method is at the command line. Run the following command, which specifies the location of the web.xml file you want to convert:

```
> java -classpath
  %CATALINA_HOME%/server/lib/jkconfig.jar;
  %CATALINA_HOME%/bin/commons-logging-api.jar;
  %CATALINA_HOME%/server/lib/tomcat-util.jar
    org.apache.jk.config.WebXml2Jk
    -context /jsp-examples
    -docBase %CATALINA_HOME%/webapps/jsp-examples
    -host localhost
```

This creates three files in WEB-INF/jk2 of the Web application specified with the -docBase switch. You can use the jk.conf file with mod_jk though it's not as efficient as the techniques used previously. The jk2.conf file is the mod_jk2 version, and you include it in Apache's httpd.conf file. The jk2map.properties file contains the mappings for workers2.properties. Copy these settings across to workers2.properties, and add the following include to Apache's httpd.conf file:

```
Include "C:/jakarta-tomcat/webapps/jsp-examples/WEB-INF/jk2/jk2.conf"
```

The second way to autogenerate settings is to use org.apache.jk.config.WebXml2Jk through Ant. You may already have a build.xml file from an earlier chapter. If that's the case, just add the task definition and the target from Listing 9-10 to it. If not, create a file called build.xml and add the code from Listing 9-10.

Listing 9-10. *Using Ant to Generate mod_jk2 Settings*

```
<project name="Jk2Application" default="jk2Generate" basedir=".">

  <taskdef name="jk2Generate"
           classname="org.apache.jk.config.WebXml2Jk"/>

  <target name="jk2Generate" description="Generate JK2 Settings">
    <jk2Generate
      docBase="C:/jakarta-tomcat-5.0.27/webapps/jsp-examples"
      context="/jsp-examples"
      host="localhost" />
  </target>
</project>
```

You must make sure that commons-logging-api.jar, tomcat-util.jar, and jkconfig.jar are in Ant's classpath. (Placing them in ANT_HOME/lib is one way to do this.) Once this is done, you simply have to run the following command to create the mod_jk2 configuration, assuming you're in the same directory as the previous build.xml file:

```
> ant
```

Testing the Final Setup

In this section, you'll see how Apache accepts every request. All the requests for any dynamic processing, such as JSP pages or servlets, will be handed over to Tomcat. Similarly, any response from them will be sent to the client through Apache.

The first step for testing will be to check the JSP examples Web application by pointing a browser at http://localhost/jsp-examples/. If everything is set up correctly, you should see the list of examples.

This shows that the integrated combination of Tomcat and Apache is working fine for serving static content. Now check whether mod_jk2 is doing its job equally well for serving dynamic content by clicking one of the examples.

After testing the deployment from a local machine, test the installation from any other machine across the network. This will make sure that the settings you made are working as expected.

Finally, visit `http://localhost/jkstatus`, and you'll see a screen similar to that in Figure 9-2. You can use various pieces of information to analyze and monitor the Tomcat-Apache bridge.

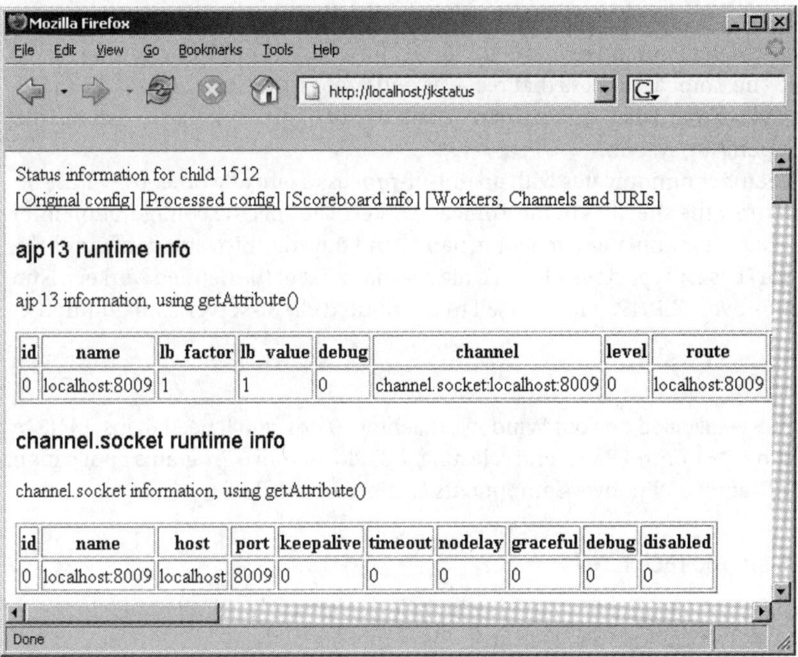

Figure 9-2. *mod_jk2's status screen*

Integrating Tomcat with IIS

IIS is Microsoft's Web server and is optimized for the Windows operating system. Why would you want to run IIS with Tomcat? You may want to do this in an environment that needs to be capable of supporting multiple development platforms, such as Microsoft's ASP and the alternative JSP. Also, you get better performance on Windows by using the Web serving capability of IIS and Tomcat as the servlet/JSP container instead of using Tomcat as both a Web server and a servlet container.

IIS is a Web server but can also process ASP, which is Microsoft's answer to server-side scripting. It doesn't have a servlet container and can't by default process JSP pages and servlets. However, you can extend IIS by adding ISAPI filters, which you can then use to configure third-party components such as servlets and JSP pages. ISAPI filters are plug-ins to IIS that filter incoming requests, perform custom processing, call other applications, and perform filtering functions on output that's to be sent to the client. The Apache group has created an ISAPI filter that can be added to IIS and configured so that IIS handles all requests except for JSP pages and servlets, which it redirects to Tomcat.

Introducing ISAPI

The ISAPI redirector that enables integration between IIS and Tomcat is available for download as a DLL called `isapi_redirector2.dll` from the usual range of Apache mirrors. ISAPI is Microsoft's answer to CGI, and it allows Microsoft to customize and extend the functionality of IIS. The `isapi_redirector2.dll` file is referred to as a *redirector* because it filters incoming URL requests and redirects some of them to Tomcat using AJP.

The filters processed by `isapi_redirector2.dll` are configurable. As this redirector is based on `mod_jk2`, these are specified in a file called `workers2.properties`, which uses the same settings as the Apache configuration described previously. This makes it extremely easy to port your Apache `mod_jk2` settings over to an IIS setup.

You can specify which incoming requests IIS should forward to Tomcat by editing the contents of this file. The Tomcat process that receives and processes requests from the ISAPI redirector is called the *worker*. The Tomcat worker exists as out of process, that is, as a distinct process within the operating system.

The ISAPI redirector communicates with an out-of-process Tomcat worker over TCP/IP using AJP and must know the specifics of the Tomcat worker. The specific configuration information could be an IP port number and machine name, and the administrator configures this information in the `workers2.properties` file. This file also has a list of the defined workers. Note that since AJP 1.3 runs over TCP/IP, it lends itself to distributed client-server configurations.

Installing IIS

Check to verify that IIS is installed on your Windows machine. If not, you'll need to install IIS by going to Start ➤ Settings ➤ Control Panel and selecting the Add/Remove Programs application. Look under the Add/Remove Windows Components section to install IIS.

Downloading the isapi_redirector2.dll

Once you have IIS on your system, the next thing to do is download the ISAPI redirector (`isapi_redirector2.dll`) from an Apache mirror. Place this file in the `CATLINA_HOME\bin` directory. Note that you can also build a copy of this `.dll` from source, but the easiest thing to do is to download the binary version.

Configuring the AJP Connector in server.xml

The AJP connector configuration in `server.xml` is already present. This makes configuration easy, as you don't need to do anything at all.

Setting the workers2.properties File

As mentioned, you set up Tomcat workers for the Web server plug-in by using the simple properties file called `workers2.properties`. This file consists of entries that will convey information about Tomcat workers to the Web server plug-in. Unlike with Apache, you can place `workers2.properties` wherever you like, though you must tell IIS where it is. You'll see how to do this in the next section. For a description of the `workers2.properties` file, see the Apache 2.0 "Setting the workers2.properties File" section.

Creating the Registry Entries

The ISAPI redirector (isapi_redirector2.dll) uses certain registry entries to initialize its configuration. These entries need to be created so that Tomcat can locate the configuration files that tell the redirector where to send incoming requests for servlets and how to log messages. Create a file called iis_redirect.reg, and edit it as follows:

```
REGEDIT4

[HKEY_LOCAL_MACHINE\SOFTWARE\Apache Software Foundation\Jakarta Isapi
Redirector\2.0]
"serverRoot"="C:\\jakarta-tomcat"
"extensionUri"="/jakarta/isapi_redirector2.dll"
"workersFile"="C:\\jakarta-tomcat\\conf\\workers2IIS.properties"
```

Don't use relative path names. Most problems with registering the isapi_redirector2.dll filter in IIS are associated with incorrect path names in the registry.

Let's take a look at each of the registry entries.

- serverRoot: This is the directory where you've installed Tomcat.
- extensionUri: This is the URL to the isapi-redirector extension. Note that jakarta is a virtual directory within IIS that you'll create later in the installation procedure.
- workersFile: This is the path to the workers2.properties file.

To create the registry entries, double-click the iis_redirect.reg file, and you'll get a warning message box. Select Yes to create the registry entries, and the script will create the values in the registry. At this point, you should open the registry using the regedt32 utility and verify the registry entry keys that were created for you under HKEY_LOCAL_MACHINE\SOFTWARE\Apache Software Foundation\Jakarta Isapi Redirector\2.0.

Note that you could also have created these entries manually, but the previous procedure creates an easy starting point. If you need to uninstall Tomcat at some point, you can remove these registry entries manually by deleting them using the regedt32 utility.

■ **Caution** You should be cautious while modifying the registry, as mistakes can prevent a Windows application from working correctly.

Configuring a Tomcat Worker

Create workers2IIS.properties as shown in Listing 9-11. You need to place this file in the directory you specified in the "Creating the Registry Entries" section. The path in the registry to this key is HKEY_LOCAL_MACHINE\SOFTWARE\Apache Software Foundation\Jakarta Isapi Redirector\2.0\workerFile. In your case, the directory is the %CATALINA_HOME%\conf directory.

Listing 9-11. *workers2IIS.properties*

```
[channel.socket:localhost:8009]

[ajp13:localhost:8009]
channel=channel.socket:localhost:8009

[status:statusWorker]
styleMode=1

[uri:/jkstatus]
group=status:statusWorker

[uri:/jsp-examples/*]
worker=ajp13:localhost:8009
```

This defines an `ajp13` worker called `localhost:8009` and a status worker called `statusWorker`. The `[uri:]` sections assign a URI to a worker. So, `/jkstatus` is assigned to `statusWorker`, and everything under `/jsp-examples` is assigned to `localhost:8009`. You set a log file when you configured the registry entries previously.

Configuration Settings for IIS

You need to create a virtual directory within IIS for the ISAPI redirector because the IIS redirector is an IIS plug-in; that is, it's a filter and an extension. IIS calls the filter function for incoming requests. If the incoming URL matches the list of filters maintained in `workers2IIS.properties`, control is transferred to the extension in the form `/jakarta/isapi_redirector2.dll`—you may remember this entry from the registry setting for the `extensionUri` that you set up. To create the virtual directory, you should do the following:

1. Open IIS Manager (Internet Services Manager).
2. Right-click Default Web Site, and select New ➤ Virtual Directory.
3. The Virtual Directory Creation Wizard will open. Use `jakarta` as the name of the virtual directory alias. Note that the name of the virtual directory has to be `jakarta` because of the previous registry entry.
4. The wizard will prompt you for a directory. Specify the directory of the installed `isapi_redirector2.dll`. This is the `bin\` directory under the root Tomcat install.
5. The wizard will prompt you for access permissions. The access permissions should be just read and execute.

Once you've created the `jakarta` virtual directory, it's a good idea to open it to review the properties you've set for the virtual directory. You can do this by right-clicking the virtual directory and selecting Properties.

You can now install the ISAPI redirector in IIS. To do this, follow these steps:

1. In IIS Manager, right-click Default Web Site, select Properties from the drop-down menu, and click it to open the Properties window.
2. In the Properties window, click the ISAPI Filters tab.
3. Click the Add button.

You'll be prompted for the name of the filter and the location of `isapi_redirector2.dll`. For the name of the filter, use `jakarta`. Use the Browse button to select `isapi_redirector2.dll`, which is in `%CATALINA_HOME%\bin` directory.

Close IIS Manager if you have it open, and restart IIS. Make sure you do this using the Services management console in the Control Panel. Don't do this using IIS Manager. You'll need to restart two services—these are the IIS Admin service and the World Wide Web Publishing service, though the console may do this automatically.

After you've restarted IIS, open up IIS Manager, check to see that there's a green arrow pointing upward next to the ISAPI redirector that you've just installed. If you don't see the green arrow, then there's a problem with the install of the ISAPI redirector. This is a common error encountered during a first install.

Check your registry entries and the configuration files. Nine times out of ten, problems with this part of the install occur because the paths set in the registry settings for `workersFile` (`workers2IIS.properties`) are wrong. If these files are in the correct locations and the registry keys are defined properly, that is, names are spelled correctly, the ISAPI redirector should load regardless of the content in these files and regardless of the values of the other registry settings. As an experiment, place a blank `workers2IIS.properties` file in the correct location and restart IIS.

Restart IIS by restarting the IIS Admin service and the World Wide Web Publishing service. Verify that the path you've specified to `isapi_redirector2.dll` when adding the filter is valid.

Testing the Final Setup

In this section, you'll see how IIS accepts every request. All the requests for any dynamic processing, such as JSP pages or servlets, will be handed over to Tomcat. Similarly, any response from them will be sent to the client through IIS.

The first step for testing will be to check the JSP examples Web application by pointing a browser at `http://localhost/jsp-examples/`. If everything is set up correctly, you should see the list of examples.

This shows that the integrated combination of Tomcat and IIS is working fine for serving static content. Now check whether the ISAPI redirector is doing its job equally well for serving dynamic content by clicking one of the examples.

After testing the deployment from a local machine, test the installation from any other machine across the network. This will make sure that the settings you made are working as expected.

Finally, visit `http://localhost/jkstatus`, and you'll see a screen similar to that in Figure 9-2. You can use various pieces of information to analyze and monitor the Tomcat-Apache bridge.

Troubleshooting the IIS Setup

If you don't see the screens described in the previous figures, then one of a number of things could have gone wrong with your setup. Verify that IIS is running. You can do this in the Services console. At a minimum, you need to have the IIS Admin service and the World Wide Web Publishing service running.

Within IIS check that you've installed the ISAPI redirector properly. If you've installed it properly, it should have a green arrow next to it.

Verify that you've defined the `jakarta` virtual directory properly. If there's something wrong with it, IIS will indicate this by flagging it with a red symbol. Check that the name of this virtual directory is indeed `jakarta`.

Look within the IIS log. The IIS log is by default located in `C:\WINNT\system32\LogFiles\W3SVC1`; you can also click the Properties button in the Web site Properties window to see where it is. By default a different log file is generated every day. In the log file you should see the following entry:

```
01:10:33 127.0.0.1 GET /jakarta/isapi_redirector2.dll 200
```

If this entry doesn't exist in the IIS log, then the ISAPI redirector isn't called by IIS. The value 200 is the HTTP status code. If the call to `isapi_redirector2.dll` exists but you're getting a status code such as 400, 404, or 500, then you have an error.

Make sure Tomcat is running and that the connector is listening on the correct port. This is port 8009 by default and is defined in the `server.xml` file. You can review this by opening a DOS prompt and running the command `netstat -a` from the command line. You should see a line similar to the following line as one of the entries:

```
TCP  localaddress:8009 foreignaddress:0  LISTENING
```

You may want to check that you don't have any additional filters defined besides the ISAPI redirector, which may be creating a conflict. If you do have additional filters defined in IIS, you may want to try removing them.

Verify the content of the `workers2IIS.properties` file. Check that you've defined the worker correctly.

Configuring Distributed Networks with Tomcat

So far, you've seen a configuration where you have both the Web server, be that IIS or Apache, and Tomcat running on the same physical server. This is useful for smaller implementations. However, in a production environment, you may be interested in a more scalable solution where you'd like to partition your architecture into multiple tiers so that the presentation layer or static HTML pages are served up by IIS or Apache on one machine and the Web applications are hosted by Tomcat workers each residing on a separate server. This makes the system more scalable because you have dedicated machines performing dedicated tasks.

In addition to scalability, you may also be interested in a distributed configuration to support multiple development and test environments, virtual hosting, and load-balanced Tomcat workers. In this section, you'll build on the previous concepts and look at the configuration changes required to build scalable distributed configurations of Web servers and Tomcat. This section deals with `mod_jk2` and its ISAPI equivalent, though the discussion is equally applicable to `mod_jk`.

First, let's look at the software on each sever. The server that has the static Web server running on it will also host the AJP module and the configuration file (`workers2.properties`). Note that the JDK and the Tomcat binaries aren't required on this server.

The server that has the full Tomcat install must have a connector and a Tomcat worker configured on it, and the Tomcat worker must be running on a known port. Note that if you had multiple Tomcat workers distributed across multiple servers servicing the same Web application, you'd want to duplicate the Web application files across all these servers.

Second, let's look at the configuration changes required. The following shows how to specify a worker on another server in `workers2.properties`:

```
[channel.socket:remoteserver:8009]

[ajp13:remoteserver:8009]
channel=channel.socket:remoteserver:8009

[status:statusWorker]
styleMode=1

[uri:/jkstatus]
group=status:statusWorker

[uri:/jsp-examples/*]
```

It's as easy as that, though this example simply uses a single Tomcat worker on a remote machine. You could have multiple Web servers that make up a Web server farm, which is load balanced using a load-balancing switch. The next section describes this scenario, which was also touched on in Chapter 7.

These configurations are possible with AJP, and the concepts remain the same whether you're using Apache or IIS as the Web server. The previous sections have covered this extensively, and the configuration file settings are identical for all servers.

Finally, notice that once you begin partitioning your architecture into Web server and application server configurations, you have paved the way for a heterogeneous system, so even though you use IIS for the Web server, your application server can be Linux based. It's now time to discuss load balancing.

Understanding Tomcat Load Balancing

On busy sites, whenever a request call is delegated from the Apache server to Tomcat, it's a good idea to route these requests to multiple Tomcat servers rather than to a single one, which you can do with `mod_jk2`. `mod_jk2` manages the task of load balancing with support for seamless sessions and round-robin scheduling.

Let's first look at the concept of a seamless session (also known as *session affinity* or a *sticky session*). When a client requests any dynamic resource, such as a JSP page, for the first time, the load balancer will route this request to any of the available Tomcat instances. Now, any further request from the same browser session should be routed to the same Tomcat container instance to keep the user session alive (see Figure 9-3).

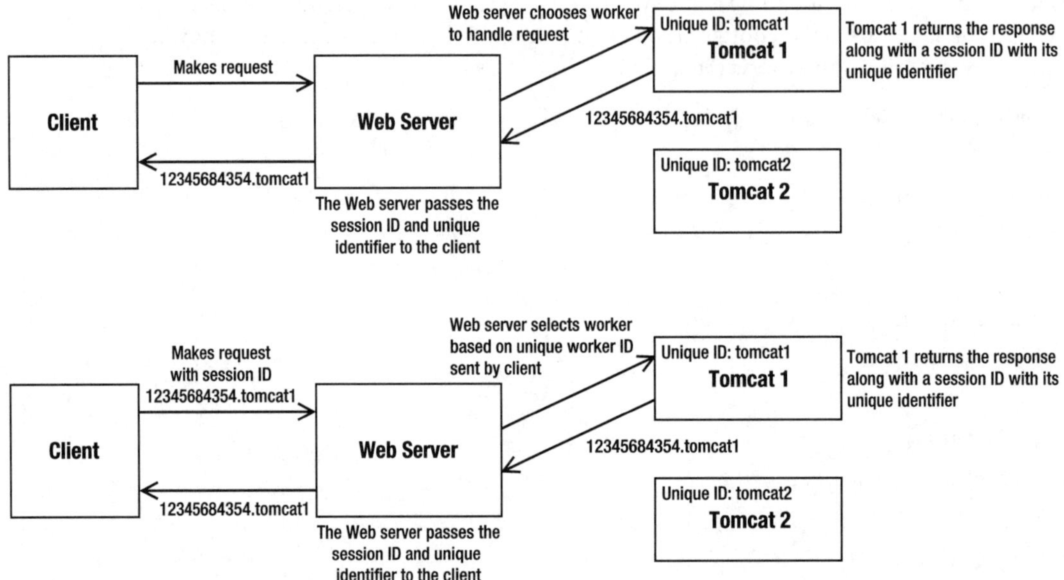

Figure 9-3. *Load balancing with a Web server*

If the maximum number of connections to that worker has been reached before this call, then `mod_jk2` waits for the appropriate worker to become free. This is known as a *seamless session* because the client sees no break in the application's function.

Here, the Tomcat instances are listening to different ports (if they're running on the same machine) or are running on different machines. You'll see how to configure Apache 1.3, Apache 2.0, and IIS before seeing how to configure Tomcat. The Tomcat settings are the same no matter which server you're using, with one exception.

Preparing for Load Balancing

The first step in setting up load balancing is to designate a load-balancing (lb) worker. The load-balancing worker is responsible for managing several actual request-processing workers. The lb worker does the following:

- Instantiates the workers in the Web server.
- Uses the workers' load balancing levels and load-balancing factors to perform weighted round-robin load balancing where a low level means a worker belongs to a preferred group and a low lb factor means a more powerful machine that can handle more requests than others in the group

- Routes requests belonging to the same session to the same Tomcat worker, thus keeping session affinity

- Identifies failed Tomcat workers, suspends requests to them, and falls back to other workers managed by the lb worker

The overall result is that workers managed by the same lb worker are load balanced (based on their lb level and factor and current user session) and covered by a fallback mechanism so that a single Tomcat process death won't bring down the entire deployment.

The Workers

In this example, you'll install and run different Tomcat instances on localhost. For this you have to install two different Tomcat instances on the test machine at `CATALINA_HOME1`, listening on port 8009, and `CATALINA_HOME2`, listening on port 8010. You Web server should also be running on this machine.

You should keep the following in mind:

- Each Tomcat instance running on the same machine should listen to a unique port. However, two Tomcat instances running on two different machines (which are participating in the same load-balancing mechanism as two workers) can listen on the same port number.

- The AJP connector of each Tomcat instance running on the same machine should listen to a unique port. However, the AJP connectors of two Tomcat instances running on two different machines (which are participating in the same load-balancing mechanism as two workers) can run on the same port.

Configuring Apache 1.3 for Load Balancing

You'll now need to define a simple `workers.properties` file for the load balancing. Here, you'll define a single worker in the `worker.list` option as the load-balancing worker. This worker will be the single access point for any requests delegated by Apache and will handle the other workers. Call it `lb`, although you can name it whatever you want.

For each Tomcat worker, define the standard parameters: the host and port on which it will be running, the load-balancing factor that should be applied, and the number of open connections accepted in the form of cache (see Listing 9-12).

Listing 9-12. *A Sample `workers.properties` File*

```
# Define the path separator appropriate to the platform we are using
# For Windows Systems
ps=\


# For Linux /Unix Systems
#ps=/
```

```
# Define the load balancing worker only, and not other workers.
worker.list=lb

# ------------------------------------------------------------------------
# First Tomcat instance running on local machine (localhost)
# ------------------------------------------------------------------------
# Set the port on which it will listen
worker.tomcat1.port=8009
# Set the host on which the Tomcat worker is running
 worker.tomcat1.host=localhost
# Set the type of worker, here we are using ajp13
worker.tomcat1.type=ajp13
# Specify the load-balancing factor, any value greater than 0
worker.tomcat1.lbfactor=10
# Specify the size of the open connection cache.
worker.tomcat1.cachesize=5

# ------------------------------------------------------------------------
# Second Tomcat instance running on local machine (localhost)
# ------------------------------------------------------------------------
# Set the port on which it will listen
worker.tomcat2.port=8010
# Set the host on which the Tomcat worker is running
worker.tomcat2.host=localhost
# Set the type of worker, here we are using ajp13
worker.tomcat2.type=ajp13
# Specify the load-balancing factor , any value greater than 0
worker.tomcat2.lbfactor=10
# Specify the size of the open connection cache.
worker.tomcat2.cachesize=5

# ------------------------
# Load Balancer worker
# ------------------------
worker.lb.type=lb
# State the comma-separated name of workers that will form part of this
# load balancing mechanism
worker.lb.balanced_workers=tomcat1, tomcat2
```

The lb worker is of type lb and uses a weighted round-robin algorithm for load balancing with support for seamless sessions as discussed earlier. If a worker dies, the lb worker will check its state over small time intervals. Until it's back online, all work is redirected to the other available workers.

The previous are the basic steps for integrating Tomcat and Apache, but perhaps the most important step is to tell Apache about the URL patterns that it should hand over to Tomcat, as in Listing 9-13.

Listing 9-13. *Mounting the JSP Examples*

```
# Mappings for the requests to JSP and servlets
JkMount /tomcatBook lb
JkMount /tomcatBook/* lb
```

mod_jk will forward any requests that match these patterns to the lb worker. Once the request processing is done, the response is sent to the corresponding client.

You now need to include the settings for mod_jk, the defined Tomcat lb worker, and a few other settings such as the location of the log file, the log level, and the mappings for the various resources that mod_jk will ask Tomcat to provide.

Insert the lines in Listing 9-14 at the bottom of Apache's httpd.conf. Of course, you could use Tomcat to generate the settings for you. Remember to change the host-level listener's jkWorker attribute to lb.

Listing 9-14. *The Final Configuration for Apache*

```
<IfModule !mod_jk.c>
  LoadModule jk_module "C:/Program Files/Apache Group/Apache/modules/mod_jk.dll"
</IfModule>

JkWorkersFile "C:/jakarta-tomcat-5.0.27/conf/workers.properties"
JkLogFile "C:/jakarta-tomcat-5.0.27/logs/mod_jk.log"

JkLogLevel info

<VirtualHost localhost>
    ServerName localhost
    JkMount /tomcatBook lb
    JkMount /tomcatBook/* lb
</VirtualHost>
```

Configuring Apache 2.0 and IIS for Load Balancing

The theory behind load balancing for Apache 2.0 and IIS is the same as for Apache 1.3, though the mechanism has been refined and of course the configuration is different. The defaults that mod_jk provides make load balancing extremely easy, as it's set up by default. You'll have to do a small amount of configuration on the Tomcat side, but it's an extremely quick process.

For Apache 2.0, create a workers2.properties file in Apache 2.0's conf directory and add the configuration shown in Listing 9-15. Do the same for IIS, but place the file in the location you specified in the registry.

Listing 9-15. *A Sample workers2.properties File*

```
[channel.socket:localhost:8009]
tomcatId=tomcat1
[channel.socket:localhost:8010]
tomcatId=tomcat2

[ajp13:localhost:8009]
channel=channel.socket:localhost:8009
[ajp13:localhost:8010]
channel=channel.socket:localhost:8010

[status:statusWorker]
styleMode=1

[uri:/jkstatus]
group=status:statusWorker

[uri:/tomcatBook/*]
```

This is almost identical to the file shown in Listing 9-9. In this case you've added another channel and worker listening to port 8010 on localhost. The Tomcat connector will append its name to each session identifier when it returns a response to the Web server. This allows the Web server to route subsequent responses to the appropriate Tomcat, as the client will also include this session identifier with the Tomcat name when it makes a request. You use the tomcatId attribute to identify which channel to use when a request comes in and thus implement sticky sessions. If the worker is busy, the Web server will wait until it's ready.

■ **Note** Remember to generate an Apache configuration file for the tomcatBook context using the generating tools mentioned previously. Include this file in httpd.conf.

You don't have anything else to do on the Web server side, bar the basic mod_jk2 configuration from earlier in the chapter. This is because all workers automatically belong to a load-balancing group called lb, which is governed by the lb:lb worker.

Load Balancing Level

mod_jk2 has added a fine-grained load-balancing mechanism that allows you to have more control over your workers. In mod_jk you simply had the load-balancing factor, which you could use to arrange servers in the order of ability to service requests. The higher the number, the more often a worker would receive a request from the Web server.

mod_jk2 builds on this with the concept of load-balancing levels. Load-balancing levels allow you to group workers together into load-balancing clusters, some of which are used only following a server failure. This wasn't possible before because the load-balancing factor is a weighting that tells the Web server how often to route requests to a certain worker, which means that all workers would get a request eventually.

The load-balancing algorithm checks the lowest level first and routes requests to those workers with the lowest balancing factor. If all the workers at a certain level fail, then the algorithm moves to the next level up and assigns requests to the workers with the lowest balancing factor. This process is repeated up the chain worker failure. Therefore, workers on higher levels will be run only if all the workers on lower levels fail.

You can set the balancing factor and balancing level as attributes of a channel or a worker. Note that a worker inherits its channel's attributes. Listing 9-16 shows an example of a load-balancing cluster.

Listing 9-16. *An Example Load-Balancing Cluster*

```
[channel.socket:localhost:8009]
tomcatId=tomcat1
level=0
[channel.socket:server1:8009]
tomcatId=tomcat2
level=1
lb_factor=0
[channel.socket:server2:8009]
tomcatId=tomcat3
level=1
lb_factor=10

[ajp13:localhost:8009]
channel=channel.socket:localhost:8009
[ajp13:server1:8009]
channel=channel.socket:server1:8009
[ajp13:server2:8009]
channel=channel.socket:server2:8009
```

In this example you define three workers, one on the local server and two on remote servers (server1 and server2). By setting tomcat1's level to 0 and the remote workers to 1, you're asking the Web server to use the local worker for all requests; should this worker fail, it should use the remote cluster. In the remote cluster, server1 has preference over server2 and will be used more often.

Configuring Tomcat for Load Balancing

For load balancing, you need to specify the jvmRoute attribute of the <Engine> directive in server.xml for each Tomcat worker. This unique ID ensures the seamless session feature is activated, and it must be unique across all the available Tomcat workers participating in the load-balancing cluster.

This unique identifier will be appended to the session ID generated for that Tomcat worker. Using this, the front-end Web server will forward any particular session request to the appropriate Tomcat worker.

This configuration is the same no matter which Web server or version of mod_jk you're using. To continue the example, add a unique jvmRoute attribute to each Tomcat worker's server.xml file, as detailed in Listing 9-17.

Listing 9-17. *Configuring Tomcat Workers for Tomcat 1 and Tomcat 2*

```
<!-- Define the top-level container in our container hierarchy -->
<!-- Tomcat 1's connector -->
<Engine name="Catalina"
        defaultHost="localhost"
        debug="0"
        jvmRoute="tomcat1">

<!-- Define the top-level container in our container hierarchy -->
<!-- Tomcat 2's connector -->
<Engine name="Catalina"
        defaultHost="localhost"
        debug="0"
        jvmRoute="tomcat2">
```

Before you run the Tomcat workers for testing, you'll need to handle the CATALINA_HOME environment variable. In most cases, when you run a single Tomcat instance, you set the CATALINA_HOME as an environment variable so that it's available once your system boots up. This can create a problem when you want to run two instances of Tomcat on the same machine. This is because each of the Tomcat instances will need a unique CATALINA_HOME variable.

You can handle this by resetting CATALINA_HOME. Edit the catalina.sh (or catalina.bat for Windows) file located in the second Tomcat's CATALINA_HOME/bin directory, and add the two lines in Listing 9-18 at the start of it to point to the appropriate directories.

Listing 9-18. *Setting* `CATALINA_HOME` *for Tomcat workers*

```
#For Linux/ Unix Systems:
#$JAVA_HOME=/usr/java/j2sdk1.4.2
#$CATALINA_HOME=/usr/java/jakarta-tomcat-X

REM For Windows:
%JAVA_HOME%=c:\j2sdk1.4.2
%CATALINA_HOME%=c:\Jakarta-tomcat-X
```

If you're using `mod_jk2`, edit `CATALINA_HOME/conf/jk2.properties` and add the following line on the second Tomcat instance:

```
channelSocket.port=8010
```

Now that you've finished configuring your load-balancing setup, you need to make sure all the Tomcat instances are up and running properly. To do this, create a file named `index.jsp` and put it in the `tomcatBook` context of Tomcat 1, as shown in Listing 9-19.

Listing 9-19. *Tomcat 1's* `index.jsp` *file*

```
<html>
  <body>
    <h1><font color="red">Session Served By Tomcat 1</font></h1>
    <table align="centre" border="1">
      <tr>
        <td>Session ID</td>
        <td>${pageContext.session.id}</td>
      </tr>
      <tr>
        <td>Created on</td>
        <td>${pageContext.session.creationTime}</td>
      </tr>
    </table>
  </body>
</html>
```

Copy this file into the `tomcatBook` context of the other Tomcat worker. To help you see which Tomcat instance has processed a request, edit `index.jsp` by changing this line

```
<h1><font color="red">Session Served By Tomcat 1</font></h1>
```

to the following for Tomcat 2:

```
<h1><font color="blue>"Session Served By Tomcat 2</font></h1>
```

Testing the Load Balancing Behavior

To test this, first verify that your Web server is serving the static content properly by browsing to the URL `http://localhost/`. You should see the default Web server `index.html` page. Now, test that Tomcat is serving the `index.jsp` page by browsing to the URL `http://localhost/tomcatBook/index.jsp`. You'll be served by one of the two Tomcat instances. If Tomcat 1 served the page, you'll get the page shown in Figure 9-4.

Figure 9-4. *Tomcat 1 serving* `index.jsp`

Similarly, if Tomcat 2 worker serves your request, you'll get the page with the blue heading and the "Session Served By Tomcat 2" message followed by its session data.

Note the session ID in the first row of the table. Refresh your browser, and you'll notice that no matter how many hits you make, the session ID remains the same. This indicates that the load balancer is keeping the current session contents intact.

Now, open another window with the same URL. This time the other Tomcat worker will handle your request. This is because the Web server is using a round-robin algorithm.

To test the fail-over aspect of load balancing, shut down one of the Tomcat workers. You'll then get output only from the remaining worker. If you start the idle worker again, the load balancer will start using it as soon as it finds that the server is up. It periodically checks the status of the worker and will start using it as soon as it's made available.

Now that you know how to configure load balancing, you use the clustering knowledge you gained in Chapter 7. You can now set up each of the Tomcat workers from this chapter as a node of the same cluster, as defined in Chapter 7. This means you can deploy Web applications across multiple Tomcat workers by dropping an application's WAR file into a node's watched deployment directory.

Summary

In this chapter you enhanced your skills for handling Web application deployment. You saw the AJP connector before going on to obtain `mod_jk`, the Apache redirector module. You looked at the binary distribution as well as how to build from source on both Windows and Unix systems. I also discussed `mod_jk2` and showed how its configuration is similar to, though much easier than, that of `mod_jk`.

You saw how `mod_jk` acts as a redirector component to route requests for dynamic content to Tomcat workers. Also, you've acquired skills to exploit the strengths of integrating Tomcat with Apache. You also saw how to configure IIS to work with Tomcat. You first saw how ISAPI works as a redirector to forward requests to Tomcat as an out-of-process worker. ISAPI communicates with Tomcat over TCP/IP using AJP.

You examined a number of ways of setting up your architecture using application servers, Web server farms, and multiple dedicated Tomcat workers to provide a more scalable architecture. In addition to this, you implemented and tested load balancing for routing traffic between multiple instances of Tomcat and an external Web server.

CHAPTER 10

Connecting to Databases Using JDBC

Many of the Web applications running on your server will process data, and most of that data will be stored in a database. The most popular databases, including MySQL, PostgreSQL, Oracle, SQL Server, Sybase, Interbase, and DB2, are based on relational concepts. You need to understand how Tomcat interacts with relational databases to better understand the requirements of your users.

In this chapter, you'll see the many situations that will arise when configuring Tomcat to work with relational databases. More important, you'll gain some hands-on experience configuring several examples. By the end of this chapter, you'll be comfortable integrating databases with Tomcat.

Introducing SQL

The Structured Query Language (SQL) is a text-based query language that you use to perform operations with data stored in a relational database. These operations include selecting data for display, inserting data into the database, deleting data from the database, and manipulating database structure.

As an admin you won't see much SQL in your Tomcat setup, because the server uses it behind the scenes to look up usernames and passwords. You will, however, have to be fairly familiar with simple SQL commands so that you can add and remove users from your Tomcat user databases. Because these are realm-related commands, they will be dealt with in Chapter 11.

Introducing JDBC

JDBC is a Java programming interface for accessing databases, which makes it the obvious choice when using databases with Tomcat. JDBC submits SQL query statements to the remote SQL processing engine (part of the database that handles multiple simultaneous connections via a connection manager), and the SQL processing engine returns the result of the query in a set of data called a *result set*. A result set is typically zero or more rows of data. You can think of result sets as temporary database tables.

Therefore, JDBC operations are designed to do the following:

- Take the JDBC API calls and transform them into a SQL query
- Submit that query to the SQL processing engine on the database
- Retrieve the result set that's returned from the query and transform it into a Java-accessible data structure

Not all statements return a result set; you may conduct a search that isn't successful, so the returned result set will be empty (called a null result set). In addition, some SQL statements, such as those you use to create tables, update data, and delete rows, don't return any result sets.

Running Basic JDBC Operations

In JDBC programming, the typical steps that a developer must follow are as follows:

1. Obtain a connection to the remote database server.
2. Create and prepare a SQL statement for execution (or call a stored procedure in the database).
3. Execute the SQL statement.
4. Obtain the returned result set (if any) and work on it.
5. Disconnect from the remote database.

It's usually the case that you'll be concerned only with the first step of this process. Once you've connected the Web server to a database, you hand the connection over to any Web applications that need it.

Establishing and Terminating Connections to Databases

Other than providing a unified way of accessing, modifying, and manipulating data in databases, JDBC also provides a unified way of connecting to databases from different vendors. While normal native connections to Oracle will be different from connections to MySQL, which will yet be different from when working with Microsoft's SQL Server, connecting to any of these databases can be accomplished using the same JDBC API calls.

As you saw in Chapter 4, JDBC, like JNDI, is simply a layer of abstraction between the native interfaces and Java (see Figure 10-1). You can see how the underlying database can be changed without the application having to worry about changing any of its settings. You have to worry about only one interface with JDBC, and JDBC deals with talking to the database in its own language.

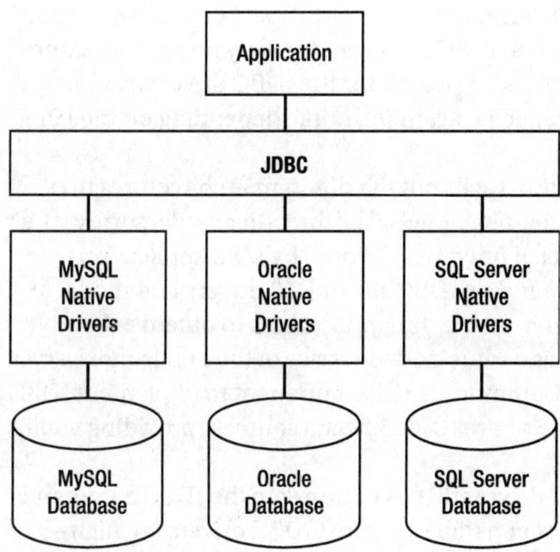

Figure 10-1. *JDBC*

JDBC uses JDBC drivers to communicate with the native database drivers, and these vary from database to database. However, application code doesn't notice the difference between drivers, because they all follow the same standard.

Which JDBC Version?

Under the JDBC 1.0 standard, the code to establish a connection to a database, as well as the code to disconnect from the database, is written by the developer. In fact, even the code to select and activate a JDBC driver is coded by the developer.

Although simple and straightforward to code, this approach creates a problem. In some cases where the driver is written by the developer, the database access code works only with specific database from the vendor. This makes it difficult to swap to a database from another vendor and removes many of the advantages of JDBC described in the previous section.

JDBC 2.0 relaxes this restriction and introduces the concept of a *data source,* which maps a name to a set of values for obtaining a database connection. A developer can obtain a connection to a data source using its name, allowing the same JDBC code to work with drivers from any vendor. Meanwhile, you can switch database vendor support by configuring a different data source. The name remains the same, but the settings have changed, so the developer doesn't need to change their code.

While data sources and connection pooling (covered in the "Database Connection Pooling" section) open new possibilities for database users, JDBC 2.0 doesn't specify how these features should be used. As a result, many architectural issues are left for the JDBC driver writer to solve—and code can quickly become vendor specific again (this time depending on the JDBC driver vendor).

JDBC 3.0 is the first specification that clearly spells out the different architectures that JDBC can operate in, including two-tier and three-tier models. The three-tier model corresponds to the application server model and the model of operation favored by J2EE applications.

The specification also attempts to accommodate JDBC 1.0 and 2.0 drivers and model of operations, while formalizing JNDI as the preferred way for applications to obtain a data source. It also formalizes connection pooling as a value-added service of the application server or servlet container. Tomcat uses the Jakarta Commons DBCP component to implement JDBC 3.0, and all data sources configured in `server.xml` are JDBC 3.0 data sources (providing you're using JDK 1.4 or newer).

Regardless of the JDBC version, the JDBC driver still has to translate the JDBC commands into native commands to connect to the different databases. Most JDBC drivers are high-performance Type IV drivers (explained in the next section). However, some legacy systems will support only the older Type I to Type III drivers. It's a good idea to gain some familiarity with the different types of JDBC driver.

Examining JDBC Driver Types

Four types of JDBC drivers exist. In general, the higher driver types represent an improvement on performance.

Type I: These are the most primitive JDBC drivers because they're just data access adapters. They adapt another data access mechanism (such as ODBC) to JDBC. These drivers completely rely on the other data access mechanism and as such have double the administrative and maintenance problems. These drivers are also typically hardware/operating system specific (because of the data access mechanism that they depend on), meaning they aren't portable at all.

Type II: These are partially written in Java and partially written in native data access languages (typically C or C++). The non-Java portion of these drivers limits the portability of the final code and platform migration possibilities. The administrative and maintenance burden of Type I still exists.

Type III: These are pure Java drivers on the client side, which gives them the portability benefit of Java. However, they rely on an external middleware engine to operate. The client code communicates with the middleware engine, and the engine talks to the different types of database. The administration and maintenance burden is somewhat reduced but is far from eliminated.

Type IV: These are 100 percent Java client drivers that talk directly to database network protocols. This results in the highest performance connection and the most portable application code. Administration and maintenance is greatly simplified (only the driver needs to be updated).

Fortunately, all the major databases have Type IV JDBC drivers available, either through the database vendors themselves or via a third-party driver vendor.

Database Connection Pooling

When a Web application accesses a remote database, it may do so through a JDBC connection. Typically, a physical JDBC connection is established between the client application and the database server via a TCP/IP connection. The action of establishing such a connection is CPU and time intensive. It involves multiple layers of software and the transmission and receipt of network data. A typical physical database connection may take seconds to establish.

Some Web applications consist of JSP pages and servlets that may need data from a database on every HTTP request. For example, an online library application will undoubtedly allow users to search the library catalog. On a heavily loaded server, the time it takes to establish, disconnect, and reestablish physical connections can substantially slow Web application performance.

To create high-performing, scalable Web applications, JDBC driver vendors and application servers are incorporating database connection pooling into their products. Connection pooling reduces expensive connection establishment time by creating a pool of physical connections when the system starts. When an application requires a connection, one of these physical connections is provided. Normally, when the application finishes using the connection, it would be disconnected. However, in the case of connection pooling, it's merely returned to the pool where it awaits the next application request.

Using Tomcat and JDBC

Tomcat provides valuable services for hosted Web applications that use JDBC connections. More specifically, Tomcat will enable running Web applications to do the following:

- Access JDBC data sources using standard JNDI lookup
- Use a connection pooling service

Providing JDBC Data Sources in Tomcat

You configure JDBC drivers as JNDI resources in Tomcat. These resources are made available during Web application run time via standard JNDI lookups. The steps are as follows:

1. First, a Web application obtains a JNDI initial context from Tomcat; it then performs a lookup on the JDBC data source by name.
2. Next, Tomcat handles the JNDI lookup by consulting the configuration files (the context XML file and `web.xml`) to determine the JDBC driver to use for obtaining a data source. Tomcat will also pool the physical connections made.

Even though no true JNDI-compatible directory services are involved, the Tomcat container emulates the action of a JNDI provider. This enables code that uses JNDI as the JDBC data source lookup mechanism to work within the Tomcat container.

Configuring JNDI JDBC Resources

Using JNDI resources in Tomcat to configure JDBC data sources is the recommended way to provide Web applications with access to JDBC connections. While other methods are possible—and you'll see at least one alternative later—this approach will lead to portable code and easily maintainable Tomcat servers.

You must perform the following steps to configure JNDI resource for a JDBC data source:

1. Add `<Resource>` and `<ResourceParams>` tags in the `<Context>` element of the context XML file or in a `<DefaultContext>` subelement of the Tomcat 5.0.*x* `<Host>` element.

2. Ensure that the application developer has defined a `<resource-ref>` element, corresponding to the previous `<Resource>`, in the `web.xml` file of the Web application using the JDBC resource.

Using the Resource and ResourceParams Elements

The `<Resource>` element specifies the JNDI resource that represents a JDBC data source, and the `<ResourceParams>` element configures the associated data source factory. You saw a JDBC data source in Chapter 7, but Listing 10-1 repeats the code for Tomcat 5.0.*x* with some extra parameters.

Listing 10-1. *Defining a JDBC Data Source for Tomcat 5.0.x*

```
<Context path="/tomcatBook"
         docBase="tomcatBook"
         crossContext="false"
         debug="0"
         reloadable="true" >

  <Resource name="jdbc/CatalogDB" auth="SERVLET"
            type="javax.sql.DataSource"/>

  <ResourceParams name="jdbc/CatalogDB">
    <parameter>
      <name>driverClassName</name>
      <value>com.mysql.jdbc.Driver</value>
    </parameter>
    <parameter>
      <name>url</name>
      <value>jdbc:mysql://localhost:3306/catalog</value>
    </parameter>
    <parameter>
      <name>username</name>
      <value>matthewm</value>
    </parameter>
```

```
    <parameter>
      <name>password</name>
      <value>m00die</value>
    </parameter>
    <parameter>
      <name>maxActive</name>
      <value>30</value>
    </parameter>
    <parameter>
      <name>maxIdle</name>
      <value>20000</value>
    </parameter>
    <parameter>
      <name>maxWait</name>
      <value>120</value>
    </parameter>
  </ResourceParams>
</Context>
```

Listing 10-2 shows the same setup for Tomcat 5.5.

Listing 10-2. *Defining a JDBC Data Source for Tomcat 5.5*

```
<Context path="/tomcatBook"
         docBase="tomcatBook"
         crossContext="false"
         debug="0"
         reloadable="true" >

  <Resource name="jdbc/CatalogDB" auth="SERVLET"
            type="javax.sql.DataSource"
            driverClassName="com.mysql.jdbc.Driver"
            url="jdbc:mysql://localhost:3306/catalog"
            username="matthewm"
            password="m00die"
            maxActive="30"
            maxIdle="20000"
            maxWait="120"/>
</Context>
```

Both these settings create a JNDI resource that the Web application can access from the context `java:comp/env/jdbc/CatalogDB`. The Web application can then use this context to look up the data source. The type of resource that will be returned during this lookup is a `javax.sql.DataSource`. It also specifies that the servlet should authenticate against the database on behalf of the Web application.

The actual name and value of the parameters depend on the data source connection factory that's used. The previous settings assume you're configuring the default DBCP factory.

The DBCP factory will work with JDBC drivers for any database and return a data source as appropriate.

Chapter 7 has more details of the attributes allowed in the <Resource> and <ResourceParams> elements.

Transactions and Distributed Transactions Support

Databases offer varying levels of support for transactions. A transaction is a unit of work composed of multiple operations but can be committed only once all its operations complete successfully. If any of the constituent operations fail, the transaction is rolled back.

When a transaction involves work that crosses multiple physical databases, it's called a *distributed transaction*. One standard that enables databases from different vendors to participate in the same distributed transaction is called XA. In the XA operation model, an external transaction manager coordinates a two-phase commit protocol between multiple resource managers (databases in this case). The two-phase commit protocol ensures that the pieces of work, scattered across multiple physical databases, either are all completed or are all rolled back.

JDBC 3.0 accommodates data sources that support XA operations. Administrators who work with XA data sources and data source factories should consult the vendor's documentation to ensure they work with Tomcat.

Testing JNDI Resource Configuration

Here you'll work through an actual example and configure a DBCP data source with a Type IV JDBC driver. You'll base your example on MySQL, as it's easily available and widely used.

■ **Note** Installing and configuring MySQL is beyond the scope of this chapter, but see Appendix B for a quick-start guide. Alternatively, see *The Definitive Guide to MySQL*, Second Edition (Apress, 2003), by Michael Kofler.

This chapter will assume that you have MySQL already configured and tested and that you have an account with privileges to create tables and add records to create the test database. The latest version of MySQL is available for download from `http://www.mysql.com`.

The Type IV JDBC driver you'll use is the Connector/J driver from MySQL. This driver is open source and is widely used by the MySQL community. You can download the latest version of the driver from `http://dev.mysql.com/downloads/connector/j/3.0.html`.

You must unzip the driver JAR from the download and use the binary JAR file. Place this file under `CATALINA_HOME/common/lib` so that the common class loader can make it available to Tomcat and all its Web applications.

Creating the MySQL Test Database

First, you'll need to create the database you'll use. This is a database of products available to buy online and will correspond to the database defined in Listings 10-1 and 10-2 previously.

Listing 10-3 shows a SQL script that will create and populate the catalog database. It's unlikely you'll have to create tables such as this normally, but it's a useful instructional exercise.

Listing 10-3. *The `createCatalogDB.sql` Script*

```
DROP TABLE IF EXISTS product;
CREATE TABLE product (
  prodid int not null,
  prodname varchar(30),
  proddesc varchar(150),
  price double(7,2)
);
INSERT INTO product VALUES (
  1,
  'Yo-Yo',
  'High-quality wooden yo-yo with your company
  name and logo imprinted on both sides.',
  3.50
);
INSERT INTO product VALUES (
  2,
  'Slinky',
  'Plastic slinky in the color of your choice with your
  company logo imprinted on closed slinky.',
  0.75
);
INSERT INTO product VALUES (
  3,
  'Envelope Cutter',
  'Small cutting tool for opening envelopes.
  Your company logo is imprinted on handle.',
  1.25
);
INSERT INTO product VALUES (
  4,
  'Padfolio',
  'Synthetic leather padfolio with company name
  and logo imprinted on cover.',
  9.50
);
INSERT INTO product VALUES (
  5,
  'Fountain Pen',
  'Attractive fountain pen sporting your company
  name on the cap.',
  1.20
);
```

```
INSERT INTO product VALUES (
  6,
  'Keychain',
  'Rubber keychain with your company name and
  logo imprinted in a variety of colors.',
  0.50
);
INSERT INTO product VALUES (
  7,
  'Ruler',
  'Wooden ruler with raised lettering containing
  your company name and logo.',
  0.25
);
INSERT INTO product VALUES (
  8,
  'Flashlight',
  'Metal flashlight in a variety of colors. Your
  company name and logo is imprinted on the handle.',
  5.0
);
```

Use createCatalogDB.sql to create the database as follows:

```
> mysql < createCatalogDB.sql
```

Now that you have the tables, you need to create a user that the developers will use to access the data in the database. Since your Web application functionality requires only read access to the data, you'll create a read-only user for developer access. This will ensure that data can't be accidentally or maliciously modified or altered.

Setting Up the Read-Only User

If you don't have privilege as the database system administrator, you'll need to seek help from the database administrator. To give a user read-only privilege on the catalog database, use the following:

```
mysql> GRANT SELECT ON catalog.*
    -> TO 'matthewm'@'localhost'
    -> IDENTIFIED BY 'm00die';
```

The developer may now use this user to access the data in the table, since in this example they won't perform any modifications to the underlying data. This is the user you saw in Listings 10-2 and 10-2.

Adding the JDBC JNDI Resource to the Server

You saw the context XML file for this example in Listings 10-1 and 10-2, so now you have to configure the Web application's settings. This is usually the developer's job, but you're filling both roles for this example. Remember that DBCP connection pooling is automatically set up. Now edit the `tomcatBook` Web application's `web.xml` file, as shown in Listing 10-4.

Listing 10-4. *A `<resource-ref>` in the `tomcatBook` Web Application's `web.xml`*

```
<!-- Describe a DataSource -->
<resource-ref>
  <description>
    Resource reference to a factory for java.sql.Connection
    instances that may be used for talking to a particular
    database that is configured in the tomcatBook.xml file.
  </description>
  <res-ref-name>
    jdbc/CatalogDB
  </res-ref-name>
  <res-type>
    javax.sql.DataSource
  </res-type>
  <res-auth>
    SERVLET
  </res-auth>
</resource-ref>
```

This `<resource-ref>` makes the `jdbc/CatalogDB` context, via JNDI APIs, available to the Web application.

Using JNDI to Look Up a Data Source

Finally, the developer will look up the data source and start querying the database. The JSP page in Listing 10-5, `lookup.jsp`, will do exactly that. Put it into the `CATALINA_HOME/webapps/tomcatBook/ch10` directory. Pay special attention to the way JNDI is used to obtain the data source in the `<sql:setDataSource>` tag.

Listing 10-5. *lookup.jsp Uses a Data Source to Obtain Data*

```
<%@ taglib prefix="c" uri="http://java.sun.com/jstl/core_rt" %>
<%@ taglib prefix="sql" uri="http://java.sun.com/jstl/sql_rt" %>

<sql:setDataSource dataSource="jdbc/CatalogDB"/>

<sql:query var="products">
  SELECT * FROM product
</sql:query>

<html>
  <head>
    <title>Online Products</title>
  </head>

  <body>
    <center>
      <h1>Products</h1>
    </center>

    <table border="1" align="center">
      <tr>
        <th>Name</th><th>Description</th><th>Price</th>
      </tr>
      <c:forEach items="${products.rows}" var="row">
        <tr>
          <td><c:out value="${row.prodname}" /></td>
          <td><c:out value="${row.proddesc}" /></td>
          <td><c:out value="${row.price}" /></td>
        </tr>
      </c:forEach>
    </table>
  </body>
</html>
```

To run this example, you need to add the JSP standard tag library (from http://jakarta.apache.org/taglibs/) to the Web application's classpath, either by placing jstl.jar and standard.jar in tomcatBook/WEB-INF/lib or in the common or shared class loader path.

The <sql:setDataSource> tag uses the jdbc/CatalogDB context to look up the JNDI resource and makes it available to the page. Behind the scenes, it's used to create a connection (actually pooled through DBCP). The JSP page then performs a SELECT * on the product table and creates an HTML table containing all the table rows.

Connect to http://localhost:8080/tomcatBook/ch10/lookup.jsp. This will compile and execute the JSP code. If everything is configured correctly and working, you should see the page as shown in Figure 10-2.

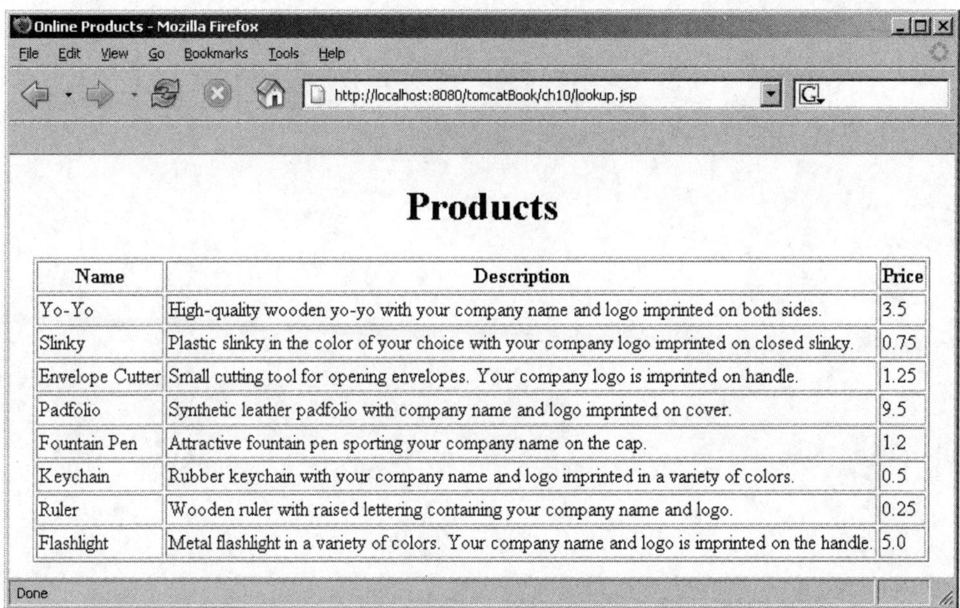

Name	Description	Price
Yo-Yo	High-quality wooden yo-yo with your company name and logo imprinted on both sides.	3.5
Slinky	Plastic slinky in the color of your choice with your company logo imprinted on closed slinky.	0.75
Envelope Cutter	Small cutting tool for opening envelopes. Your company logo is imprinted on handle.	1.25
Padfolio	Synthetic leather padfolio with company name and logo imprinted on cover.	9.5
Fountain Pen	Attractive fountain pen sporting your company name on the cap.	1.2
Keychain	Rubber keychain with your company name and logo imprinted in a variety of colors.	0.5
Ruler	Wooden ruler with raised lettering containing your company name and logo.	0.25
Flashlight	Metal flashlight in a variety of colors. Your company name and logo is imprinted on the handle.	5.0

Figure 10-2. *A JSP page that uses a JDBC data source to obtain data*

Summary

In this chapter, you saw JDBC connectivity in the context of Tomcat. The most obvious interaction is the need of Web applications to connect to relational database sources.

I discussed Java's support for accessing relational database management systems (RDBMSs) in the form of JDBC. I covered the JDBC version evolution, and I talked briefly about the different types of JDBC drivers that are available.

Next, you saw the recommended way of providing a JDBC data source to Web applications, which involved the configuration of JNDI resources in the Tomcat configuration file. In addition, Tomcat also provides a database connection pooling service through the Jakarta Commons DBCP project.

CHAPTER 11

Working with User Authentication

This chapter and the next deal with Tomcat security, though this chapter deals exclusively with access to the server's resources. Chapter 12 covers securing data transfer and securing the machine on which the server runs. When users attempt to access a restricted resource on the server, Tomcat challenges them to produce user details to confirm that they are who they say they are. This is *authentication*.

Once a user is authenticated, the server must then determine whether this user is authorized to view the restricted resource requested. This is *authorization*. Both of these concepts make up the security policy of a server.

Tomcat uses realms to implement and enforce specific security policies, some of which developers specify, but all of which you administer. A realm itself doesn't enforce security policies; it's a depository of user information that allows the server, or sometimes an application, to enforce a security policy.

Looking at Realms

As mentioned, a *realm* is a depository of user information that authenticates and authorizes users. As befits a standard data access mechanism in Java, realms present a standard interface to Tomcat, no matter what the underlying data store (see Figure 11-1).

As you can see, realms are another layer of abstraction on top of sources of data. In the case of databases (accessed with JDBC) and JNDI resources, a realm is a layer of abstraction on top of a layer of abstraction. Thus, Tomcat can authenticate against any JNDI or JDBC data source on any platform that supports it. This allows you to use existing personnel databases that may be running on back-end or directory servers.

Realms, as standard abstractions of underlying data, must provide a standard interface to Tomcat, which in turn means that the underlying data must conform to a standard format. In other words, each underlying set of data must have the following, though it may contain many other pieces of information:

- A username
- A password
- The roles assigned to the user

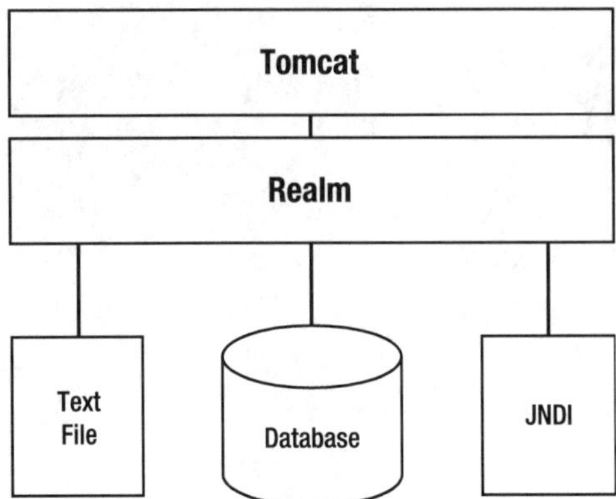

Figure 11-1. *A realm is an abstraction of the data store.*

Understanding Container-Managed Security

Container-managed security puts the onus on the Web server for enforcing and implementing security policies. This means developers don't need to write code to use authentication and authorization (though they can if they want); they can rely on the servlet container to do the authentication for them.

By delegating authentication and authorization to the server, developers can write general-purpose code that can apply to many user roles. If they want to restrict access to this general-purpose code, they ask the administrator to implement container-managed security and place a security policy between the users and the resources. Therefore, this code can be protected from unauthorized access without any changes in the application. Further, the restriction can be altered without changing the application if need dictates it.

Let's look at an example of what container-managed security provides for Web application developers and administrators. Imagine a Web application that enables employees in a company to view their performance reviews online. The application also enables supervisors to add reviews. This application must ensure the following:

- An employee is authenticated before seeing the confidential information.
- A supervisor is authenticated before seeing and adding employee records.

In a traditional Web application, the Web application developer would write the authentication routines and place them in the application's logic. Once a user has been authenticated, they must also be authorized, which means more application-specific code to determine which sections of the applications a supervisor can access and which sections a worker can access. But suppose company policy changes and human resources now has responsibility for adding the performance reviews. You have to rewrite code to stop supervisors viewing reviews and to allow human resources to add reviews.

With container-managed security, the administrator handles this change. All the mappings of users to roles and roles to access rights are placed in server configuration files and as such aren't hard-coded. When human resources is given access to the review-adding process, the administrator maps the new relationship in the configuration file, and the developers don't need to do anything. Figure 11-2 shows this process.

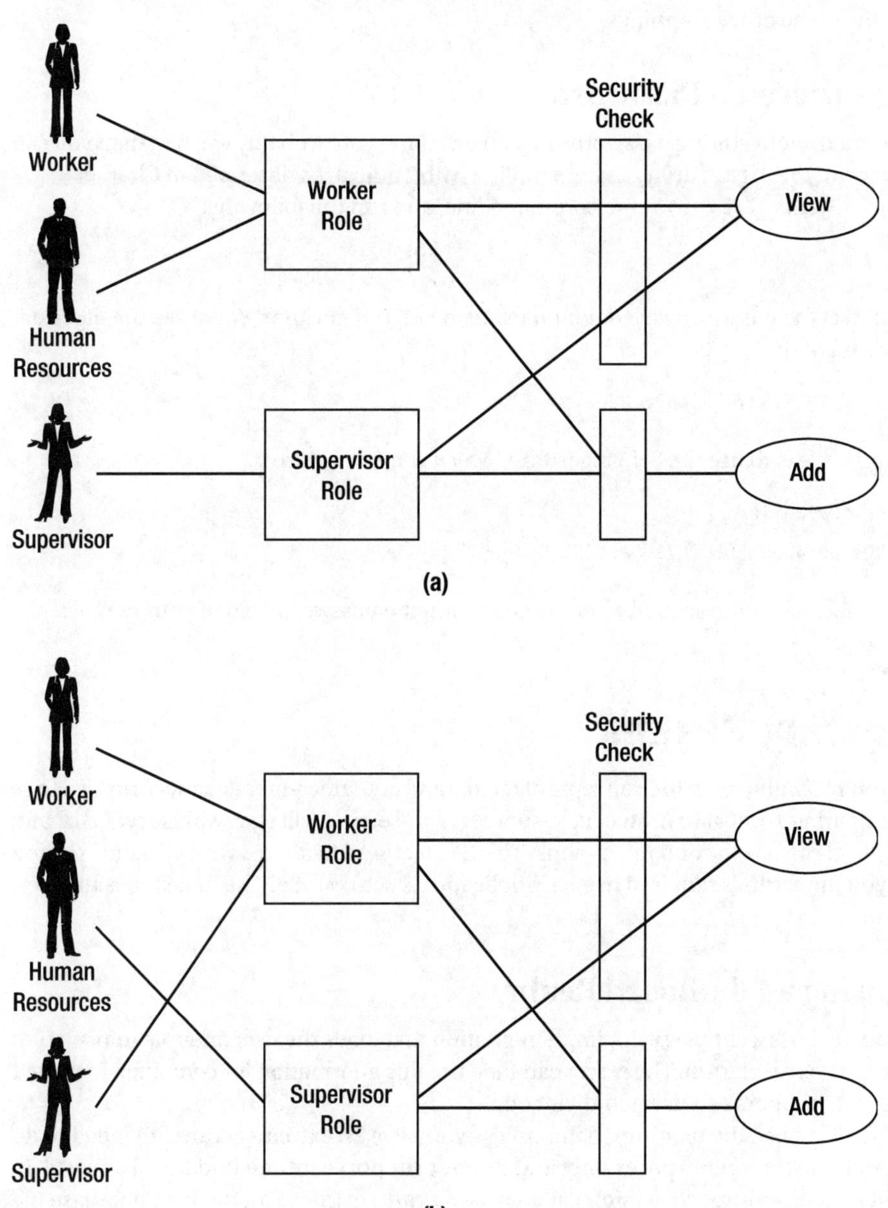

Figure 11-2. *(a) The manager can view and add reviews. (b) The human resources team can now view and add reviews, but the supervisor can't.*

In Figure 11-2 (a) the worker and the human resources team can only view the reviews because they're mapped to the worker role. Managers can view and add reviews because they're mapped to the supervisor role. In Figure 11-2 (b) members of the human resources team can now view and add reviews because they're now mapped to the supervisor role. The supervisor is now mapped to the worker role and can only view the reviews. This shows how easy it is to reassign users to roles without changing an application's logic. It'd be just as easy to change any of the other mappings.

Storing a Digested Password

If you're worried about storing passwords in plain text (and you probably will be), then you can digest them with the `digest` utility that's supplied with Tomcat, as described in Chapter 3. Navigate to `CATALINA_HOME/bin` at the command line, and run the following:

```
> digest -a md5 admin
```

This digests the password called *admin* using the MD5 algorithm. You'll see the digested password as follows:

```
admin:21232f297a57a5a743894a0e4a801fc3
```

An alternative is to use the SHA algorithm, which is more secure.

```
> digest -a sha admin
admin:d033e22ae348aeb5660fc2140aec35850c4da997
```

You can then copy the section after the colon into the password field of your realm's password store.

Configuring Realms

Now that you're familiar with the concepts of realms and container-managed security, it's time to start configuring Tomcat to protect its resources. This section will start with `server.xml` and the settings you can use to configure realms. The "Protecting a Resource with a Realm" section will show you the settings required in each application's `web.xml` file. The first stop is the file-based realm.

Configuring a File-Based Realm

The memory realm is a simple realm implementation that loads the user and role information into memory at server startup. The server can then use this information for container-managed security, and developers can use it in their code.

You shouldn't use the memory realm unless you have an extremely pressing need to do so. It's for demonstration purposes only and doesn't support runtime updates. Tomcat 4.1 introduced a much-improved version called a *user database* (more on the user database in the next section).

The memory realm configuration element in server.xml can have attributes specified in Table 11-1.

Table 11-1. *A Memory Realm's Attributes*

Attribute	Description	Required?
className	The class that implements the memory realm. It must be set to org.apache.catalina.realm.MemoryRealm.	Yes
debug	Tomcat 5.0.*x* only. The level of the debugging message that will be sent to the log. The default is zero.	No
digest	The digest algorithm used to store the password. By default, passwords are stored in plain text.	No
pathname	The XML file that will be the source of data for the memory realm. The default is CATALINA_HOME/conf/tomcat-users.xml.	No

A memory realm is configured in the default server.xml, but it's commented out. This reflects the concerns mentioned previously. Listing 11-1 shows the relevant section.

Listing 11-1. *The Memory Realm in server.xml*

```
<!--
<Realm className="org.apache.catalina.realm.MemoryRealm" />
-->
```

This specifies a memory realm that uses the CATALINA_HOME/conf/tomcat-users.xml file. It's at the engine level, so it will be used in all Web applications running in that engine. It will also use the logger associated with that engine, be that a logger component or a Log4J implementation. If you want to use or test this implementation, remember to comment out any other realms in server.xml.

If you need to specify your own set of users, passwords, and roles for a memory realm, add them to tomcat-users.xml, as shown in Listing 11-2.

Listing 11-2. *The tomcat-users.xml File*

```
<?xml version='1.0' encoding='utf-8'?>
<tomcat-users>
  <role rolename="tomcat"/>
  <role rolename="role1"/>
  <role rolename="admin"/>
  <user username="admin" password="admin" roles="admin"/>
  <user username="tomcat" password="tomcat" roles="tomcat"/>
  <user username="role1" password="tomcat" roles="role1"/>
  <user username="both" password="tomcat" roles="tomcat,role1"/>
</tomcat-users>
```

As has already been noted, this memory realm isn't configured by default. Instead, a greatly improved memory realm implementation called a *user database* has superseded this primitive memory realm implementation. The old memory realm is retained for backward compatibility (which is still no excuse to use it).

If you're using a digested password, you should copy the digested output of the digest script into the password attribute of the appropriate `<user>` element in `tomcat-users.xml`, as shown in Listing 11-3.

Listing 11-3. *A Digested Password Is Added for the Admin User*

```
<?xml version='1.0' encoding='utf-8'?>
<tomcat-users>
  <role rolename="tomcat"/>
  <role rolename="role1"/>
  <role rolename="admin"/>
  <user username="admin"
        password="d033e22ae348aeb5660fc2140aec35850c4da997"
        roles="admin"/>
  <user username="tomcat" password="tomcat" roles="tomcat"/>
  <user username="role1" password="tomcat" roles="role1"/>
  <user username="both" password="tomcat" roles="tomcat,role1"/>
</tomcat-users>
```

When Tomcat asks for a password and you've set it up to use digested passwords, it digests whatever users enter as their passwords and compares them to the values stored in the realm (see Figure 11-3).

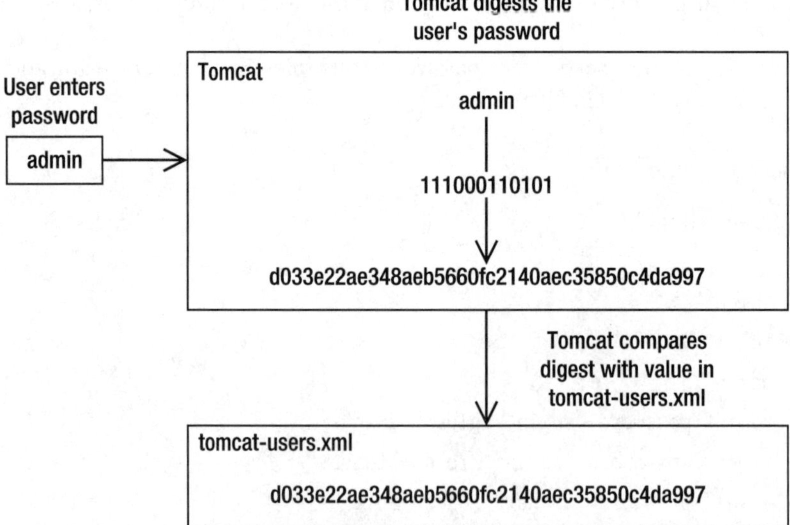

Figure 11-3. *Tomcat using digested passwords*

You can see that it's important to tell Tomcat to digest the password entered so that it can make a proper comparison. If Tomcat doesn't know to digest the password, then it won't authenticate the user.

You'll see how to protect a Web application in the "Protecting a Resource with a Realm" section.

Configuring a User Database Realm

A user database is a greatly enhanced implementation of a memory realm. Though it may not seem like much (it still uses `tomcat-users.xml`, for instance), it does offer three large improvements:

- You can now change the user information programmatically during the lifetime of the engine. This allows you to build administrative utilities. Note that this doesn't mean you can edit the file manually and expect the changes to be reflected instantly. You'll have to restart the server in that case.
- Upon modification and shutdown, the user database can save any changes to the `tomcat-users.xml` data file for use in the future.
- You can alter the username, password, and role mapping with the `admin` Web interface utility as described in the next section.

In the default `server.xml`, the user database is already configured in place of the legacy memory realm implementation, which you may have uncommented earlier. The user database is usually configured in the `<GlobalNamingResources>` element as a JNDI resource that's available to all applications on the server. Unlike the memory realm, which is implicitly used in configuring each Web application, the user database must be configured for each Web application. Listing 11-4 shows the user database global settings as configured in Tomcat 5.0.*x*'s `server.xml`. Tomcat 5.5 uses attributes of the `<Resource>` element rather than a `<ResourceParams>` element.

Listing 11-4. *The Global Settings for the Default User Database in* `server.xml`

```
<!-- Global JNDI resources -->
<GlobalNamingResources>

  <!-- Editable user database that can also be used by
       UserDatabaseRealm to authenticate users -->
  <Resource name="UserDatabase" auth="Container"
            type="org.apache.catalina.UserDatabase"
            description="User database that can be updated and saved">
  </Resource>
  <ResourceParams name="UserDatabase">
    <parameter>
      <name>factory</name>
      <value>org.apache.catalina.users.MemoryUserDatabaseFactory</value>
    </parameter>
```

```
    <parameter>
      <name>pathname</name>
      <value>conf/tomcat-users.xml</value>
    </parameter>
  </ResourceParams>

</GlobalNamingResources>
```

This makes the user database called `UserDatabase` accessible through JNDI lookup, relative to the `java:comp/env` naming context. The `factory` parameter sets the class that will return a user database to Tomcat for use in authentication.

This configuration also allows you to reference the user database in a later scope. For example, you can use the user database as a realm at the engine level as the default `server.xml` file does. Listing 11-5 shows this situation.

Listing 11-5. *Adding a User Database*

```
<!-- This realm uses the UserDatabase configured in the global JNDI
     resources under the key "UserDatabase".  Any edits
     that are performed against this UserDatabase are immediately
     available for use by the Realm.  -->

<Realm className="org.apache.catalina.realm.UserDatabaseRealm"
       debug="0" resourceName="UserDatabase"/>
```

This realm has all the same attributes as the memory realm, save the addition of the `resourceName` attribute. For example, if you wanted to use message digests with this realm, you'd set it up as in Listing 11-6.

Listing 11-6. *A User Database That Uses Digested Passwords*

```
<Realm className="org.apache.catalina.realm.UserDatabaseRealm"
       debug="0" resourceName="UserDatabase"
       digest="sha"/>
```

This will allow you to use the admin user from Listing 11-3. If you didn't set the `digest` attribute in this case, then Tomcat would make a comparison between the plain password entered by a user and the digested password stored in the realm. Setting the `digest` attribute makes Tomcat digest the password before comparing it every time the user enters it.

As noted previously, you can alter this realm while the server is running, which is a vast improvement over the memory realm. You can, if you like, write an application that manipulates this file to add, remove, and modify users, though Tomcat's `admin` application does just that. You saw the `admin` application in Chapter 6 but not in any great detail. I'll now show you how to use the `admin` application to work with user databases.

Configuring User Databases with the Admin Application

To add a new user database start Tomcat, then visit the `admin` application via the URL `http://localhost:8080/admin/`. You may have to set up appropriate users for this application if you haven't followed the steps in Chapter 6, which simply tell you to add an admin user to `tomcat-users.xml`. When you visit the `admin` application, you'll see the screen shown in Figure 11-4.

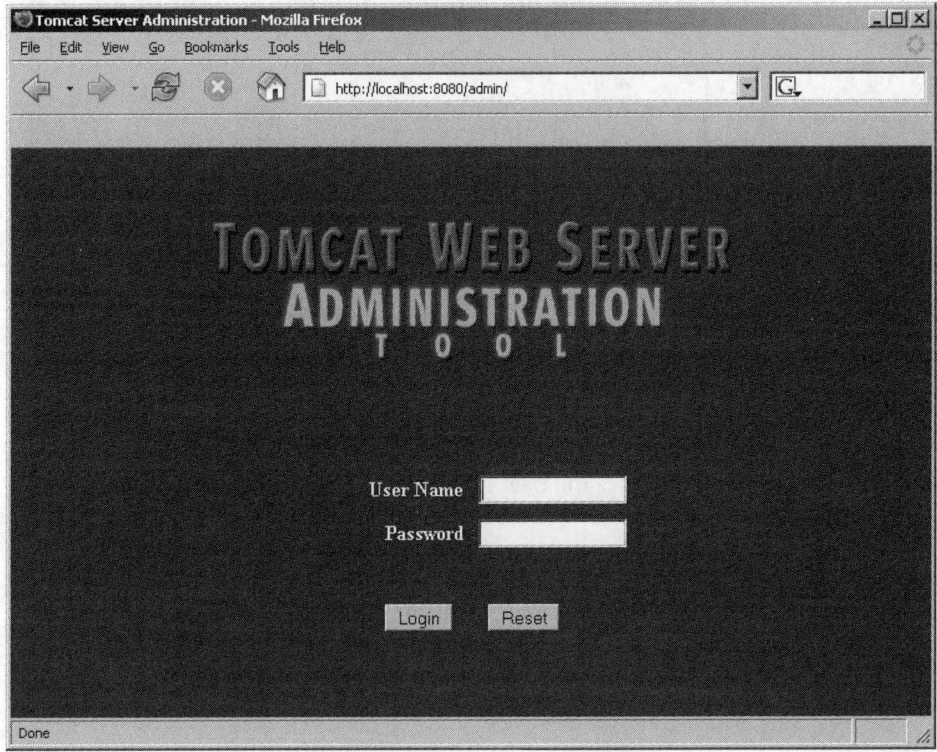

Figure 11-4. *The Tomcat admin application*

Log in using the details of a user with the admin role. You'll see the `admin` Web interface. Click the User Databases link in the left pane, and you'll see the screen shown in Figure 11-5.

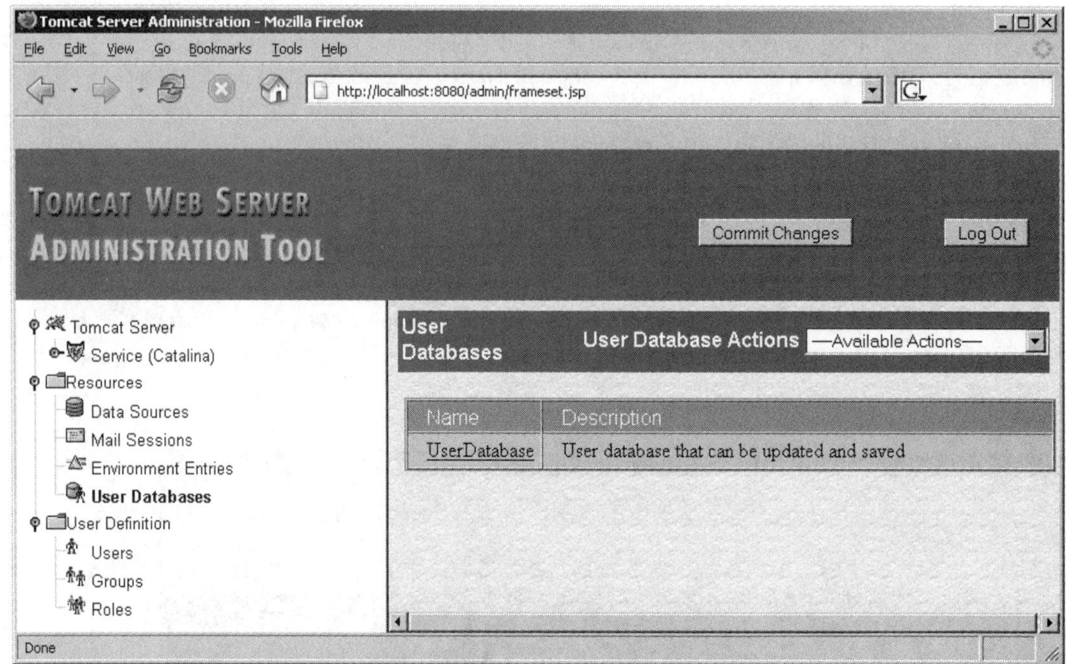

Figure 11-5. *User databases in the Tomcat `admin` application*

This corresponds to the user database entry as defined in Listing 11-4, right down to the description. Click the user database's name, and you'll see a screen like Figure 11-6.

This is the default user database as defined in `server.xml`. Only one user database factory for user databases exists, so you can't edit that setting. The others allow you to change the location of the user information from the default `tomcat-users.xml` file and change the description.

To add a new user database, click the User Database Actions box and select Create New User Database. You'll see a blank version of the screen in Figure 11-6, with the factory already filled in. Enter the details you require, and click Save. Once you've clicked Save, Tomcat holds the configuration in memory. When you've made all the changes you want to make to the server configuration, click the Commit Changes button at the top of the Web interface. Any comments you had in `server.xml` will be lost, as Tomcat overwrites the entire file. The good news is that Tomcat will create a backup of the old `server.xml` file with the date appended to the filename.

■ **Note** When you click Commit Changes, the `admin` application will restart the server. This means you'll have to log in again once the server has restarted. If you attempt any actions while the restart is in progress, you'll receive multiple errors in multiple frames. You don't have to click Commit Changes to update the user database, as described next.

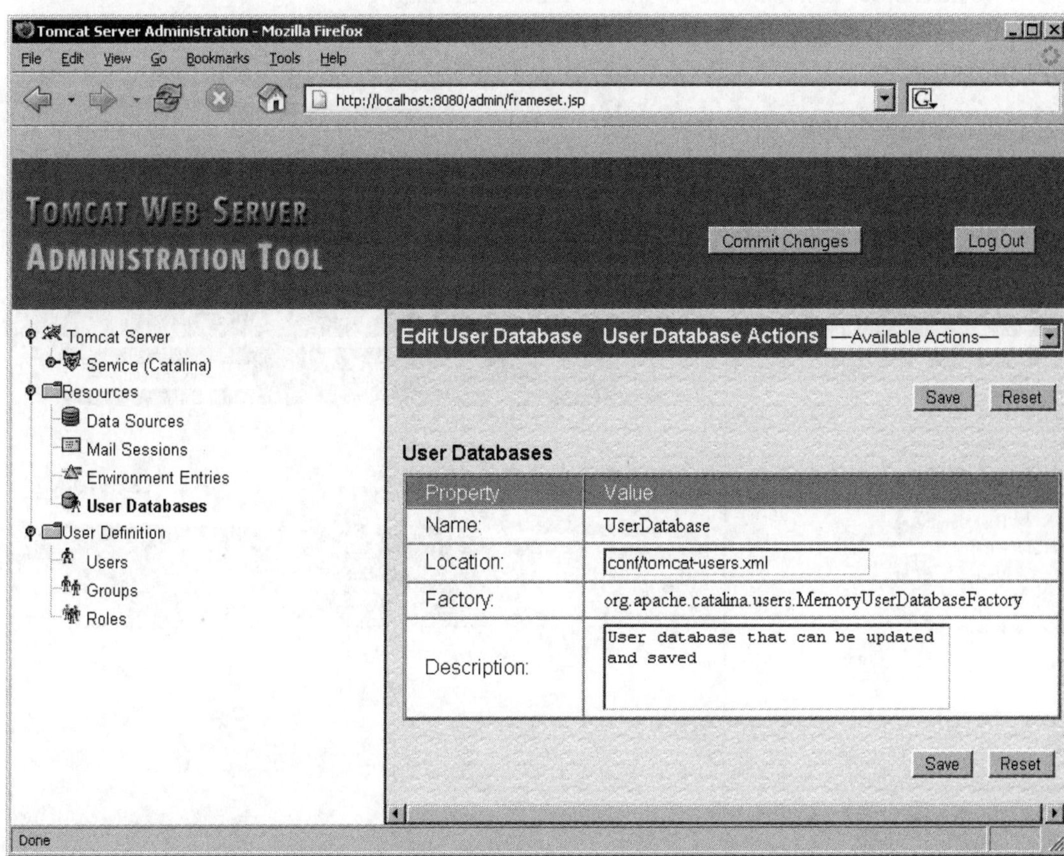

Figure 11-6. *Editing the default user database*

You can also delete user databases if you no longer require them. Click the User Database Actions box, and select Delete User Databases. You'll see a list of user databases and their descriptions along with a checkbox, as shown in Figure 11-7.

In Tomcat 5.0.*x*, you can't delete the default user database, as indicated by the star, but you can delete any of the others listed. Tomcat 5.5 allows you to remove any user database. Select the checkbox of the user database you want to delete, and click Save. That's the theory anyway. As things stand, this function of the `admin` application is fairly flaky, so you may have to delete your user databases by hand for the time being.

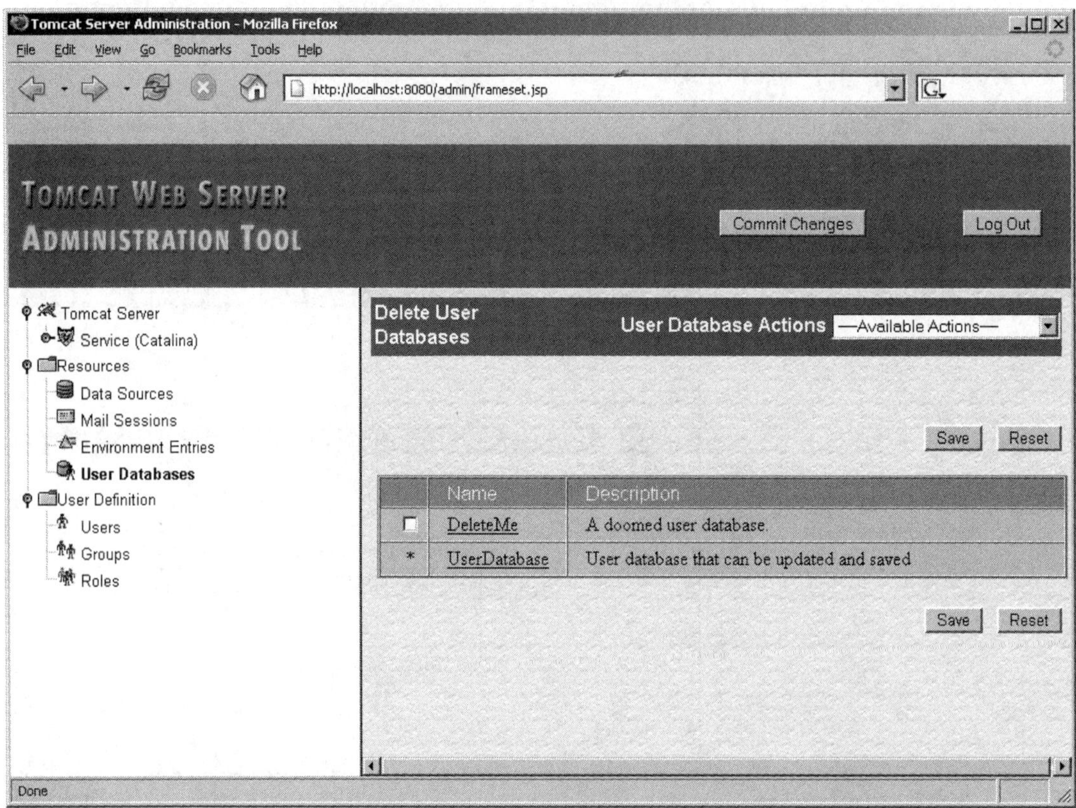

Figure 11-7. *Deleting a user database*

Editing the User Database with the Admin Application

To edit the user database, click the Users item in the tree view on the left; you'll see a screen like Figure 11-8.

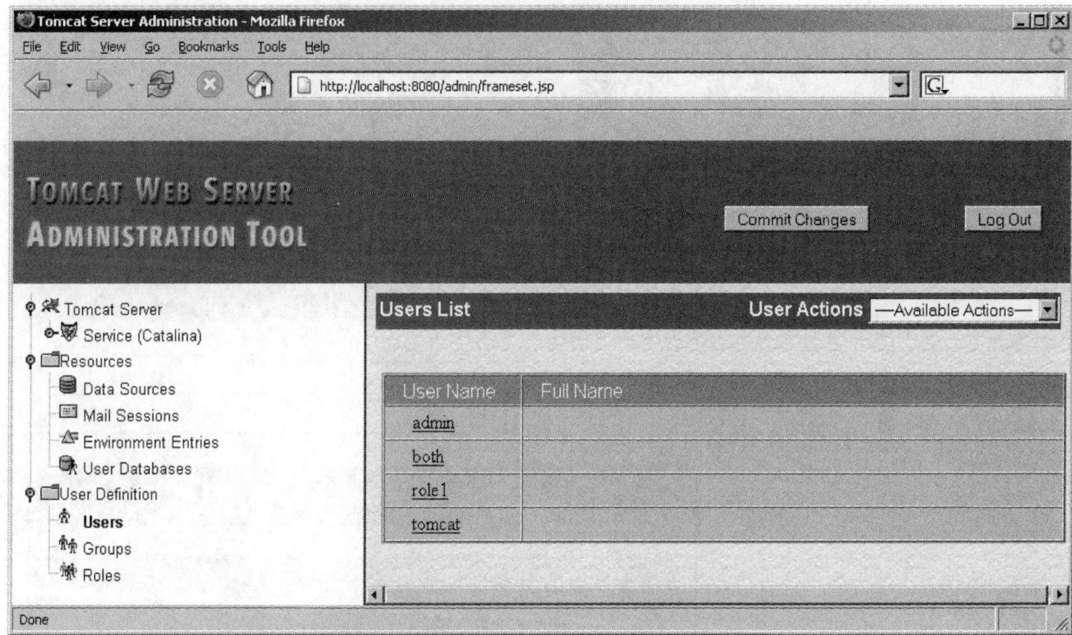

Figure 11-8. *Viewing users with the* `admin` *application*

It's worth noticing that the list of users shown in the table on the right is the same as the list of users shown in Listing 11-2, where an example `tomcat-users.xml` file is shown.

To edit a user, click a name. You can change the password, add a full name or description, and change the roles (see Figure 11-9).

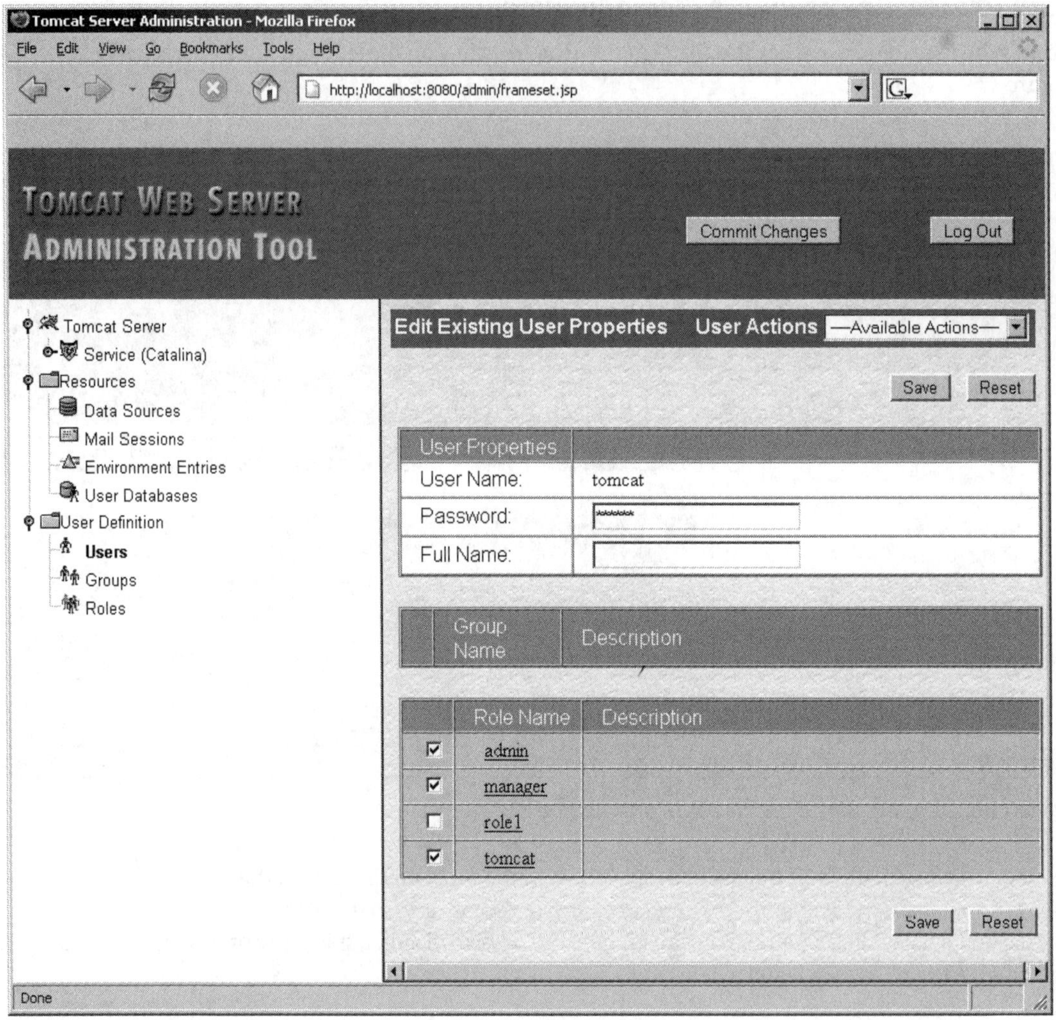

Figure 11-9. *Editing a user's details*

Any changes you make will be written to `tomcat-users.xml` (or whichever realm you're using) once you click Save. As with all the actions of the `admin` application, any changes will remove comments from the user database file. This is because the `admin` application writes a new file every time, so "modifying the user database" is a slight misnomer; you're really specifying new values to replace the old user database, which the `admin` application will overwrite. You don't have a backup in this case, though.

To create a new user, click the User Actions box and select Create New User. You'll see a screen like in Figure 11-10.

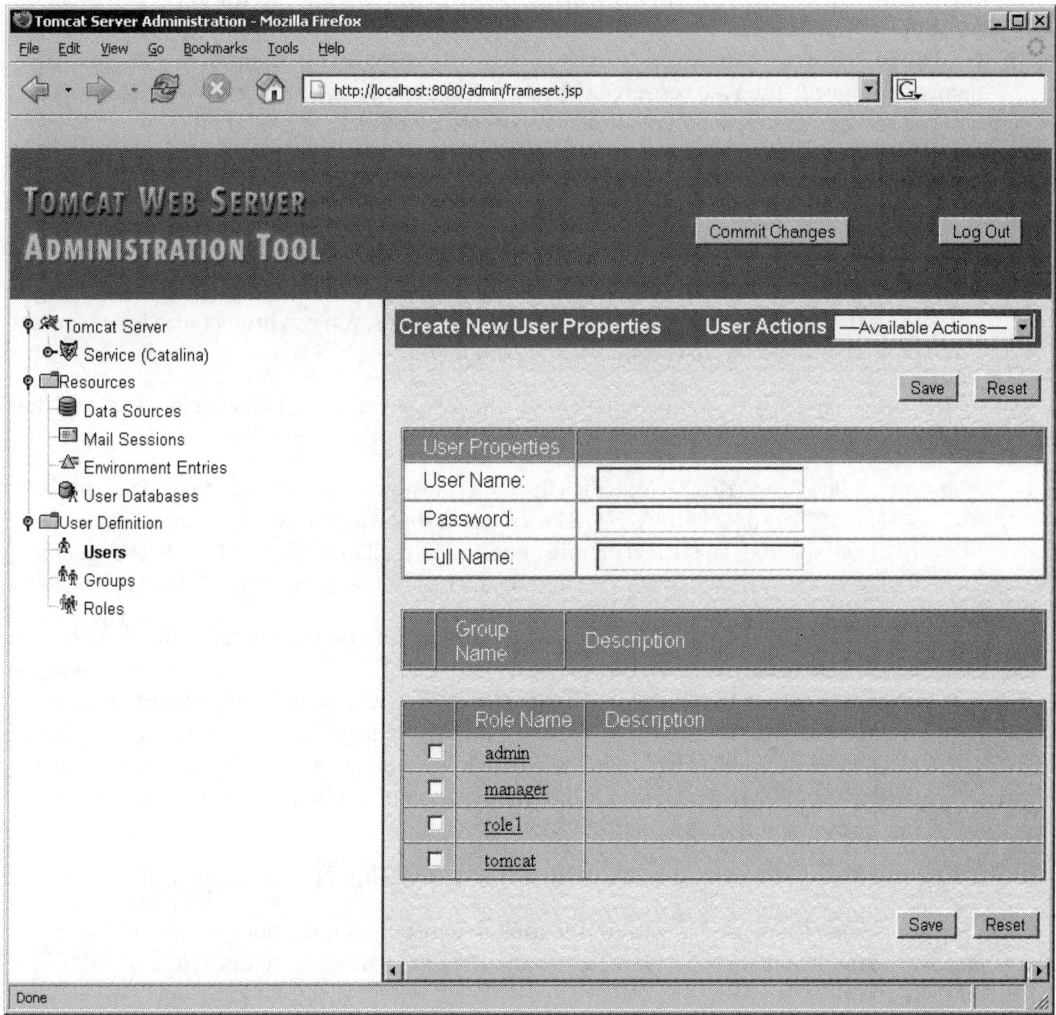

Figure 11-10. *Creating a new user*

Click the Save button. After clicking Save, open `tomcat-users.xml` and check that your new user has been added. You don't need to click Commit Changes in this case, unless you've made changes elsewhere and want to restart the server and overwrite `server.xml`. Your user is now available to Tomcat for authentication. If you gave the user the admin role, log out of the `admin` application and try to log in as the new user. Their details should allow you to access the `admin` application.

Protecting a Resource with a Realm

It's usually a Web application developer who will specify which resources need to be protected, though you'll have your own applications you want to protect, such as the admin and manager Web applications.

You saw the important security-related elements of web.xml in Chapter 5. You use these elements to specify the Web resource to protect and the way in which you want to protect it.

The security-related elements from web.xml are as follows:

- <security-constraint>: Protects a group of Web resources and specifies the role that a user must have before accessing the resource.
- <web-resource-collection>: A subelement of <security-constraint>. This specifies the Web resources that this security constraint protects. This can be a URL pattern using wildcard notation or an HTTP method. In other words, you can protect physical resources or protect access from certain access methods.
- <auth-constraint>: A subelement of <security-constraint>. This specifies the roles that are allowed to access resources covered by this security constraint.
- <user-data-constraint>: Specifies the data transport security constraint. This can be NONE, INTEGRAL, or CONFIDENTIAL. NONE specifies that no transport guarantee is required. INTEGRAL specifies that the data must not be changed in transit. CONFIDENTIAL specifies that others may not view the date in transit. The last two mean that HTTPS must be used.
- <login-config>: Specifies the type of authentication Tomcat should perform. The choices are BASIC, DIGEST, FORM, or SSL client methods for authentication. BASIC uses the browser's password request box but transmits the username and password in unencrypted text. DIGEST uses the browser's password request box and encryption. This isn't always well supported by browsers. FORM allows you to specify a custom login form, like the admin application. The SSL client methods require digital certificates. You'll learn more about them in Chapter 12.
- <security-role>: Specifies the security roles used within this Web application.

You've seen these used in various incarnations throughout the book so far, but I won't discuss them in detail until Chapter 12 because they're security configuration, not realm configuration.

However, Listing 11-7 shows how to set up basic protection for the ch11 directory of the tomcatBook Web application.

Listing 11-7. *A Simple Security Setup*

```
<?xml version="1.0" encoding="ISO-8859-1"?>
<web-app xmlns="http://java.sun.com/xml/ns/j2ee"
        xmlns:xsi="http://www.w3.org/2001/XMLSchema-instance"
        xsi:schemaLocation="http://java.sun.com/xml/ns/j2ee
        http://java.sun.com/xml/ns/j2ee/web-app_2_4.xsd" version="2.4">
```

```
<!-- Describe a DataSource -->
<resource-ref>
  <description>
    Resource reference to a factory for java.sql.Connection
    instances that may be used for talking to a particular
    database that is configured in the tomcatBook.xml file.
  </description>
  <res-ref-name>
    jdbc/CatalogDB
  </res-ref-name>
  <res-type>
    javax.sql.DataSource
  </res-type>
  <res-auth>
    SERVLET
  </res-auth>
</resource-ref>

<!-- Define a Security Constraint on this application -->
<security-constraint>
  <web-resource-collection>
    <web-resource-name>Tomcat Book Application</web-resource-name>
    <url-pattern>/ch11/*</url-pattern>
  </web-resource-collection>
  <auth-constraint>
     <role-name>tomcat</role-name>
  </auth-constraint>
</security-constraint>

<!-- Define the Login Configuration for this Application -->
<login-config>
  <auth-method>BASIC</auth-method>
  <realm-name>Tomcat Book Application</realm-name>
</login-config>

<!-- Security roles referenced by this Web application -->
<security-role>
  <description>
```

```
      The role that is required to log in to the TomcatBook application
    </description>
    <role-name>tomcat</role-name>
  </security-role>
</web-app>
```

Configuring a JDBC Realm

Now that you're familiar with realms in general, and file-based realms in particular, it's time to introduce JDBC realms. JDBC realms use relational databases as their data storage mechanism and can be extremely useful if you have an existing user database that contains usernames and passwords. They're even better if the database already contains the roles each user has. Even if this isn't the case, you can easily add another table to the database.

JDBC realms allow you to seamlessly integrate Tomcat into your existing network infrastructure. You gain all the advantages of using a common database for all your users, which include making database maintenance easy, making code maintenance easy, and removing the need to rewrite any application code. Like the user database, a JDBC realm is up-to-date and reflects any changes in your common database.

Even if you don't have a common database, a JDBC realm is a good option for your realm, especially if you have any database applications running on your server. Using the same database server as Tomcat's Web applications won't adversely affect performance and brings some of the advantages outlined previously, namely ease of maintenance. JDBC realms are robust, and you can easily secure databases against unauthorized entry. It's certainly more difficult for casual observers to view user information in a database than it is to view it in a text file residing in Tomcat's directory structure.

Creating a JDBC Realm's Data Store

JDBC realms are designed to be integrated with existing user databases, and as such their configuration maps to a common user database setup. Each of the configuration parameters you saw in `tomcat-users.xml` has a corresponding parameter in a JDBC realm, so a database should contain a username column, a user password column, and a user role column associated with a username. Following good database design, the username and password should be stored in one table and the username and role should be stored in another table, as shown in Figure 11-11.

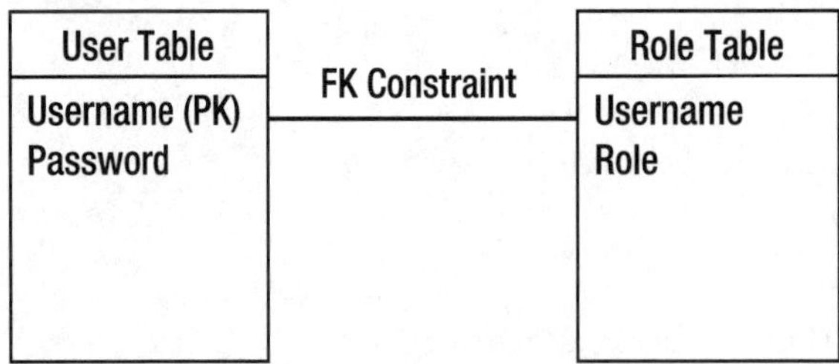

Figure 11-11. *The JDBC realm table schema*

The user table has a username field, which is the primary key, and a password field. This ensures that all usernames are unique, as should be the case in any existing database. The role table also has a username field, which is linked to `user.username` with a foreign key constraint to enforce relational integrity. There's no primary key, though you should use a compound primary key if your database allows it, either of which means there may be more than one role assigned to a username in the role table. Each combination is given its own row.

These tables and fields don't have to follow any naming conventions because you can configure the JDBC realm to use any table and fields you want. This is all part of the graceful integration that makes JDBC realms so easy to use.

You configure JDBC realm definitions in a realm element at the level of any container component, just like the file-based realms previously described. Table 11-2 shows the JDBC realm's attributes.

Table 11-2. *The JDBC Realm Attributes*

Attribute	Description	Required?
`className`	The Java class that implements the JDBC realm. This must be `org.apache.catalina.realm.JDBCRealm`.	Yes
`connectionName`	The JDBC connection username to be used.	Yes
`connectionPassword`	The JDBC connection password to be used.	Yes
`connectionURL`	The JDBC connection URL used to access the database instance.	Yes
`debug`	Tomcat 5.0.*x* only. Controls the level of debugging information that's printed to the log file. The default is zero.	No
`digest`	Specifies the digest algorithm for the password (as used by the `java.security.MessageDigest` class). The default is plain text.	No
`driverName`	The JDBC driver.	Yes
`userTable`	The name of the users table in the database.	Yes
`userNameCol`	The username column in the `userTable` table and the `userRoleTable` table.	Yes
`userCredCol`	The password column in the `userTable`.	Yes
`userRoleTable`	The user role table in the database.	Yes
`roleNameCol`	The role column in the `userRoleTable`.	Yes

As you can see, it's a straightforward task to specify the database server, the user and role tables, and the username, password, and role columns. `server.xml` contains three JDBC realms by default: MySQL, Oracle, and ODBC. Let's examine how to work with MySQL before looking at ODBC.

Configuring a MySQL JDBC Realm

Listing 11-8 shows the default MySQL setting in `server.xml`. You shouldn't change its `className` and `driverName` attributes because they're required when using a MySQL JDBC realm. You should make sure that the MySQL driver is in Tomcat's classpath. For details of obtaining and installing a MySQL driver, see Chapter 10.

You should note, however, that the MySQL driver is no longer called `org.gjt.mm.mysql.Driver`, though this class is still supplied in the driver JAR file for backward compatibility. You should use `com.mysql.jdbc.Driver` for all other purposes.

Listing 11-8. *The Default MySQL JDBC Realm in* `server.xml`

```
<!--
<Realm  className="org.apache.catalina.realm.JDBCRealm" debug="99"
        driverName="org.gjt.mm.mysql.Driver"
        connectionURL="jdbc:mysql://localhost/authority"
        connectionName="test" connectionPassword="test"
        userTable="users" userNameCol="user_name" userCredCol="user_pass"
        userRoleTable="user_roles" roleNameCol="role_name" />
-->
```

Before you change any of these values, you should ensure you have a database ready. In this example you'll be replicating the `tomcat-users.xml` file from Listing 11-3, digested admin password and all. Listing 11-9 shows a SQL script (`realmDB.sql`) that will create the database, the tables, and the columns. It will also insert the user data from Listing 11-3.

Listing 11-9. *A SQL Script to Set Up the JDBC Realm in MySQL*

```
CREATE DATABASE realmDB;
USE realmDB;

CREATE TABLE deptusers (
  apressusername VARCHAR(15) NOT NULL PRIMARY KEY,
  password     VARCHAR(40) NOT NULL
) TYPE=InnoDB;

CREATE TABLE deptroles (
  apressusername VARCHAR(15) NOT NULL,
  apressrole     VARCHAR(15) NOT NULL,
  PRIMARY KEY (apressusername, apressrole),
  FOREIGN KEY (apressusername) REFERENCES deptusers(apressusername)
    ON DELETE CASCADE
) TYPE=InnoDB;
```

```
INSERT INTO deptusers VALUES ('tomcat', 'tomcat');
INSERT INTO deptusers VALUES ('both', 'tomcat');
INSERT INTO deptusers VALUES ('role1', 'tomcat');
INSERT INTO deptusers VALUES ('admin',
'd033e22ae348aeb5660fc2140aec35850c4da997');

INSERT INTO deptroles VALUES ('tomcat', 'tomcat');
INSERT INTO deptroles VALUES ('both', 'tomcat');
INSERT INTO deptroles VALUES ('both', 'role1');
INSERT INTO deptroles VALUES ('role1', 'role1');
INSERT INTO deptroles VALUES ('admin', 'admin');
```

MySQL provides `MD5()` and `SHA()` functions to digest passwords as they're placed into the database. The `SHA()` function is available only in MySQL 4.0.2 onward, so you still have to use Tomcat's digest script to calculate the digest if you have an older version. Change the digested line to the following as appropriate if you want to use these functions:

```
# Can be used in all versions of MySQL
INSERT INTO deptusers VALUES ('admin', MD5('admin'));
# MySQL 4.0.2 onwards
INSERT INTO deptusers VALUES ('admin', SHA('admin'));
```

Remember to delete this script when you've finished, though.

Versions of MySQL older than 3.23.44 don't support foreign keys, but they will parse the script, and newer versions of the MySQL 3.23 series must use InnoDB tables as specified in Listing 11-9. MySQL 4 uses InnoDB tables by default. The absence of foreign key support isn't too big a problem; you must just be careful when modifying the database.

To check whether InnoDB tables are enabled on your server, run the following in MySQL:

```
mysql> SHOW VARIABLES LIKE 'have_%';
```

If InnoDB tables are enabled, you'll see the following:

```
+---------------+-------+
| Variable_name | Value |
+---------------+-------+
| have_bdb      | YES   |
| have_gemini   | NO    |
| have_innodb   | YES   |
| have_isam     | YES   |
| have_raid     | NO    |
| have_openssl  | NO    |
+---------------+-------+
```

```
6 rows in set (0.00 sec)
```

If the have_innodb variable is set to DISABLED, then your server has the potential to use InnoDB tables, and you'll have to configure them. Add the following line under the [mysqld] section to your my.ini file (through the MySQL admin interface) on Windows or your MYSQL_HOME/data/my.cnf file on other platforms:

```
innodb_data_file_path = ibdata1:30M:autoextend
```

This creates a 30MB store for InnoDB tables in the MYSQL_HOME/data directory that grows if required. Restart the server, and check that InnoDB tables are enabled.

To run the realmDB.sql script, log into the MySQL server and run the following, assuming the script is in MySQL's bin directory:

```
mysql> \. ./realmDB.sql
```

You should create a user in MySQL that will allow Tomcat to read the values in the user database. This follows a similar pattern to the read-only user you created in Chapter 10. You could even use the same read-only user if you wanted, though you still have to execute a new GRANT command. The following creates a tomcat read-only user in the MySQL privileges database:

```
mysql> GRANT SELECT ON realmDB.*
    -> TO 'tomcat'@'localhost'
    -> IDENTIFIED BY 'meow';
```

Now that you've prepared the database, you should create the realm definition in server.xml. Listing 11-10 shows the settings for the realmDB database, though you should change the connectionName and connectionPassword attributes if you have a different username and password than the ones just shown. Comment out any other realm definitions.

Listing 11-10. *The Example MySQL JDBC Realm Configuration*

```
<Realm className="org.apache.catalina.realm.JDBCRealm" debug="99"
       driverName="com.mysql.jdbc.Driver"
       connectionURL="jdbc:mysql://localhost/realmDB"
       connectionName="tomcat" connectionPassword="meow"
       userTable="deptusers" userNameCol="apressusername"
       userCredCol="password"
       userRoleTable="deptroles" roleNameCol="apressrole"
       digest="sha"
/>
```

You should now test the realm by visiting a protected resource, such as the `admin` application. If the setup was successful, you'll be able to log in using the admin user as before. Open the Service node, and click the Realm node. You'll see that Tomcat is using the MySQL JDBC realm for authentication, as shown in Figure 11-12.

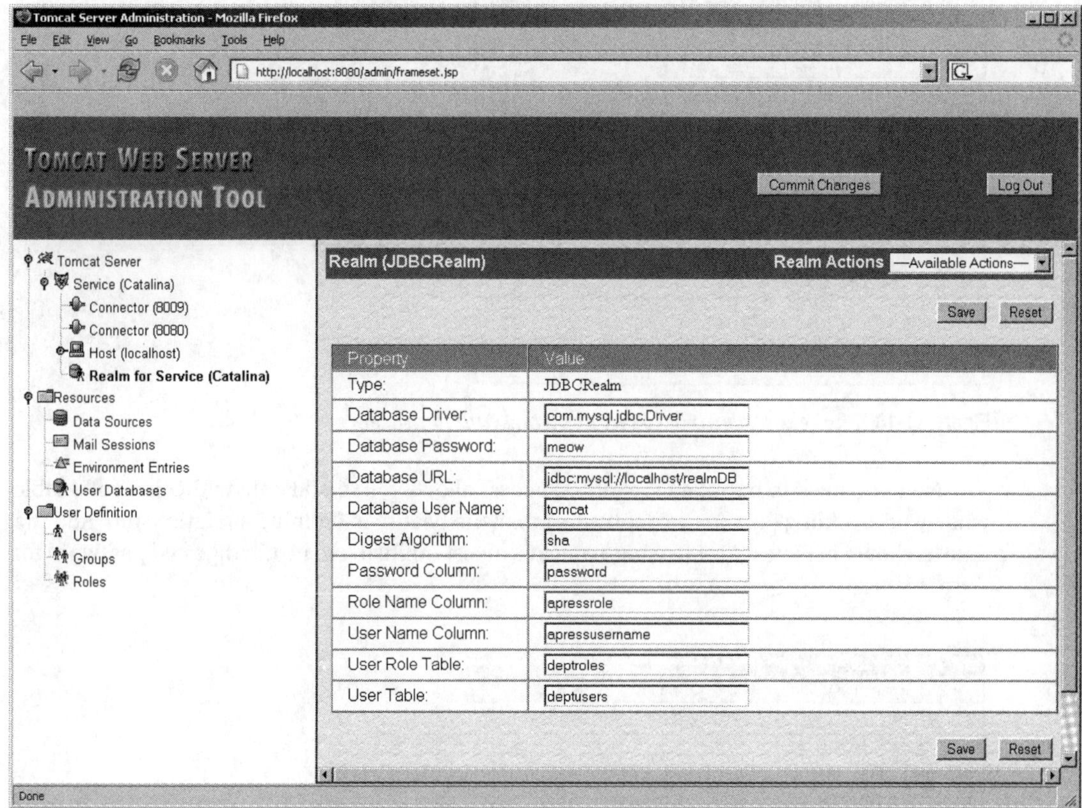

Figure 11-12. *The* `admin` *application shows that Tomcat is using the new realm.*

Configuring an ODBC JDBC Realm

For this example you'll use an Access database as the ODBC data source, though SQL server or Excel spreadsheets are just as easy. Create the two tables as described in the previous section, with a relationship as shown in Figure 11-13.

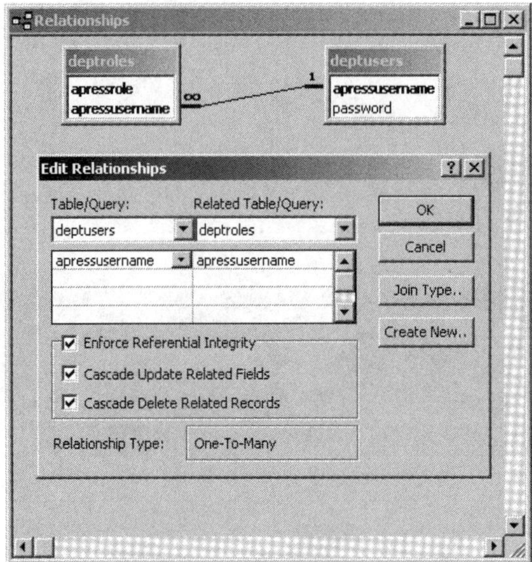

Figure 11-13. *The relationship between deptroles and deptusers*

Now you need to populate the tables. Access allows you to add data to the deptroles table while you're adding data to the deptusers table: the beauty of defining a relationship. Add the data as shown in Figure 11-14, using Tomcat's digest utility to create the digested password for the `admin` user.

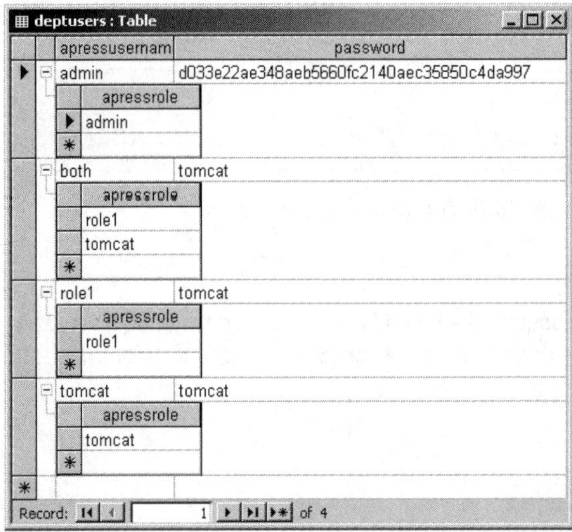

Figure 11-14. *The data in deptroles and deptusers*

Of course, you may already have data you can use. The final step of configuration for Access is to add a Windows data source. Click Start ➤ Settings ➤ Control Panel ➤ Administrative Tools ➤ Data Sources (ODBC). Choose a System DSN, and click Add.

Choose an Access (`*.mdb`) driver, and fill in the details as shown in Figure 11-15; you can browse to the database by clicking Select.

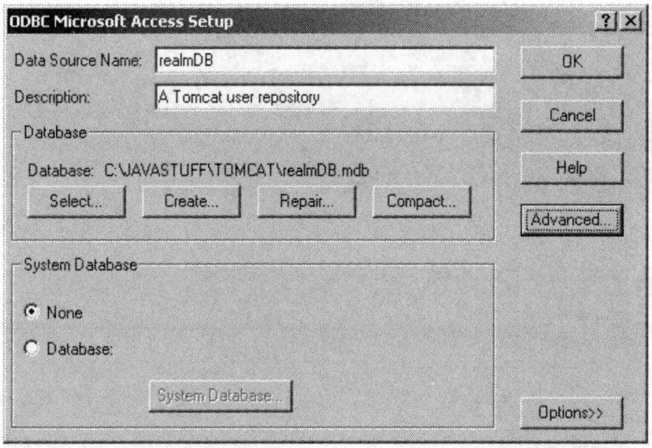

Figure 11-15. *Configuring an ODBC data source*

Click Advanced to set a username and password. In this case, enter the username **tomcat** and the password **meow**.

The JDBC ODBC driver is part of the Java distribution, so you don't need to add any JAR files to Tomcat's classpath. This just leaves the realm configuration in `server.xml`. Comment out any other realms, and add the definition as shown in Listing 11-11.

Listing 11-11. *A JDBC Realm Using an ODBC Data Source*

```
<Realm className="org.apache.catalina.realm.JDBCRealm" debug="99"
       driverName="sun.jdbc.odbc.JdbcOdbcDriver"
       connectionURL="jdbc:odbc:realmDB"
       connectionName="tomcat" connectionPassword="meow"
       userTable="deptusers" userNameCol="apressusername"
       userCredCol="password"
       userRoleTable="deptroles" roleNameCol="apressrole"
       digest="sha"
/>
```

You shouldn't change the `className` or `driverName` options because they're standard for ODBC JDBC realms. The `connectionURL` option is the name of the ODBC data source you configured earlier, and the other settings correspond to the database and user details you added. The password for the admin Tomcat user is digested with the SHA algorithm, so enter the digest attribute **sha**.

Start Tomcat, and attempt to log into the `admin` application using this setup. If all went well, you'll be able to log in successfully. Open the Service node, and click the Realm node. You'll see that Tomcat is using the ODBC JDBC realm for authentication, as shown in Figure 11-16.

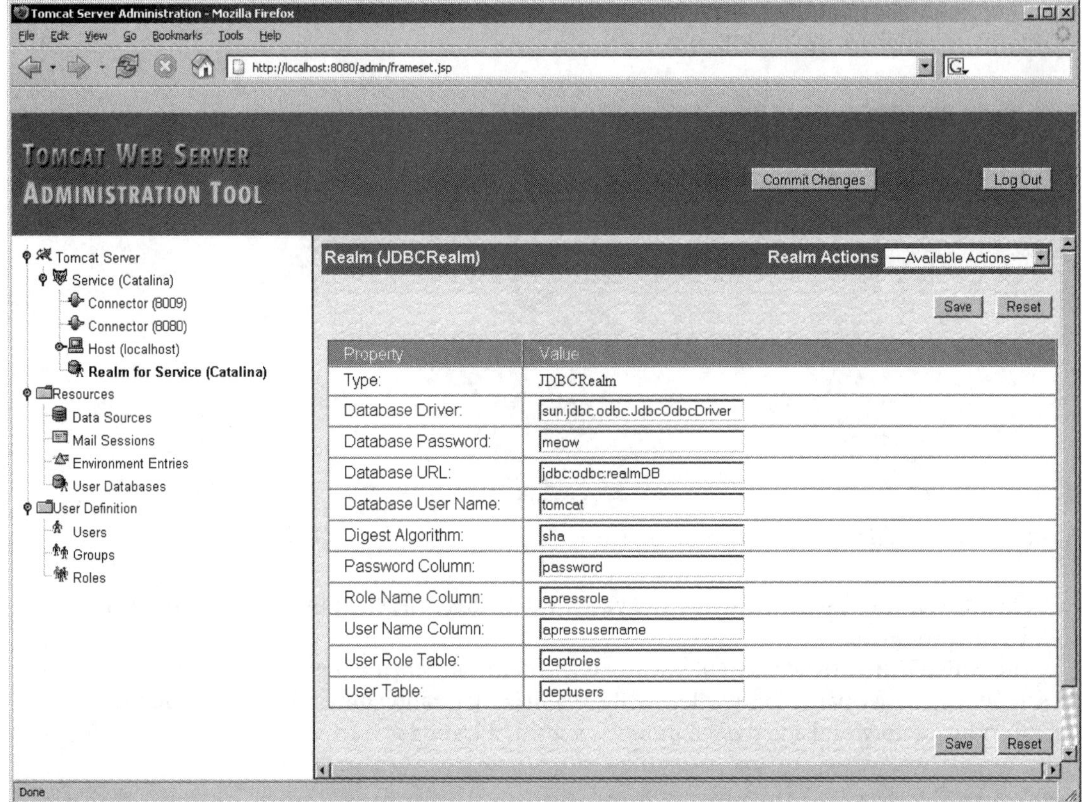

Figure 11-16. *The* `admin` *application shows that Tomcat is using the new realm.*

Configuring JNDI Realms

JNDI realms also allow you to use existing data, this time in the form of directory services. To use a JNDI realm, you must be able to map the configuration attributes to an existing directory schema. This is similar to the process of mapping database tables and columns to Tomcat login details. Table 11-3 shows the attributes for the JNDI realm.

Table 11-3. *The JNDI Realm's Attributes*

Attribute	Description	Required?
`className`	Class name of the JNDI realm implementation. Must be `org.apache.catalina.realm.JNDIRealm`.	Yes
`connectionName`	The username used to log into the directory service. Not required if simple binding is in use.	No
`connectionPassword`	The password used to log into the directory service. Not required if simple binding is in use.	No
`connectionURL`	The URL of the directory service.	Yes

Table 11-3. *The JNDI Realm's Attributes (Continued)*

Attribute	Description	Required?
`contextFactory`	The class used to create the context for the JNDI connection. The standard JNDI LDAP provider is sufficient in most cases.	No
`debug`	The level of debugging messages that will be logged.	No
`digest`	Specifies the digest algorithm used to digest the user's password. This attribute is ignored if you don't specify `userPassword`.	No
`roleBase`	The base element for role searches. The default is the top-level element.	No
`roleName`	The name of the directory attribute that contains the role name.	No
`roleSearch`	An LDAP pattern for searching the directory for roles. The `{0}` placeholder inserts the user's distinguished name, and `{1}` inserts the username. Often these are the same.	No
`roleSubtree`	If set to `true`, a subtree search will be conducted for the role. The default is `false`.	No
`userBase`	The base element for user searches using the `userSearch` attribute. This isn't used if you're using the `userPattern` expression. The default is the top-level element in the directory context.	No
`userPassword`	The name of the user element's directory attribute that contains the password information.	No
`userPattern`	An LDAP pattern for searching the directory for a user entry. The `{0}` placeholder inserts the username entered by the user.	No
`userRoleName`	The name of an attribute in the user's directory entry containing zero or more roles assigned to the user. If `userRoleName` isn't specified, all the roles for a user derive from the role search.	No
`userSearch`	The LDAP filter expression for searching for a user's directory entry. `{0}` inserts the username as entered by the user. Use this property (along with the `userBase` and `userSubtree` properties) instead of `userPattern` to search the directory for the user's entry.	No
`userSubtree`	Set to `true` if you want to search the entire subtree of the element specified by the `userBase` property for the user's entry. The default value of `false` causes only the top level to be searched. Not used if you're using the `userPattern` expression.	No

Let's see some of these attributes in action, because JNDI realms are slightly more complicated than the other realm types.

Setting Up a Directory Server

If you don't already have a directory server, then you may want to install OpenLDAP (`http://www.openldap.org`). It's a free, open-source directory server that uses Lightweight Directory Access Protocol (LDAP), and you can use its services via a JNDI driver, which means you can also use it as a JNDI realm data repository. Download the server, and install it in a convenient location (`LDAP_HOME` for the purposes of this discussion). A Windows binary is available at `http://download.bergmans.us/openldap/`.

The main configuration file is `LDAP_HOME/slapd.conf`. The default file already contains a number of settings, none of which you should have to change. However, you may need to add some settings. Listing 11-12 shows the minimum you'll require (using OpenLDAP 2.2).

Listing 11-12. *The Settings in slapd.conf*

```
ucdata-path C:/openldap/ucdata
include C:/openldap/etc/schema/core.schema
include C:/openldap/etc/schema/cosine.schema
include C:/openldap/etc/schema/inetorgperson.schema

pidfile C:/openldap/var/slapd.pid
argsfile C:/openldap/var/slapd.args

database bdb
suffix dc="mycompany,dc=com"
rootdn "cn=Manager,dc=mycompany,dc=com"
rootpw secret
directory C:/openldap/var/openldap-data
```

You should, of course, change the paths to suit your system. The `include` directives at the beginning of the file include object definitions that you'll use when adding users and roles to the directory. The `suffix` attribute specifies the domain in which this directory server is running, and the `rootdn` and `rootpw` attributes set the admin user and password for this directory server. The directory attribute specifies where the directory files will be stored.

Once you've modified `slapd.conf`, start the directory server.

```
> slapd -d 1
```

The directory server will listen on port 339 (the default LDAP port) and will report at debug level 1. Now that the directory server is running, you can add entries to the directory using LDAP Data Interchange Format (LDIF). LDIF is a text-based directory description format that's processed by client tools so that directory entries can be added.

Again, you'll replicate the information in `tomcat-users.xml` in LDIF. Create a file called `realmDB.ldif`, and add the entries shown in Listing 11-13.

Listing 11-13. *The Users and Roles from `tomcat-users.xml` in LDIF*

```
# Define top-level entry
dn: dc=mycompany,dc=com
objectClass: dcObject
objectClass: organization
dc: mycompany
o: mycompany

# Define an entry to contain people
# searches for users are based on this entry
dn: ou=people,dc=mycompany,dc=com
objectClass: organizationalUnit
ou: people

# Define a user entry for tomcat
dn: uid=tomcat,ou=people,dc=mycompany,dc=com
objectClass: inetOrgPerson
uid: tomcat
sn: tomcat
cn: tomcat user
userPassword: tomcat

# Define a user entry for role1
dn: uid=role1,ou=people,dc=mycompany,dc=com
objectClass: inetOrgPerson
uid: role1
sn: role1
cn: role1 user
userPassword: tomcat

# Define a user entry for both
dn: uid=both,ou=people,dc=mycompany,dc=com
objectClass: inetOrgPerson
uid: both
sn: both
cn: both user
userPassword: tomcat
```

```
# Define a user entry for admin
dn: uid=admin,ou=people,dc=mycompany,dc=com
objectClass: inetOrgPerson
uid: admin
sn: admin
cn: admin user
userPassword: d033e22ae348aeb5660fc2140aec35850c4da997

# Define an entry to contain LDAP groups
# searches for roles are based on this entry
dn: ou=groups,dc=mycompany,dc=com
objectClass: organizationalUnit
ou: groups

# Define an entry for the "tomcat" role
dn: cn=tomcat,ou=groups,dc=mycompany,dc=com
objectClass: groupOfUniqueNames
cn: tomcat
uniqueMember: uid=tomcat,ou=people,dc=mycompany,dc=com
uniqueMember: uid=both,ou=people,dc=mycompany,dc=com

# Define an entry for the "role1" role
dn: cn=role1,ou=groups,dc=mycompany,dc=com
objectClass: groupOfUniqueNames
cn: role1
uniqueMember: uid=role1,ou=people,dc=mycompany,dc=com
uniqueMember: uid=both,ou=people,dc=mycompany,dc=com

# Define an entry for the "admin" role
dn: cn=admin,ou=groups,dc=mycompany,dc=com
objectClass: groupOfUniqueNames
cn: admin
uniqueMember: uid=admin,ou=people,dc=mycompany,dc=com
```

Here you've added the users to the people group, which is part of the `mycompany.com` domain. Table 11-4 shows what each of the user attributes means.

Table 11-4. *Attributes for a User Entry*

Attribute	Description
cn	This user's common name, which can be used as a description.
dn	The user's distinguished name, which makes it unique within the directory. This is used when searching for a user.
objectClass	The object that models this user. The inetOrgPerson is a standard definition of a person with common attributes, such as e-mail addresses and telephone numbers.
sn	The user's surname.
uid	The unique username for this person.
userPassword	The password of this user.

The roles are added to a groups called *groups* and follow the same pattern as the users. The uniqueMember attribute specifies a member of that role using the user's distinguished name. If you're interested in seeing how objects and attributes are linked together, examine the *.schema files in LDAP_HOME/etc/schema.

You have two choices for adding these entries to the directory: online or offline. You should create the database online using LDAP only when creating small databases (1 to 2,000 entries) because it uses the directory server to create the database. Clients can also access the database while an online operation is in progress, meaning that large, slow updates will result in problems. The offline method creates the database files directly without going through the directory server.

To add the entries to the directory online, use the ldapadd utility that comes with OpenLDAP:

```
> ldapadd -x -D "cn=Manager,dc=mycompany,dc=com" -w secret -f realmDB.ldif
adding new entry "dc=mycompany,dc=com"
adding new entry "ou=people,dc=mycompany,dc=com"
adding new entry "uid=tomcat,ou=people,dc=mycompany,dc=com"
adding new entry "uid=role1,ou=people,dc=mycompany,dc=com"
adding new entry "uid=both,ou=people,dc=mycompany,dc=com"
adding new entry "uid=admin,ou=people,dc=mycompany,dc=com"
adding new entry "ou=groups,dc=mycompany,dc=com"
adding new entry "cn=tomcat,ou=groups,dc=mycompany,dc=com"
adding new entry "cn=role1,ou=groups,dc=mycompany,dc=com"
adding new entry "cn=admin,ou=groups,dc=mycompany,dc=com"
```

The -x switch tells the ldapadd client to connect to the directory server using the simple bind method, as opposed to an encrypted method. In this case, the username and password are sent in plain text. -D specifies the bind distinguished name, essentially the username for the domain you're configuring, and -w specifies the password. The -f switch specifies the LDIF file to use for creating the directory entries.

To add the entries offline, use the slapadd utility.

```
> slapadd -v -l realmDB.ldif -f slapd.conf
added: "dc=mycompany,dc=com" (00000001)
added: "ou=people,dc=mycompany,dc=com" (00000002)
added: "uid=tomcat,ou=people,dc=mycompany,dc=com" (00000003)
added: "uid=role1,ou=people,dc=mycompany,dc=com" (00000004)
added: "uid=both,ou=people,dc=mycompany,dc=com" (00000005)
added: "uid=admin,ou=people,dc=mycompany,dc=com" (00000006)
added: "ou=groups,dc=mycompany,dc=com" (00000007)
added: "cn=tomcat,ou=groups,dc=mycompany,dc=com" (00000008)
added: "cn=role1,ou=groups,dc=mycompany,dc=com" (00000009)
added: "cn=admin,ou=groups,dc=mycompany,dc=com" (0000000a)
```

-v specifies verbose mode, -l specifies the LDIF file, and -f is the slapd configuration file.

To test that your entries are in the directory, use the ldapsearch tool, as follows, where -b is the base distinguished name to search:

```
> ldapsearch -b "dc=mycompany,dc=com"
```

If the search is successful, you'll see output that's similar to realmDB.ldif with the passwords scrambled.

To delete the entries, use ldapdelete with the -r switch to do a recursive delete.

```
> ldapdelete -x -D "cn=Manager,dc=mycompany,dc=com"
-w secret -r "dc=mycompany, dc=com"
```

Adding the JNDI Realm

You now need to configure the realm in Tomcat's server.xml file. Listing 11-14 shows a realm definition that will connect to the directory server with an anonymous login and search for users and roles according to the username entered by the user:

Listing 11-14. *A JNDI Realm in server.xml*

```
<Realm className="org.apache.catalina.realm.JNDIRealm" debug="99"
       connectionURL="ldap://localhost:389"
       userPassword="userPassword"
       userPattern="uid={0},ou=people,dc=mycompany,dc=com"
       roleBase="ou=groups,dc=mycompany,dc=com"
       roleName="cn"
       roleSearch="(uniqueMember={0})"
       digest="sha"
/>
```

You shouldn't change the className or connectionURL attributes because they're standard for JNDI realms. The userPassword attribute specifies which attribute in a user's directory entry should be used for password comparison when trying to log into an application.

The userPattern attribute tells the driver which pattern should be used when searching for a user. If you look at the previous realmDB.ldif file, you'll see that each user is specified with a distinguished name in the form given in this attribute. When the user types in their username, it will be substituted in this string and the result will be used to search for that user. If that user is found then they have been authenticated for the purposes of this realm. However, they still must be authorized.

The role* attributes combine in the search for a user role. roleBase tells the directory server where to begin the search, in this case with the groups organizational unit. The roleName attribute specifies which attribute in a role's entry should be used to identify its name. Once a role has been identified with this directory attribute, the attribute specified in roleSearch is used to confirm that a user is a member of that role.

The digest attribute is used as in other realms.

Start Tomcat, and attempt to log into the admin application using this setup. If all went well, you'll be able to log in successfully. Open the Service node, and click the Realm node. You'll see that Tomcat is using the JNDI realm for authentication, as shown in Figure 11-17.

For a further insight into the communication between Tomcat and the directory server, examine the log for the service component. You should see something similar to Listing 11-15.

Listing 11-15. *The Communication Between Tomcat and the Directory Server*

```
JNDIRealm[Catalina]: Connecting to URL ldap://localhost:389
JNDIRealm[Catalina]: lookupUser(admin)
JNDIRealm[Catalina]:   dn=uid=admin,ou=people,dc=mycompany,dc=com
JNDIRealm[Catalina]:   retrieving attribute userPassword
JNDIRealm[Catalina]:   validating credentials
JNDIRealm[Catalina]: Username admin successfully authenticated
JNDIRealm[Catalina]:   getRoles(uid=admin,ou=people,dc=mycompany,dc=com)
JNDIRealm[Catalina]:   Searching role base 'ou=groups,dc=mycompany,dc=com' for
attribute 'cn'
JNDIRealm[Catalina]:   With filter expression
'(uniqueMember=uid=admin,ou=people,dc=mycompany,dc=com)'
JNDIRealm[Catalina]:   retrieving values for attribute cn
JNDIRealm[Catalina]:   Returning 1 roles
JNDIRealm[Catalina]:   Found role admin
```

Here you can see the two steps mentioned previously. The directory server authenticates the user by looking up the user's distinguished name, using the string built with the username. The directory server finds the user and retrieves the password attribute for comparison by Tomcat. Tomcat validates the user's credentials and tells the directory server that it can authenticate the user, which it does.

The directory server then tries to find a role that's associated with this user and returns the value of the cn attribute. This value is then used by Tomcat to authorize the user's access to the resource. Note how all the attribute values in this communication were specified in server.xml.

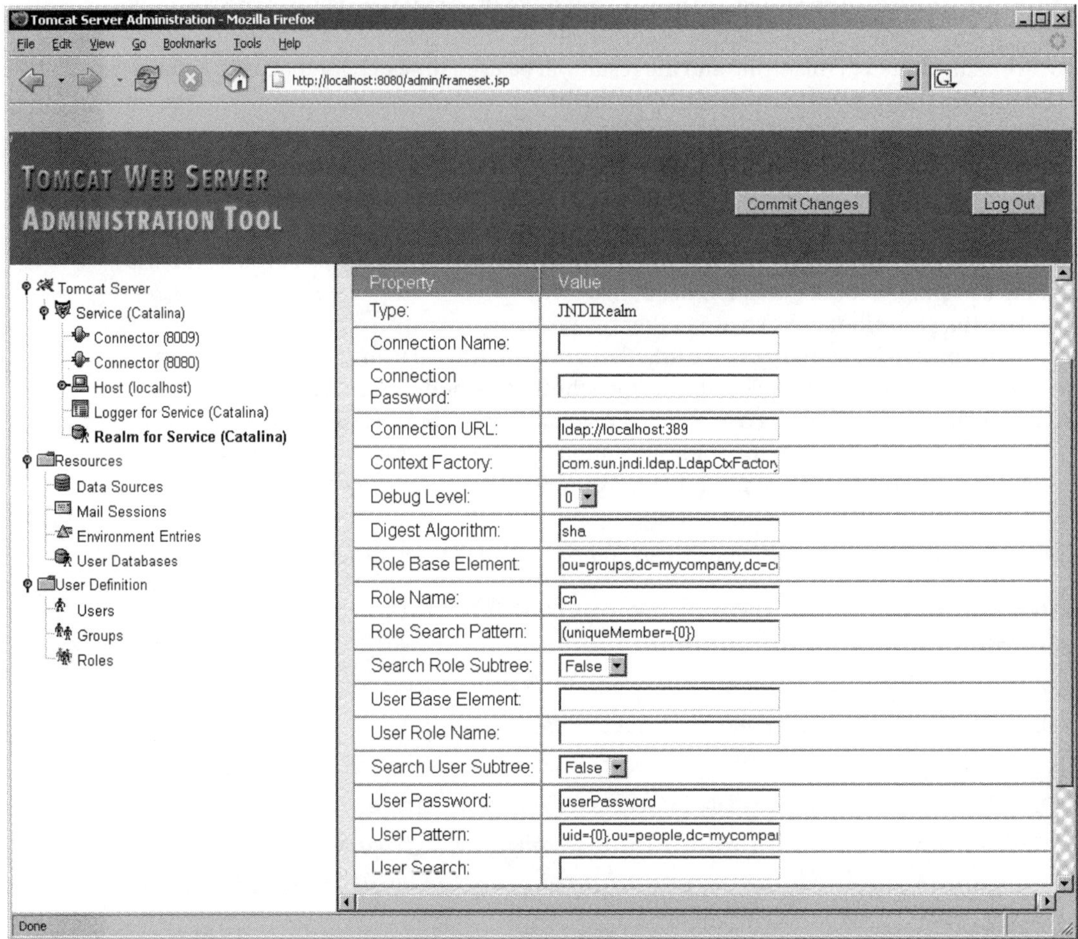

Figure 11-17. *The* admin *application shows that Tomcat is using the new realm.*

Summary

In this chapter you saw how realms provide a Web application with an authentication mechanism, as well as container-managed security. Many different types of realm implementations exist. You saw JDBC realms, JNDI realms, memory realms, and user database realms.

CHAPTER 12

Securing Tomcat

Security is the most important aspect of your job as an administrator; a server that's compromised can't serve any content and could possibly lead to loss of commercial secrets, financial details, or dignity. Securing a server includes many aspects, such as securing the file system, securing the databases, and securing the Tomcat server.

You can think of security as several layers, each of which is as important as the other. If your Tomcat server does somehow become compromised, you want to be sure that the file system, and all the information stored on it, isn't compromised along with Tomcat.

This chapter will deal with Windows file system issues to start and then cover Unix file system issues. Once you've learned about these specifics, you'll learn about general Tomcat security issues equally applicable to both operating systems.

Securing the Windows File System

In this section you'll see how to secure your server's file system against malicious intruders who could read and execute sensitive files. You may already know these techniques if you're a seasoned admin, so feel free to move on to the Tomcat-specific sections.

Windows implements a file system security architecture that uses permissions. You can use file system permissions to control the files users are allowed to view, execute, and manipulate. This means that users can't access the file system in any way without being given explicit permission to do so.

Windows has several different file system types, as shown in Table 12-1.

Table 12-1. *Windows File System Types*

File System Type	Description
FAT	All early versions of Windows are based on the File Allocation Table (FAT) file system. FAT is capable of associating bytes with files and directories but not much more. FAT is the reason for good old filenames that couldn't be longer than eight characters.
NTFS	The NT file system (NTFS) is better than FAT in every way, as it was developed for Microsoft's enterprise NT systems. The latest incarnation of NTFS (available on Windows 2000/XP) supports permissions and encryption, long filenames, networking, disk quotas, and so on. NTFS also stores files in a much more efficient way than FAT and is much more reliable.

Table 12-1. *Windows File System Types (Continued)*

File System Type	Description
FAT32	FAT can handle only up to 2 gigabytes of information, so it's unusable with any decent modern computer. NTFS was intrinsically linked with the Windows NT family, so it was inappropriate for Windows 9*x*. As a result, Microsoft created FAT32, which supports 2 terabytes of space and stores data in a more efficient way. FAT32 is available on Windows 95, Windows 98, Windows ME, Windows 2000, and Windows XP.

As you can see, only NTFS is appropriate for this discussion, as no other Windows file system supports security features such as encryption or permissions. This also means that if you run Tomcat on Windows, and you want to implement security properly, you'll have to use the NTFS file system and thus Windows 2000/XP. This isn't to say that you could run a decent server setup on another operating system, but your file system will be more vulnerable.

■ **Note** Your Windows 2000/XP setup may use the FAT32 file system. It's fairly straightforward to change this, however.

Right-click your C: drive (or equivalent), and select Properties. You will see the properties page, as in Figure 12-1.

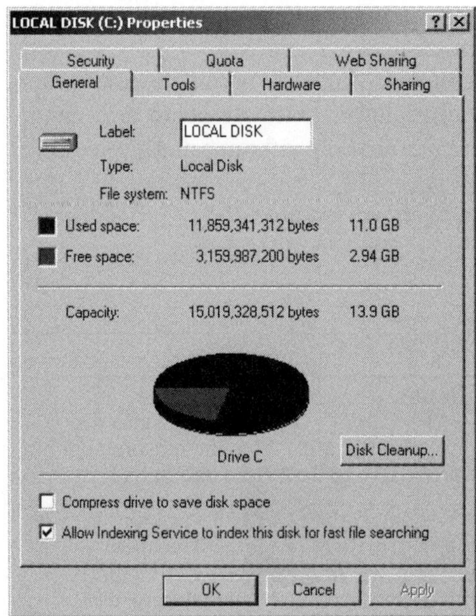

Figure 12-1. *The properties page showing the file system type*

In this case, the drive in question uses the NTFS file system. If your drive uses FAT32, you can upgrade your file system with the `convert` command-line conversion utility.

```
> convert C: /FS:NTFS
```

Replace C: with your hard drive as appropriate. This utility is designed to be fail-safe and won't damage your data; but if you are in any way concerned and have vital data, then you should back up your drive before you run the command. Also, once you've converted a file system to NTFS, you can't convert it back to FAT32.

You must have some disk space free if you want to convert your file system, because the convert utility will need space to work with to build the NTFS structures. The amount of space depends mainly on the initial size of the drive and the number of files and directories on the drive. The details are on `http://support.microsoft.com/default.aspx?scid=KB;en-us;q156560`, but Table 12-2 shows a summary and the calculation for the drive shown in Figure 12-1.

Table 12-2. *Calculating the Space Needed for an NTFS Conversion*

Component of Calculation	Value for Drive C: in Figure 12-1 (in Bytes)
The size of the volume in bytes divided by 100. If this value is less than 1,048,576, use 1,048,576. If it's larger than 4,194,304, use 4,194,304.	4,194,304
The size of the volume in bytes divided by 803.	18,704,021
The number of files and directories on the volume multiplied by 1280.	184,695,040
Add 196,096.	196,096
Total (bytes)	**207,789,461**
Total (megabytes)	**198.16**

This calculation shows that you don't need a huge amount of space on a drive for a successful conversion, though this largely depends on the number of files you have. One way to calculate this is to use the following command:

```
C:\> dir /S
```

This will cycle through all the files and directories on C: and display the totals, as shown in Figure 12-2.

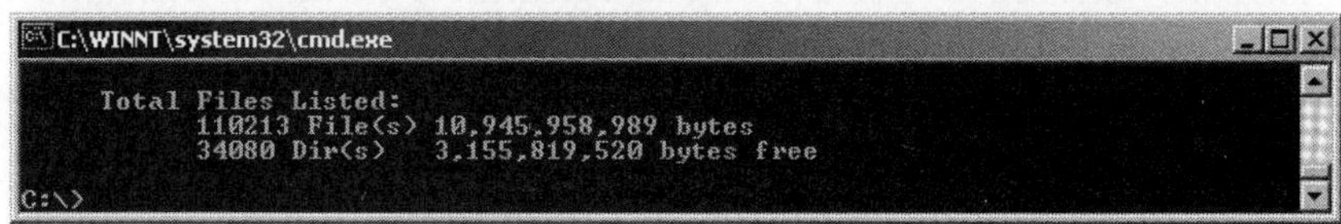

Figure 12-2. *The total number of files and directories on C:*

Now that you have an NTFS file system, let's discuss the individual NTFS permissions you can use. The permissions are divided into two categories: folder permissions and file permissions. Table 12-3 describes folder permissions, and Table 12-4 describes file permissions.

Table 12-3. *Folder Permissions for Windows*

Permission	Actions Permitted
Read	View files and subfolders; view folder ownership, permissions, and file system attributes (read-only, hidden, and so on).
Write	Create files and subfolders; view folder ownership and permissions, change folder attributes.
List Folder Contents	View names of files and subfolders in folder.
Read and Execute	Move through folder to get to subfolders and files; includes permissions from Read and List Folder Contents.
Modify	Delete the folder; rename the folder; includes permissions from Read and Execute and Write.
Full Control	Includes all other folder permissions; delete files and subfolders; take ownership; change permissions.

Table 12-4. *File Permissions for Windows*

Permission	Actions Permitted
Read	View the file contents; view file ownership, permissions, and file system attributes.
Write	Overwrite the file; view file ownership and permissions; change file attributes.
Read and Execute	Execute the file; includes permissions from Read.
Modify	Modify file; delete file; includes permissions from Read and Execute and Write.
Full Control	Includes all other file permissions; take ownership; change permissions.

Controlling Users, Groups, and Owners in Windows

To use these permissions, you need to consider how to assign them to the various users who will be accessing your operating system.

Working with Users

Anyone who wants to log onto a Windows system must know an account name and its associated password. Each user can be assigned one or more of the permissions you saw previously and thus be granted authority to manipulate objects (files or directories) in the file system.

Working with Groups

Windows allows you to add users to a group. Groups can then receive permissions with all the users who belong to a group sharing those permissions.

Working with Owners

Finally, Windows has the concept of a file/directory owner. An owner is a user who ultimately has complete control over what permissions other users or groups have for a given resource, regardless of what permissions the user has been granted.

Working with Superusers

This discussion wouldn't be complete without including one additional detail. Windows has superuser accounts, which have complete and unrestricted access to your system, regardless of any other permission that has been set. On Windows, the default superuser account is called *Administrator*.

The password for this account should be well chosen and extremely well guarded. You're advised not to use these accounts for your day-to-day operations, as any virus or other malicious program may inadvertently execute when running and this account has complete control of your system.

Creating Users and Groups in Windows

You now need to create users and groups to implement the details mentioned earlier. To do this, select Control Panel ➤ Administrative Tools ➤ Computer Management to open the console, as shown in Figure 12-3.

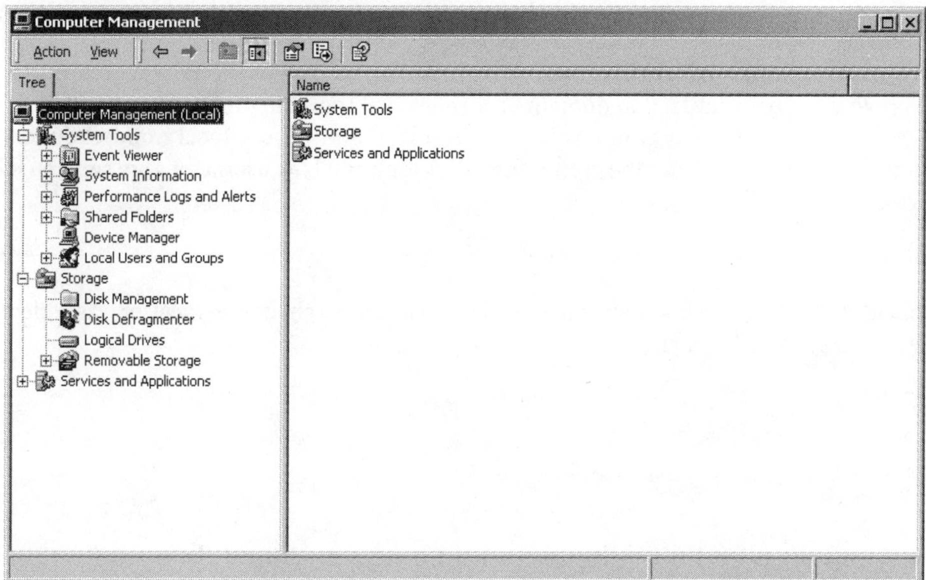

Figure 12-3. *The Computer Management tool*

Now, click the Local Users and Groups icon. You can add, modify, and delete users and groups by selecting either of the two folders revealed and right-clicking the list of users or groups shown on the right.

Command-Line Users and Groups

In addition to the graphical user interface (GUI), Windows also has some command-line utilities for working with users and groups. You won't see how to use it in detail here because the GUI is easier, though the command-line tools allow you to automate user and group tasks.

You have two utilities for working with groups at the command line: `net group` and `net localgroup`. Their syntax is identical, except that they operate on domain users and local users, respectively, though you can induce `net localgroup` to work with domain users by adding the `/DOMAIN` switch to all commands. To list existing groups on the local machine, use the following:

```
C:\>net localgroup
```

The equivalent `net group` command will list groups in the current NT domain.

To add a group to the local machine, run the following, where `"Tomcat Group"` is the name of the new group:

```
C:\>net localgroup "Tomcat Group" /ADD
```

If you wanted to add a description for this group, run the following, where the description is always in quotes:

```
C:\>net localgroup "Tomcat Group" /ADD /COMMENT:"A Tomcat group"
```

To delete the same group, run the following:

```
C:\>net localgroup "Tomcat Group" /DELETE
```

You can also use these utilities to add users to groups. When adding a user with `net localgroup`, make sure that the user exists, that domain users have their domain prefix (for example, `TOMCAT\matthewm`), and that any groups you're adding to this group aren't local groups. You can specify more than one user after the group's name, as long as all the usernames are separated by spaces.

```
C:\>net localgroup "Tomcat Group" matthewm /ADD
```

This adds the local user matthewm to the Tomcat Group. To check that the user was added successfully, run the following:

```
C:\>net localgroup "Tomcat Group"
Alias name     Tomcat Group
Comment        A Tomcat group

Members
-----------------------------------
matthewm
```

To add a user account at the command line, use the net user command. This is a powerful command, though you'll see only its basic functions here. To add a new user called *tomcat* with a specified password of meow, run the following:

```
C:\>net user tomcat meow /ADD
```

If you're uneasy about displaying passwords in plain text on the screen, you can ask for a password prompt. The following won't display the password as you type it in:

```
C:\>net user tomcat * /ADD
Type a password for the user:
Retype the password to confirm:
```

Again, you can add a description to this user with the same utility.

```
C:\>net user tomcat /ADD /COMMENT:"A Tomcat user"
```

To check the user's details, just supply their username to the net user command.

```
C:\>net user tomcat
User name                    tomcat
Full Name
Comment                      A Tomcat user
User's comment
Country code                 000 (System Default)
Account active               Yes
Account expires              Never

Password last set            10/22/2004 5:49 PM
Password expires             12/4/2004 4:37 PM
Password changeable          10/22/2004 5:49 PM
Password required            Yes
User may change password     Yes

Workstations allowed         All
Logon script
User profile
Home directory
Last logon                   Never

Logon hours allowed          All

Local Group Memberships      *Tomcat Group         *Users
Global Group memberships     *None
```

You can of course set all these parameters shown. See `http://www.microsoft.com/WINDOWSXP/home/using/productdoc/en/net_user.asp` for more details.

To delete the tomcat user, run the following:

```
C:\>net user tomcat /DELETE
```

If you delete the user, it will be removed from any groups of which it was a member.

Microsoft also provides the `addusers` utility for creating users from a comma-delimited file. However, this is provided only in the Windows Resource Kit. See `http://support.microsoft.com/default.aspx?scid=kb;en-us;199878` for more details.

Assigning Permissions in Windows

Windows gives you much more flexibility when assigning permissions than Unix does. However, this flexibility comes with a steep price: your security configuration can rapidly deteriorate into chaos if you aren't careful. The Unix model, on the other hand, trades the complexity of Windows for a simplicity that's easy to understand and easy to administer.

You have two ways to manipulate a file's permissions in Windows: a GUI and a command-line interface. To view permissions in the GUI, open Windows Explorer, pick the file or directory whose permissions you want to view, right-click it, and choose Properties. Click the Security tab of the resulting window, and you'll see something similar to Figure 12-4.

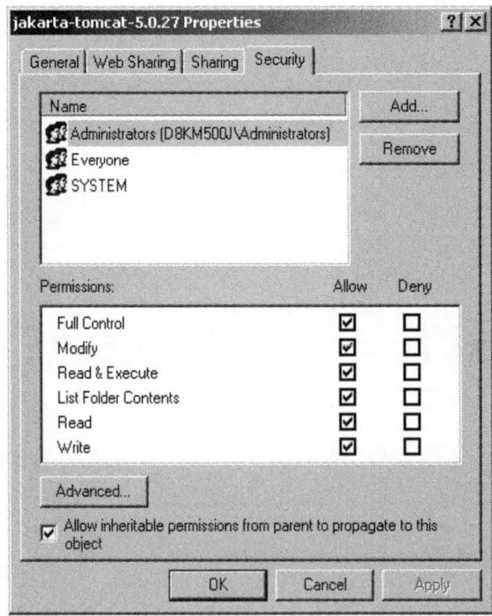

Figure 12-4. *A directory's permissions*

The top section has all the users and groups with explicit permissions for this object. If you click a user or a group, the Permissions section will show the permissions assigned.

The default configurations of Windows XP Professional often hide this Security tab. To enable it, go to Control Panel ➤ Folder Options. Click the View tab, scroll to the bottom of the Advanced Settings list, and uncheck the Use Simple File Sharing (Recommended) option.

Inherited Permissions

Some checkboxes that accompany permissions are disabled, which indicates that the permissions in question have been inherited from a parent folder. By default, all files and directories inherit the permissions that have been assigned to their parent object.

Permission inheritance is recursive, so a folder inherits permissions from its parent, all the way to the root directory of the file system. When a file or folder inherits a permission, you can't clear the Allow checkbox. You can, however, explicitly deny a permission with the Deny checkbox. Deny settings always override Allow settings, for this reason.

You can also turn off permission inheritance for an object. To do so, uncheck the Allow inheritable permissions from parent to propagate to this object box, and you'll no longer inherit permissions and can explicitly define them all for your objects.

Group Permissions

A user may inherit permissions from group membership. This means you may want to assign additional explicit permissions to a user over and above their group permissions. Therefore, you can allow certain users to have access to a file while other members of their group don't.

In the event that you assign conflicting permissions, through multiple group membership, permission denials always take precedence over permission allowances.

Verifying Permissions

Windows provides a feature that you can use to verify a user's permissions. You can do this by clicking the Advanced button and selecting the Permissions tab from the Access Control Settings window that appears. You can then select a group or user to verify by double-clicking or clicking View/Edit..., as shown in Figure 12-5.

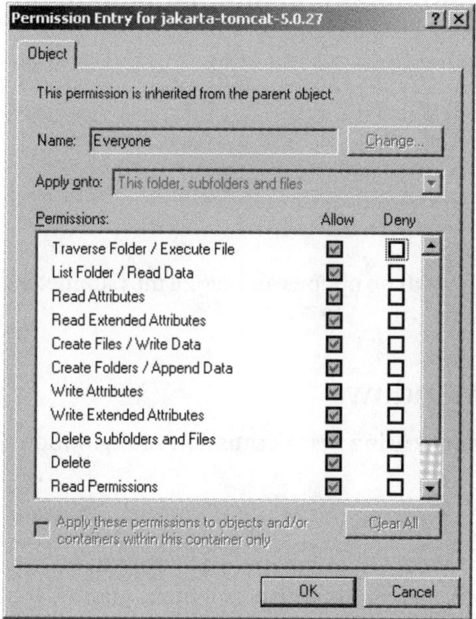

Figure 12-5. *Verifying a group's permissions*

You can now verify permissions, even if they were obtained via inheritance or group membership. You should note that the permissions here are more numerous and have different names than in other dialog boxes. Windows 2000 added some additional, finer-grained permissions to the NTFS security model.

Command-Line Permissions

In addition to the GUI, Windows has the `cacls` command-line utility, which you can use to modify permissions. You won't see how to use it in detail here, though, because the GUI is easier and has more features.

You can view the permissions for the Tomcat folder with the following:

```
C:\>cacls jakarta-tomcat
C:\jakarta-tomcat Everyone:(OI)(CI)F
                  NT AUTHORITY\SYSTEM:(OI)(CI)F
                  BUILTIN\Administrators:(OI)(CI)F
```

Here `F` donates full control for these groups. You can use the same utility to deny or change access.

```
C:\>cacls jakarta-tomcat /E /P Everyone:R
processed dir: C:\jakarta-tomcat
```

The `/E` switch indicates that this command should edit the configuration, not overwrite it. `/P` sets a permission, in this case to `R`, which is read access. Check that this command has worked with the following:

```
C:\>cacls jakarta-tomcat
C:\jakarta-tomcat Everyone:(OI)(CI)R
                  NT AUTHORITY\SYSTEM:(OI)(CI)F
                  BUILTIN\Administrators:(OI)(CI)F
```

To revoke access for a user, run the following:

```
C:\>cacls jakarta-tomcat /E /R Everyone
```

For more information on `cacls`, you can execute it with no options and see all the parameters it supports.

Planning Security Permissions in Windows

Now it's time to talk about how to secure your system by using wise permission configurations.

Separate Tomcat Account

Some users run Tomcat with their normal user account or with the superuser account, both of which are bad ideas. If Tomcat is ever compromised, it could use the permissions granted to the account that started it (such as your own account or the all-powerful superuser account) to wreak havoc. Therefore, you vastly improve the security of your file system by creating a special user account just for running Tomcat. This account should be assigned only those permissions necessary to run Tomcat and nothing more.

Suggested Account Settings for Windows

You should create a new user named *tomcat*. Make sure that the tomcat account doesn't belong to any groups, including the default user group. Also, make sure you give the account a password. Windows can't use the tomcat account to launch services without you giving it a password. For maximum security, the password should be at least six characters long and consist of mixed-case letters, numbers, and special characters.

The only way for Tomcat to run as a user in Windows is if it's installed as a service. Chapter 3 covered this process. You'll need to give it permissions to run services and nothing else.

Windows exposes many additional permissions, mostly unrelated to the file system. These permissions are defined in a security policy. Windows security policies may be defined on the machine itself (a local security policy) or may be defined in a central network location (a domain security policy).

You can modify your machine's local security policy by selecting Control Panel ➤ Administrative Tools ➤ Local Security Policy. You will see a screen similar to that in Figure 12-6.

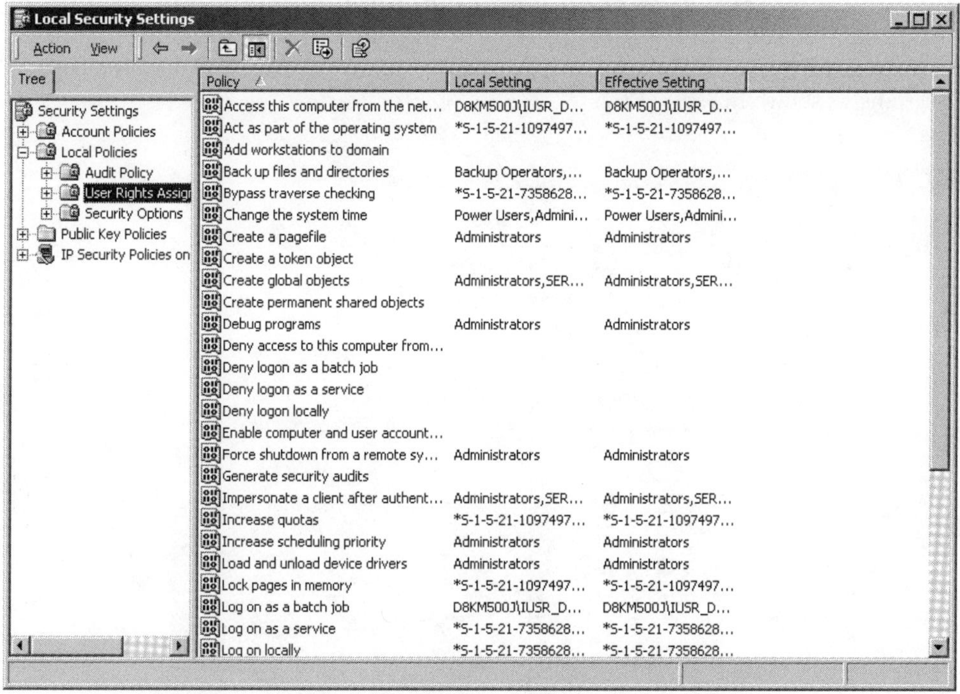

Figure 12-6. *The local security policy settings*

You'll need to make two changes to your local security policy.

- **Disable the tomcat account's ability to log in**: Although tomcat's lack of membership in any group implicitly denies tomcat this ability, you should still explicitly deny this privilege. Double-click the Deny Logon Locally setting in the Policy column. In the screen that appears, add the tomcat account. Do the same for the following policies: Deny Access to This Computer from the Network, Deny Logon As a Batch Job, and Deny Logon Through Terminal Services, if it's present.
- **Grant permission to tomcat to run services**: Double-click Log On As a Service, and add tomcat to this policy.

When Tomcat was installed as a service, it should start automatically. Check Chapter 2 for details.

Configuring File Permissions in Windows

Up until now you've created a special tomcat account and instructed your operating system to launch the Tomcat service with your tomcat account. You now need to configure your file system's permissions.

Your tomcat user account will by default be given read access to many locations on the file system. So the best place to start is revoking all file system permissions for the root directory of all your drives. You can accomplish this by going to My Computer and viewing the properties for each hard disk partition. In the Security tab, add the tomcat account and disable all of its permissions, as shown in Figure 12-7.

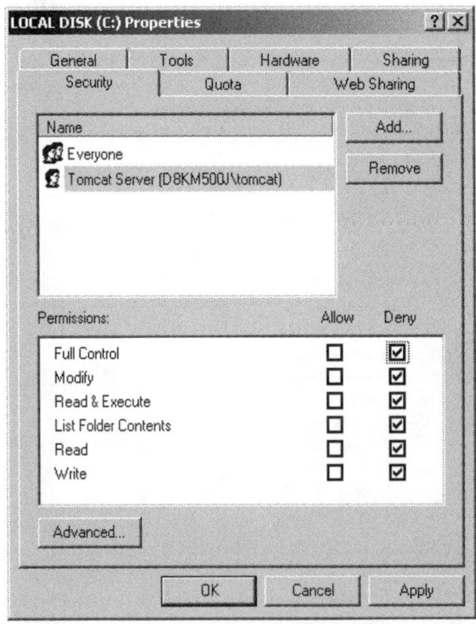

Figure 12-7. *The tomcat user is denied all rights.*

Now you need to grant read access to the JDK directory so that Java can execute Tomcat. Locate the directory where you've installed Java (identified by the `%JAVA_HOME%` variable) and give the tomcat account the Read & Execute, List Folder Contents, and Read permissions. Depending on where you've installed your JDK, you may first need to set the folder not to inherit security permissions from its parent. The best way to do this is to instruct Windows to copy (not remove) the formerly inherited permissions and then remove any conflicting entry for the tomcat account.

Finally, you need to grant various permissions to the Tomcat directory hierarchy, as shown in Table 12-5.

Table 12-5. *Assigning Permissions to Tomcat's Directories*

Tomcat Directories	Permissions for Tomcat Account
`%CATALINA_HOME%` `%CATALINA_HOME%\bin`	Allow: Read & Execute, List Folder Contents, and Read

`%CATALINA_HOME%\common`
`%CATALINA_HOME%\server`
`%CATALINA_HOME%\shared`
`%CATALINA_HOME%\webapps`
	Deny: Write

`%CATALINA_HOME%\conf`	Allow: Read & Execute, List Folder Contents, Read, Write (only if using the `admin` application or a user database) Deny: Write (otherwise)

`%CATALINA_HOME%\logs`
`%CATALINA_HOME%\temp`
`%CATALINA_HOME%\work`
	Allow: Modify, Read & Execute, List Folder Contents, Read, Write

Everything is read-only except those locations that Tomcat needs to modify: the `conf` directory where the `admin` application may edit `server.xml` and context XML files, the `temp` directory for temporary files, the `logs` directory, and the `work` directory for Tomcat's own temporary working files.

The next few pages are devoted to Unix issues, so feel free to skip to the "Examining General Tomcat Security Principles" section.

Securing the Unix File System

You'll now see how to secure your server's file system against malicious intruders who may read and execute sensitive files. You may already know these techniques if you're a seasoned admin, so feel free to move on to the Tomcat-specific sections.

Security has always been inherent in the Unix file system. The Unix permissions are the same for directories and files because a directory is considered to be a special kind of file. Table 12-6 describes these permissions.

Table 12-6. *File Permissions for Unix*

Permission	Actions Permitted
Read	View the contents of the file or directory.
Write	Modify or delete if a file; create files if a directory.
Execute	Execution if a file; access for directories.

Controlling Users, Groups, and Owners in Unix

To use these permissions, you need to consider how to assign these permissions to the various users who will be accessing your operating system.

Working with Users

Anyone who wants to log onto a Unix system must know an account name and its associated password. Each user can be assigned one or more of the permissions you saw previously and thus be granted authority to manipulate objects (files or directories) in the file system.

Working with Groups

Unix allows you to add users to a group. Groups can then receive permissions with all the users who belong to a group sharing those permissions.

Working with Owners

Finally, Unix has the concept of a file/directory owner. An owner is a user who ultimately has complete control over what permissions other users or groups have for a given resource, regardless of what permissions the user has been granted.

Working with Superusers

This discussion wouldn't be complete without including one additional detail. Unix has so-called superuser accounts. These accounts have complete and unrestricted access to your system, regardless of any other permission that has been set. On Unix, the default superuser account is called *root*.

The password for this account should be well chosen and extremely well guarded. You're advised not to use these accounts for your day-to-day operations, as any virus or other malicious program may inadvertently execute when running and this account has complete control of your system.

Creating Users and Groups in Unix

On Unix you use command-line utilities to create and manipulate users and groups. Although these are Linux utilities, they have analogs in other Unix-like operating systems, which will offer similar functionality. All these commands require you to be logged in as root.

Alternatively, because of the caveats on superuser accounts expressed previously, you can use the `sudo` command, which allows you to run commands as if you were logged in as root (or any user you want to configure). This effect wears off after five minutes, though this can also be configured, and you're returned to your old user permissions. This ensures that you don't leave a root-enabled terminal unattended for longer than five minutes and that, since you use your own password, you don't have to use the root password in public.

To run a command under sudo, simply append the appropriate command and supply your password.

```
$ sudo useradd lauraj -g users
```

sudo gives you many other features, most of which can be used to give auditable responsibility to other users. See http://www.courtesan.com/sudo/ for more details.

You can determine which groups a user belongs to with the groups command, which displays its results as the username followed by the user's groups.

```
$ groups matthewm
matthewm : users abusers
```

You add new users with the useradd utility.

```
$ useradd lauraj
```

This creates a new user in a group with the same name as the user. You can specify which group a user should belong to with the -g parameter, though the group must exist for any of the group assignment commands to work.

```
$ useradd lauraj -g users
```

Use the -G parameter to add a user to multiple groups and separate each group by a comma.

You can modify the groups to which an existing user belongs with the usermod command. It takes the same -g and -G parameters as the useradd command. The following example of the usermod command will make user matthewm belong only to the users group:

```
$ usermod -g users -G "" matthewm
```

You can delete users using the userdel command.

```
$ userdel matthewm
```

You can create groups with the groupadd command.

```
$ groupadd abusers
```

You can delete groups with the groupdel command.

```
$ groupdel lovers
```

Assigning Permissions in Unix

The Unix model of security isn't as flexible as the Windows model, though it trades the complexity of Windows for a simplicity that's easy to understand and easy to administer.

Setting Permissions in Unix

To view permissions in Unix, all you need is the ls utility. The following command will display the contents of a directory complete with permissions information:

```
$ ls -l
```

The -l parameter tells the ls command to display the long file directory format, which includes the permissions. The output of this command looks like the following:

```
$ ls -l
drwxr-xr-x 2 tomcat tomcat 4096 Oct 22 18:38 bin
```

You'll see a series of columns that correspond to each file or directory in the current directory. You're concerned only with the first, third, fourth, and last columns. Let's define each of those, and drop out the other columns that are irrelevant to the discussion.

```
Permissions Owner Group Filename
========================================
drwxr-xr-x tomcat tomcat bin
```

Now, let's break down the values of each entry in the permissions column. The permissions column itself can be viewed as four separate columns: file type, owner permissions, group permissions, and permissions for other users. Let's take the first and last files from the previous list and break down the permissions column for each.

```
File Type Owner Group Other P. Filename
=======================================================
d rwx r-x r-x bin
```

The first subcolumn of the permissions column dictates the file type, such as d for directory, l for link, or - for a normal file. All of the remaining columns display whether the owner, group, or other users have read (r), write (w), or executable (x) access to that file (remember that for directories, the executable property indicates whether the user has access to the directory). In the previous case, all three of these groups have read and execute rights, but only the owner of the bin directory can write to the directory.

Changing Permissions

You use the chmod utility to change the permissions of a file. For example, you can change the permissions of a file so that every user can read and write to it by running chmod with the following parameters:

```
$ chmod u=rw,g=rw,o=rw file01
```

The u parameter sets the permissions for the owner of the file, the g parameter sets the permissions for the group associated with the file, and o sets the permissions for everyone else. You can use one, two, or all three of these parameters. The following is the result of the operation:

```
$ chmod u=rw,g=rw,o=rw file01
$ ls -l | grep file01
-rw-rw-rw- ... file01
```

Table 12-7 describes the chmod command in more detail.

Table 12-7. *chmod's Parameters*

chmod **Parameter**	**Description**
[u,g,o,a]=[r,w,x]	This is the parameter you saw in the previous example. On the left side of the equals sign, you choose one of the following to which you can assign permissions: the owner (u), group (g), others (o), or all three of these (a). On the right side, you choose from: read permission, write permission, or execute permission. You can combine the permissions on the right as also shown. You can issue this parameter multiple times if each instance is separated by a comma. Here are some examples: a=rw u=rwx,g=rx,o=rx
[u,g,o,a][+,-][r,w,x]	This parameter is the same as the previous one, except it either adds or removes a permission from existing permissions. For example, to remove the group's write permission without altering its other permissions, you'd use the following parameter: g-w
-R	This is the recursive parameter, meaning that the permission assignments will be made to the directory and any of its subdirectories and files, and any of their subdirectories, and so forth.

Changing Ownership

You can use the chown command to change the owner of a file and the group with which the file is associated.

```
$ chown user[:group] filename
```

So, if you want to change the owner of the LICENSE file from tomcat to bobcat, you'd issue this command:

```
$ chown bobcat LICENSE
```

Unix actually stores two more pieces of metadata with every file that relate to security. These are the SUID and SGUI bits. If a file has the SUID bit set, it indicates that users who execute the file will execute it as though they are the owners of the file. For example, if a file named program was owned by root and it had the SUID bit set, and if another user executed program, the operating system would execute program as though the user were root.

The SGID bit is similar. Any file with the SGID bit will make the user who executes that file a member of the group associated with the file for that file's execution.

You can set the SUID and SGID bits with the chmod utility. The syntax is as follows:

```
$ chmod u+s [filename] (sets the SUID bit)
$ chmod g+s [filename] (sets the SGID bit)
```

The SUID and SGID bits show up in the executable column of the permissions of each file as an s, as follows:

```
-rwsr-sr-x 2 tomcat tomcat 4096 Aug 25 01:28 program01
```

Of course, you should use the SUID/SGID bits with great caution.

Planning Security Permissions

Now it's time to talk about how to secure your system by using wise permissions configurations.

Separate Tomcat Account

Some users run Tomcat with their normal user account or with the superuser account, both of which are bad ideas. If Tomcat ever becomes compromised, it could use the permissions granted to the account that started it (such as your own account or the all-powerful superuser account) to wreak havoc. Therefore, you vastly improve the security of your file system by creating a special user account just for running Tomcat. This distinct account should be assigned only those permissions necessary to run Tomcat and nothing more.

Suggested Account Settings for Unix

Create an account for running Tomcat called *tomcat*. You should include tomcat in only one group, also named *tomcat*. Because you'll want to run Tomcat as a daemon, you shouldn't let console logins use this account. Disabling login ability is often achieved by starring the account's password.

Here are two examples of this technique. The first example is from a BSD-like system that doesn't use a shadow password file.

```
/etc/passwd:
tomcat:*:23102:100:Tomcat:/:/bin/csh
```

The second example is from a Linux system that does use a shadow password file.

```
/etc/passwd:
tomcat:x:502:502:Tomcat:/:/bin/bash
/etc/shadow:
tomcat:*:12040:0:99999:7:::
```

Note how the password column has been given an asterisk (*). This means you can't log into this account.

The various Unix operating systems have several mechanisms for creating and configuring daemons. Chapter 2 discussed this procedure.

Configuring File Permissions in Unix

Up until now you've created a special tomcat account and instructed your operating system to launch the service with your tomcat account. You now need to configure your file system's permissions.

Table 12-8 shows the recommended directory and owner/group and file permission combinations.

Table 12-8. *Assigning Permissions to Tomcat's Directories*

Directory/File	Owner/Group	Permissions
`$CATALINA_HOME`	`root/tomcat`	`rwxr-x---`
`$CATALINA_HOME/bin`	`root/tomcat`	`rwxr-x---`
`$CATALINA_HOME/bin/*.sh`	`root/tomcat`	`rwxr-x---`
`$CATALINA_HOME/common`	`root/tomcat`	`rwxr-x---`
`$CATALINA_HOME/conf`	`root/tomcat`	`rwxrwx---` (only if using the `admin` application or a user database) `rwxr-x---` (otherwise)
`$CATALINA_HOME/logs`	`root/tomcat`	`rwxrwx---`
`$CATALINA_HOME/logs/*.*`	`root/tomcat r`	`w-rw----`
`$CATALINA_HOME/server`	`root/tomcat`	`rwxr-x---`
`$CATALINA_HOME/shared`	`root/tomcat`	`rwxr-x---`
`$CATALINA_HOME/temp`	`root/tomcat`	`rwxrwx---`
`$CATALINA_HOME/webapps`	`root/tomcat`	`rwxr-x---`
`$CATALINA_HOME/work`	`root/tomcat`	`rwxrwx---`

If not otherwise indicated, all files in the listed directories should have the same ownership as their parent directory and have `rw-r-----` permissions.

Examining General Tomcat Security Principles

Now that you've secured your file system against attack, you should consider a few other security issues before tackling Tomcat's configuration files. All but one of these applies to Windows and Unix.

Retaining Tomcat's Administration Tools

Because `tomcat-users.xml` stores your username and password for Tomcat's management applications, you may want to switch to a different realm, as discussed in Chapter 11. Otherwise, a hacker may view this file and gain access to your Tomcat management applications (though you can also digest the passwords). Because the tomcat account has only read access to the `webapps` directory, the hacker couldn't modify your Web applications, but the hacker could stop or reload your Web applications on demand. Thus, if you use the Tomcat realms that use tomcat-users.xml, you should consider removing the admin and manager Web applications.

If you use the admin application to change server.xml or users in tomcat-users.xml, then you must have write access to the directory. This also means a hacker can write to this directory and carry out any of the commands that the admin tool can and so may be able to add context XML files for malicious code. This also applies to user databases because they need write access to tomcat-users.xml.

If this bothers you, remove the admin tool, should it be installed, and use a JDBC or JNDI realm (or even the memory realm if you want; it doesn't require write access to any files).

Read-Only webapps Directory

You'll note that you've set read-only permissions on the webapps directory. This is to prevent hackers from modifying your Web applications. This also means, however, that you may not be able to use WAR files when running Tomcat with the tomcat account, since Tomcat won't be able to expand the WAR into the file system. Thus, you'll need to unzip the WAR file yourself when you deploy it, run Tomcat as root from the console when you deploy new WAR files for the first time, or set the containing host's unpackWARs attribute to false.

This also means that Web applications can't write to their directories. This is recommended in the Servlet specification because it's assumed that some servlet containers will run unexpanded WAR files and would thus not be able to write changes to the Web application's file system (it doesn't have one). This is the case if unpackWARs is set to false.

Securing Your Files

You should review your operating system for any additional files stored on the server that should be secured. You should consider either moving these files to another server or ensuring that the tomcat account doesn't have any permissions for them. On Windows, add the tomcat user to the Security tab for the file or directory and explicitly click the Deny checkboxes. In Unix, set the permissions for others to nothing (-rwx).

Knowing If You've Been Violated

Despite your best efforts, it's possible that a hacker may exploit Tomcat (or another service) and modify your file system in some unimagined way. Intrusion detection systems can help you detect when your file system has been tampered with. Tripwire is one of these programs, and Red Hat includes instructions for installing and configuring Tripwire in its Official Red Hat Linux Reference Guide.

If you're not using Red Hat Linux, see http://www.tripwire.com for more information.

Read-Only File Systems

Some operating systems support read-only file systems. In this concept, available only to Unix-like operating systems, you configure two separate file systems. The first file system, a root file system, contains your operating system configured just the way you need it, with a Tomcat daemon. You then make this file system read-only (or for ultimate security, transfer it to a read-only medium, such as a CD or a hard drive that you can make read-only). The second file system is contained on a read-write medium and contains your Tomcat installation and other files that must be modified.

Should you want to take this (highly secure) step, you'll need to find documentation for your specific operating system. No standard Unix way exists to achieve this functionality. You must exercise caution if you attempt this route; once you mark your root file system as read-only, you'll need a boot disk to make any changes.

Securing Tomcat's Default Configuration

In this section, you'll tighten up the default installation by editing the configuration files and managing the Web applications that come with Tomcat. This will remove some of the most vulnerable entry points for attacks against the server.

As detailed earlier, the `admin` application and user databases are the main causes of concern. If you don't use either of these, then you may keep and use the `manager` application, if you have considered the previous options. Without access to the manager password or write access to `server.xml`, a hacker can't access the manager application.

If you don't take these steps, it's safer to place the `manager` folder and its contents outside of Tomcat's directory structure (you should consider doing this anyway). This means an intruder can't enable it by just adding an entry to `tomcat-users.xml`. However, it's still possible to enable the application by modifying the `server.xml` file and modifying the manager context's `docBase` attribute. As long as the `manager` folder is on the same machine as the server installation, it's possible to set up the manager again (though it's more difficult if you have appropriate permissions set).

You should always remove the example Web applications (`jsp-examples` and `servlets-examples`) on a development server. They aren't necessary for Tomcat to run and take up disk space if nothing else. Likewise, unless you're using WebDAV, you should remove the `webdav` Web application.

The Tomcat documentation is now provided as a Web application named `tomcat-docs`, which is an entirely static Web application with no JSP pages or servlets. Whether you leave this in place is up to you, as it may be useful for developers to have a local copy of the documentation, whether to save network traffic or in case of problems connecting to the outside world.

It may also be worth disabling the default `ROOT` Web application if you don't have one of your own. If your applications will be accessed by a Web application context name, then it may be worth replacing the contents of the `ROOT` folder with an empty `index.html` file. You can then supply an empty Web application that would show access restriction error messages to clients who attempt to access the directory.

Alternatively, you can also disable unauthorized access to the Web application. Thus, it's possible to restrict access to the ROOT application to internal clients, such as the developer group, using valves or filters.

Securing Tomcat's Permissions

Configuring your file system for maximum security is an important part of securing your Tomcat deployment, but it's only half of the picture. By using Java's security manager architecture, you can restrict those features of the Java language that Tomcat is able to access.

The Java Security Manager

The Java security manager architecture allows you to impose fine-grained security restrictions to all Java applications. This security architecture is turned off by default, but you can turn it on at any time. In the following sections you'll see the security manager architecture in general terms and then look at how this architecture specifically applies to Tomcat.

Overview of the Security Manager

The security manager architecture works on the notion of permissions (just as the file system does). Once the security manager is turned on, applications must have explicit permission to perform certain security-sensitive tasks, such as creating a custom class loader or opening a socket to servers.

To use the security manager effectively, it's therefore necessary to know how applications can be given permissions and what the possible permissions are.

Granting Permissions to Applications

Policy files are the mechanism that the security manager uses to grant permissions to applications. Policy files are nothing more than simple text files composed of individual actions that applications can perform.

A policy file is composed of grant entries, as shown in Listing 12-1.

Listing 12-1. *A Policy File*

```
// first grant entry
grant {
  permission java.lang.RuntimePermission "stopThread";
}

// second grant entry
grant codeBase "file:${java.home}/lib/ext/*" {
  permission java.security.AllPermission;
};
```

The first grant entry demonstrates the simplicity of the syntax. It grants all applications the ability to access the deprecated `Thread.stop()` method.

The second grant entry illustrates that code in specific locations can also be granted permissions. This is useful when you want to extend permissions to certain trusted code while denying permissions to all other code. In this case, all code in the `JAVA_HOME/lib/ext` directory is granted all permissions, which disables the security manager architecture for that code.

Writing Grant Entries

Each grant entry must be composed of the following syntax:

```
grant codeBase "URL" {
  // this is a comment
  permission permission_class_name "target_name", "action";
  ...
};
```

Note that comments in policy files must begin with // on each line. As you saw in the first grant entry, the codeBase attribute is optional. codeBase specifies a URL to which all the permissions should apply. Table 12-9 describes the syntax.

Table 12-9. *The codeBase Attribute's Syntax*

codeBase Example	Description
file:/C:/myapp/	This assigns the permissions in the grant block to the c:\myapp directory. Note that the slash (/) indicates that only class files in the directory will receive the permissions, not any JAR files or subdirectories.
http://java.sun.com/*	All code from the specified URL will be granted the permissions. In this case, the /* at the end of the URL indicates that all class files and JAR files will be assigned the permissions, but not any subdirectories.
file:/matthewm/-	All code in the /matthewm directory will be granted the permissions in the grant block. The /- indicates that all class files and JAR files in the directory and its subdirectories will be assigned the permissions.

Within the grant block, one or more permissions can be assigned. A permission consists of a permission class name and, in some cases, an additional target that identifies a specific permission within the permission class. Some permission targets can additionally take parameters, called *actions*. Listing 12-2 shows examples of permissions.

Listing 12-2. *Example Permissions*

```
grant {
  // allows applications to listen on all ports
  permission java.net.SocketPermission "localhost", "listen";

  // allows applications to read the "java.version" property
  permission java.util.PropertyPermission "java.version", "read";
}
```

Special classes that ultimately inherit from the abstract class `java.security.Permission` define permissions. Most permission classes define special targets that represent a security permission that can be turned on and off.

Nineteen different permission classes offer control over various permissions. Table 12-10 describes these classes to demonstrate what's possible with permissions but doesn't provide an extensive listing of the permission targets. You can view the complete list of permission classes and their targets at `http://java.sun.com/j2se/1.4/docs/guide/security/permissions.html`.

Table 12-10. *Permissions for Policy Files*

Permission Class	Description
`java.security.AllPermission`	By granting this permission, all other permissions are also granted. Granting this permission is the same as disabling the security manager for the affected code.
`java.security.SecurityPermission`	Allows programmatic access to various security features of the Java language.
`java.security.UnresolvedPermission`	This permission class isn't defined in policy files; rather, it's used as a placeholder for when a policy file makes reference to a user-defined permission class that hadn't been loaded at the time of processing the policy file. This permission is relevant only to those interacting with the security manager system programmatically at run time.
`java.awt.AWTPermission`	Controls various AWT permissions.
`java.io.FilePermission`	Restricts read, write, execute, and delete access to files in specified paths.
`java.io.SerializablePermission`	Allows serialization permissions.
`java.lang.reflect.ReflectPermission`	Allows applications to circumvent the public and private mechanism's access checks and reflectively access any method.
`java.lang.RuntimePermission`	Allows access to key runtime features, such as creating class loaders, exiting the VM, and reassigning stdin, stdout, and stderr.
`java.net.NetPermission`	Allows various network permissions.
`java.net.SocketPermission`	Allows incoming socket connections, outgoing connections, listening on ports, and resolving hostnames. These permissions can be defined on specific hostnames and port combinations.
`java.sql.SQLPermission`	While this sounds intriguing, don't get too excited; it controls only a single permission: setting the JDBC log output writer. This file is considered sensitive because it may contain usernames and passwords.

Table 12-10. *Permissions for Policy Files (Continued)*

Permission Class	Description
java.util.PropertyPermission	Controls whether properties can be read from or written to.
java.util.logging.LoggingPermission	Allows the ability to configure the logging system.
javax.net.ssl.SSLPermission	Allows the ability to access SSL-related network functionality.
javax.security.auth.AuthPermission	Controls authentication permissions.
javax.security.auth.PrivateCredentialPermission	Controls various security permissions.
javax.security.auth.kerberos.DelegationPermission	Controls various security permissions related to the Kerberos protocol.
javax.security.auth.kerberos.ServicePermission	Controls various security permissions related to the Kerberos protocol.
javax.sound.sampled.AudioPermission	Controls access to the sound system.

Enabling the Security Manager System

You can enable the security manager system by passing the -Djava.security.manager parameter to the JVM at startup, as follows:

```
> java -Djava.security.manager MyClass
```

By default, Java looks for JAVA_HOME/lib/security/java.policy to determine what permissions to grant when the security manager is turned on. For more information on enabling the security manager and using your own policy files, see http://java.sun.com/j2se/1.4/docs/guide/security/PolicyFiles.html.

Using the Security Manager with Tomcat

Now that I've covered the basics of the security manager system, it's time to talk about how to use it with Tomcat.

Enabling Tomcat's Security Manager

The preferred way to start Tomcat with the security manager enabled on Unix systems is the following:

```
$ $CATALINA_HOME/bin/catalina.sh start -security
```

On Windows systems, you'd issue this command:

```
> %CATALINA_HOME%\bin\catalina start -security
```

Tomcat's Policy File

Tomcat uses the CATALINA_HOME/conf/catalina.policy file to determine its own permissions and those of its Web applications. Listing 12-3, Listing 12-4, and Listing 12-5 show this file in full. Note that it's divided into three sections: system code permissions, Catalina code permissions, and Web application code permissions.

Tomcat's policy file grants all permissions to javac, which compiles JSP pages into servlets, and it also grants all permissions to any Java standard extensions. Four grant lines are used instead of two to deal with multiple path possibilities. Note that you may need to add additional grants to this section if your JVM uses different paths for its standard extensions (Mac OS X needs additional grants, for example) and you're actually putting JARs or classes in those paths.

Listing 12-3. *The System Code Permissions from Tomcat's Default Policy File*

```
// ========== SYSTEM CODE PERMISSIONS
=========================================


// These permissions apply to javac
grant codeBase "file:${java.home}/lib/-" {
        permission java.security.AllPermission;
};

// These permissions apply to all shared system extensions
grant codeBase "file:${java.home}/jre/lib/ext/-" {
        permission java.security.AllPermission;
};

// These permissions apply to javac when ${java.home] points at $JAVA_HOME/jre
grant codeBase "file:${java.home}/../lib/-" {
        permission java.security.AllPermission;
};

// These permissions apply to all shared system extensions when
// ${java.home} points at $JAVA_HOME/jre
grant codeBase "file:${java.home}/lib/ext/-" {
        permission java.security.AllPermission;
};
```

Note that Catalina grants all permissions to the following:

- Tomcat's startup classes (CATALINA_HOME/bin/bootstrap.jar)
- The common class loader files (CATALINA_HOME/common/lib and CATALINA_HOME/common/classes)
- The server class loader files (CATALINA_HOME/server/lib and CATALINA_HOME/server/classes)

Listing 12-4. *The Catalina Code Permissions from Tomcat's Default Policy File*

```
// ======== CATALINA CODE PERMISSIONS
=======================================



// These permissions apply to the launcher code
grant codeBase "file:${catalina.home}/bin/commons-launcher.jar" {
        permission java.security.AllPermission;
};

// These permissions apply to the daemon code
grant codeBase "file:${catalina.home}/bin/commons-daemon.jar" {
        permission java.security.AllPermission;
};

// These permissions apply to the commons-logging API
grant codeBase "file:${catalina.home}/bin/commons-logging-api.jar" {
        permission java.security.AllPermission;
};

// These permissions apply to the server startup code
grant codeBase "file:${catalina.home}/bin/bootstrap.jar" {
        permission java.security.AllPermission;
};

// These permissions apply to the JMX server
grant codeBase "file:${catalina.home}/bin/jmx.jar" {
        permission java.security.AllPermission;
};
```

```
// These permissions apply to the servlet API classes
// and those that are shared across all class loaders
// located in the "common" directory
grant codeBase "file:${catalina.home}/common/-" {
        permission java.security.AllPermission;
};

// These permissions apply to the container's core code, plus any additional
// libraries installed in the "server" directory
grant codeBase "file:${catalina.home}/server/-" {
        permission java.security.AllPermission;
};
```

Tomcat allows read access to various system properties. Note also the following grant:

```
    permission java.lang.RuntimePermission
"accessClassInPackage.org.apache.jasper.runtime";
```

The `accessClassInPackage.*` target of `RuntimePermission` allows classes to see other classes to which they wouldn't normally have access. In this case, Tomcat is giving all Web applications access to the `org.apache.jasper.runtime.*` package.

Listing 12-5. *The Web Application Permissions from Tomcat's Default Policy File*

```
// ======== WEB APPLICATION PERMISSIONS
=====================================

// These permissions are granted by default to all Web applications
// In addition, a Web application will be given a read FilePermission
// and JndiPermission for all files and directories in its document root.
grant {
    // Required for JNDI lookup of named JDBC DataSources and
    // javamail named MimePart DataSource used to send mail
    permission java.util.PropertyPermission "java.home", "read";
    permission java.util.PropertyPermission "java.naming.*", "read";
    permission java.util.PropertyPermission "javax.sql.*", "read";

    // OS Specific properties to allow read access
    permission java.util.PropertyPermission "os.name", "read";
    permission java.util.PropertyPermission "os.version", "read";
    permission java.util.PropertyPermission "os.arch", "read";
```

```
    permission java.util.PropertyPermission "file.separator", "read";
    permission java.util.PropertyPermission "path.separator", "read";
    permission java.util.PropertyPermission "line.separator", "read";

    // JVM properties to allow read access
    permission java.util.PropertyPermission "java.version", "read";
    permission java.util.PropertyPermission "java.vendor", "read";
    permission java.util.PropertyPermission "java.vendor.url", "read";
    permission java.util.PropertyPermission "java.class.version", "read";
    permission java.util.PropertyPermission "java.specification.version", "read";
    permission java.util.PropertyPermission "java.specification.vendor", "read";
    permission java.util.PropertyPermission "java.specification.name", "read";

    permission java.util.PropertyPermission "java.vm.specification.version", "read";
    permission java.util.PropertyPermission "java.vm.specification.vendor", "read";
    permission java.util.PropertyPermission "java.vm.specification.name", "read";
    permission java.util.PropertyPermission "java.vm.version", "read";
    permission java.util.PropertyPermission "java.vm.vendor", "read";
    permission java.util.PropertyPermission "java.vm.name", "read";

    // Required for OpenJMX
    permission java.lang.RuntimePermission "getAttribute";

    // Allow read of JAXP compliant XML parser debug
    permission java.util.PropertyPermission "jaxp.debug", "read";

    // Precompiled JSPs need access to this package.
    permission java.lang.RuntimePermission
"accessClassInPackage.org.apache.jasper.runtime";
    permission java.lang.RuntimePermission
"accessClassInPackage.org.apache.jasper.runtime.*";

};
```

Recommended Security Manager Practices

Now that you know how to turn on the security manager with Tomcat and where Tomcat stores its policy file, you can look at recommended practices for granting permissions to your applications.

Use the Security Manager

If you don't turn on Tomcat's security manager, any JSP page or class file is free to perform any action it likes. This includes opening unauthorized connections to other network hosts, destroying your file system, or even abnormally terminating Tomcat by issuing the `System.exit()` command.

To maintain a secure Tomcat installation, you should assume that at some point a hacker will be able to deploy malicious code into one of Tomcat's Web applications. By turning the security manager on, you gain explicit control over what Web applications are allowed to do.

Regulating Common Code

Placing code into Tomcat's common class loader directories (`CATALINA_HOME/common/classes` and `CATALINA_HOME/common/lib`) is a good way to share common libraries among Web applications. However, because of Tomcat's liberal permission grants for this class loader (all permissions are granted), you may want to think twice before you make a habit out of placing code in this class loader.

You must do either of the following:

- Ensure that all code placed in this class loader is trusted.
- Place the code in the shared class loader. This class loader isn't covered by the security manager by default and is therefore restricted in its actions.

Example Grants

As mentioned, turning the security manager on gives you complete control over what Web applications are allowed to do. The flip side of this security coin is that Web applications will find themselves unable to do some things that they may have taken for granted before. Consider the following tasks that are unauthorized with Tomcat's default policy configuration:

- Creating a class loader
- Accessing a database via a socket (for example, the MySQL JDBC driver establishing a connection with a MySQL database)
- Sending an e-mail via the JavaMail API
- Reading or writing to files outside a Web application's directory

Creating a Class Loader

Listing 12-6 shows how to give a specific Web application the ability to create a class loader.

Listing 12-6. *Allowing Class Loader Creation*

```
grant codeBase "file:${catalina.home}/webapps/tomcatBook/WEB-INF/-" {
  permission java.lang.RuntimePermission "createClassLoader";
};
```

This is an extremely dangerous permission to grant. Applications that can instantiate their own class loaders can, by definition, load their own classes. As mentioned earlier, malicious classes could then be used to compromise your system in a number of ways.

Opening Socket Connections to Databases

Listing 12-7 shows how to allow all Web applications access to a specific database running on the host `db.server.com` on port 54321.

Listing 12-7. *Allowing a Database Connection*

```
grant codeBase "file:${catalina.home}/webapps/-" {
  permission java.net.SocketPermission "db.server.com:54321", "connect";
};
```

This example allows all code in all Web applications to connect to `db.server.com:54321`. If this is too much of a security risk for you, you have a few alternative options.

First, explicitly assign permission to each Web application's JDBC driver individually, as shown in Listing 12-8.

Listing 12-8. *Enabling a Web Application to Make a Database Connection*

```
grant codeBase "file:${catalina.home}/webapps/tomcatBook/WEB-INF/lib/JDBC.jar" {
  permission java.net.SocketPermission "db.server.com:54321", "connect";
};
```

Second, place the JDBC driver into the common class loader, which has all permissions granted to it. This means the driver can access the database, but the Web application can't.

Sending an E-mail with JavaMail

To send e-mail, Web applications need access to port 25 on an SMTP server. Listing 12-9 shows how to grant this permission to all classes in a Web application.

Listing 12-9. *Allowing Access to an SMTP Server*

```
grant codeBase "file:${catalina.home}/webapps/myWebApp/WEB-INF/classes/-" {
  permission java.net.SocketPermission "mail.server.com:25", "connect";
};
```

Reading or Writing to Files Outside a Web Application's Directory

If you want to use your operating system to control file access, rather than Java's permissions, you can give your Web applications free rein once again, as in Listing 12-10.

Listing 12-10. *Allowing Access to All Files*

```
grant {
  java.io.FilePermission "<<ALL FILES>>", "read,write,execute,delete";
};
```

If you don't grant at least some file permissions to your Web application, your Web applications will be shut out from accessing your file system. You should still secure it with your operating system's file permissions, because, even though your Web applications may be shut out, Tomcat itself has full permissions, and should a malicious hacker modify Tomcat somehow, they could still access your file system.

Using Security Realms

Recall that a realm is a programming interface that's used to authenticate users and implement container-managed security based on roles. The actual mapping of users to roles can be specified at deployment time—and can be changed dynamically without having to change the application code. I introduced realms in Chapter 11 but deferred a detailed discussion of the Web application-specific configuration to this chapter.

When protecting a resource, you must know which roles are to have access to it. This information is stored in the Web application's `web.xml` file in the `<security-constraint>` element. The application's developer should provide you with this information, but it's a good idea to be familiar with the options that can be used in a Web application.

These settings are usually the developer's job, and you just have to set up the server appropriately. However, the `admin` and `manager` applications are also protected resources, and you're in sole charge of them and may want to change their configuration.

Adding Settings to web.xml

The `<web-resource-collection>` element of `web.xml` is a convenient place to group Web resources together so that security can be applied uniformly. You specify the name of the resource and the URL patterns to cover inside this element, which is a subelement of `<security-constraint>`.

The `<role-name>` subelement of `<auth-constraint>`, itself a subelement of `<security-constraint>`, specifies a role that's allowed to access this section of the Web application. Any user belonging to this role may log in, providing they give a valid password. This is the domain of the administrator, as users and roles are defined in realms in `server.xml`. The Web application doesn't care what realm is used, as long as the user is configured in one of them.

Listing 12-11 shows the relevant section of the `admin` application's `web.xml` file.

Listing 12-11. *The Section of* `web.xml` *That Protects a Web Application*

```
<!-- Security is active on entire directory -->
<security-constraint>
  <display-name>
    Tomcat Server Configuration Security Constraint
  </display-name>
  <web-resource-collection>
    <web-resource-name>Protected Area</web-resource-name>
    <!-- Define the context-relative URL(s) to be protected -->
    <url-pattern>*.jsp</url-pattern>
    <url-pattern>*.do</url-pattern>
    <url-pattern>*.html</url-pattern>
  </web-resource-collection>
  <auth-constraint>
    <!-- Anyone with one of the listed roles may access this area -->
    <role-name>admin</role-name>
  </auth-constraint>
</security-constraint>
```

Here three patterns have been covered by the constraint: `*.jsp`, `*.do`, and `*.html`. This means any request for a file matching these patterns will be challenged. Tomcat will then authenticate the user and allow them to view the resource if they have the role specified, which in this case is `admin`.

Another element in `web.xml` has an association with realms. This is the `<login-config>` element that specifies how Tomcat challenges a user when they request a resource. Listing 12-12 shows the `admin` application's entry.

Listing 12-12. *The Section of* `web.xml` *That Specifies a Login Mechanism*

```
<!-- Login configuration uses form-based authentication -->
<login-config>
  <auth-method>FORM</auth-method>
  <realm-name>
    Tomcat Server Configuration Form-Based Authentication Area
  </realm-name>
  <form-login-config>
    <form-login-page>/login.jsp</form-login-page>
    <form-error-page>/error.jsp</form-error-page>
  </form-login-config>
</login-config>
```

`<login-config>` sets the type of login and authentication that the application needs. In this case, the application has form-based authentication, which means Tomcat will use the form page specified instead of the user's browser. This may also be BASIC, DIGEST, or CLIENT-CERT.

Choosing Form-Based Authentication

Form-based authentication is a good option for a few reasons.

- The server handles the user information. In the other forms of authentication, the browser may cache the authentication information. While this is convenient for the user, it isn't as secure as the server holding the information.
- BASIC authentication is easy to decode because the user information is sent as a plain, base64-encoded string.
- Not all browsers supported DIGEST authentication, so you can't guarantee that all clients will be able to authenticate. However, if the application is in a closed environment, such as a corporate intranet, it's easier to control the choice of browser. Internet Explorer, Mozilla, Firefox, and Konqueror all support DIGEST authentication.
- DIGEST authentication doesn't work if the passwords are digested on the Tomcat side because of the way that the DIGEST mechanism calculates its digest. The browser first calculates a digest of the username, the password, the URL, the HTTP method, and a random string sent to it by the server. Likewise, the server creates a digest using the same information and then compares the two digests. However, as the password is already digested on the server, and thus different from the version entered into the browser, the two digests will be different and authentication will fail. In other words, Tomcat is creating a message digest of a message digest.
- JDBC realms don't currently work with DIGEST authentication. Some of the algorithms to digest the password from the database aren't yet implemented.
- CLIENT-AUTH is really necessary only in business-to-business transactions, so it doesn't appear in most Web applications that you'll see.

The one drawback of form-based login for the manager application is that you can't run manager commands with Ant because it can authenticate only using BASIC authentication.

Using Custom Login and Error Pages

If you want to add form-based authentication to a Web application in place of some other type supplied by the developers, Listing 12-13 shows an example.

Listing 12-13. *An Example Form for Login*

```
<%@ taglib prefix="c" uri="http://java.sun.com/jstl/core_rt" %>
<c:url value="j_security_check" var="j_security_check"/>
<html>
  <head><title>Please Log In</title>
```

```
  <body>
    <form method="POST"
          action='${j_security_check}' >
      <table border="0" cellspacing="5">
        <tr>
          <th align="right">Username:</th>
          <td align="left"><input type="text" name="j_username"></td>
        </tr>
        <tr>
          <th align="right">Password:</th>
          <td align="left"><input type="password" name="j_password"></td>
        </tr>
        <tr>
          <td align="right"><input type="submit" value="Log In"></td>
          <td align="left"><input type="reset"></td>
        </tr>
      </table>
    </form>
  </body>
</html>
```

The important values here are j_security_check, j_username, and j_password. Your form must submit to the special j_security_check URL (here encoded using the core JSTL tag library to allow for browsers that don't use cookies), with the two special parameter names. This URL is part of the authentication mechanism and will authenticate the user.

Listing 12-14 shows an example error page that's displayed to users if they fail to log in correctly, though you could quite easily use the original page.

Listing 12-14. *A Login Error Page*

```
<%@ taglib prefix="c" uri="http://java.sun.com/jstl/core_rt" %>
<c:url value="ch12/login.jsp" var="login"/>
<html>
  <head><title>Error: Login Failure</title></head>
  <body>
    Login failed, please try
    <a href='${login}'>again</a>.
  </body>
</html>
```

This is simple and gives a link for the user to return to the login page following a failure.

Place these files in a Web application, and update the links appropriately. The following examples will assume you've placed them in `tomcatBook/ch12`. Listing 12-15 shows the `web.xml` entry to protect the entire Web application.

Listing 12-15. *An Example `web.xml` Entry to Protect the `tomcatBook` Web Application*

```
<!-- Define a Security Constraint on this Application -->
<security-constraint>
  <web-resource-collection>
    <web-resource-name>Tomcat Book Application</web-resource-name>
    <url-pattern>/*</url-pattern>
  </web-resource-collection>
  <auth-constraint>
     <role-name>tomcat</role-name>
  </auth-constraint>
</security-constraint>

<!-- Define the Login Configuration for this Application -->
<login-config>
  <auth-method>FORM</auth-method>
  <realm-name>Tomcat Book Application</realm-name>
  <form-login-config>
    <form-login-page>/ch12/login.jsp</form-login-page>
    <form-error-page>/ch12/error.jsp</form-error-page>
  </form-login-config>
</login-config>

<!-- Security roles referenced by this Web application -->
<security-role>
  <description>
    The role that's required to log in to the Tomcat Book Application
  </description>
  <role-name>tomcat</role-name>
</security-role>
```

Now whenever you try to access a page in the tomcatBook application for the first time, you'll have to enter user details in the ch12/login.jsp page. If you provide the wrong details or have the wrong role, then you'll see the ch12/error.jsp page. This security constraint will use whichever realm you've configured (see Chapter 11 for details of configuring realms).

Using the Secure Sockets Layer

SSL is a protocol that allows clients and servers in a network environment to communicate securely. In addition to encryption of data (and hence secure communication), SSL provides for authentication.

The security protocols on which SSL is based are public key encryption and symmetric key encryption. Public key encryption uses a pair of encryption keys to encode a message—a public key that's public and a private key that isn't disclosed to anyone else. Anyone wanting to send a message to an application that has a known public key encrypts it with that key. Only the corresponding private key can decrypt the message, and thus the transmission is secure. Symmetric key encryption, on the other hand, uses the same secret key for both encryption and decryption. This algorithm, however, needs a reliable way to exchange the secret key between the two end points in the transmission.

When a client opens an SSL connection with a server, an SSL handshake is performed. The procedure for an SSL handshake is as follows:

1. The server sends its digital certificate. This contains the public key of the server, information about the server, the authority that issued the server's certificate, and the use-by date of the certificate.

2. The client then authenticates the server based on the validity of the certificate and trustworthiness of the authority that issued the certificate. Certificates issued by well-known (and trusted) certificate authorities (CAs), such as VeriSign and Thawte, are recognized by most Web browsers. If the certificate can't be validated, the user is warned, and they can choose to either accept the certificate or deny it.

3. A session key is then generated and exchanged over the connection. The connection is now secured by the public key encryption mechanism, which means that the exchange is secure. The session key is a symmetric key and is used for the duration of the session to encrypt all subsequent data transmissions.

The server configuration may also require the client to present its own authentication details. In this situation, another step is introduced in the SSL handshake. Such a requirement isn't common and is used only in some business-to-business application environments.

The HTTP over SSL (HTTPS) protocol uses SSL as a layer under HTTP. Transport Layer Security (TLS) is the Internet Engineering Task Force (IETF) version of the SSL protocol. It's defined by RFC 2246 (http://www.ietf.org/rfc/rfc2246.txt) and is intended to eventually supersede SSL.

Adding support for SSL or TLS in Tomcat is a four-step process.

1. Download and install an SSL/TLS implementation (not necessary for JDK 1.4 and newer).
2. Create the certificate keystore containing a self-signed certificate, which is generated by you and isn't guaranteed by anyone else, such as a CA.
3. Obtain a certificate from a CA such as VeriSign (`http://www.verisign.com`), Thawte (`http://www.thawte.com`), or Trustcenter.de (`http://www.trustcenter.de`). Use your self-signed certificate to generate a certificate-signing request, and submit it to the CA to get a certificate digitally signed by them. This certificate, when presented to a user, guarantees that you are who you claim to be. If you're using Tomcat in a test/development environment, you can skip this step. You'd need a certificate for a production deployment, though, as users may not be willing to accept a self-signed certificate.
4. Make the Tomcat configuration changes for SSL.

Installing JSSE

Java Secure Socket Implementation (JSSE) is Sun's implementation of the SSL and TLS protocols. JSSE is available for free but isn't open source. For more information on JSSE, see `http://java.sun.com/products/jsse/`. You have to install JSSE if you're using JDK 1.2 or 1.3. JDK 1.4 and newer includes JSSE, so you should skip the following step if you have JDK 1.4 installed.

Download JSSE from `http://java.sun.com/products/jsse/`. The three JSSE JAR files (`jsse.jar`, `jnet.jar`, and `jcert.jar`) need to be in Tomcat's classpath. Copy them to the `JAVA_HOME/jre/lib/ext` directory.

Preparing the Certificate Keystore

You may have seen how to prepare a keystore in Chapter 9, but here's a reminder:

```
> JAVA_HOME\bin\keytool -genkey -alias tomcat -keyalg RSA
```

The `-genkey` option specifies that a key pair (private key, public key) should be created. This key pair is enclosed in a self-signed certificate. The `-keyalg` option specifies the algorithm (which in this case is RSA) to be used for the key pair. All keystore entries are accessed via unique aliases using the `-alias` option—here the alias is tomcat. The `keytool` command will ask for a password, which you should take the usual precautions with.

The default name for the keystore file is `.keystore`, and it's stored in the home directory of the user who runs the `keytool` command. This directory will vary depending on the operating system. For example, if you install Tomcat as a user called *tomcat* on Linux, the keystore file will be in `/home/tomcat`. Similarly, if you install it as the tomcat user on Windows, the keystore file would be in `C:\Documents and Settings\tomcat`. You can also specify an alternative keystore filename and password using the `-keystore` and `-keypass` options.

```
> JAVA_HOME/bin/keytool -genkey -alias tomcat -keyalg RSA
  -keypass somepass -keystore /path/to/keystorefile
```

Here's an example run of the keytool:

```
> keytool -genkey -alias tomcat -keyalg RSA
Enter keystore password:  tomcat
What is your first and last name?
  [Unknown]:  localhost
What is the name of your organizational unit?
  [Unknown]:  Editorial
What is the name of your organization?
  [Unknown]:  Java
What is the name of your City or Locality?
  [Unknown]:  Glasgow
What is the name of your State or Province?
  [Unknown]:  Scotland
What is the two-letter country code for this unit?
  [Unknown]:  UK
Is CN=localhost, OU=Editorial, O=Java, L=Glasgow, ST=Scotland, C=UK correct?
  [no]:  yes

Enter key password for <tomcat>
        (RETURN if same as keystore password):
```

Note that the first field you're asked for is the domain name of your server, which becomes the common name (CN). This needs to be of the format `www.domainname.com`, `hostname.domainname.com`, or just `domainname.com`. This name is embedded in the certificate. The CN should be the fully qualified hostname for the machine where Tomcat is deployed. If this isn't so, then users will get a warning message in their Web browsers when they try to access a secure page from your Web site, as you saw in Chapter 9.

If this is a test/development environment or you don't want a certificate from a CA, you can stop here. You're now ready to make Tomcat-related setup changes. If you were deploying in a production environment, you'd need to get a certificate that's validated by a CA.

Installing a Certificate from a Certificate Authority

First, create a local certificate as before using the `keytool` command.

```
> keytool -genkey -alias tomcat -keyalg RSA -keystore <keystore_filename>
```

Next, use this certificate to create a certificate signing request (CSR).

```
> keytool -certreq -keyalg RSA -alias tomcat -file certreq.csr -keystore <
keystore_filename>
```

If the keystore file is the default (that is, a file named .keystore in the home directory), then you can omit the -keystore <keystore_filename> option.

The -certreq option creates a CSR file called certreq.csr that you can submit to the CA to get a certificate. The file will be in the directory where you ran the keytool command previously. Getting a certificate requires payment to the CA for the authentication services. Some CAs have test certificates available for download at no cost, which are usually valid only for a short time.

To submit your CSR, go to the CA of your choice and paste the contents of the file into the form provided there. Then follow the instructions.

Importing the Certificate

After you have the certificate from the CA, you need to get the *chain certificate* (also called the *root certificate*) from them. You can download this from the following sites (depending on the CA):

- http://www.verisign.com/support/install/intermediate.html
- http://www.trustcenter.de/set_en.htm
- http://www.thawte.com/roots/

The chain certificate is a self-signed certificate from the CA that contains its well-known public key. You can view the contents of a certificate using the -printcert option.

```
> keytool -printcert -file /path/to/certificate
```

This is good practice before you import a third-party certificate into the keystore. You then import the chain certificate into the keystore.

```
> keytool -import -alias root -keystore <keystore_filename>
  -trustcacerts -file <filename_of_the_chain_certificate>
```

And finally, import the new certificate.

```
> keytool -import -alias tomcat -keystore <keystore_filename>
  -trustcacerts -file <certificate_filename>
```

Here, the <filename_of_the_chain_certificate> contains the chain certificate you got from the CA. As mentioned earlier, the -keystore <keystore_filename> option isn't required if the keystore file has a default name (.keystore). You're now ready to make Tomcat-related setup changes.

Protecting Resources with SSL

You can protect resources with SSL just as you can protect resources with authentication constraints. The <user-data-constraint> subelement of <security-constraint> in web.xml specifies the guaranteed integrity of the data flowing between the client and the server for this resource. There are three levels of integrity: NONE, INTEGRAL, and CONFIDENTIAL.

NONE means there's no guarantee that the data hasn't been intercepted and tampered with, and INTEGRAL guarantees the integrity of the data, meaning that the data hasn't been interfered with. The strongest guarantee is CONFIDENTIAL, which guarantees that a third party hasn't intercepted the data. If you specify INTEGRAL or CONFIDENTIAL, the server will use SSL for all requests to this resource by redirecting the client to the SSL port of the server. The redirection port is configured in the redirectPort attribute of the HTTP connector.

For your secure resource, you want to be sure that all the data you transfer is safe, so you'll use the CONFIDENTIAL level. Simply add the element in Listing 12-16 to the <security-constraint> in your web.xml file from the previous example.

Listing 12-16. *Guaranteeing the Integrity of Data with a Security Constraint*

```
<security-constraint>
  ...
  <user-data-constraint>
    <description>
     Constrain the user data transport for the whole application
    </description>
    <transport-guarantee>CONFIDENTIAL</transport-guarantee>
  </user-data-constraint>
</security-constraint>
```

This will force all requests for your secure Web application to use HTTPS, even if the original request came in over HTTP. This is the only setup required in web.xml.

Configuring the SSL Connector

The setup procedure for an SSL connector is straightforward. You've already seen its attributes in Chapter 4, so this section covers how to configure a connector for the keystore you created earlier.

Modify the default SSL HTTP connector, and add the location and password of the keystore if appropriate (see Listing 12-17).

Listing 12-17. *Configuring an SSL Connector*

```
<!-- Define a SSL Coyote HTTP/1.1 Connector on port 8443 -->
<Connector port="8443"
           maxThreads="150" minSpareThreads="25" maxSpareThreads="75"
           enableLookups="false" disableUploadTimeout="true"
           acceptCount="100" debug="0" scheme="https" secure="true"
           clientAuth="false" sslProtocol="TLS"
           keystorePass="tomcat"/>
```

Now start Tomcat, and point a browser to http://localhost/tomcatBook/. You'll be presented with a warning about the suspicious certificate (note that this warning may vary depending on your browser).

You can choose to view the certificate to see the details of the issuer. These details will match those you specified when you created the certificate. Before you proceed your browser will give you the option to install this certificate forever (you'll have to view the certificate with Internet Explorer to do this), which means that you trust this site and won't be shown the security warning again. An additional warning will be given if you didn't use the domain name of your server.

Once you've confirmed you're happy with accepting this certificate, you'll see the login page from Listing 12-13, only this time your session will be conducted over SSL. To confirm this, examine the URL. It should be https://localhost:8443/tomcatBook/. Tomcat knows to redirect you to this port for SSL because of the redirectPort="8443" setting in the default HTTP connector.

Using SSL with the Apache Web Server

You've seen how the stand-alone HTTP connector handles SSL. Another approach that's more widely used is to have a dedicated Web server handle the SSL-related functionality. This is a more stable configuration and has better performance. In this configuration, the communication between the user's browser and Web server is encrypted over SSL, but the communication between the Web server and Tomcat isn't.

Before you can configure Apache, you need to create a private key and certificate. This is a separate process from Tomcat's because the keytool command creates a propriety keystore format (maintained by Sun) that Apache can't use. To create a private key and a certificate for Apache, you need the OpenSSL library from http://www.openssl.org.

If you're using Windows, you should visit http://hunter.campbus.com and download the Apache/OpenSSL combination for your Apache installation. You don't need to install the whole bundle but will need the openssl utility and the libeay32.dll, ssleay32.dll, and mod_ssl.so files. Place the first three (openssl, libeay32.dll, and ssleay32.dll) in Apache's bin directory and mod_ssl.so in Apache's modules directory.

If you don't have an openssl.cnf file, create one with contents similar to those shown in Listing 12-18. These are the certificate details you would have entered in the previous keytool examples.

Listing 12-18. *The openssl.cnf File Setting Your Server's Certificate Properties*

```
[ req ]
default_bits = 1024
distinguished_name = req_distinguished_name
attributes         = req_attributes

[ req_distinguished_name ]
countryName                  = Country Name (2 letter code)
countryName_default          = UK
countryName_min              = 2
```

```
countryName_max                = 2

stateOrProvinceName            = State or Province Name (full name)
stateOrProvinceName_default    = Scotland

localityName                   = Locality Name (eg, city)
localityName_default           = Glasgow

organizationName               = Organization Name (eg, company)
organizationName_default       = Java

organizationalUnitName         = Organizational Unit Name (eg, section)
organizationalUnitName_default = Editorial

commonName                     = Common Name (eg, YOUR name)
commonName_default             = localhost
commonName_max                 = 64

emailAddress                   = Email Address
emailAddress_max               = 40

[ req_attributes ]
challengePassword              = A challenge password
challengePassword_min          = 4
challengePassword_max          = 20
```

Then run the following to create a private key:

```
> openssl genrsa -des3 1024 > ./certs/localhost.key
Loading 'screen' into random state - done
Generating RSA private key, 1024 bit long modulus
...++++++
...............++++++
e is 65537 (0x10001)
Enter pass phrase:
Verifying - Enter pass phrase:
```

This will create the `localhost.key` key file in the `certs` directory with password protection. You'll have to provide this password to enable SSL when you start or restart Apache. If you don't want to use a password to protect this file (more on this later), then omit the `-des3` switch.

Now create a CSR, which you can use to request a certificate from a CA or create a self-signed certificate.

```
> openssl req -new -key ./certs/localhost.key
  -out ./certs/localhost.csr -config openssl.cnf
Enter pass phrase for ./certs/localhost.key:
You are about to be asked to enter information that will be incorporated
into your certificate request.
What you are about to enter is what is called a Distinguished Name or a DN.
There are quite a few fields but you can leave some blank
For some fields there will be a default value,
If you enter '.', the field will be left blank.
-----
Country Name (2 letter code) [UK]:
State or Province Name (full name) [Scotland]:
Locality Name (eg, city) [Glasgow]:
Organization Name (eg, company) [Java]:
Organizational Unit Name (eg, section) [Editorial]:
Common Name (eg, YOUR name) [localhost]:
Email Address []:

Please enter the following 'extra' attributes
to be sent with your certificate request
A challenge password []:tomcat
```

This creates the `localhost.csr` file in the `certs` directory. Note the default values from `openssl.cnf`. Provide the password for the private key as appropriate. The final step is to create the certificate.

```
>openssl req -x509 -key ./certs/localhost.key -in ./certs/localhost.csr
  -out ./certs/localhost.crt
Enter pass phrase for ./certs/localhost.key:
```

This creates the `localhost.crt` certificate in the `certs` directory. You're now ready to configure Apache and Tomcat.

Deploying a Web Application

Begin by configuring Apache. If you're responding to user requests on port 80 (the default HTTP port) and the SSL port (default value 443), Apache needs to listen on both these ports. In this example you'll protect the `tomcatBook` Web application with Apache's SSL and leave the default Apache files unprotected.

```
# Listen on port 80 and 443 (the SSL port)
Listen 80
Listen 443

# Use name-based virtual hosts on these ports
NameVirtualHost *:80
NameVirtualHost *:443
```

You now have to make the SSL-related settings in Apache.

```
<VirtualHost *:443>
  # The name of this host
  ServerName localhost

  # Switch on SSL for this host
  SSLEngine on

  # The path to the certificate
  SSLCertificateFile /path/to/certs/localhost.crt

  # The path to the private key
  SSLCertificateKeyFile /path/to/certs/localhost.key

  # You are protecting the tomcatBook webapp
  # so enable the connector settings
  Include /path/to/tomcatBook/WEB-INF/jk2/jk2.conf"
</VirtualHost>
```

Here you create a virtual host listening on the SSL port (443) for protecting the `tomcatBook` Web application. You switch on SSL for this host and set the locations of the certificate and the private key. Assuming that you've enabled `mod_jk2` and have generated the settings using the techniques from Chapter 9, you then include the settings for the `tomcatBook` Web application.

Next, you need to configure the non-SSL host for Apache's static files.

```
<VirtualHost *:80>
  ServerName localhost
  DocumentRoot /path/to/Apache2/htdocs
</VirtualHost>
```

A final point to consider is running Apache and SSL on Windows. The default private key password prompt doesn't work on Windows, so you must either configure a private key without password protection or configure a script or utility to provide the password. Both scenarios have inherent problems, so you must make sure that both files (the private key or the utility) are heavily protected.

To specify the file that will give the key password to Apache, set the following outside your virtual host definitions:

```
SSLPassPhraseDialog exec:bin/password.bat
```

This points to the password batch file in Apache's bin directory. Listing 12-19 shows the password batch file.

Listing 12-19. *The `password.bat` File That Sends the Key Password to Tomcat*

```
@echo tomcat
```

There's no more to it than that (providing that tomcat is your key password), though this doesn't do any checking as to whom is running the script and for which domain. If more than one domain were to use this file, and each domain had a different password, then you'd have to check the domain name. Apache sends this information as `servername:port` as the first argument to the script and the appropriate algorithm as the second argument. Listing 12-20 shows an example batch file that does this for the server you have configured.

Listing 12-20. *The `password.bat` File That Sends the Key Password to Tomcat*

```
@echo off
if "%1" == "localhost:443" @echo tomcat
```

Here you check that the first argument matches the name and port of the server. If this is the case, then you echo the password to `stdout`.

Listing 12-21 shows an example `workers2.properties` file for this setup.

Listing 12-21. *The `workers2.properties` file using Apache's SSL functionality*

```
# Define the channel
[channel.socket:localhost:8009]

# Define the worker
[ajp13:localhost:8009]
channel=channel.socket:localhost:8009

# Uri mapping
[uri:localhost:443/tomcatBook/*]
group=ajp13:localhost:8009
```

The important thing to note here is the URI mapping. Only requests to the `tomcatBook` Web application that also map to the server name and the SSL port will be passed on to Tomcat.

Testing the Installation

After making these changes, restart Tomcat and Apache. You should be able to access the secure Tomcat Web application through `https://localhost/tomcatBook` and the nonsecure Apache files through `http://localhost`.

A common problem in the setup is related to SSL configuration on Apache. Apache may fail to start or not serve up SSL content. If you face this problem, first check the new directives added to `httpd.conf`.

```
> apache/bin/apache -t
```

This should uncover any errors related to directive syntax. Next, look for Apache error messages logged in `APACHE_HOME/logs/error.log`. You can control logging via the `LogLevel` Apache directive.

```
LogLevel debug
```

The log levels are `debug`, `trace`, `info`, `warn`, `error`, and `none`. A debug level of `none` turns off all logging. The log levels are in order of priority, and setting logging to a certain level shows messages of that and higher levels. For example, the `warn` level shows warnings and error messages.

Summary

In this chapter, you looked at various security topics with respect to Tomcat. First you looked at general security: removing or disabling the default Web applications and locking up the file system. Both of these procedures are common practice in all server installations, so they should fit into your general security policy without too much trouble.

Then you moved on to the Tomcat-specific security. You examined Java's security manager and its role in controlling access to system resources. Tomcat can take advantage of this feature to prevent Web applications from carrying out potentially dangerous actions. A rogue servlet could easily take down the file system if you don't take measures to restrict access.

You then learned how to put realms into practice with Tomcat's security constraints. You saw the different kinds of login mechanism you can use, as well as their strengths and weaknesses. You then saw how to force SSL connections for groups of Web resources on the Tomcat server. SSL prevents third parties from listening in on your data transfers between the server and the client. When dealing with sensitive data it's always wise to use SSL. The final topic was securing the data channel between Tomcat and the client using Apache's SSL abilities.

CHAPTER 13

Implementing Shared Tomcat Hosting

This chapter shows how you can use Tomcat to implement shared hosting, which means that many hosts can run on the same server and thus share resources. Shared hosting has been a popular and useful part of the Apache Web server's architecture for a long time, and Tomcat has an analogous mechanism.

In this chapter, a Web site refers to the contents of a distinct fully qualified domain name (FQDN), which is served by a Web server. A FQDN consists of two parts: a host name and a domain name. For example, the FQDN `www.apress.com` consists of the host name `www` and the domain name `apress.com`. The domain name can have other hosts, such as `mail` or `java`. The FQDNs would be `mail.apress.com` and `java.apress.com`.

A standard Web server in its default configuration allows only one domain to be served from the machine. In this case, if you wanted to serve hundreds of domains from your servers, you would have to set up hundreds of computers to serve all these Web sites. This is clearly not a scalable solution.

Also, IP addresses are a scarce resource. A Web-hosting provider gets a limited number of IP addresses from its connectivity providers for hosting. Using one IP address for every Web host would quickly eat up all the allocated IP addresses. To overcome these limitations, virtual hosting uses all your available resources, be they services, IP addresses, or other computing resources, in an optimal way.

Examining Virtual Hosting

You have two ways to implement virtual hosting:

- **IP-based virtual hosting**: Based on machines with multiple distinct IP addresses, every domain is allocated one IP address. The Web server listens to each of these network interfaces and serves resources from the relevant domain based on the IP address on which the request had arrived.

- **Name-based virtual hosting**: The Web server listens on a single IP addresses and serves resources from the relevant Web site, based on the HTTP request headers from the Web client.

IP-Based Virtual Hosting

In this form of virtual hosting, the machine is configured to have the same number of IP addresses as the hosts it's to serve. So a machine hosting ten Web sites needs ten IP addresses. You configure these additional IP addresses either by adding physical network interfaces to the machine or, as is more common, by adding aliased network interfaces to the computer.

Normally when you add a network interface card (NIC) to your machine, you configure it with a single IP address, which you then use in various services. However, it's possible to configure the same NIC with more than one IP address. Adding these additional IP addresses involves using operating system–specific commands for creating a virtual interface and then configuring it with a virtual IP address. This process normally involves using a physical NIC and adding virtual interfaces on top, a process known as *aliasing*.

Configuring Aliasing for Windows

Windows versions from Windows NT onward support aliasing and therefore IP-based virtual hosting. Each flavor of Windows has slightly different ways to configure this, but they're similar enough that you'll be able to transfer the example shown here to your version.

This example uses Windows 2000 Professional. Open Control Panel ➤ Network and Dial-up Connections, and double-click the network interface you want to configure. For example, this may be your local area network connection. You'll see a properties dialog box similar to that in Figure 13-1.

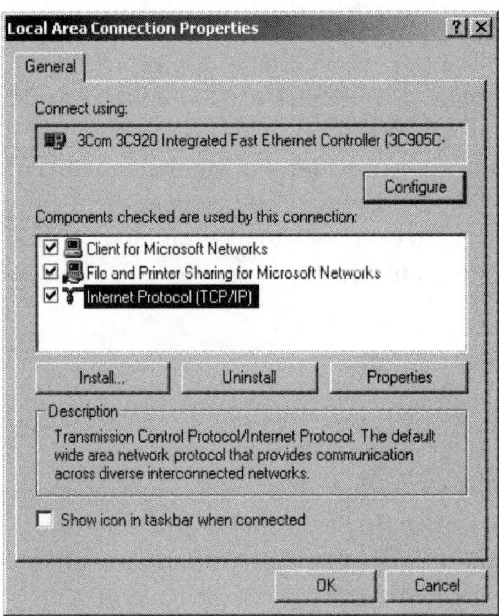

Figure 13-1. *The network properties dialog box*

Select the TCP/IP component as shown, and click Properties. The TCP/IP properties box allows you to specify a main IP address and DNS servers for this network interface. If there's no IP address, enter a value that's appropriate for your network, as shown in Figure 13-2. The default subnet mask should be sufficient.

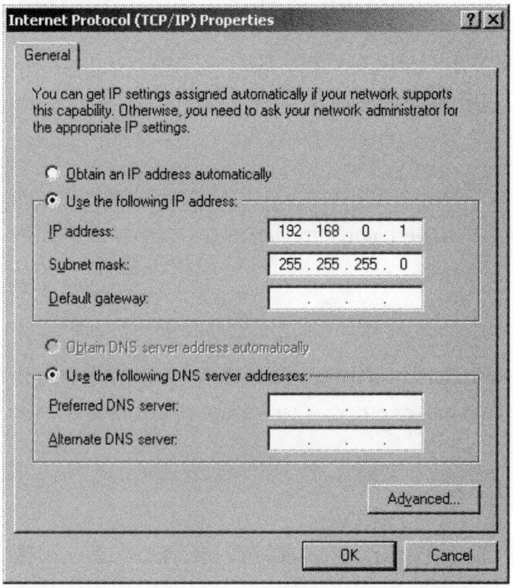

Figure 13-2. *The TCP/IP properties dialog box*

To add further IP addresses, click Advanced. You'll see that the IP address you just entered listed in the top pane of the resultant dialog box. To add further IP addresses, click Add and enter another value. You'll see the new IP address that has been added to the list, as in Figure 13-3. This computer will now listen on 192.168.0.1 and 192.168.0.2.

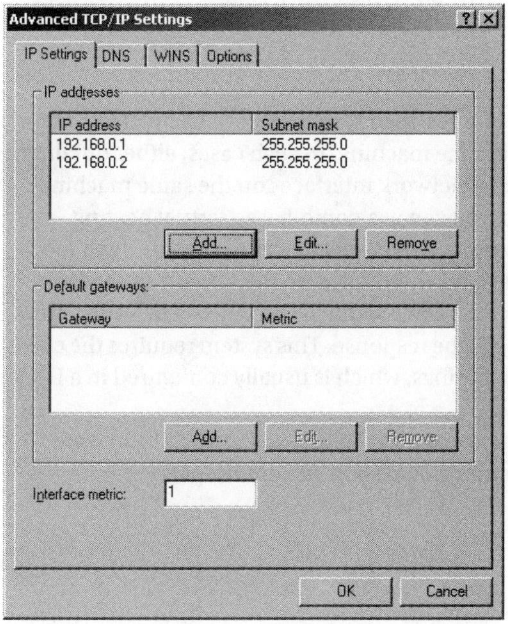

Figure 13-3. *The Advanced TCP/IP Settings dialog box*

Configuring Aliasing for Unix

To set network interface options on Unix-like systems, you use the `ifconfig` utility. On most systems, to check which network interfaces are installed, run `ifconfig` with the `-a` switch.

```
# ifconfig -a
```

If this doesn't work, try `netstat -i`.

Once you know which network interfaces are installed, you can view the details of a specific interface with the following:

```
# ifconfig interface_name
```

To set the IP address of a network interface, specify the interface's name, followed by the IP address, options such as the `netmask`, and the `up` parameter. So, to set the IP address of `eth0` to 192.168.0.1, run the following:

```
# ifconfig eth0 192.168.0.1 netmask 255.255.255.0 up
```

`eth0` will now be listening on the new IP address. To turn the network interface off, use the `down` parameter:

```
# ifconfig eth0 down
```

To add an additional IP address to a network interface to implement aliasing, run the following:

```
# ifconfig eth0:1 192.168.0.2
```

`eth0` will now listen on 192.168.0.1 and 192.168.0.2.

Name-Based Virtual Hosting

While IP-based virtual hosts help maximize resources, they're still not feasible in places where hundreds of domains need to be hosted on the same machine. In such cases, either obtaining one IP address for each host or configuring many network interfaces on the same machine becomes a logistical nightmare. In these cases, you can use name-based virtual hosting.

An HTTP 1.1 request contains the Host: header, which specifies the host on which the requested resource resides. When such a request is sent to a server, the server can read the Host: header and determine which of its hosts the client would like to reach. The server then processes the request accordingly and sends back the response. This system requires the client to first look up a list of IP address/hostname mappings, which is usually configured in a DNS server. Figure 13-4 shows this process.

You can see how this makes more efficient use of the available resources. If you were limited to one host for one IP address, the Internet would soon run out of space.

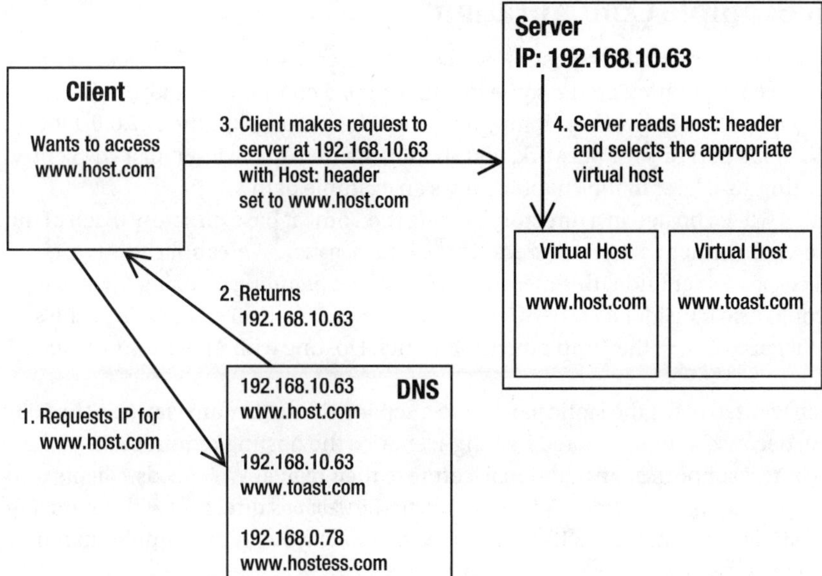

Figure 13-4. *Name-based virtual hosting*

Name-based virtual hosting does have some problems.

- SSL connections aren't on HTTP, so the Host: header can't be extracted in advance. Therefore, it isn't possible to have multiple SSL servers running on the same IP address. For this reason, each SSL-enabled Web site needs to be configured on a unique IP address.
- Older Web clients and many Web access software libraries still use the old HTTP 1.0 protocol. Since they don't send the Host: header to the Web server, name-based virtual hosting wouldn't work properly with them. However, these clients are pretty rare, so this isn't as big a consideration as it used to be.

Implementing Virtual Hosting with Tomcat

Tomcat can work either in stand-alone mode, in which it serves static pages along with JSP pages/servlets, or in conjunction with a Web server such as Apache. Chapter 9 and Chapter 12 have more details on this.

If Tomcat is to provide virtual hosting support, then when a request comes for a particular resource on one of Tomcat's virtual hosts, Tomcat should be able to successfully obtain the host that the request was for and fetch the required resource from the host's document base.

When working in conjunction with another Web server like Apache, the Web server handles the virtual hosts and processing of subsequent static pages, as you saw in Chapter 12. Tomcat then handles the servlets and JSP pages while distinguishing the various hosts involved.

Creating an Example Configuration

You'll configure Tomcat to serve three hosts: `www.tomcatbook.com`, `www.catalinabook.com`, and `www.jasperbook.com`, each running on the same machine with a common IP address. This machine may be part of your network, or it may be the local machine with the 127.0.0.1 local loopback address. If it's part of your network, you should ensure you have set up a DNS entry for each host. (Listing 13-8 later in the chapter shows an example of this.)

These domains will be hosted in a directory outside the Tomcat base directory. Each of the domains has its own document area in `/home/sites/<domain-name>`. Web applications are deployed in the `webapps` folder under this hierarchy. If you were planning on using Apache with this setup, you could also consider a `/home/sites/<domain-name>/web` directory as Apache's document root. I'll get to this in the "Implementing Virtual Hosting with Apache and Tomcat" section.

You may even want to place the static pages into a separate directory anyway (say the `ROOT` Web application), because in many shared hosting scenarios the hosting requirement of the clients includes Tomcat support, as an additional feature to their regular Web needs. Clients who want to add Web applications can drop their WAR files in the `webapps` directory without mixing them up with the static content. Figure 13-5 shows the general layout of the sample shared hosts on the Tomcat server.

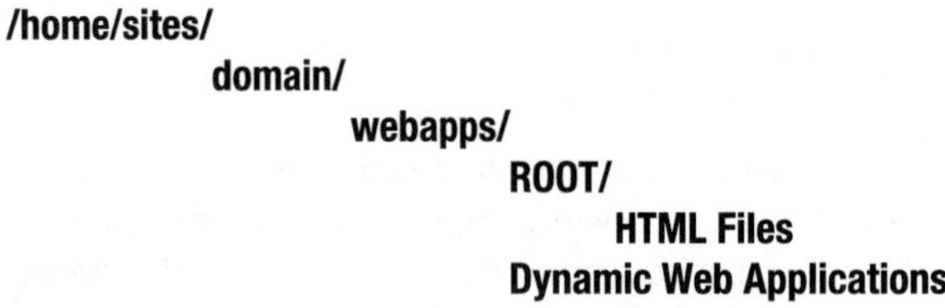

Figure 13-5. *The general layout of the example shared hosts*

You'll need a way to identify which host you have accessed to determine if your configuration is correct. Therefore, each host should have a `ROOT` Web application with an `index.html` file that points to a JSP page in the dynamic section, as shown in Listing 13-1.

Listing 13-1. *The `index.hml` Page for Shared Hosting*

```
<html>
  <head><title>Welcome to catalinabook.com</title>

  <body>
    <h1>Welcome to catalinabook.com</h1>
    <hr/>
    <p>
      Click <a href="jsp/index.jsp">here</a>
      to access the dynamic section of the site.
    </p>
  </body>
</html>
```

Remember to change the name of the host. Feel free to change these setup details to suit your own server hosting policy. Just remember to change the settings as given in Listing 13-5 accordingly.

The JSP page is common to all the hosts and should be placed in the `jsp` Web application. Listing 13-2 shows this page.

Listing 13-2. *The `index.jsp` Page That's Common to All the Hosts*

```
<html>
  <head>
    <title>
      Welcome to ${pageContext.servletContext.servletContextName}
    </title>

  <body>
    <h1>Welcome to ${pageContext.servletContext.servletContextName}</h1>
    <hr/>
  </body>
</html>
```

The EL segments obtain the name of the host so that you can see that the virtual hosting is working and that JSP pages are producing dynamic content. The `servletContextName` property is set in each Web application's `web.xml` file.

Finally, you don't necessarily need a `web.xml` file for each of these simple Web applications, though to follow good practice you should add one such as is shown in Listing 13-3 and Listing 13-4.

Listing 13-3. *A `web.xml` for the `ROOT` Web Application*

```
<?xml version="1.0" encoding="ISO-8859-1"?>
<web-app xmlns="http://java.sun.com/xml/ns/j2ee"
        xmlns:xsi="http://www.w3.org/2001/XMLSchema-instance"
        xsi:schemaLocation="http://java.sun.com/xml/ns/j2ee
        http://java.sun.com/xml/ns/j2ee/web-app_2_4.xsd" version="2.4">

  <display-name>ROOT web application</display-name>
  <description>
    Users should place their static HTML files here.
  </description>
</web-app>
```

You should change the <display-name> setting for each host as follows. This will be displayed to show that each host is serving a different dynamic page.

Listing 13-4. *A web.xml for the jsp Web Application*

```
<?xml version="1.0" encoding="ISO-8859-1"?>
<web-app xmlns="http://java.sun.com/xml/ns/j2ee"
         xmlns:xsi="http://www.w3.org/2001/XMLSchema-instance"
         xsi:schemaLocation="http://java.sun.com/xml/ns/j2ee
         http://java.sun.com/xml/ns/j2ee/web-app_2_4.xsd" version="2.4">

  <display-name>the jsp web application on catalinabook.com</display-name>
  <description>
    A dynamic web application.
  </description>
</web-app>
```

You now have all you need to implement virtual hosting. Figure 13-6 shows you how your final configuration should look for each host.

```
webapps/
        ROOT/
             index.html
             WEB-INF/
                     web.xml
        jsp/
           index.jsp
           WEB-INF/
                   web.xml
```

Figure 13-6. *The final Web application configuration*

Here you can see that the static HTML files are separated from any dynamic content. You can then host static Web sites alongside dynamic Web sites by placing subdirectories in the ROOT Web application should you choose to do so.

Setting Up the Virtual Hosting

You define virtual hosts in `server.xml`. For this example you'll see a complete `server.xml` file written from scratch. Feel free to add the settings to your existing `server.xml`.

Listing 13-5 shows the setup for the first virtual host. To add the other two, simply duplicate the settings appropriately.

Listing 13-5. *Creating a Virtual Host in server.xml*

```
<Server port="8005" shutdown="SHUTDOWN">
  <Service name="Virtual Hosting Tomcat">

    <Connector port="8080"
               maxThreads="150" minSpareThreads="25" maxSpareThreads="75"
               enableLookups="false" redirectPort="8443" acceptCount="100"
               debug="0" connectionTimeout="20000"
               disableUploadTimeout="true" />

    <Engine name="Catalina" defaultHost="www.catalinabook.com">

      <!-- Global logger unless overridden at lower levels -->
      <!-- Tomcat 5.0.x only -->
      <Logger className="org.apache.catalina.logger.FileLogger"
              prefix="catalina_log." suffix=".txt"
              timestamp="true"/>

      <Host name="www.catalinabook.com" debug="0"
            appBase="C:/home/sites/catalinabook.com/webapps"
            unpackWARs="true">

        <Valve className="org.apache.catalina.valves.AccessLogValve"
               directory="C:/home/sites/catalinabook.com/logs"
               prefix="catalinabook.com.access."
               suffix=".log"
               pattern="common"/>

         <!-- Tomcat 5.0.x only -->
         <Logger className="org.apache.catalina.logger.FileLogger"
                 directory="C:/home/sites/catalinabook.com/logs"
                 prefix="catalinabook.com."
                 suffix=".log"
                 timestamp="true"/>
      </Host>
      <!-- The other two virtual hosts go here -->
    </Engine>
  </Service>
</Server>
```

The connector is copied from the default `server.xml` file and listens for HTTP requests on port 8080 as usual. The engine setting configures `www.catalinabook.com` as the default host. The engine examines the HTTP headers, especially the Host: header, and determines which of the virtual host definitions should receive the request. If none of the virtual host seems to match the request headers, the engine passes on the request to the default host. The value of this attribute must match a `<Host>` definition in the engine. Then the host setting assigns a home directory for `webapps` and sets an access log and a general log.

For Tomcat 5.5 logging, follow the instructions in Chapter 4 to set up Log4J and then place the file in Listing 13-6 in `CATALINA_HOME/common/classes`.

Listing 13-6. *`log4j.properties` Logging File for Virtual Hosting*

```
#-------------------------------#
# Set the root logger for Tomcat #
#-------------------------------#

log4j.rootLogger=INFO, TomcatINFO, TomcatERROR

#---------------------------------------------#
# Send all INFO messages and above to a file  #
#---------------------------------------------#

log4j.appender.TomcatINFO=org.apache.log4j.FileAppender
log4j.appender.TomcatINFO.File=C:/jakarta-tomcat-5.5.3/logs/catalina_log.txt

# Use the simple layout
log4j.appender.TomcatINFO.layout=org.apache.log4j.SimpleLayout

#--------------------------------------------------#
# Send all ERROR messages and above to the console #
#--------------------------------------------------#

log4j.appender.TomcatERROR=org.apache.log4j.ConsoleAppender
log4j.appender.TomcatERROR.Target=System.out
log4j.appender.TomcatERROR.layout=org.apache.log4j.PatternLayout
log4j.appender.TomcatERROR.layout.ConversionPattern=%p: %m: %d{ABSOLUTE} %n
log4j.appender.TomcatERROR.Threshold=ERROR
```

```
#--------------------------------------------#
# Define a log for the catalinabook.com host #
#--------------------------------------------#

log4j.logger.org.apache.catalina.core.ContainerBase.
[Catalina].[www.catalinabook.com]=INFO,catalinabook

# Log to a file
log4j.appender.catalinabook=org.apache.log4j.FileAppender
log4j.appender.catalinabook.
File=C:/home/sites/catalinabook.com/logs/catalinabook.com.log

# Use the simple layout
log4j.appender.catalinabook.layout=org.apache.log4j.SimpleLayout

#------------------------------------------#
# Define a log for the jasperbook.com host #
#------------------------------------------#

log4j.logger.org.apache.catalina.core.ContainerBase.
[Catalina].[www.jasperbook.com]=INFO,jasperbook

# Log to a file
log4j.appender.jasperbook=org.apache.log4j.FileAppender
log4j.appender.jasperbook.File=C:/home/sites/jasperbook.com/logs/jasperbook.com.log

# Use the simple layout
log4j.appender.jasperbook.layout=org.apache.log4j.SimpleLayout

#------------------------------------------#
# Define a log for the tomcatbook.com host #
#------------------------------------------#

log4j.logger.org.apache.catalina.core.ContainerBase.
[Catalina].[www.tomcatbook.com]=INFO,tomcatbook
```

```
# Log to a file
log4j.appender.tomcatbook=org.apache.log4j.FileAppender
log4j.appender.tomcatbook.File=C:/home/sites/tomcatbook.com/logs/tomcatbook.com.log

# Use the simple layout
log4j.appender.tomcatbook.layout=org.apache.log4j.SimpleLayout
```

This file sets the same loggers as the <Logger> components in Listing 13-5.

To configure contexts for catalinabook.com, place a context XML file in CATALINA_HOME/conf/Catalina/www.catalinabook.com. Note the name of the host is the name of the last directory. Listing 13-7 shows the jsp.xml configuration file, and Listing 13-8 shows the ROOT.xml configuration file.

Listing 13-7. *The jsp.xml Configuration File*

```
<Context path="/jsp" docBase="jsp" debug="0" />
```

Listing 13-8. *The ROOT.xml Configuration File*

```
<Context displayName="Welcome to Tomcat" docBase="ROOT" path="" />
```

These files are common to all the Web applications, so place them in CATALINA_HOME/conf/Catalina/www.jasperbook.com and CATALINA_HOME/conf/Catalina/www.tomcatbook.com as well.

Testing the Virtual Hosting

If you don't have your DNS server set up to point to your machine, you can alter your local hosts file to simulate a DNS server. On Unix systems this is the /etc/hosts file, and on Windows it's WinNT/system32/drivers/etc/hosts (or equivalent on older systems). Listing 13-9 shows the entries in the hosts file that map the three hosts to your local machine's IP address.

Listing 13-9. *An Example Hosts File*

```
127.0.0.1       localhost
127.0.0.1       www.catalinabook.com
127.0.0.1       www.jasperbook.com
127.0.0.1       www.tomcatbook.com
```

Start Tomcat, and browse to one of the virtual hosts as shown in Figure 13-7. Remember that Tomcat is still listening on port 8080.

Here you can see that the correct index page is shown for www.jasperbook.com. Click the link to try the JSP page, as shown in Figure 13-8.

Again, this is the expected behavior, so the dynamic part of the virtual host is working. Try the other hosts to confirm that they're also working and examine their access logs.

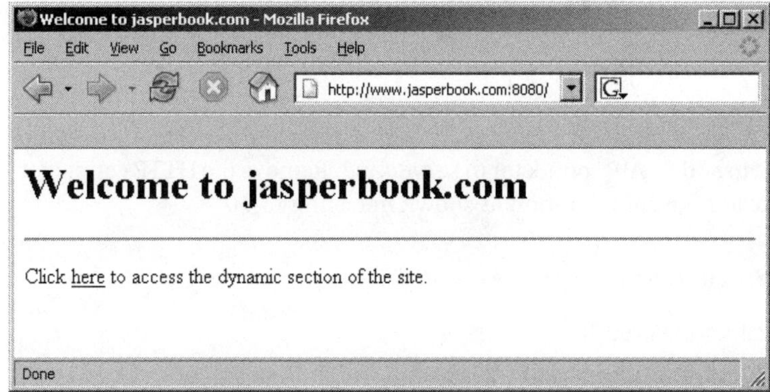

Figure 13-7. *The index page of* `www.jasperbook.com`

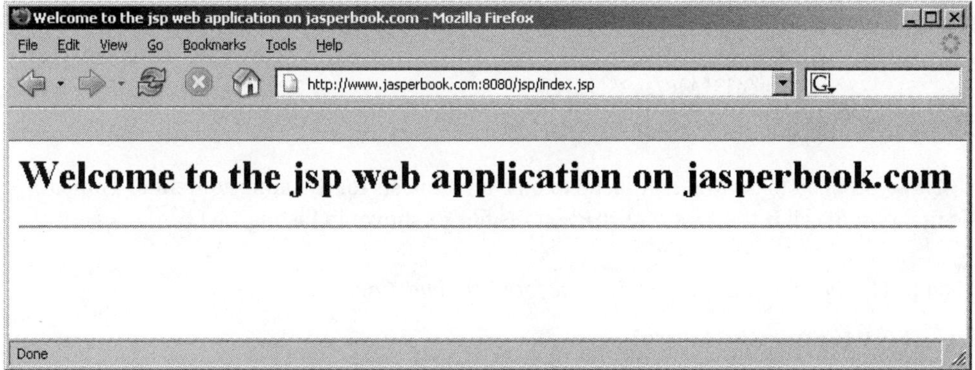

Figure 13-8. *The dynamic JSP page of www.jasperbook.com*

You should then check that the `defaultHost` setting of the `<Engine>` element is working properly. Try to access the dynamic section on IP address 127.0.0.1 (or whatever you've set your machine's IP address to be). You should see the `www.catalinabook.com` page, as shown in Figure 13-9.

Figure 13-9. *Accessing the default host using an IP address*

Implementing Virtual Hosting with Apache and Tomcat

If you want to use Apache to serve the static files of your virtual hosts and Tomcat to serve the dynamic content, you need to add an AJP connector to `server.xml`. Remove the HTTP connector from your `server.xml`, and add the configuration as shown in Listing 13-10.

Listing 13-10. *Adding an AJP Connector to* `server.xml`

```
<Server port="8005" shutdown="SHUTDOWN">
  <Service name="Virtual Hosting Tomcat with Apache">

    <!-- Define a Coyote/JK2 AJP 1.3 Connector on port 8009 -->
    <Connector port="8009"
               enableLookups="false" debug="0"
               protocol="AJP/1.3" />
<!-- The rest of the file remains the same -->
```

Now you need to configure Apache to pass all requests for dynamic content to Tomcat. The first port of call is the `workers2.properties` file, as shown in Listing 13-11.

Listing 13-11. *The* `workers2.properties` *File for virtual hosting*

```
[channel.socket:localhost:8009]

# define the worker
[ajp13:localhost:8009]
channel=channel.socket:localhost:8009

# Uri mapping
[uri:/*.jsp]
group=ajp13:localhost:8009
```

Here you instruct Apache to pass all requests for `*.jsp` files to Tomcat. Tomcat will then process them according to the virtual host they're requesting. To serve static files from Apache, you first need to generate the settings for each Web application using Ant or a similar tool (see Chapter 9 for details). Listing 13-12 shows a sample `jk2.conf` file as generated by Ant.

Listing 13-12. *The* `jk2.conf` *File for* `www.catalinabook.com`

```
# Must be included in a virtual host context for www.catalinabook.com
Alias /jsp "C:/home/sites/catalinabook.com/webapps/jsp"
<Directory "C:/home/sites/catalinabook.com/webapps/jsp" >
  Options Indexes FollowSymLinks
  DirectoryIndex
  AddHandler jakarta-servlet2 .jsp
</Directory>

<Location "/jsp/WEB-INF" >
  AllowOverride None
  Deny from all
</Location>

<Location "/jsp/META-INF" >
  AllowOverride None
  Deny from all
</Location>
```

As the comment at the beginning of this file says, you must include this file in the appropriate virtual host definition to protect Tomcat's files. Apache's virtual hosts must match Tomcat's virtual hosts so that there's a seamless integration of static pages and dynamic content. In this case you'll use the Web directory for static content instead of the `ROOT` Web application. Figure 13-10 shows this configuration.

```
webapps/
        jsp/
            index.jsp
            WEB-INF/
                    web.xml
web/
    index.html
```

Figure 13-10. *The virtual hosting configuration when using Apache*

Therefore, the Apache setup will be as shown in Listing 13-13.

Listing 13-13. *The Apache Setup for Virtual Hosting with Tomcat*

```
NameVirtualHost www.catalinabook.com
NameVirtualHost www.jasperbook.com
NameVirtualHost www.tomcatbook.com

<VirtualHost www.catalinabook.com>
  ServerName www.catalinabook.com

  DocumentRoot "C:/home/sites/catalinabook.com/web"

  Include "C:/home/sites/catalinabook.com/webapps/jsp/WEB-INF/jk2/jk2.conf"
</VirtualHost>

<VirtualHost www.jasperbook.com>
  ServerName www.jasperbook.com

  DocumentRoot "C:/home/sites/jasperbook.com/web"

  Include "C:/home/sites/jasperbook.com/webapps/jsp/WEB-INF/jk2/jk2.conf"
</VirtualHost>

<VirtualHost www.tomcatbook.com>
  ServerName www.tomcatbook.com

  DocumentRoot "C:/home/sites/tomcatbook.com/web"

  Include "C:/home/sites/tomcatbook.com/webapps/jsp/WEB-INF/jk2/jk2.conf"
</VirtualHost>
```

Each virtual host corresponds to a Tomcat virtual host and has a document root corresponding to the Web directory in the host's installation directory. Any requests that don't match the setting in `workers2.properties` (that is, any non-JSP pages) will be served from here. If you want to continue to use the `ROOT` directory, you can change the `DocumentRoot` directive to point to it.

To test the setup, copy `index.html` from each host's `ROOT` directory into its Web directory and change it as shown in Listing 13-14.

Listing 13-14. *The Index File Served by Apache*

```
<html>
  <head><title>Welcome to catalinabook.com</title>

  <body>
    <h1>Welcome to catalinabook.com on Apache</h1>
    <hr/>
    <p>
      Click <a href="jsp/index.jsp">here</a>
      to access the dynamic section of the site.
    </p>
  </body>
</html>
```

The JSP pages stay the same because they're still served by Tomcat. Now start Apache, and restart Tomcat. Browse to `http://www.catalinabook.com`, and you should see the index page as served by Apache (see Figure 13-11).

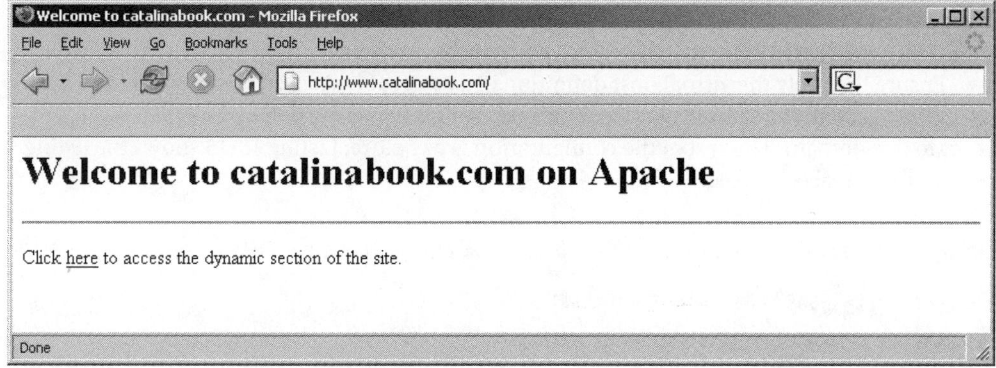

Figure 13-11. *The index page on the Apache server*

If you click the link to the dynamic section, you'll see the JSP page as before.

Setting a JVM for Each Virtual Host

In the previous example all the virtual hosts are in the same request-processing engine, so trusted contexts in these virtual hosts (which can access Tomcat internal objects, load/unload other Web applications, and so on), such as the `manager` Web application, have access to the common Tomcat internal classes and can encroach on each other's territory.

One possible solution is to set up one `<Engine>` per virtual host in the same `server.xml` file. Since each `<Service>` container element in the file can have only one child `<Engine>` element, this would mean adding one service per virtual host with the accompanying engine. Also, since every service has its own set of connectors, this requires setting up different connectors listening on different ports for each engine. Therefore, you'll have to use Apache as a front end.

While the previous technique removes the problem of sharing information between the virtual hosts, a relaxed Tomcat security policy can still give one domain enough privileges to bring down the whole Tomcat process. The more secure, albeit more resource-intensive, solution to these security problems is to have one Tomcat process per virtual host.

Tomcat depends on two environment variables to find its internal classes and the configuration-specific files.

- `CATALINA_HOME` is needed for Tomcat to function properly. Tomcat uses this variable to find its internal classes and libraries.
- `CATALINA_BASE` is used by Tomcat to find the location of the configuration files and directories, such as the Web application directories. If `CATALINA_BASE` isn't set, it defaults to the value of `CATALINA_HOME`.

Therefore, to maintain separate Tomcat processes, all you have to do is set the value of `CATALINA_BASE` to a different area of the disk for each server instance. Each server has its own `server.xml` file, which contains only one virtual host definition, different connector port numbers, and different directories for logs, scratch areas, and so on.

For the previous three virtual hosts, you'd store their configurations in directories under `/home/sites/<domain-name>/catalina`. So in this case, `www.catalinabook.com`'s `CATALINA_BASE` would be `/home/sites/www.catalinabook.com/catalina`, `www.jasperbook.com`'s `CATALINA_BASE` would be `/home/sites/www.jasperbook.com/catalina`, and `www.tomcatbook.com`'s `CATALINA_BASE` would be `/home/sites/www.tomcatbook.com/catalina`.

Ensure that only the virtual host definition of `www.catalinabook.com` is present in `/home/sites/www.catalinabook.com/catalina/conf/server.xml`, and the default host of the `<Engine>` is set to this domain. The rest of the configuration is as before. Listing 13-15 shows the listing for `www.catalinabooks.com`.

Listing 13-15. *`server.xml` for `www.catalinabooks.com` Using a Separate JVM*

```
<Server port="8005" shutdown="SHUTDOWN">
  <Service name="Virtual Hosting Tomcat">

    <!-- Define a Coyote/JK2 AJP 1.3 Connector on port 8009 -->
    <Connector port="8009"
               enableLookups="false" debug="0"
               protocol="AJP/1.3" />

    <Engine name="Catalina" defaultHost="www.catalinabook.com">
```

```
      <!-- Global logger unless overridden at lower levels -->
      <!-- Tomcat 5.0.x only -->
      <!--
      <Logger className="org.apache.catalina.logger.FileLogger"
              prefix="catalina_log." suffix=".txt"
              timestamp="true"/>
      -->

      <Host name="www.catalinabook.com" debug="0"
            appBase="C:/home/sites/catalinabook.com/webapps"
            unpackWARs="true">

        <Valve className="org.apache.catalina.valves.AccessLogValve"
               directory="C:/home/sites/catalinabook.com/logs"
               prefix="catalinabook.com.access."
               suffix=".log"
               pattern="common"/>

        <!-- Tomcat 5.0.x only -->
        <!--
        <Logger className="org.apache.catalina.logger.FileLogger"
                directory="C:/home/sites/catalinabook.com/logs"
                prefix="catalinabook.com."
                suffix=".log"
                timestamp="true"/>
        -->
      </Host>
    </Engine>
  </Service>
</Server>
```

For the `server.xml` file of `www.jasperbook.com` and `www.tomcatbook.com`, do the following:

1. Change the `<Server>` port to 8105 and 8205, respectively.
2. Change the AJP connector to port 8010 and 8011, respectively.
3. Ensure that only one virtual host definition is present and the default host of the `<Engine>` element is set to this domain

You'll also have to have a directory for the Web application context XML files for each engine/host pair. Create a CATALINA_BASE/conf/Catalina/www.catalinabook.com directory, and copy jsp.xml and ROOT.xml there. Repeat this for the other two hosts. Figure 13-12 shows the final directory structure for www.catalinabook.com.

```
home/
    sites/
        catalinabook.com/
                    catalina/
                        conf/
                            server.xml
                            Catalina/
                                www.catalinabook.com/
                                        jsp.xml
                                        ROOT.xml
                    logs/
                    web/
                    webapps/
                        jsp/
                            WEB-INF/
                        ROOT/
                            WEB-INF/
```

Figure 13-12. *The directory structure for the* www.catalinabook.com *host*

You'll have to modify (or, in the case of Tomcat 5.5, create) the jk2.properties file in /home/sites/<domain-name>/catalina/conf to contain the following line, with the appropriate port for the virtual host:

```
# The setting for www.tomcatbook.com
channelSocket.port=8011
```

The only change on the Apache side is in workers2.properties, because the three virtual hosts are already set up in Apache's httpd.conf file. Create a new workers2.properties file, as shown in Listing 13-16.

Listing 13-16. *The `workers2.properties` File for Separate Virtual Hosts*

```
# Only at beginning. In production comment it out.
[logger.apache2]
level=DEBUG

# Socket channels.
[channel.socket:localhost:8009]
[channel.socket:localhost:8010]
[channel.socket:localhost:8011]

# Define the workers.
[ajp13:localhost:8009]
channel=channel.socket:localhost:8009

[ajp13:localhost:8010]
channel=channel.socket:localhost:8010

[ajp13:localhost:8011]
channel=channel.socket:localhost:8011

# Uri mappings.
[uri:www.catalinabook.com/*.jsp]
group=ajp13:localhost:8009

[uri:www.jasperbook.com/*.jsp]
group=ajp13:localhost:8010

[uri:www.tomcatbook.com/*.jsp]
group=ajp13:localhost:8011
```

The three workers correspond to the three hosts you've already configured in Tomcat. Notice the corresponding port numbers.

You now need to start each of the instances with a new CATALINA_BASE each time. Run the batch file shown in Listing 13-17 if you're on Windows.

Listing 13-17. *Running the Three Virtual Hosts Using a Windows Batch File*

```
@echo Running three Tomcat workers
set CATALINA_BASE=C:\home\sites\catalinabook.com\catalina
start /B catalina start

set CATALINA_BASE=C:\home\sites\jasperbook.com\catalina
start /B catalina start

set CATALINA_BASE=C:\home\sites\tomcatbook.com\catalina
start /B catalina start
```

Run the batch file shown in Listing 13-18 if you're on a Unix-like system.

Listing 13-18. *Running the Three Virtual Hosts Using a Unix Shell Script*

```
CATALINA_BASE=/home/sites/catalinabook.com/catalina
catalina start

CATALINA_BASE=/home/sites/jasperbook.com/catalina
catalina start

CATALINA_BASE=/home/sites/tomcatbook.com/catalina
catalina start
```

Now stop all the instances of Apache and Tomcat, and start the Tomcat instances using the earlier script. Now start Apache, and test the installation as you did for the previous Apache examples. You should see no change in functionality.

Summary

In this chapter you learned about various topics related to using Tomcat in a shared hosting scenario. You initially looked at the concept of shared hosting and the various types of shared hosting that are possible.

You configured Tomcat to work as a stand-alone Web server and as a servlet/JSP engine for Apache. You could configure Apache to use the mod_jk2 connector to communicate with Tomcat. You then examined some common security enhancements for using virtual hosts with Tomcat.

CHAPTER 14

Testing Tomcat's Performance

Before you can confidently move your test server into production, meaning that it will be completely open to the elements, you have to have some idea of how it will respond to heavy usage. Ignorance is no defense in this situation; you must be sure of your server's ability to cope with real life. The most effective way of doing this, bar having hundreds of third-world offshore testers bombard the server, is to run an automated load test.

An automated server load test simulates client requests so that a server is exposed to large amounts of activity in an environment you control. Load testing therefore helps you understand the scalability and performance limits of your server before it's exposed to a heavy production load.

Server load testing tests the scalability of the server and thus the ability of the system to handle an increased load without degradation of performance or reliability. Scalability is how well a solution to a problem will work when the size of the problem increases. In the case of Web applications, scalability is the ability of the server to handle the jump from a small number of clients to a large number of clients. This usually involves the addition of hardware, though a well-configured system is the first line of defense. Scalability is intrinsically linked to performance, and a scalable system is one that has an increase in performance proportional to the new resources added, be they network equipment, high-performance databases, bandwidth, or hardware.

Preparing for Load Testing

You need to make several decisions when setting up and configuring Tomcat that will affect the scalability of your installation.

Configuring Java's Memory

The JVM sets its own memory usage, but you can configure the limits that it uses at the command line. These settings alter the JVM's heap, which is where object instances are stored.

You should remember two very important switches when you set up a Tomcat instance.

- `-Xmx<size>`: The maximum heap size for the JVM
- `-Xms<size>`: The initial heap size for the JVM

If you don't explicitly set these parameters, the JVM will use its defaults, which are a minimum of 2MB and a maximum of 64MB for JDK 1.4 and JDK 5.

Setting the Maximum Heap Size

Maximum heap size is the upper limit of RAM that the JVM will allocate to the heap. To set the maximum heap size to 256MB, use the following switch:

```
-Xmx256m
```

To specify memory size in GB, use the letter g instead of m.

In a data-intensive application with long-lived objects, memory usage can build up quickly. If an application's memory requirement exceeds the maximum heap size of the JVM, the JVM will first default to virtual memory and then fail with and throw a `java.lang.OutOfMemory` error. This gives you systemwide protection, but you must be careful when setting maximum heap size. You should always make sure your system has enough memory to comply with the JVM setting because you shouldn't rely on the virtual memory mechanism to save your server.

Setting the Minimum Heap Size

You use the initial heap size setting to allocate memory to the Java heap at JVM startup. In a memory-intensive, heavily loaded application, initial heap size can be important; if the JVM starts with a very small heap size and it receives a large number requests that require large object instantiations, it will struggle to keep up with the memory allocation needs and may not recover in some situations. In this case it's often useful to set the minimum heap size to be the same as the maximum heap size. This will ensure there isn't a performance hit from a large number of object instantiations at once. For example, the following sets the minimum and maximum heap sizes to 256Mb:

```
-Xms256m -Xmx256m
```

Something to bear in mind when doing this is that setting the heap size to a value that's as large as your server will allow isn't always a good idea. This may cause otherwise unexplainable pauses in the applications running on the server. It could also cause poor average server performance. Both of these phenomena are caused by the garbage collector, which runs only when memory is exhausted and then runs through the entire system. If your server handles heavy-duty applications and has a large heap, then the garbage collector has more work to do.

One possible solution to this problem is to pass the following command-line option to the Java executable:

```
-Xincgc
```

This forces the garbage collector to run in incremental mode, meaning it runs more often but checks through smaller amounts of memory. You should monitor this carefully because there may be a small performance hit with this method too.

Lowering the size of the heap may also help this situation, as would a combination of both these techniques. These are prime examples of why you should load test your server before it goes into production. Otherwise, you wouldn't know which of these settings was most appropriate for the Web applications on your server.

Configuring Tomcat's Connectors

Several connector parameters may affect your server's performance. The following are the performance-critical attributes of the `<Connector>` element. For an exhaustive discussion of these elements, see Chapter 9.

The acceptCount Attribute

`acceptCount` sets the number of connections that the server will accept while waiting for a free processor. Incoming connections over this limit will be refused. While you may be tempted to increase this to a very high number, a high setting may cause your system to run out of free file descriptors, which can cause processes—or under extreme circumstances, operating systems—to crash or become unstable. The default is `10`.

The enableLookups Attribute

This setting tells Tomcat to resolve each request's host name. This is useful when viewing log files, but it puts extra load on the server and the network. You should therefore use it with caution. The default is `true`.

The maxProcessors Attribute

The `maxProcessors` attribute imposes a limit on the number of threads the server will start, regardless of the server load. If the server receives more simultaneous requests for a given connection than the value of this setting, the requests will block until a thread is freed to handle them. If this number is set too high, heavily loaded sites run the risk of a performance slowdown as the JVM struggles to manage the large number of threads and network connections that will be created.

You can monitor thread count with operating system–specific tools, such as `ps` in Unix-like systems. If the number of threads approaches the `maxProcessors` setting, followed by a server performance slowdown, you should increase this setting and repeat the experiment. The default is `20`.

The minProcessors Attribute

A processor is a thread that handles requests for a connector on a given port. Setting the `minProcessors` attribute too high can produce a large number of unnecessary threads, which will put an extra burden on the JVM. Setting it too low can cause delays when servicing requests that come in soon after server startup because the server will have to spawn a separate thread for incoming requests if it's already servicing the number of clients equal to this setting.

As with the `maxProcessors` attribute, you can monitor the thread count with operating system–specific tools. If you see the number of threads increasing rapidly before reaching a plateau, the number of threads reached at the plateau makes a good general `minProcessors` setting. The default is `5`.

Configuring Application Sessions

Tomcat's default session manager is very fast because it stores its data in memory, as discussed in Chapter 7. This implies a trade-off between speed and the memory consumption on the server. However, the problem when working with sessions is that they're configured at the application level in `web.xml`, using the `<session-timeout>` subelement of the `<session-config>` element. This means developers are in charge of them in the beginning and may have their own reasons for configuring them they way they are.

You must weigh the needs of your server against the needs of the developer's application and its users. Ultimately, you have responsibility for the application once it's deployed on your server, so you have the means and the authority to change the session settings as appropriate.

In extreme cases, such as data-entry applications or point-of-sale systems, where sessions need to be active for hours at a time, it may be worthwhile to use Tomcat's persistent session manager. Reactivation of the sessions will be sluggish in terms of performance, but the memory trade-off may prove to be worth the cost. Chapter 7 also covered the persistent session manager.

Altering Tomcat's Deployment Architecture

The simplest Tomcat setup with a single stand-alone Tomcat server using an HTTP connector is usually appropriate for very small installations. However, as load increases and applications become resource intensive, the deployment architecture can make or break a server's performance.

It's possible, under certain conditions, for the JVM to become a bottleneck, even if a single server is sufficient. The JVM isn't optimized for dealing with huge amounts of memory, so breaking it into multiple processes on the same system may help, as discussed in Chapter 13.

If application performance is constrained by the limits of the operating system or server hardware, it may be necessary to load balance two or more application servers, as discussed in Chapter 9.

While Tomcat has an HTTP connector, it isn't optimized as an HTTP server. Bringing Apache or other supported Web servers into the picture would increase performance, as they're designed for handling only HTTP requests, as discussed in Chapter 9.

Working with a Developer's Code

A well-configured server is no match for inefficient application code deployed within it. The best weapon in this situation is a clear understanding of the performance of your server when it's unencumbered with sluggish code. Regardless of what the reality is, the onus is always on you as the server administrator to identify the bottleneck. Thorough pre-application load testing and analysis will allow you to cast off undeserved blame and quickly identify application performance bottlenecks as and when they appear.

Load Testing with JMeter

The first thing you're going to need for load testing, unless you have the aforementioned army of Web-savvy coolies, is some software to help you simulate a heavy load.

You have a number of options, including open-source software, commercial packages, and home-brewed efforts (which are universally a mistake). In this case, as the rest of the book focuses on open-source software, you need not look very far. Tomcat's sister project, Apache JMeter, fits the bill quite nicely.

JMeter is capable of load testing FTP sites, JDBC data sources, and Java objects, but this chapter will focus on load testing HTTP servers and applications.

Installing and Running JMeter

JMeter's home page is located at `http://jakarta.apache.org/jmeter/`. Download the distribution, and unpack it to a convenient location. Starting JMeter is as simple as entering the `bin` directory and running either `jmeter.bat` (on Windows) or the `jmeter` shell script (on Unix-style systems).

Making and Understanding Test Plans

Having started JMeter, you'll see JMeter's interface, as shown in Figure 14-1.

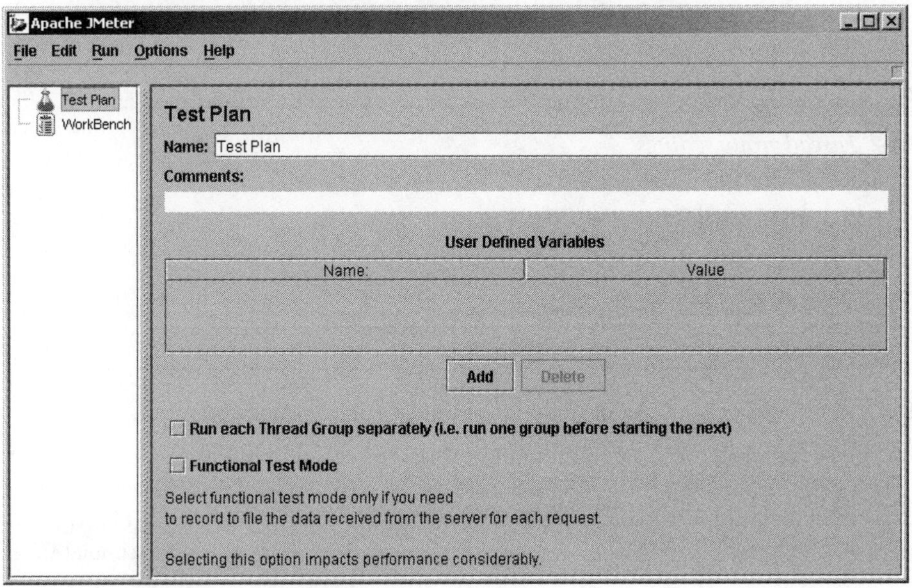

Figure 14-1. *The JMeter interface*

JMeter's user interface consists of a tree in the left pane, representing the list of items and actions you can add, and a right pane that provides configuration forms and output windows for items from the left pane.

The test plan is at the heart of any JMeter session and is a list of actions you want JMeter to perform. You can add elements to the test plan by right-clicking its node and selecting Add from the pop-up menu.

The first element in a test plan is a thread group. Right-click the Test Plan node in the left pane, and select Add. You can now click its icon in the left pane to expose the thread group configuration pane, as shown in Figure 14-2. Leave the default configuration values to keep your first run simple.

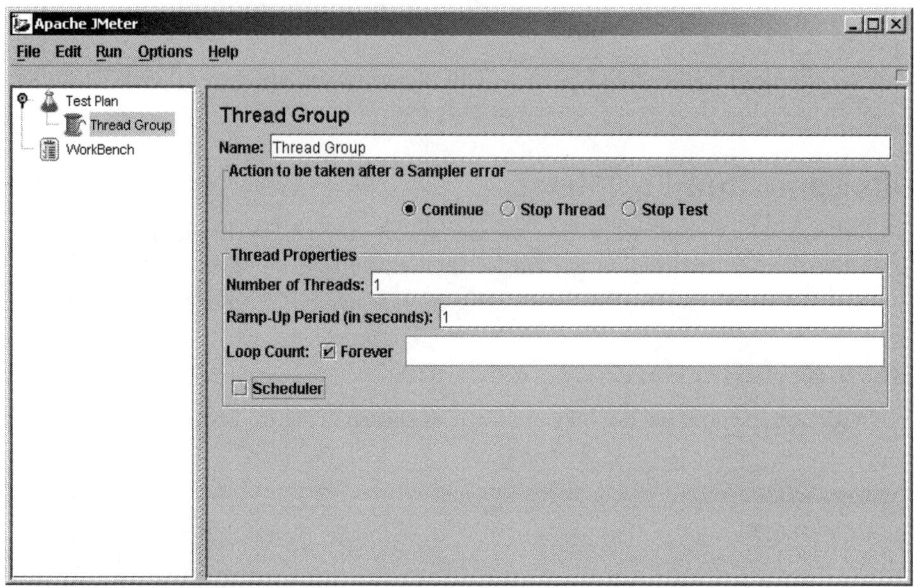

Figure 14-2. *Thread group settings*

Table 14-1 describes the available options.

Table 14-1. *The Options for a Thread Group*

Option	Description
Name	If you had multiple thread groups, it's useful to choose descriptive names that reflect their purposes.
Action to Be Taken After a Sampler Error	A sampler tells JMeter to send requests to a server. You can configure its behavior if there was any kind of error.
Number of Threads	The number of threads you'd like the thread group to spawn to carry out its work. If you wanted to simulate a heavy load, you'd want to increase this number to simulate simultaneous users.
Ramp-Up Period (in seconds)	JMeter will start with one thread and will add threads evenly over the course of the specified period until the number of threads configured has been reached.
Loop Count	The number of times you want JMeter to execute the elements of this thread group. The default is forever, which means the elements of the test plan will execute until you tell them to stop.
Scheduler	You can schedule the test to run at a more convenient time if resources are at a premium.

Now that you have a thread group, you're ready to start doing something with it. Right-click the Thread Group icon to view the Add menu. Select Simple Controller, and then add an HTTP request sampler, as shown in Figure 14-3.

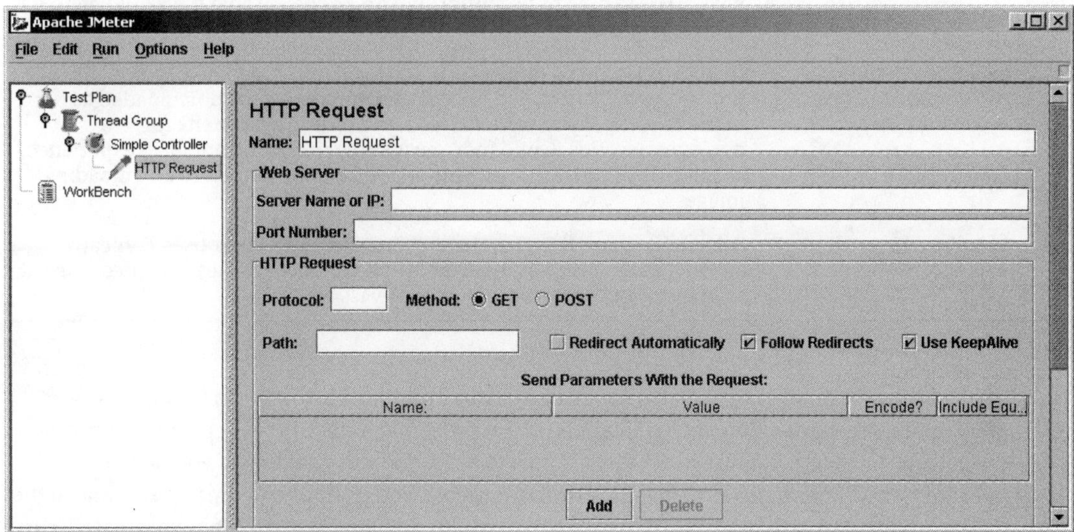

Figure 14-3. *HTTP request group settings*

Table 14-2 describes the configuration options available for an HTTP request sampler.

Table 14-2. *The Options for an HTTP Request Sampler*

Option	Description
Name	This is the same as in the thread group configuration.
Server Name or IP	A resolvable host name or IP address of the server you want to test.
Port Number	The port number of the HTTP server. The standard is 80 unless specifically configured differently.
Protocol	HTTP or HTTPS.
Method	Sets whether the test should send a GET or a POST request, which depends on what the page you're requesting is expecting.
Path	The URI of the page you're going to test.
Parameters	If you're testing a dynamic application, the page may expect some parameters to be submitted along with the request. For example, if you're testing the shopping cart functionality of an online store, you may send a model number for the product to add to your shopping cart.
Filename	Some Web applications accept file uploads via HTTP POST. This setting specifies which file you'd like to upload with the request.
Parameter Name	The file will be uploaded as a key-value pair. This is the name of the key that the Web application will use to reference the file in the request.

Table 14-2. *The Options for an HTTP Request Sampler (Continued)*

Option	Description
MIME Type	The type of the file you're uploading. For example, an HTML file would have a MIME type of text/html, and an Adobe Acrobat file would be application/pdf.
Retrieve All Embedded Resources from HTML Files	If this is set, when a request is made for a Web page, the page will be parsed and all embedded images and applets will be downloaded as part of the request. If you were to test a graphics-intensive site for performance, this would more accurately reflect the end user experience, as the bulk of the response time would be apportioned to downloading images.
Use As Monitor	Select this to use this sampler as a monitor. A monitor uses Tomcat's status servlet to request data on the server's general health. You can use it to monitor the server and react to any issues.

Keep this simple by filling in only the bare minimum number of fields for this first test. Assuming you have a Tomcat installation on the same machine from which you're running JMeter, set the server name to `localhost`, port to `8080`, and the path to `/`. If you were to run JMeter on a different physical machine from the server, you'd simply set the server name to the appropriate host or IP address of the server you wanted to load test. All other parameters can remain unchanged for now.

You have now done enough to start testing Tomcat's performance. You can start the test by selecting Run ➤ Start from the menu bar. However, the example isn't very practical so far, since you have no way to capture or view the results of the test.

JMeter separates the execution of a test plan from the collection and analysis of the test plan's results. You can accomplish this with the Observer or, as it's sometimes called, Event Listener design pattern. This is reflected in the JMeter interface by its use of the listener terminology. Controllers are responsible for performing actions, and listeners are responsible for reacting to those actions. Thus, if you want access to the results of a test plan, you must use one of the JMeter listeners.

To finish the simple test plan, right-click the Thread Group icon, and select Add ➤ Listener ➤ View Results Tree. Select the View Results Tree icon in the left pane to show its output window. You don't need to add any configuration for this listener. When running a test with a view results tree listener, you can watch each response as it's received from the server. Selecting the response from the bottom-left area of the right pane, you'll see the actual data returned in the bottom-right area of that pane.

Before starting the test, you should save the test plan. Right-click the Test Plan icon in the left pane, and choose Save As from the pop-up menu. For consistency, use the default `.jmx` extension when saving your test plan.

Now, click the View Results Tree icon, and choose Start from the Run menu on the menu bar. You should see the Root node in the bottom-left pane change to a folder icon as test results start to come in. Click that node to open it, revealing the individual test results contained within. Selecting any of the results will change the bottom-right pane to show you the results of the request (including response code and load time) under the Sampler result tab, the actual request made under the Request tab, and the data received in the response under the Response data tab. Select Run ➤ Stop to finish the test.

Figure 14-4 shows the completed test plan with the view results tree listener activated.

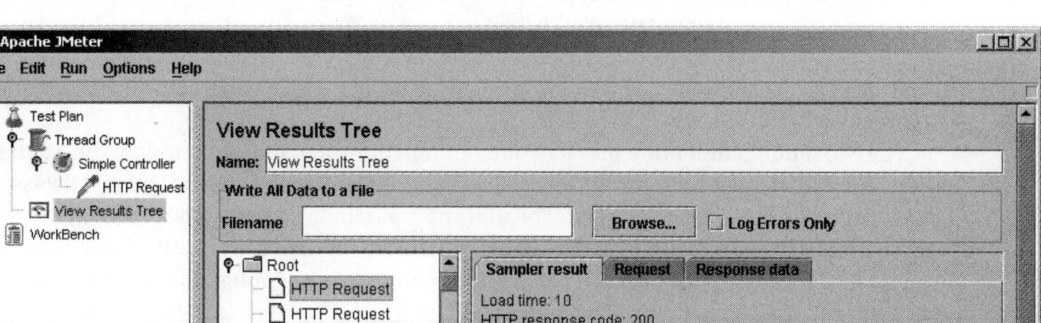

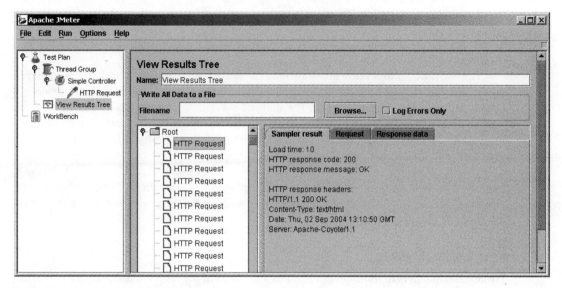

Figure 14-4. *The results of the simple test*

Examining JMeter's Features

You now know how to load test a Web server and how to view the results of the test. You can get some idea of how well your Tomcat server is responding to the test in terms of load time and stability. If you were content to manually click through each result in the View Results Tree window and inspect the full page, this might be enough. Fortunately, JMeter provides many more features to aid you in capturing and analyzing load data. JMeter has five major feature types:

- Configuration element
- Listener
- Logic controller
- Sampler
- Timer

Though JMeter can test many different types of server, I'll cover only HTTP-related settings in the sections to follow.

Using Timer Features

In the previous example, JMeter spawns one thread and makes requests as fast as it and the server being tested can keep up. In real-world cases, it may not make sense to pound the server with a constant onslaught of requests. Only in exceptional cases will a server be faced with a large number of simultaneous requests with no delay in between.

To spare your server the full brunt of this load, and to make the load more representative of the real world, you can add a timer to your thread group. This will introduce some intelligent logic that regulates the frequency and speed of each thread's requests. JMeter includes four types of timers—two random timers and two constant timers.

The constant throughput timer allows you to specify how many requests you want to make per minute, and the constant timer inserts a delay between each request for a given thread. These are just two different ways of saying the same thing, so take your pick as to which one you prefer.

The two random timers are the Gaussian random timer and uniform random timer. These timers simulate real-world traffic more accurately by inserting randomly calculated delays between the requests for each thread. The uniform random timer appends a random delay to a configurable constant delay, and the Gaussian random timer uses a statistical calculation to generate a pseudo-random delay. Each random timer takes a configurable constant time to which its random calculation will be appended.

To add a timer, right-click a thread group, select Timer from the Add menu, and choose the timer you want. Timers will affect the entire thread group to which they're added but won't affect peer thread groups. Adding more than one timer to a thread group will have a cumulative effect on the delay between requests.

Using Listener Features

JMeter uses listeners to monitor and react to the results of the requests it sends. The previous example used the view results tree listener to show the data returned from the server, the response time, the HTTP response code, and the HTTP response message. You add a listener by right-clicking a thread group and selecting the desired listener from the Add ➤ Listener menu.

The listener listens only to the activity of the thread group to which it's added. So, if you have two thread groups in your test plan, thread group A and thread group B, a listener added to thread group B will be oblivious to anything that happens in the scope of thread group A. Table 14-3 lists the listeners currently provided by default with JMeter.

Table 14-3. *JMeter's Listeners*

Listener	Description
Assertion Results	The output of the assertion elements of a sampler.
Graph Full Results	A cumulative graph of the response times of each request made.
Graph Results	A simple graph view, plotting individual data points, mean response time, and standard deviation of response time for all requests in its parent thread group.
Mailer Visualizer	Sends an e-mail to a specified e-mail address if a certain number of failures occur. You must add `mail.jar` to JMeter's `lib` directory to add this listener.
Monitor Results	This listener shows you the results of any monitored samplers.
Simple Data Writer	Writes the results to a file in CSV format.
Spline Visualizer	A graph view of all data points made during a test plan run. Shows the results as an interpolated curve.
Aggregate Report	Each request sampler is given an entry in a table, and the totals and averages are calculated in real time.

Table 14-3. *JMeter's Listeners (Continued)*

Listener	Description
View Results in Table	Provides a real-time view of the test results.
View Results Tree	Organizes the results into a tree.

You can group each listener into one of three categories:

- Visualization listeners
- Data listeners
- Other listeners

Visualization Listeners

Graph Full Results, Graph Results, and Spline Visualizer all create graphical, real-time depictions of the test results. Graph Results is the simplest and most popular of these, plotting mean response time, standard deviation, and individual data points.

Data Listeners

Simple Data Writer, View Results in Table, Aggregate Report, and View Results Tree capture the raw data, response time, and return codes returned from the server. While View Results in Table and View Results Tree are useful as status checkers while running tests, Simple Data Writer is perhaps the most important of the listeners. Simple Data Writer listeners perform the simple task of logging response time to a file, as well as logging response codes and other information. This is an important tool, because it allows you to keep your data for posterity as well as to import the data into other more sophisticated tools for more detailed analysis.

■ **Note** All the listeners, except the Monitor Results listener, can use the Simple Data Writer listener as well. When you configure one of these elements, add the filename of the results file as you would for a Simple Data Writer listener.

You can save the data as an XML file or as a CSV file. The following setting is in the `jmeter.properties` file:

```
jmeter.save.saveservice.output_format=xml
```

The Simple Data Writer listener offers the following configuration options:

- **Name**: A descriptive name for the simple data writer element as it will appear in the test plan.
- **Filename**: The path to the output file to be created by the file reporter. If you supply a relative path, it's relative to `JMETER_HOME/bin`.

The Monitor Results Listener

If you want to monitor the server's overall performance, you can use the Monitor Results listener. This listener allows you to monitor multiple Tomcat servers from one console, using the manager application's status servlet.

It's a good idea to create a new thread group for a Monitor Results listener. Name it Server Status Thread Group, and add an HTTP request sampler. Set the host name, port, and protocol as normal. Now set the path to `/manager/status`, and add a request parameter called *XML* and set it to `true`. Finally, check the Use As Monitor box. The XML parameter will cause the status servlet to return its response in an XML format that JMeter can translate into monitoring information. Figure 14-5 shows this setup.

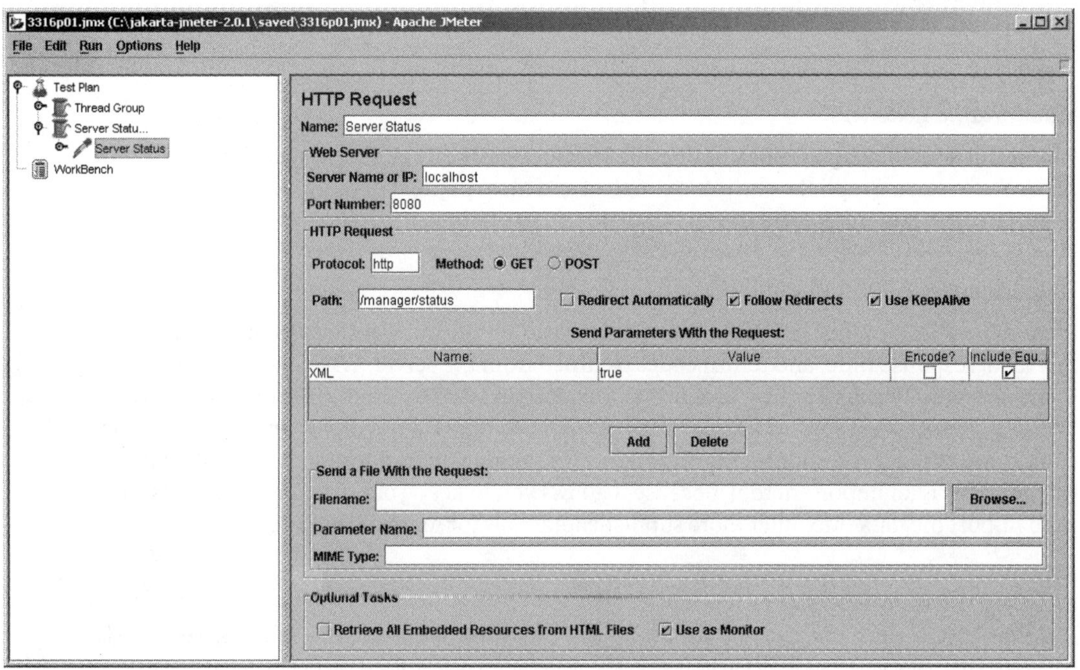

Figure 14-5. *The HTTP request sampler for the Monitor Results listener*

The manager application is protected by authentication, so you'll have to send your authentication information along with your request. To do this, add an HTTP authorization manager configuration element to the HTTP request sampler using the Add menu. Set the Base URL to `http://servername:port/manager`, and the Username and Password properties to a user with the manager role.

Finally, add a monitor results listener and a constant timer, set to 5,000 milliseconds. After all, you don't want to drown your server with the monitoring tool.

When you run the test, check the Monitor Results listener to see how your server is performing. The Health tab will show a summary of the server's performance, with a colored icon indicating general health and a load bar that tells you the relative load. The Performance tab breaks down the server's performance.

The Assertion Results Listener

You use assertions to test if the response contains the data that you expect. If you want to see the results of your assertions, add an Assertion Results listener to your thread group. It will show you the URL of the request and the result of the assertion as applied to the response.

The Mailer Visualizer Listener

If you want to be informed of any successes or failures in your test plan, then you should configure a Mailer Visualizer listener. Fill in your details as shown in Figure 14-6.

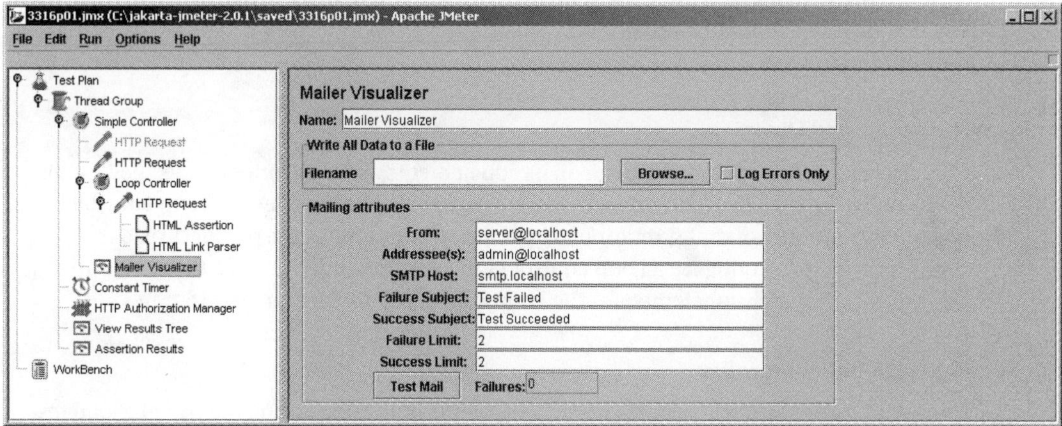

Figure 14-6. *A Mailer Visualizer listener*

Using a Logic Controller Feature

A logic controller's primary purpose is to manage the execution flow of a test plan. They're containers for other executable test plan elements. Logic controllers that are added to a thread group—or even as a subnode of another logic controller—will be treated by their parent execution context as a single node to be executed. Elements added beneath logic controller nodes will be executed according to the rules of the specific logic controller to which they're added.

Like thread groups, logic controllers create a separate namespace for listeners, timers, and other elements, which are context specific. You can think of logic controllers as the closest approximation JMeter test plans have for the while, for, and function constructs of typical programming languages.

The Interleave Controller

The Interleave controller will execute one of its subelements each time its parent container loops. It will execute them in the order in which they're listed in the configuration tree. For example, if you were to create an Interleave controller with four elements under a thread group set to loop 14 times, JMeter would execute the entire set of Interleave controller subelements three times and would then execute only the first two subelements a fourth time (4 + 4 + 4 +2 = 14).

Interleave controllers are good for testing a sequential process, where each request depends on the previous request for successful completion. An obvious example is an online shopping application, where a user searches for an item, adds it to their shopping cart, enters credit card details, and finalizes the order.

The Simple Controller

The Simple controller is a container for other elements and provides no special functionality. You can use the Simple controller to organize test elements in much the same way as you use folders on a file system to organize their contents.

If you were to load test a site with a nontrivial amount of functionality, it would make sense to use Simple controller elements to separate the tested functionality into related modules to ensure a maintainable test plan. This enhances the maintainability of the test plan in the same way that dividing large software projects into modules and functions enhances the maintainability of the software.

The Loop Controller

The Loop controller will loop through all its subelements as many times as specified in the Loop controller's configuration panel. Therefore, any elements under the Loop controller will execute this number of times, multiplied by the number of times the parent thread is set to loop. If you were to configure a Loop controller to loop four times under a thread group that loops four times, each subelement of the Loop controller will be executed 16 times.

The Once Only Controller

The Once Only controller executes its child elements only once during the run of a load test. You can use this controller to execute an initial login, create an application entity on which other tests depend (for example, creating an order in a sales application so you can manipulate it with other requests), or perform any other operation that needs to happen only once.

Using Assertions

Even if your application is giving subsecond responses, you have no cause to celebrate if its output is invalid. An assertion gives you a way to validate the actual data returned as a result of each request so that you can be sure the server is both responsive and reliable. Assertions are created as subelements of samplers, such as the HTTP request sampler. An assertion is a declaration of some truth you want to test against.

You could declare, for example, that the resulting output should contain the word *Hello*. When this assertion exists, the response of the HTTP request to which it is added will be checked for the existence of *Hello* and will throw an assertion failure if the string isn't present.

Given the simple HTML file in Listing 14-1, you'll build an assertion that validates its output during load testing. Call it `hello.html` and place it in the `tomcatBook` Web application's `ch14` folder.

Listing 14-1. *A Sample HTML Page for Testing Assertions*

```
<html>
  <body>
    Hello, World!
  </body>
</html>
```

The first step is to build an HTTP request sampler into the test plan that will access the file's URL. After creating the HTTP request sampler, you can now right-click the HTTP Request icon, and then choose Assertions ➤ Response Assertion from the Add menu. Select the new assertion, and add a new pattern, as shown in Figure 14-7.

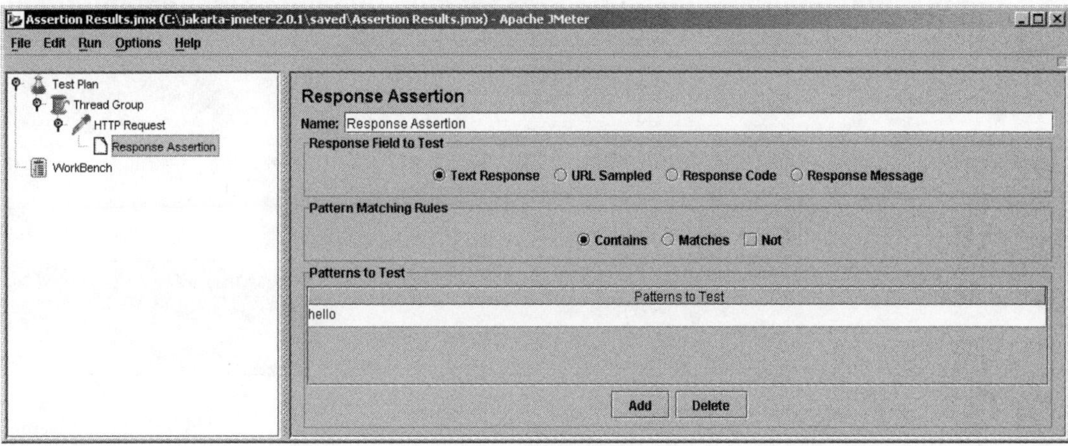

Figure 14-7. *A response assertion*

JMeter assertions accept Perl-style regular expressions, so the assertion you've added will match occurrences of the string *Hello*. *Hello, World* is a matching occurrence of this regular expression, so the assertion should pass.

In this example, the Contains option tests that the page contains the pattern you've added. If you wanted to check the entire Web page, you could use the Matches option, which would check that the page returned directly matches the pattern you add.

Add an assertion results listener to the thread group, and run the test. You should see the results, as in Figure 14-8.

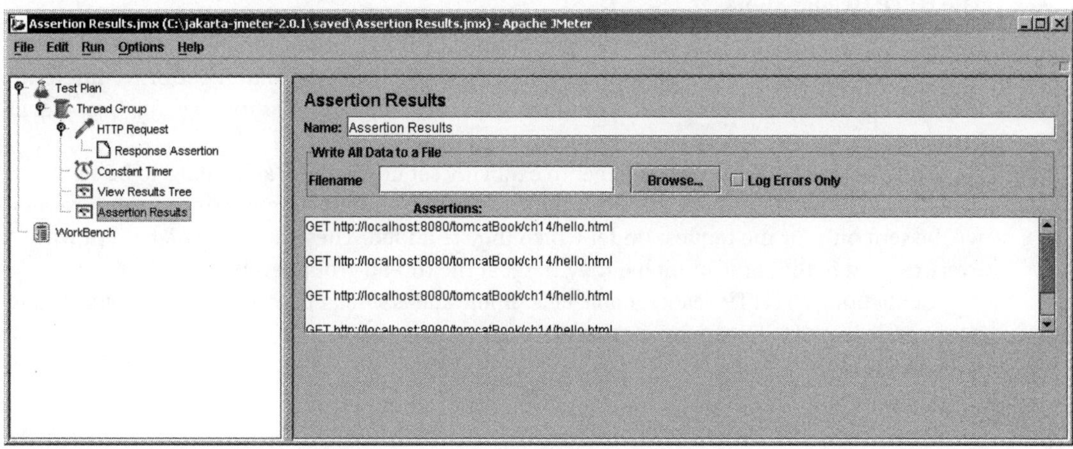

Figure 14-8. *Viewing successful assertions*

The results of the assertion don't show any assertion failures, so the tests were successful. If they were to fail, you would see something similar to Figure 14-9.

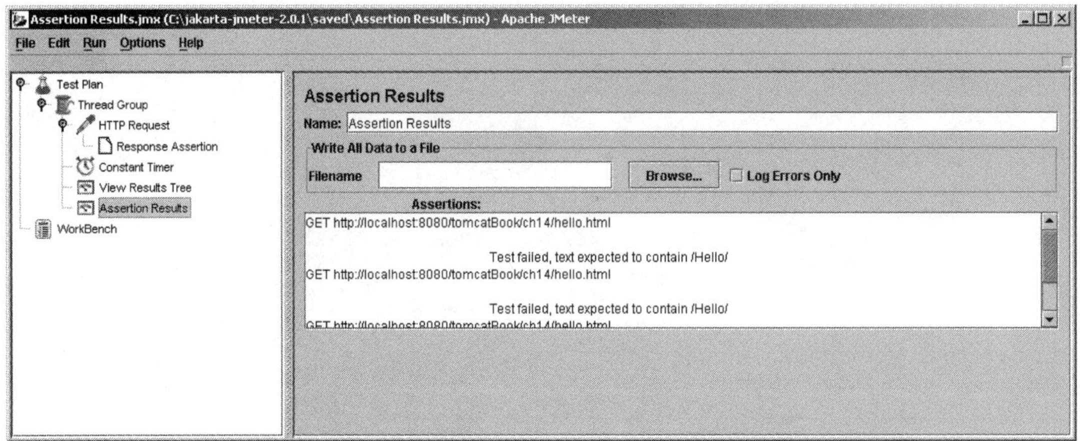

Figure 14-9. *Viewing unsuccessful assertions*

You can test many different aspects of a response, including its response code and the contents of the entire response. If you want to validate your HTML, add an HTML assertion and select the strictness of the test. Assertions also exist for testing the server response time and the size of the response.

Using a Configuration Element

A configuration element's job is to modify requests in some way. They offer a pluggable way to add request modification logic from various types of default values to automatic building of requests.

The HTTP Header Manager

In some cases, application testing will require specific HTTP headers to be set to get a valid reflection of true application performance. For example, if an application performs different actions depending on the browser type making the request, it's necessary to set the User-Agent header when making test requests.

You use the HTTP header manager to explicitly set header keys and values to be sent as part of each request. If added as a node under an HTTP request element, the custom headers will be sent only for the request under which they're added. These headers will be sent with every request in the same branch if they're set at the thread group level.

Configuring an HTTP header manager is simple and is similar to configuring the name/value parameters in an HTTP request element.

The HTTP Authorization Manager

The HTTP authorization manager handles requests that require HTTP authentication. Like the HTTP header managers, they can be added directly underneath an HTTP request element or to an entire branch of a tree. Their configuration parameters are simple, accepting a base URL from which it will attempt to send authentication credentials, plus the obligatory username and password. You saw this element in action in "The Monitor Results Listener."

The HTTP Cookie Manager

Like HTTP authorization managers and HTTP header managers, HTTP cookie managers can accept a hard-coded list of cookies that should be sent for every request. In this way, you can simulate a browser that has previously visited a site. Additionally, HTTP cookie managers can mimic a browser's ability to receive, store, and resend cookies. So, for example, if a cookie is dynamically assigned to each visitor, the HTTP cookie manager will receive it and resend it with every appropriate subsequent request.

You can also add HTTP cookie managers to a thread group or directly to an HTTP request element, depending on the scope of its intended influence.

The HTTP Request Defaults

In most cases, each test plan will be created for a single-server environment or online application. Because of this, you'll find yourself typing the same server name, port, path, or parameters into each new HTTP request sampler you add to the test plan. HTTP request defaults eliminate this duplication of work by allowing you to specify defaults for many of the HTTP request element's configuration parameters. After adding the defaults, you can leave these fields blank in any HTTP request element in the same thread group.

For example, if you were load testing an application that follows the Model View Controller design pattern, with all traffic flowing through a single HTTP servlet, you may have a common base URL for every request like this: `http://loadtest.apress.com/Router/`.

This servlet will provide access to different functionality in the application via a request parameter such as the following:

```
http://localhost:8080/Router?action=addToCart
http://localhost:8080/Router?action=checkOut
```

The server name, port, protocol, and path are common to all HTTP requests that access this application, with only the request parameters varying. In such a case, you could add an HTTP request defaults element, as shown in Figure 14-10.

Any requests that are in the same thread group will inherit these settings unless they're explicitly overridden in their own configurations. To access any `addToCart` and `checkOut` features of your imaginary application, you'd need to add HTTP request elements, leaving all configuration options blank except for the addition of the action parameter and corresponding values. In a large load test scenario with potentially tens of HTTP requests, this will really save you time and give your fingers a break from typing.

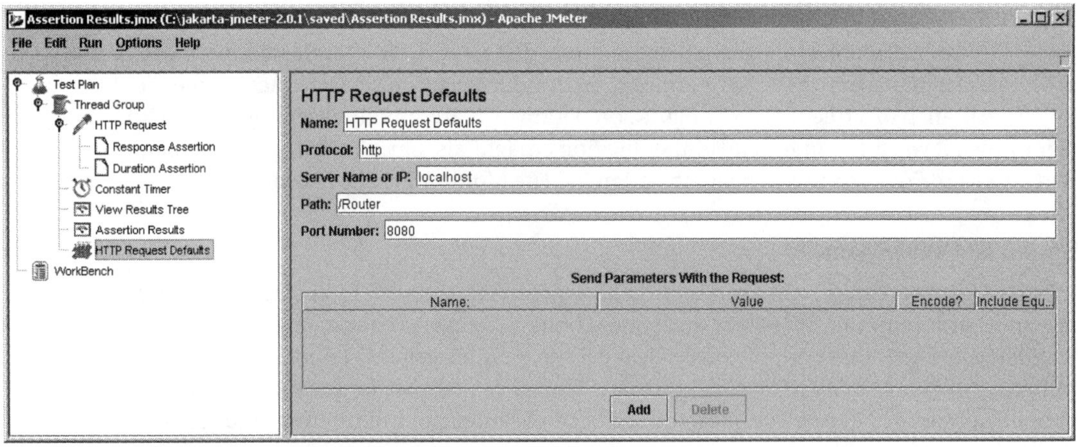

Figure 14-10. *Setting default values for HTTP tests*

Using Preprocessor Elements

You use the preprocessor elements to modify a sampler's request before it's sent to the server and they can extract links from a Web page or options from a form. Once JMeter has this information it can use it to iteratively follow each link or submit each option. Other functionality includes adding a counter before each request and adding user variables before each request to test different behavior depending on the variable sent to the server.

Creating a Web Spider

If you want to run through your application to check that all your links work and are valid, you can use JMeter as a Web spider. To do this, create a simple controller and an HTTP request sampler. In this example you'll use the JSP examples Web application, so set the path to `/jsp-examples/`. Add a constant timer if you don't want to burden your server too much.

Now that you have the initial request set up, you can then use its results to modify subsequent requests. However, if you put settings (in the form of regular expressions) into the original request to be modified by subsequent requests, then the original request won't return meaningful results because Tomcat won't recognize them. If the original request doesn't return meaningful results, then the subsequent requests can't be modified. To solve this, you must use another HTTP request sampler to work on the new requests.

Add another HTTP request sampler with the path set to `.*`. This matches any links found in the response returned by the previous requests and fills in the values for this request. For this to work, though, you must add an HTML link parser to this HTTP request sampler. You don't have to configure any extra settings on this component. If you want to see the results of the link parser, you should add a listener. If you're testing for valid links, you could add an assertion, as shown in Figure 14-11.

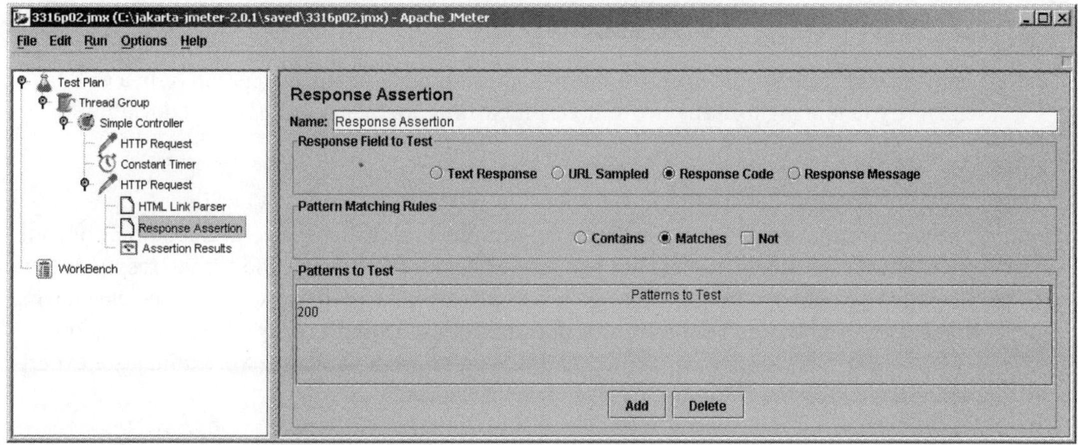

Figure 14-11. *A response assertion to test that a resource exists*

To see if all the links on your site link to existing resources, add an assertion listener and run the test. You'll see each link from the `jsp-examples` Web application executed in turn and will be told if any don't exist. Rename one of the files to see what happens.

Using Post-Processor Elements

Post-processor elements act after a request has finished. You can use them to save the responses to a file for your reference, stop the test if an error occurred, or create a running summary. To use this functionality, add a post-processor to a sampler.

Generating Summaries

To generate a running summary of a test, add a Generate Summary Results post-processor element to an HTTP request sampler. You can view the summary in stdout, in JMeter's log file, or in both. You can configure where the summary is sent, and how often it is compiled, in `jmeter.properties`. The following sends the summary to the JMeter log file but not to stdout:

```
summariser.interval=300
summariser.out=false
summariser.log=true
```

The `summariser.interval` setting is the number of seconds between summaries. The default is 180 (that is, three minutes). The other two settings aren't mutually exclusive, and you can set them both to `true` if you want. Here's an example of the summary:

```
2004/10/25 23:31:03 INFO  - jmeter.reporters.Summariser:
Generate Summary Results =    22 in    86s =    0.3/s
Avg:     3 Min:     0 Max:    20 Err:     0 (0.0%)
```

Here, 22 responses were returned in 86 seconds, which is 0.3 responses per second. The average response time was 3 milliseconds, with response times ranging from 0 to 20 milliseconds.

Interpreting Test Results

You now have the data in whichever format you wanted it, be that in a graph or in a CSV file. What are you looking for? The two simplest measures are mean and standard deviation.

Examining the Mean

The *mean* is the average response time for a sample. It indicates the central tendency of your server's performance. But what about variation? If your server has a good mean response time but a huge amount of variation among the samples, you'll end up with the average user having a decent experience and the occasional user or request having a really bad (or really good) experience. It's this kind of variation that drives an unpredictable and frustrating user experience. A good measure of variation is standard deviation.

Examining the Standard Deviation

Standard deviation is a measure of how widely values in a sample are dispersed from the mean value. Hence, a higher standard deviation indicates more variance in response time. You have many ways to splice and dice performance data. Sometimes, mentally comparing two samples is enough. Other times, it may make sense to delve into more complex statistical tools, such as regression analysis, for predictive modeling of a process's performance. Although a description of these statistical methods is beyond the scope of this book, you can find many online and printed statistics resources at `http://www.prndata.com/statistics_sites.htm`.

Summary

Load testing is an important but often overlooked activity of the system administrator. It can help you to make initial architectural decisions as well as to validate the decisions you've previously made. In this chapter, you examined the following topics:

- Scalability, the ability of a system to handle increased load without experiencing performance problems or reliability issues, is driven by many factors. In a Tomcat installation, some of those factors are server hardware, software configuration, and deployment architecture.
- JMeter is an open-source load tester, which is part of the Jakarta project. I covered JMeter load testing techniques from the simple to the advanced.
- Server load testing and application load testing require different approaches. They're tightly coupled, and it's up to the server administrator to gauge how application code affects server performance and to understand which factors contribute to performance issues.

The open-source world also has more to offer in terms of load testing tools. For example, the Grinder (`http://grinder.sourceforge.net`) is a well-established Java tool. A great resource for finding the latest in open-source load testing tools is the FreshMeat.net open-source software archive site, which includes a category specifically for these kinds of tools at `http://freshmeat.net/browse/863/`.

Additionally, many testing resources are available on the Web. A great place to look for a list of sites is the Open Directory Software Testing list (`http://www.dmoz.org/Computers/Programming/Software_Testing/`), which is a directory of sites that focus on testing topics.

APPENDIX A

Tomcat's Log4J Loggers

This appendix lists Tomcat's built-in loggers for use with Log4J (see Chapter 4 for details).

Tomcat 5.0.*x* Log4J Loggers

These are the Tomcat 5.0.*x* Log4J loggers:

```
org.apache.catalina.authenticator.AuthenticatorBase
org.apache.catalina.authenticator.BasicAuthenticator
org.apache.catalina.authenticator.DigestAuthenticator
org.apache.catalina.authenticator.FormAuthenticator
org.apache.catalina.cluster.deploy.FarmWarDeployer
org.apache.catalina.cluster.deploy.WarWatcher
org.apache.catalina.cluster.io.XByteBuffer
org.apache.catalina.cluster.mcast.McastService
org.apache.catalina.cluster.mcast.McastServiceImpl
org.apache.catalina.cluster.session.DeltaManager
org.apache.catalina.cluster.session.DeltaSession
org.apache.catalina.cluster.session.SimpleTcpReplicationManager
org.apache.catalina.cluster.tcp.AsyncSocketSender
org.apache.catalina.cluster.tcp.Jdk13ReplicationListener
org.apache.catalina.cluster.tcp.PooledSocketSender
org.apache.catalina.cluster.tcp.ReplicationListener
org.apache.catalina.cluster.tcp.ReplicationTransmitter
org.apache.catalina.cluster.tcp.ReplicationValve
org.apache.catalina.cluster.tcp.SimpleTcpCluster
org.apache.catalina.cluster.tcp.SocketSender
org.apache.catalina.cluster.tcp.TcpReplicationThread
org.apache.catalina.cluster.tcp.WorkerThread
org.apache.catalina.cluster.util.SmartQueue
org.apache.catalina.core.ApplicationContextFacade
org.apache.catalina.core.ApplicationDispatcher
org.apache.catalina.core.ApplicationFilterConfig
org.apache.catalina.core.ContainerBase
org.apache.catalina.core.NamingContextListener
org.apache.catalina.core.StandardContext
org.apache.catalina.core.StandardContextValve
```

```
org.apache.catalina.core.StandardEngine
org.apache.catalina.core.StandardHost
org.apache.catalina.core.StandardHostDeployer
org.apache.catalina.core.StandardHostValve
org.apache.catalina.core.StandardPipeline
org.apache.catalina.core.StandardServer
org.apache.catalina.core.StandardService
org.apache.catalina.core.StandardWrapper
org.apache.catalina.core.StandardWrapperValve
org.apache.catalina.loader.WebappClassLoader
org.apache.catalina.loader.WebappLoader
org.apache.catalina.logger.LoggerBase
org.apache.catalina.mbeans.GlobalResourcesLifecycleListener
org.apache.catalina.mbeans.MBeanUtils
org.apache.catalina.mbeans.ServerLifecycleListener
org.apache.catalina.realm.JAASCallbackHandler
org.apache.catalina.realm.JAASMemoryLoginModule
org.apache.catalina.realm.JAASRealm
org.apache.catalina.realm.MemoryRealm
org.apache.catalina.realm.RealmBase
org.apache.catalina.security.SecurityConfig
org.apache.catalina.security.SecurityUtil
org.apache.catalina.session.ManagerBase
org.apache.catalina.session.PersistentManagerBase
org.apache.catalina.startup.Catalina
org.apache.catalina.startup.ContextConfig
org.apache.catalina.startup.DigesterFactory
org.apache.catalina.startup.Embedded
org.apache.catalina.startup.HostConfig
org.apache.catalina.startup.TldConfig
org.apache.catalina.util.ExtensionValidator
org.apache.catalina.valves.ExtendedAccessLogValve
org.apache.catalina.valves.ValveBase
org.apache.coyote.http11.Http11Processor
org.apache.coyote.http11.Http11Protocol
org.apache.coyote.tomcat5.CoyoteAdapter
org.apache.coyote.tomcat5.CoyoteConnector
org.apache.coyote.tomcat5.MapperListener
org.apache.jasper.EmbeddedServletOptions
org.apache.jasper.JspC
org.apache.jasper.compiler.Compiler
org.apache.jasper.compiler.JspConfig
org.apache.jasper.compiler.JspReader
org.apache.jasper.compiler.JspRuntimeContext
org.apache.jasper.compiler.TagLibraryInfoImpl
org.apache.jasper.compiler.TldLocationsCache
org.apache.jasper.runtime.JspFactoryImpl
```

```
org.apache.jasper.runtime.PageContextImpl
org.apache.jasper.security.SecurityClassLoad
org.apache.jasper.servlet.JspServlet
org.apache.jasper.servlet.JspServletWrapper
org.apache.jasper.xmlparser.ParserUtils
org.apache.jk.apr.AprImpl
org.apache.jk.common.ChannelJni
org.apache.jk.common.ChannelSocket
org.apache.jk.common.ChannelUn
org.apache.jk.common.HandlerDispatch
org.apache.jk.common.HandlerRequest
org.apache.jk.common.JkInputStream
org.apache.jk.common.JkMX
org.apache.jk.common.JniHandler
org.apache.jk.common.ModJkMX
org.apache.jk.common.MsgAjp
org.apache.jk.common.Shm
org.apache.jk.config.WebXml2Jk
org.apache.jk.server.JkCoyoteHandler
org.apache.jk.server.JkMain
org.apache.naming.NamingContext
org.apache.naming.ant.JndiProperties
org.apache.naming.ant.JndiSet
org.apache.naming.modules.cache.ProxyDirContext
org.apache.naming.modules.fs.FileDirContext
org.apache.naming.modules.fs.fsURLContextFactory
org.apache.naming.modules.java.ContextBindings
org.apache.naming.util.DomXml
org.apache.tomcat.util.compat.Jdk14Compat
org.apache.tomcat.util.compat.JdkCompat
org.apache.tomcat.util.http.mapper.Mapper
org.apache.tomcat.util.net.PoolTcpEndpoint
org.apache.tomcat.util.net.SSLImplementation
org.apache.tomcat.util.net.jsse.JSSE14Support
org.apache.tomcat.util.net.jsse.JSSEImplementation
org.apache.tomcat.util.net.jsse.JSSESocketFactory
org.apache.tomcat.util.net.jsse.JSSESupport
org.apache.tomcat.util.net.puretls.PureTLSSocketFactory
org.apache.tomcat.util.net.puretls.PureTLSSupport
org.apache.tomcat.util.threads.ThreadPool
```

Tomcat 5.5 Log4J Loggers

These are the Tomcat 5.5 Log4J loggers:

```
org.apache.ajp.Ajp13Packet
org.apache.ajp.Logger
```

```
org.apache.ajp.NegociationHandler
org.apache.ajp.test.TestAjp13
org.apache.ajp.tomcat4.config.BaseJkConfig
org.apache.catalina.authenticator.AuthenticatorBase
org.apache.catalina.authenticator.BasicAuthenticator
org.apache.catalina.authenticator.DigestAuthenticator
org.apache.catalina.authenticator.FormAuthenticator
org.apache.catalina.cluster.deploy.FarmWarDeployer
org.apache.catalina.cluster.deploy.WarWatcher
org.apache.catalina.cluster.io.XByteBuffer
org.apache.catalina.cluster.mcast.McastService
org.apache.catalina.cluster.mcast.McastServiceImpl
org.apache.catalina.cluster.session.DeltaManager
org.apache.catalina.cluster.session.DeltaSession
org.apache.catalina.cluster.session.SimpleTcpReplicationManager
org.apache.catalina.cluster.tcp.AsyncSocketSender
org.apache.catalina.cluster.tcp.Jdk13ReplicationListener
org.apache.catalina.cluster.tcp.PooledSocketSender
org.apache.catalina.cluster.tcp.ReplicationListener
org.apache.catalina.cluster.tcp.ReplicationTransmitter
org.apache.catalina.cluster.tcp.ReplicationValve
org.apache.catalina.cluster.tcp.SimpleTcpCluster
org.apache.catalina.cluster.tcp.SocketSender
org.apache.catalina.cluster.tcp.TcpReplicationThread
org.apache.catalina.cluster.tcp.WorkerThread
org.apache.catalina.cluster.util.SmartQueue
org.apache.catalina.connector.Connector
org.apache.catalina.connector.CoyoteAdapter
org.apache.catalina.connector.MapperListener
org.apache.catalina.core.ApplicationContextFacade
org.apache.catalina.core.ApplicationDispatcher
org.apache.catalina.core.ApplicationFilterConfig
org.apache.catalina.core.ContainerBase
org.apache.catalina.core.NamingContextListener
org.apache.catalina.core.StandardContext
org.apache.catalina.core.StandardContextValve
org.apache.catalina.core.StandardEngine
org.apache.catalina.core.StandardHost
org.apache.catalina.core.StandardHostValve
org.apache.catalina.core.StandardPipeline
org.apache.catalina.core.StandardServer
org.apache.catalina.core.StandardService
org.apache.catalina.core.StandardWrapper
org.apache.catalina.core.StandardWrapperValve
org.apache.catalina.loader.WebappClassLoader
org.apache.catalina.loader.WebappLoader
org.apache.catalina.mbeans.GlobalResourcesLifecycleListener
```

```
org.apache.catalina.mbeans.MBeanFactory
org.apache.catalina.mbeans.MBeanUtils
org.apache.catalina.mbeans.ServerLifecycleListener
org.apache.catalina.realm.JAASCallbackHandler
org.apache.catalina.realm.JAASMemoryLoginModule
org.apache.catalina.realm.JAASRealm
org.apache.catalina.realm.MemoryRealm
org.apache.catalina.realm.RealmBase
org.apache.catalina.security.SecurityConfig
org.apache.catalina.security.SecurityUtil
org.apache.catalina.session.ManagerBase
org.apache.catalina.session.PersistentManagerBase
org.apache.catalina.startup.Bootstrap
org.apache.catalina.startup.Catalina
org.apache.catalina.startup.CatalinaProperties
org.apache.catalina.startup.ClassLoaderFactory
org.apache.catalina.startup.ContextConfig
org.apache.catalina.startup.DigesterFactory
org.apache.catalina.startup.Embedded
org.apache.catalina.startup.EngineConfig
org.apache.catalina.startup.HostConfig
org.apache.catalina.startup.TldConfig
org.apache.catalina.startup.Tool
org.apache.catalina.startup.UserConfig
org.apache.catalina.util.CGIProcessEnvironment
org.apache.catalina.util.ExtensionValidator
org.apache.catalina.util.ProcessEnvironment
org.apache.catalina.util.ProcessHelper
org.apache.catalina.util.StringManager
org.apache.catalina.valves.ExtendedAccessLogValve
org.apache.catalina.valves.ValveBase
org.apache.coyote.http11.Http11Processor
org.apache.coyote.http11.Http11Protocol
org.apache.coyote.http11.RandomAdapter
org.apache.coyote.tomcat4.OutputBuffer
org.apache.jasper.EmbeddedServletOptions
org.apache.jasper.JspC
org.apache.jasper.compiler.Compiler
org.apache.jasper.compiler.JspConfig
org.apache.jasper.compiler.JspReader
org.apache.jasper.compiler.JspRuntimeContext
org.apache.jasper.compiler.SmapUtil
org.apache.jasper.compiler.TagLibraryInfoImpl
org.apache.jasper.compiler.TldLocationsCache
org.apache.jasper.runtime.HttpJspBase
org.apache.jasper.runtime.JspFactoryImpl
org.apache.jasper.runtime.PageContextImpl
```

```
org.apache.jasper.security.SecurityClassLoad
org.apache.jasper.servlet.JspServlet
org.apache.jasper.servlet.JspServletWrapper
org.apache.jasper.xmlparser.ParserUtils
org.apache.jasper.xmlparser.UCSReader
org.apache.jasper.xmlparser.UTF8Reader
org.apache.jk.apr.AprImpl
org.apache.jk.common.ChannelJni
org.apache.jk.common.ChannelSocket
org.apache.jk.common.ChannelUn
org.apache.jk.common.HandlerDispatch
org.apache.jk.common.HandlerRequest
org.apache.jk.common.JkInputStream
org.apache.jk.common.JkMX
org.apache.jk.common.JniHandler
org.apache.jk.common.ModJkMX
org.apache.jk.common.MsgAjp
org.apache.jk.common.Shm
org.apache.jk.common.Shm14
org.apache.jk.config.WebXml2Jk
org.apache.jk.server.JkCoyoteHandler
org.apache.jk.server.JkMain
org.apache.naming.NamingContext
org.apache.naming.ant.JndiProperties
org.apache.naming.ant.JndiSet
org.apache.naming.modules.cache.ProxyDirContext
org.apache.naming.modules.fs.FileDirContext
org.apache.naming.modules.fs.fsURLContextFactory
org.apache.naming.modules.java.ContextBindings
org.apache.naming.resources.FileDirContext
org.apache.naming.resources.WARDirContext
org.apache.naming.util.DomXml
org.apache.tomcat.util.IntrospectionUtils
org.apache.tomcat.util.buf.B2CConverter
org.apache.tomcat.util.buf.Base64
org.apache.tomcat.util.buf.C2BConverter
org.apache.tomcat.util.buf.UDecoder
org.apache.tomcat.util.buf.UEncoder
org.apache.tomcat.util.buf.UTF8Decoder
org.apache.tomcat.util.collections.SimpleHashtable
org.apache.tomcat.util.collections.SimplePool
org.apache.tomcat.util.compat.Jdk14Compat
org.apache.tomcat.util.compat.JdkCompat
org.apache.tomcat.util.digester.Digester
org.apache.tomcat.util.digester.GenericParser
org.apache.tomcat.util.digester.XercesParser
org.apache.tomcat.util.http.Cookies
```

```
org.apache.tomcat.util.http.Parameters
org.apache.tomcat.util.http.ServerCookie
org.apache.tomcat.util.http.mapper.Mapper
org.apache.tomcat.util.net.PoolTcpEndpoint
org.apache.tomcat.util.net.SSLImplementation
org.apache.tomcat.util.net.jsse.JSSE14Support
org.apache.tomcat.util.net.jsse.JSSEImplementation
org.apache.tomcat.util.net.jsse.JSSESocketFactory
org.apache.tomcat.util.net.jsse.JSSESupport
org.apache.tomcat.util.net.puretls.PureTLSSocketFactory
org.apache.tomcat.util.net.puretls.PureTLSSupport
org.apache.tomcat.util.threads.Expirer
org.apache.tomcat.util.threads.Reaper
org.apache.tomcat.util.threads.ThreadPool
```

APPENDIX B

■ ■ ■

Installing MySQL

This appendix is a quick-start guide to installing and running MySQL on Windows and Linux/Unix. To start, download the appropriate MySQL installer from `http://mysql.com/downloads/`. Windows users have a choice of an MSI installer or a zipped file. Linux and Unix users have a huge array of binary installations as well as the source code.

Installing MySQL on Windows

If you're using the installer, unzip the file to a suitable location and double-click the setup program in your desktop or Windows Explorer. After reading the standard introductory screens, choose the directory in which to install MySQL. Unless you have a really good reason not to, it's better to install it in the default directory. On the next screen, choose the Typical installation unless you're extremely short of space on your hard drive.

As with Tomcat, Windows 9*x*/ME users will need to run the `mysqld.exe` program as an application, but Windows NT/2000/XP users have the option to install it as a service. You can unzip and use the zipped file without using an installer.

To test the installation, open a DOS prompt and run the following command (run all commands from the `bin` subdirectory of the MySQL installation):

```
> mysqlshow
```

This will list the databases that come with MySQL. You're now ready to work with MySQL, so you can skip ahead to the "Working with MySQL" section.

Installing MySQL on Linux and Unix

As noted, you have a number of options for installing MySQL on Linux and Unix. The MySQL binaries are available as generic, precompiled binaries for a number of systems, as RPM packages, and as source bundles. The method you use for installation is up to you. In the following sections you'll see how to install from the RPM package and from source.

Creating a User for MySQL

The MySQL server will be running as a process on your system. Since MySQL must create and manipulate files to maintain the database, and it's potentially able to accept connections from remote computers, you must create a unique user and group for MySQL.

```
# groupadd mysql
# useradd -g mysql mysql
```

This creates the mysql group using the groupadd command. The useradd command adds a user to the group specified with the -g switch.

Installing MySQL from the RPM Package

Download the following packages to an appropriate place:

- MySQL: The base server package
- MySQL-bench: MySQL benchmarks and test suite
- MySQL-client: MySQL client applications
- MySQL-devel: Header files and libraries for development
- MySQL-shared: MySQL client shared libraries
- MySQL-Max: The server version that includes InnoDB tables (see Chapter 11 for details on this)

Before you begin the install, make sure you've logged on as root. To install the RPM packages, use the RPM package manager application. You have two options with this: you could use the graphical package manager of your choice, or you could place all the RPM files in a single directory and (making sure you are root) execute the following:

```
# rpm -i *.rpm
```

This will unpack the packages and install all the files into their correct places for your distribution.

To test the installation, run the following command (run all commands from the bin subdirectory of the MySQL installation):

```
> mysqlshow
```

This will list the databases that come with MySQL. You're now ready to begin working with MySQL, so you can skip ahead to the "Working with MySQL" section.

Installing MySQL from Source

You can find the entire MySQL source code in a single tarball that will have a name similar to mysql-4.0.x.tar.gz.

Compiling MySQL is a relatively simple operation. If you're familiar with compiling open-source products, there will be no surprises for you here; even if this is your first attempt in compiling and installing an open-source product, you should have no real difficulty.

The MySQL build scripts will give an error if you're missing any of the required development utilities. If this happens, you'll need to install the missing development tools and try again. Linux distributions generally ship with a suitable development environment containing the GNU tools from the Free Software Foundation.

Note At the time of writing there were some issues with compiling certain versions of the GNU C/C++ compiler, especially versions 2.96 and 3.0. Check the MySQL Web site for the latest news on compiler compatibility; also read the release notes of the tarball you downloaded.

Transfer the source tarball to the target machine, and place it in an appropriate directory for compiling. This shouldn't be the final location of your MySQL installation.

Unpack the tarball to extract the source code.

```
$ tar zxvf mysql-4.0.x.tar.gz
```

You must use the GNU version of the `tar` utility for this to work. On systems without GNU `tar`, you may need a two-step extraction to decompress the tarball.

```
$ gunzip mysql-4.0.x.tar.gz
$ tar xvf mysql-4.0.x.tar
```

However, Solaris's version of `tar` causes problems with the decompression, so you should install GNU `tar` instead.

The extraction process will make a new directory, related to the version of MySQL you're building. Move into that directory.

```
$ cd mysql-4.0.x
```

In this directory, you'll find a file, `INSTALL-SOURCE`, that contains detailed manual build instructions. This can be useful in the unlikely event that the automated method outlined in this appendix fails for some reason.

The build process uses the `configure` configuration script to tailor the build parameters to your specific environment. To accept all defaults, you can simply run `configure` without arguments.

```
$ ./configure
```

The configuration script can take a number of parameters that alter the features built into MySQL. One of these features is the ability to use different implementations for its database tables. You can choose table types optimized for speed or features such as transactions. You will use the InnoDB table type in Chapter 11, so you need to tell the configuration script to include support for this table type.

```
$ ./configure --with-innodb
```

For a full list of options, you can use the `--help` argument.

Once the compilation is configured, you can build the software with the `make` utility.

```
$ make
```

If all goes well, you should see a large number of compilations proceeding. When `make` has finished, you need to copy the programs to their final resting places. Use the `make install` command to do this, but you need to be root first.

```
$ su
# make install
```

Now you have a complete but empty installation of MySQL in the directory /usr/local/mysql and its subdirectories. You have another couple of steps to take before you're ready to use MySQL. The initial database doesn't contain any user definitions or privileges that MySQL will use to control access to your data. To create the privilege tables, you need to run a script provided for this purpose. Again, this must be run as root after moving into the /usr/local/mysql directory.

```
# scripts/mysql_install_db
```

The MySQL files need to have the correct ownership set that's to be owned by the MySQL user. After using make install, all the files are owned by root. You want root to own everything except the /var subdirectory, and you do this by using the recursive form of chmod and chgrp.

```
# chown -R root /usr/local/mysql
# chown -R mysql /usr/local/mysql/var
# chgrp -R mysql /usr/local/mysql
```

You're now in much the same situation as you would have been had you installed MySQL from binary packages. Now it's time to turn your attention to setting up MySQL to run.

To start the MySQL server, execute the following:

```
# /etc/rc.d/init.d/mysql start
```

To stop the server, run the following:

```
# /etc/rc.d/init.d/mysql stop
```

To test the installation, run the following command (run all commands from the bin subdirectory of the MySQL installation):

```
> mysqlshow
```

This will list the databases that come with MySQL. You're now ready to begin working with MySQL.

Working with MySQL

Now that you've installed MySQL, set the MySQL root password. (It's blank by default.) Failure to do so will leave your MySQL server, and ultimately your entire machine, open to malicious attacks. To do this, run the following command from the command line and substitute your preferred password:

```
> mysqladmin -u root password sc00bI
```

Once you've done this, the mysql command will start a command-line client program that lets you issue SQL commands to the database server. When administering MySQL, you should use the root admin user, so issue the following to ensure that MySQL prompts you for your password:

```
mysql -u root -p
```

You should see some status messages about the version of MySQL and a prompt such as in Figure B-1.

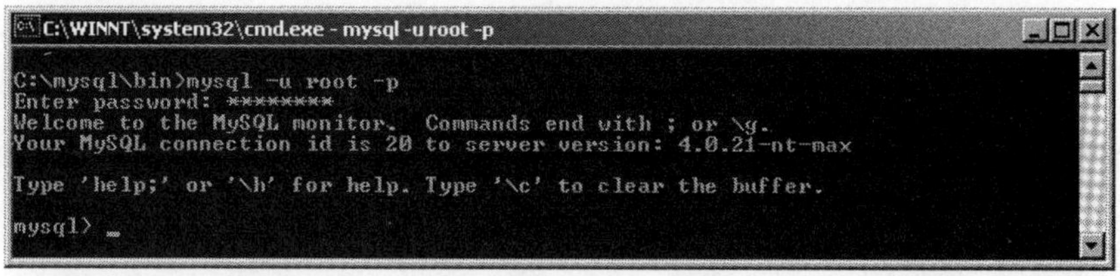

```
C:\WINNT\system32\cmd.exe - mysql -u root -p

C:\mysql\bin>mysql -u root -p
Enter password: ********
Welcome to the MySQL monitor.  Commands end with ; or \g.
Your MySQL connection id is 20 to server version: 4.0.21-nt-max

Type 'help;' or '\h' for help. Type '\c' to clear the buffer.

mysql> _
```

Figure B-1. *The MySQL command-line tool*

You can use the `\q` or `exit` command to exit from the MySQL client.

Now you should create a database. Run the following at the MySQL prompt:

```
mysql> CREATE DATABASE catalog;
```

To add some data to the `catalog` database, start by typing the following at the prompt:

```
mysql> USE catalog;
Database changed
```

You're now in the `catalog` database, which has no tables and no data. Type the following at the prompt:

```
mysql> CREATE TABLE product (
    -> prodid int not null,
    -> prodname varchar(30)
    -> );
```

The `->` prompt means you haven't finished a SQL statement. This isn't a problem, because SQL statements can span multiple lines.

If you see a prompt such as `'>`, it means you have an opening apostrophe that hasn't been closed. Similarly, `">` means you have an opening quote mark that hasn't been closed. Apostrophes must always balance out and so must quote marks.

To view details of your new table, type the following:

```
mysql> DESCRIBE product;
+----------+-------------+------+-----+---------+-------+
| Field    | Type        | Null | Key | Default | Extra |
+----------+-------------+------+-----+---------+-------+
| prodid   | int(11)     |      |     | 0       |       |
| prodname | varchar(30) | YES  |     | NULL    |       |
+----------+-------------+------+-----+---------+-------+
2 rows in set (0.10 sec)
```

To insert a row of data into your table, type the following:

```
mysql> INSERT INTO product VALUES (
    -> 1,
    -> 'Yo-Yo'
    -> );
```

Now that you have some data in your database, run a SELECT command to access it.

```
mysql> SELECT * FROM product;
+--------+----------+
| prodid | prodname |
+--------+----------+
|      1 | Yo-Yo    |
+--------+----------+
1 row in set (0.02 sec)
```

This is quite a labor-intensive process. However, there is a better way. Save all the previous commands in a file called mysqlTest.sql, as shown in Listing B-1. The addition of the EXISTS commands ensure that you can change and reuse this script without having to alter the database beforehand.

Listing B-1. *mysqlTest.sql*

```
CREATE DATABASE IF NOT EXISTS catalog;

USE catalog;

DROP TABLE IF EXISTS product;

CREATE TABLE product (
  prodid int not null,
  prodname varchar(30)
);

DESCRIBE product;

INSERT INTO product VALUES (
  1,
  'Yo-Yo'
);

SELECT * FROM product;
```

You can use this file in two ways. The first is to direct the mysql binary to use it as an input.

```
> mysql -u root -p < ./scripts/3316/mysqlTest.sql
```

This will produce the required results, in that the table will be created and the data will be entered. However, the DESCRIBE and SELECT commands won't produce very nice output.

The second way to use the file is from within the mysql binary.

```
mysql> \. ./scripts/3316/mysqlTest.sql
```

The following are the results:

```
mysql> \. ./scripts/3316/mysqlTest.sql
Database changed
Query OK, 0 rows affected (0.01 sec)

Query OK, 0 rows affected (0.07 sec)

+----------+-------------+------+-----+---------+-------+
| Field    | Type        | Null | Key | Default | Extra |
+----------+-------------+------+-----+---------+-------+
| prodid   | int(11)     |      |     | 0       |       |
| prodname | varchar(30) | YES  |     | NULL    |       |
+----------+-------------+------+-----+---------+-------+
2 rows in set (0.01 sec)

Query OK, 1 row affected (0.00 sec)

+--------+----------+
| prodid | prodname |
+--------+----------+
|      1 | Yo-Yo    |
+--------+----------+
1 row in set (0.00 sec)
```

As you can see, each command runs in turn.

To give users access to your database, you can use the mysql binary to grant access privileges. The following command grants the user matthewm read-only (SELECT) access to all the tables in the catalog database when connecting from localhost.

```
mysql> GRANT SELECT ON catalog.*
    -> TO 'matthewm'@'localhost'
    -> IDENTIFIED BY 'mOOdie';
```

catalog.* indicates all tables within the catalog database. To grant access to a single table, you can use catalog.product. The user being granted privileges has the form user'@'hostname where the host name may be replaced by % to indicate all hosts.

Resources

This appendix is a cursory look at installing and using MySQL. You should consult dedicated resources such as *The Definitive Guide to MySQL*, Second Edition (Apress, 2003), by Michael Kofler or the MySQL Web site (http://www.mysql.com), which is an excellent resource.

INDEX

E

F

G

J

N

O

R

T

U

V

W

X

Z